SPIRIT MARRIAGE

"Megan Rose offers a well-researched path to meaningful, long-term relationships in the unseen realm. This is the book to read if you are interested in developing intimacy with spirits close to you and being relationally well about it."

PAVINI MORAY, PH.D., SEX AND RELATIONSHIP EDUCATOR,
FOUNDER OF WELLCELIUM, AND HOST OF
THE *BESPOKEN BONES* PODCAST

"Broadens our usual conceptions about romantic love to include the dimension of the more-than-human. In tending and nourishing these sacred connections we step into traditions long suppressed or ignored but vital to our rounder sense of what it means to love and be loved."

CRAIG CHALQUIST, PH.D., AUTHOR OF
TERRAPSYCHOLOGICAL INQUIRY

"An inspired and inspiring exploration of the phenomenon of the *Hieros Gamos,* and how it can contribute to the spiritual regeneration of human life on Earth. Regardless of whether you think you will ever enter into a spirit marriage— or are already in one—you will find Rose's book to be a heartfelt and deeply engaging exploration of this widespread spiritual practice. Read it, and prepare for new and compelling insights into the spiritual destiny of humanity."

BRUCE MACLENNAN, PH.D., AUTHOR OF *THE WISDOM OF HYPATIA*

"Have you heard the call of the Beloved? You are not alone. Megan Rose captures stories of people in loving relationships with spirits and provides a road map to enter into a relationship for those who have heard the call. She combines insights gained from these interviews with her extensive academic and magical training to arrive at a profound and nuanced understanding of the experience. *Spirit Marriage* is that rare book that grants voice to what has been hidden and encourages those who dare to follow the call to love."

BRANDY WILLIAMS, AUTHOR OF *PRACTICAL MAGIC FOR BEGINNERS*

"There is a certain amount of intimacy in all forms of ʃ
small part of the community of practitioners the contac

T0323051

beloved spouse. *Spirit Marriage* is the first book to explore this phenomenon in depth. The book is particularly valuable because it contains stories from the lives of beings engaged in spirit marriages today."

IVO DOMINGUEZ JR., AUTHOR OF *THE FOUR ELEMENTS OF THE WISE*

"Megan Rose's exploration of this widely practiced but little-known phenomenon is illuminated with impeccable scholarship and a deep intuition born of her own experiences in this area. I know of no finer book on this important topic. It belongs in the library of anyone seeking to understand the emerging possibilities of connection and collaboration with allies in the realms of Spirit."

DAVID SPANGLER, SPIRITUAL DIRECTOR OF THE
LORIAN ASSOCIATION AND AUTHOR OF *APPRENTICED TO SPIRIT*

"*Spirit Marriage* is not only a guidebook to forming bonded relationships with Spirit, it is an invitation to awaken our own spiritual potential."

SALICROW, PSYCHIC MEDIUM AND AUTHOR OF
THE PATH OF ELEMENTAL WITCHCRAFT

"Megan Rose takes us on an engaging journey through the history of spirit marriage, from its ancient roots to contemporary accounts of its modern-day practitioners. An important and illuminating study of a fascinating subject!"

VERE CHAPPELL, AUTHOR OF *SEXUAL OUTLAW, EROTIC MYSTIC*

"It is through her embodiment of the three 'keys' of devotion, discernment, and discipline that the book becomes a catalyst for the reader's own journey of divine or extraordinary embodiment. This book will phenomenologically alter you."

MONICA MODY, PH.D., POET, AUTHOR, AND ADJUNCT PROFESSOR
AT THE CALIFORNIA INSTITUTE OF INTEGRAL STUDIES

"This is a book that deserves careful reading with an open mind, not something to dismiss out of hand. It comes from the personal experience of the author and is not a new viewpoint—relationships between humans and other level beings have been recorded down the ages. An interesting and thought-provoking book."

DOLORES ASHCROFT-NOWICKI, AUTHOR OF
THE RITUAL MAGIC WORKBOOK AND *THE SHINING PATHS*

SPIRIT MARRIAGE

Intimate Relationships with Otherworldly Beings

A Sacred Planet Book

MEGAN ROSE, Ph.D.

Bear & Company
Rochester, Vermont

Bear & Company
One Park Street
Rochester, Vermont 05767
www.BearandCompanyBooks.com

Text stock is SFI certified

Bear & Company is a division of Inner Traditions International

Sacred Planet Books are curated by Richard Grossinger, Inner Traditions editorial board member and cofounder and former publisher of North Atlantic Books. The Sacred Planet collection, published under the umbrella of the Inner Traditions family of imprints, is comprised of works on the themes of consciousness, cosmology, alternative medicine, dreams, climate, permaculture, alchemy, shamanic studies, oracles, astrology, crystals, hyperobjects, locutions, and subtle bodies.

This book is intended as an informational guide. The remedies, approaches, and techniques described herein are meant to supplement, and not to be a substitute for, professional medical care or treatment. They should not be used to treat a serious ailment without prior consultation with a qualified health care professional.

Cataloging-in-Publication Data for this title is available from the Library of Congress

ISBN 978-1-59143-415-3 (print)
ISBN 978-1-59143-416-0 (ebook)

Printed and bound in the United States by Lake Book Manufacturing, Inc. The text stock is SFI certified. The Sustainable Forestry Initiative® program promotes sustainable forest management.

10 9 8 7 6 5 4 3 2 1

Text design and layout by Virginia Scott Bowman
This book was typeset in Garamond Premier Pro with Alchemist and Acherus Grotesque used as the display typefaces

To send correspondence to the author of this book, mail a first-class letter to the author c/o Inner Traditions • Bear & Company, One Park Street, Rochester, VT 05767, and we will forward the communication, or contact the author directly at **www.drmeganrose.com**

*

*This research is dedicated to Ida Craddock
and all who seek deeper contact with the denizens
of extraordinary reality.*

Contents

PART III

The Future

✳

Foreword

Orion Foxwood

To the Sub-Prior

That which is neither ill nor well.
That which belongs not to Heaven nor to hell,
A wreath of the mist, a bubble of the stream,
'Twixt a waking thought and a sleeping dream;
A form that men spy
With the half-shut eye.
In the beams of the setting sun, am I.

SIR WALTER SCOTT

There are many reasons why I am honored to write this foreword for *Spirit Marriage: Intimate Relationships with Otherworldly Beings* by Megan Rose, Ph.D. First and foremost, it is written by a dedicated and accomplished seer, priestess, and spiritual advisor. Many academics have written on topics such as spirit possession, but few and cherished are those who write with academic clarity, years of personal experience, and rigorous training on the subject of human-spirit companionship and symbiosis. Megan is one of those rare treasures and her book reflects sound research, deep understanding, and the type of clarity that will make it a classic for the researcher and practitioner alike. To these qualities, Megan offers a broad survey of types of spirit-beings encountered, traditional and contemporary approaches to the topic, and a view into the benefits and challenges of these companionships. Additionally, she offers us a rare glimpse into the lived experience of her research subjects as well as herself, and into subtleties that can only be known by experience. There is an old saying, "See and you will know, but do and you will understand—therein lies the difference between knowledge and wisdom." This is wisdom in your hands.

AN IN-SPIRITED LIFE

I have been in a spirit marriage for well over twenty years. In those years I have gleaned transformative wisdom from traditional folkloric material and revealed information that came through from my spirit companion as well as personal revelation. In fact, there was so much powerful material that I created a seven-year Faery Seership apprenticeship program that fosters these kinds of relationships for hundreds of people worldwide. Their lives have been deeply enriched by the material, and the spirit contacts that have been nurtured during the trainings have led my apprentices to become cocreative agents of change—especially as it relates to ecology and ancestral healing.

My own life with an ancient nonphysical being led me to push off from all that was familiar, and journey into ancient and often uncharted landscapes of the soul of humanity, Earth, and the cosmos. My spirit marriage has expanded my positive impact on the world in ways I could never have imagined. Layers upon layers of wisdom have been gleaned from this profound symbiosis.

My spirit wife, Brigh, and I have tested each other, as her nature had to recalibrate my nature to ensure that we could cocreate together in a healthy way. Conversely, I did not just accept her as benevolent, helpful, or real. You see, when a powerful being like Brigh approaches it is foolhardy to surrender or share your interior until you are clear that: (1) they are real; (2) they are benevolent and/or do not come to do harm; (3) they are helpful; (4) they are accurate and relevant; and (5) they can demonstrate this to not only the human counterpart but to many other witnesses. Brigh has done this in manifold ways. It is my hope that everyone who finds themselves in a potential spirit encounter—where a long-term or permanent merging and mingling of essence is possible—will develop this level of clarity as well.

Because of Brigh it has become normal for me to know of important scientific insights prior to any contact with the science behind them and often before the discovery has been released by the scientific community. Once, while teaching a group of over four hundred people, an astrophysicist approached me and asked if I had studied or been to school for astrophysics. I exclaimed, "No, not at all." To which he responded, "You sure are speaking about it, and quite accurately, though using metaphors."

When he asked how I had come to this knowledge my response was, "I know it the way any seer, shaman, or other mediator of spiritual wisdom knows—I ask, I wait, I allow myself to know." You see, the universe is very interactive. It withholds nothing to those who ask and then allow themselves to know. Many a genius has reported that their moment of revelation felt as if something or someone had guided them or whispered into their ear the answer—a discovery, pertinent directions, a warning alert, or the right selection among various options.

THE ORIGINS OF GENIUS

The Mystic's Prayer

Lay me to sleep in sheltering flame,
O Master of the Hidden Fire!
Wash pure my heart, and cleanse for me My soul's desire.
In flame of sunrise bathe my mind, O Master of the
Hidden Fire,
That, when I wake, clear-eyed may be My soul's desire.
FIONA MACLEOD[1]

Whether it is the "fire in the head" (a sudden flash of illumination) of the Celtic tradition, or an inner-heating force that reveals the spiritual light of vision and inspiration, or a spiritual force or a spiritual being that is mediated or indwelled by a human host, profound wisdom and healing is often found in the spirit or invisible realm. In ancient Rome, when a person had an uncommonly high intellect, its source was thought to be a particularly potent guiding spirit known as a *genius.* Thus to this day we refer to a brilliant person as a genius.

We all have these helpful spirits but most of us never allow ourselves to be open to them. And when they do come through, too often they are called *demons*—a word derived from the Greek word *daemon,* which originally denoted a divine being, not an infernal one.

In this book many types of informing spirits are discussed. They include human ancestral, faery, divine, and more. Each spirit marriage has its own nuances, challenges, and benefits, and each has changed its human counterpart forever. In the spirit marriage accounts relayed herein, Megan gives ample room for each individual subject to invite the reader into the intimacy of their spirit marriage, sharing information often closed to others who are not appropriately trained, initiated, and part of their community or culture. I can assure you, I shared aspects of my Faery marriage that I never discussed with anyone but my apprentices. Why am I sharing it now? Because it's time to pull back the curtain, and because Megan was the right person to receive this material and share it with the world. She feels, as I do, that spirit and human partnerships have always been important to the spiritual and intellectual development of humanity. The farseeing eyes of the ancient, immortal, divine, unseen, human ancestral, and other beings are crucial if we are to see outside of our limits and beyond time.

Now more than ever we need clarity, as runaway human technology, overpopulation, ecological threats, and increasingly complex diseases and other maladies affect the destiny of humanity and our planet. We need the wisdom of the past, a sage view of the future, and a vision that is inclusive. We need to view the world and all its beings in ways that are transcendent, ancestral, and internal. We also need objective views that are as intelligent as humans, but can also see beyond the illusion of isolation, the desire for possessions and power, fear or resentment of change, and the desire for absolutes. We need spirit sight that is disentangled from our issues, one that sees, cares, loves, and wants us whole, healed, and evolved and living in a healthy world for us, our ancestors, our descendants, and other beings yet to come.

WHY THIS SUBJECT, WHY NOW, AND WHY THIS BOOK?

There are three overarching reasons why I feel that the subject of human and spirit symbiosis, or marriage, is important. It is relevant; it is necessary; and it is timely.

Its *relevance* is in the different lenses it provides for understanding that there are modes of existence beyond the range of our "normal" senses. These modes can offer information, insight, and understanding that may give new perspectives and answers to the dilemmas of our world, particularly those that derive from invisible modes of life such as ancestral traumas, ecological concerns, spiritual ailments, and the invisible connections between visible things. There is also the illusive concept called consciousness, which challenges scientists. There are many things science does not understand about consciousness, including what it really is and where it comes from. Nor does science understand that everything in the universe is conscious. It seems that the great conceptual hurdle for contemporary science is to consider that consciousness is a dynamic that is ever present in everything. It does not need any nervous system to perceive it, body to contain it, or eye to behold it. Our sciences are already considering the ranges of life that we will encounter when we journey past familiar elements of our Earth-based periodic table, into ranges of light beyond the spectrum of our sun—when we set foot onto other worlds. There are vistas of awareness far beneath our consensus range here on Earth and in the heavens beyond. We invent mechanical antennae to receive signals in greater ranges.

Perhaps nature and the evolution of humanity has already placed those capacities in some of us, where it lay dormant until necessity, opportunity, and resources awaken it. The message, messenger, and medium now come together in a symbiosis of intelligence where humans and other beings are the bridge to a new humanity—sharing information and insights that pass into us on a stream that never ends.

Then there is the very *necessary* need to understand and engage with conscious life on other worlds, which will be a challenge as we prepare to travel to them. The springboard for understanding other worlds starts here on Earth where we need a deeper understanding of each other, our shared past, and the invisible but felt connection between us and all Earth life. Our senses and sensibilities need to be refined, and that's an inside job. Inner contacts see the necessary invisible wounds and the possibilities that exist to resensitize us to each other and return us to our roots. Our inner senses have dulled to the subtle rhythms of our lives that are intertwined with each other, but they can be brought outward and awakened with the help of those who are fully awake in consciousness.

Finally, the *time* is now. The bottom line is that humans are moving rapidly into an era of expanded and fluid states of consciousness, and we must perceive the invisible relationships between visible things if we are to grow with our own destiny. We are *human-becoming;* we are not finished growing in our understanding of healing, the intimate workings of our planet, the causes and cures for maladies likely induced by human technology, and actions that impact nature in ways we cannot see. If we are to thrive and if we are to save our Earth from a forthcoming extinction event, then we must perceive beyond the perspectives that challenge the life of our species and our world. The eyes that are invisible see what is invisible to our eye, whereas the ear that extends beyond the audible may hear a silent tongue of wisdom. Our ancestors held in highest esteem those who heard beyond the range of sound, who were guided by ancient forces, who knew the very beginning of life, and whose reach was into the unfolding future—for they knew the unknowable.

Perhaps the "invisibles" will guide all things toward their highest potential if we allow them. More cocreative relationships are emerging, with information that answers many questions and guidance that is sound. Perhaps the time to know beyond knowing, sense beyond feeling, and dance in balance to a tune of helpful harmony is *now*. This book offers insights from finely tuned human instruments of the eternal, who historically often come forth in times of great change. I think we have arrived at that place of change where we must thread the pearls of knowing with an integrative cord that is woven of a finer thread. This finer thread is made of the invisible that becomes visible, silence that becomes sound, darkness that becomes color. It is ripe with uncontaminated inspiration.

I end this foreword with a quote from Albert Einstein, "Everything is determined, the beginning as well as the end, by forces over which we have no control. It is determined for the insect, as well as for the star. Human beings, vegetables, or cosmic dust, we all dance to a mysterious tune, intoned in the distance by an invisible piper."[2]

Through spirit marriages, the song of this piper is placed within our voice, but only if we ask and allow. Let us become what has never been and leap to vistas yet unknown. All that is visible begins as being invisible. Our ancestors had a more expanded experience of all life as sentient, interpenetrating, and imbued with a fluid expression of gender, shape, and power, and expressed as seen, unseen, and the thresholds in between. Tribal, indigenous, and folk culture still have living awareness of this. Formal religion may have retained some glimmerings, but it too often pales, drained by fear, overintellectualism, humano-centrism, and a belief that matter and spirit are at odds and humanity is the treasured child caught in the middle.

A great deal of lore and wisdom has been lost in the wars of religion, the displacement and genocide of indigenous people, the rejection of the spiritual for the intellectual, and the demonization and trivialization of the existence and helpfulness of the "unseen company." However, my elders used to say to me, "No wisdom leaves the world and love is eternal." And my mother advised, "God left everything in the hands of helpful spirits." The book you hold in your hands represents a collective treasury of wisdom that fulfills these two wise statements. Perhaps you will feel a kindred spirit in its message, for you may have already felt

a sacred hand upon your shoulder,
a holy whisper in your ears,
a fire within that makes you bolder.
An unseen hand that wipes your tears.

ORION FOXWOOD
AUTHOR, TRADITIONAL WITCH, AND FAERY SEER
NEW CARROLLTON, MARYLAND
OCTOBER 31, 2021

Preface

This is a love story—a love story disguised as a piece of scholarly research. Or maybe it's a piece of scholarly research about *true* love; the kind of love one can only find within one's True Self. Either way, the jury is still out on ultimately what genre of literature wants to fully lay claim to this book, as it is both academic and esoteric. Erudite and down-to-Earth. Visionary and embodied. You get the picture. This research, as the poet once said, "contains multitudes."

I began this research inquiry out of necessity. I am by training and inclination a practitioner-scholar of subaltern, or oppressed, spiritualities. I have been studying and practicing them since 1994 when, while attending seminary at the Graduate Theological Union in Berkeley, California, I discovered the world-altering purview of women's spirituality and Paganism. Although in my undergraduate work I had already identified myself as a feminist, it had never occurred to me that the very religions I was devoting good time and money to studying might be built on the shoulders of other spiritual traditions that in many cases were supplanted—often persecuted into nonexistence—by dominator religions. This was a revelation, and I vowed to question and deconstruct every assumption I held about my own spiritual experiences. In short, I became an agnostic mystic with a penchant for Paganism.

Then in 2002 I began to experience numinous encounters with what seemed to be a spirit lover, primarily in my dreams. What was remarkable about this phenomenon was the felt-sense knowing I had of a separate presence, something extraordinary that felt different from my experiences of other dream figures. I choose *not* to reduce the presence of a recurring dream being to gestalt or metaphor. Initially, when these kinds of extraordinary beings first began to show up in my dreams, I did look at how they might represent aspects of myself. Yet over time I began to determine that these dreams were different from the more psychological dreams I was having—those in which I was rehashing old stories, working out problems, dealing with relationships, and so forth. These extraordinary dreams included visitations, prophecies, lucid consciousness, and other parapsychological phenomena. In addition, they were almost always accompanied by a deep sense of wholeness, heart-opening, and oftentimes orgasm, which I understand to be Kundalini Shakti rising and releasing.

These experiences led me to an in-depth study of sacred sexuality, also called erotic mysticism. Since then I have received training in the yogic practices of Shakta Tantra, the Taoist practices of sexual alchemy, and the Western Hermetic practices of sex magick. In 2007 I was initiated as a Ceremonial Magician within a Western Hermetic lineage, and in 2010 I began my apprenticeship as a Faery Seership practitioner. I have also done an introductory study of the African Traditional religion of the Dagara people of Burkina Faso, as well as the folk magic traditions of the American South—known as conjure, hoodoo, and rootwork. I began exploring these traditions because each one had something to teach me about spirit lovers and spirit marriage.

I take the presence of my dream figures—particularly ones that elicit a somatic response—seriously. I have come to the conclusion that when a spirit contact visits in a dream, it is a bona fide extraordinary being with its own energy signature, felt-sense, attitude, personality, and agenda—just like that of any human person. This is similar to the conclusion that ethnographer Irving Hallowell arrived at in his research with the Ojibwa people. He came to the understanding of "the Ojibwa concept of personhood as relational: persons were not classified according to whether they were human or physical, but rather according to their capacity to engage in relationships with other persons."[1] Over the years I have searched for spiritual and esoteric systems that would help me contextualize this phenomenon. I am particularly interested in those living traditions in which the relationship with a spirit lover is still practiced. This personal inquiry, which I elaborate upon in greater detail in my personal story "The Erotic Mystic," in chapters 12 and 13, forms the basis of *Spirit Marriage*.

The challenge I faced in 2002 when I experienced first contact was that very few books or articles explicitly discussed spirit marriage as a living practice and its importance as a spiritual undertaking. So I decided to undertake that research both for myself and for future readers who I imagined might be encountering some of the same phenomenon I was. After independently researching as much of the literature and tradition of spirit marriage as I could, I decided to undertake a formal study of spirit marriage as a doctoral student to give my research a container, a cauldron within which I could grow this fledgling inquiry into a full-blown undertaking—namely to write this book.

I also decided that instead of just looking at the past history of spirit marriage in religion, anthropology, folklore, and the like, I needed to understand how it was currently being practiced and why. This is because I was absolutely positive that I was not the only contemporary person having these kinds of extraordinary encounters. I sought out practitioners (whom I call my *coresearchers* for reasons we'll unpack later) from well-established lineage traditions. I felt that they could significantly expand upon my understanding of this rarely discussed and often hidden tradition as well as contribute this knowledge to the field of religious studies. I also wanted to contribute to the growing field of Earth-based spirituality, or Animism, by elaborating on this practice in marginalized, sometimes called subaltern, traditions: Traditional Witchcraft, African Diaspora religion, African

Traditional religion, and Goddess*-centered Eastern Tantra. As such, this research sheds light on a practice sacred to these traditions, offering academic, psychological, and spiritual context—and perhaps guiding readers who may encounter or wish to cultivate similar experiences for themselves.

---

*Throughout this piece I have intentionally chosen to capitalize terms like Goddess, Creatrix, and Divine Feminine to emphasize the belief in the equality, and in some cases primacy, of deity as female. I have also chosen to capitalize the term Gods when referring to non-monotheistic deities to emphasize the equality of all deities.

Acknowledgments

I am deeply grateful to the friends, colleagues, and family who have supported the decades-long research that became this book. To Ryan Indigo Warman and Jonathan Jay Levine, for your love, support, and stalwart belief in me and my work. To Emily Shurr, for your friendship, encouragement, and vision for this project as well as your keen editor's eye. To my coresearchers, for your openness and participation. To Orion Foxwood, for your continued love, wisdom, and power. To my early readers, Richard Power and Lillie Falco-Adkins, for your encouragement. To Brandy Williams, for your insightful suggestions and practitioner's eye. To Rob Brezsny, for your belief in this work and timely connections. To Richard Grossinger for championing this project. To the team at Inner Traditions/Bear and Co. for your willingness to take on a first-time author who was dead-set on writing a tome!

To the Albion 8 (Salicrow, Jewels Aradia, Pam Kimball, Henry Austin, Dennis Loreman, JJ, and Indi), my compatriots in the *wyrd*, for holding the container for me to go deep. To Lisa Christie, Craig Chalquist, David Spangler, Marguerite Rigoglioso, and Randy Conner for your skillful guidance and academic excellence which lay the foundation for this book. To Monica Mody, S. K. Thoth, Lila Angelique, and the Entheosis Institute, for your love and brilliance. To the House of Brigh, the Kali kula, Janice Craig, Elizabeth Bast, Cynthia Morrow, Ro Loughran, Patti O'Luanaigh, the Mystic Midway, the Reclaiming

Community, the San Francisco Theosophical Society, the Seven Sisters Mystery School, the Quimera Tribe, the Temple of Awakening Divinity, the Temples of Ma'at and Thoth-Hathor, the Santa Cruz Wisdom Intensive, the Boat of Soul, the Yoga Kula Berkeley, the Damanhur Federation, and the Findhorn Foundation for teaching, training, and community-building with me.

Feminizing and Decolonizing Our Perceptions of Reality

Spirit marriage is a form of embodied spirituality and a transpersonal phenomenon. To put it as clearly as I can, it is the bonded or intimate relationship between a human and a subtle or discarnate entity such as a deity, spirit, or extraordinary intelligence.

In this practice, the consciousness of the practitioner is linked or wedded to a specific entity, and the two beings share a cocreative consciousness forthwith. This practice has appeared in many cultures, among a strikingly large number of religious traditions ranging from African indigenous spirituality to Tantric yoga to Christian mysticism. The practice of union with a spirit can manifest in many different forms—channeling, possession, sexual encounters, visitations, and the like. However, for the purposes of this book, I have limited my definition of spirit marriage* to practitioners who have gone through a ritual or ceremony of union, designed to align them with a particular spirit.

The term *invisible* is often used to describe the realms of spirit, but

---

*The term *Godspouse* is also used in contemporary Pagan circles to describe this phenomenon. I prefer Spirit Marriage insomuch as it is gender neutral and, as we shall see, deities aren't the only entities to which humans can be wed.

my research indicates reports of spirit-beings taking on human form, thereby rendering them corporeal and visible to the human eye, as well as manifesting in nature. Therefore, the adjectives *invisible, incorporeal,* and *nonhuman* are technically inaccurate descriptors of these beings. The terms *otherworldly, supernatural,* and *paranormal* are also problematic in that they could imply that these beings do not share our world, are not a part of nature, or behave abnormally, rendering them alien rather than native.* Similarly, I find the term *nonordinary* problematic insomuch as it is phrased in the negative and suggests that encounters such as these might not be a typical way of perceiving—whereas my research suggests just the opposite. Therefore, I have mostly chosen to use the term *extraordinary,* which Merriam-Webster defines as "1a: going beyond what is usual, regular, or customary; 1b: exceptional to a very marked extent."

The practice of spirit marriage has allegedly been with us since the dawn of civilization. Through folklore and mythology we hear of its ancient roots. We first start to see textual records of the practice in the ancient Mesopotamian sacred marriage, where it is reportedly undertaken to aid humans in the development and expansion of consciousness, both spiritual and everyday.[1] It is said to result in the development of extrasensory perception (ESP), esoteric revelation, and personal and societal transformation. Quite lofty outcomes! With that in mind, in this book we're going to explore the possibility that spirit marriage is a viable means of personal and planetary evolution, and to investigate why it has seemingly been marginalized and obfuscated throughout history.

Personally I believe that spirit marriage has the potential to be a kind of liberation spirituality. At crucial moments in history it seems that it has offered spiritual empowerment, cocreative engagement, and conscious evolution to its practitioners. And in cases wherein dominant religions and their God(s) are mediated by a human oppressor,

---

*For a further discussion on terminology see the chapter "The Problematic Paranormal: Supernatural or Natural?" in Jack Hunter's book *Engaging the Anomalous: Collected Essays on Anthropology, the Paranormal, Mediumship and Extraordinary Experience.*

many have chosen to offer themselves to what they contend are spirits that predate or dwell outside the oppressive regime; beings that are believed to have a higher authority and more power than their human persecutors. In fact, I once had a mentor tell me that if the Gods you're worshipping don't seem to be on your side, then you need to choose new Gods!

However, not all spirit marriages are undertaken to free someone from oppression. In fact, most seem to be undertaken at the request of the spirit who wishes to cocreate with a human. This book will demonstrate how spirit marriage offers a means to personal agency, individuation of the Self, and an avenue for personal awakening—often against widespread cultural oppression and religious intolerance.

Spirit marriage currently can be found as a living practice in the African Diaspora traditions of Haitian Vodou and New Orleans Voodoo; the folkloric Faery tradition of Faery Seership; the African Traditional religion of the Dagara people in Burkina Faso; and in Indo-Tibetan Tantric sadhana.* These are all traditions that have experienced colonialism, religious oppression, and/or persecution. Because of this history I tread lightly in seeking to interview spirit marriage practitioners. I wanted to be invited in as someone my interviewees would trust and respect, and not seen as an outsider trying to project my own opinion or ideas on the subject. Fortunately, because I am both a scholar and a practitioner of subaltern spiritualities, I was very graciously given access to the personal stories and experiences of contemporary spirit marriage practitioners. These stories illuminate and elucidate upon the living, breathing practice of "marrying the Gods."

When I began this inquiry, I also included achievement of

---

*This list, however, is currently growing as more practitioners come forward with their stories, notably the God Spouse tradition of Norse Heathenry. And although I focused my research on marginalized spiritual and religious traditions, the Catholic *Rite of Consecration to a Life of Virginity,* wherein a woman mystically espouses herself to Christ, also falls within this purview. (See Judith Stegman's thesis, "Virginial Chastity in the Consecrated Virgin," and the "Ecclesiae Sponae Imago," the commentary by Pope Francis on the entire body of existing law on the Order of Virgins, for further elaboration.)

Knowledge and Conversation with the Holy Guardian Angel by a Ceremonial Magician as a kind of spirit marriage,[2] the logic being that it expresses a form of divine union. Over the years my opinion has evolved, alternating between the Holy Guardian Angel (HGA) practice *not qualifying* for inclusion (because can someone *really* marry themselves?) and then, by the end of the research process, again *qualifying* (because marrying one's HGA *is* an extraordinary union, albeit not necessarily an erotic one). I will discuss this in greater detail in chapter 14, "Cultivating a Spirit Marriage," however, and in any event, I have decided to include it (the achievement of Knowledge and Conversation with the Holy Guardian Angel) as an outlier example of what union with Spirit might look like through the spiritual technology of embodying the Divine Self.*

One of my not-so-subtle goals in writing this book, particularly from the perspective of a practitioner-scholar, is to offer a much needed counterpoint to traditional academic scholarship. That type of scholarship tends to invalidate and deny the occurrence of extraordinary spiritual encounters by assuming Western scientistic reality as the norm. Research and reporting from within a colonialist framework tend to devalue the embodied and numinous experience of the practitioners in favor of a psycho-social analysis of the phenomenon.

Therefore I'm using a decolonizing indigenous research framework to reclaim the embodied spiritual experience of spirit marriage practitioners, particularly in the subaltern spiritual context.[3] I'm arguing that, in most instances, the practice of spirit marriage involves personal awakening, the establishment of self-worth, and the claiming of sovereignty in a world that in many cases relegates members of marginalized traditions to categories of slave, evil-doer, or subversive influence. Further, I demonstrate that in most cases, the practice of spirit marriage has been

---

*Research on embodying the Divine Self is a topic that merits its own book. In this work I have sought to explore the concept and practice of Divine Self embodiment as it specifically relates to spirit marriage as I have defined it, leaving the literature and history of the practice of Divine Self embodiment for later research.

upheld predominantly through oral tradition or in the *twilight* or coded language of metaphor—only revealed to the trusted initiate—so as to preserve the practice of spirit marriage against the overarching tide of religious and cultural persecution.

I'm not interested in answering the question "Are spirits real?" Nor am I interested in deconstructing views on reality versus nonreality. Instead, I'm embracing the worldview of an *enchanted universe,* which assumes that parapsychological phenomena and transpersonal encounters within an indigenous and ecofeminist framework are valid and worthy of serious study.[4] Following the precedent set by transpersonal anthropologists, ethnographers, and animist psychologists, I assume that these experiences are completely real for my coresearchers, who deserve the kind of respect that any religious studies scholar would afford a mainstream religion.

As paranthropologist* Jack Hunter observes, "The ultimate aim of this type of approach, then, is to interpret religious, spiritual and paranormal beliefs and experiences from a perspective that does not, from the very outset, reduce the complexity of the phenomenon or ignore the significance of personal, subjective experience."[5] Instead, following American ecofeminist philosopher Caroline Merchant's clarion call in *The Death of Nature,*[6] which critiques modern scientific method as a specifically masculinist endeavor, I seek to reclaim the organic and feminist nature of extraordinary experience. I do this though a willingness to listen with an open mind and to enter the extraordinary worldview of my coresearchers as much as possible.

Common assumptions within masculinist science require distance and quantification for validation of content. These same assumptions underpin the hetero-masculinist worldview. In this approach both scientism and mainstream religion agree. In fact, both areas have become allies and, as such, suppress and marginalize the subaltern

---

*A term minted by anthropologist Jack Hunter, *paranthropology* is the study of the paranormal using an open-minded social-scientific approach to anomalous phenomena.

stories of extraordinary spiritual and mystical experience. Therefore, from a feminist-indigenous approach, I have allowed my coresearchers' accounts, their beliefs, and their experiences to inform this research, instead of attempting to shoehorn their stories into some prescribed category of psychological diagnosis that fits neatly into a Western scientistic framework.

Craig Chalquist is a terrapsychologist,* depth psychologist, and faculty member in East-West psychology at the California Institute of Integral Studies in California. As such, he promotes a philosophy of being called *enchantivism*. Enchantivism is an activist approach that seeks to inspire deep societal change. It does this either locally or more widely by working with story, myth, dream, and the presence of place to inspire and envision alternative possibilities for our future as a species and a planet. I am specifically taking an enchantivist approach with the material I present in this book. In so doing, I seek to "make lasting change by sharing reenchanting stories about our relations with ourselves, each other, and our ailing but still-beautiful planet; and then letting these stories lead us into creative and thoughtful responses to how things are."7

I argue that the primary goal of spirit marriage is not only liberation and transformation of the individual but ultimately the transformation of society and evolution of the planet. I take the position that spirit marriage practices have led and continue to lead to the development of a cocreative consciousness between humanity and other-than-human intelligences—a partnership that helps the human species evolve, through the cultivation of extraordinary powers, acceleration of our evolutionary development, and progression of the human race, all of which is articulated further in the pages of this book.

Spirit Marriage has been divided into three parts: Past, Present, and Future. The Past deals primarily with the historical, folkloric, and reli-

---

*A terrapsychologist is someone who embraces the practice of terrapsychology, which is a growing field of imaginative studies, ideas, and practices for reenchanting our relations with the natural world and therefore with each other and ourselves.

gious accounts of spirit marriage as they've been documented and as they've impacted various cultures. I think it's important to give a historical overview so that the reader may better understand the current manifestation of spirit marriage in our culture today. This work, being first of its kind and highly transgressive, necessitates giving you a solid foundation before throwing you willy-nilly into the initiatory energy of the stories. I hope you will indulge me as I wear my scholar hat—never to lecture, always to illuminate!

The Present tells the stories of ten contemporary practitioners of spirit marriage. These stories are based on conversations in which both the spirit-spouse and the practitioner were invited to tell me their story. They are powerful transmissions, heavy with encoded language, metaphor, and lineage teachings often given only to the adept. Perhaps as you read them you may hear the voice of one of the spirits reach out and beckon you into relationship.

Finally, the Future takes these stories and weaves them into guidelines, recommendations, and precautions for how one might evolve a spirit marriage relationship oneself.

The bottom line is that hidden within this research is magic—magic that is meant to please your intellect, delight your senses, and inspire a sense of wonder and awe at the extraordinary capacity of humans to love beyond the bounded notions of what's deemed "normal" or "real." This is a magical book written not only by me but by all the extraordinary beings—human and Otherworldly—who cocreated it with me. And like all books of magic, if you allow it, it will transform you, leave you altered, quickened, and hopefully awakened to the extraordinary nature of your being.

PART I

The Past

✴

**A Druid chant for waking
the living memory of Earth**

. . . .

Earth Mother,
we honor your body,
Earth Mother,
we honor your bones,
Earth Mother,
we enter your body,
Earth Mother,
we sing to your stones.
Awake, Awake, Awaken.
Awake, Awake, Awaken.

1
Hidden in Plain Sight

*A*s we explore the history of spirit marriage in the next few chapters, we'll discover that the practice has been alive and well since the beginning of recorded time, and it continues to this day to shape our evolution as a species. We're also going to explore some of the best-concealed evidence in history, folklore, religion, and the like as to the prevalence of spirit marriage transculturally. And if you are a history buff like I am, you will find it a bit of a jaw-dropping good time!

A TRANSCULTURAL PHENOMENON

Sifting through the transcultural evidence of spirit marriage found in academic and religious literature, mythology, and folklore makes it pretty clear that the concept and practice of spirit marriage has existed since the dawn of civilization. Spirit marriage appears on almost every continent and is still practiced today. According to my research, the phenomenon of the spirit-spouse or spirit lover—an entity to which a human is psychically bonded—appears to be a widespread element of embodied spiritual practice distributed throughout most continents and in many disparate cultures. The spirit-spouse typically visits a person in dreams or nonordinary states; female shamans have even reported that they can give birth to spirit children conceived through these entities.[1]

The person dreaming will habitually dream of having a spouse who is both Otherworldly and able to assist in waking-world activities.

Through the intersection of human and divine coupling, the human is reportedly transfigured into a kind of suprahuman being, now endowed with mediumistic capabilities, and in some cases becoming the progenitor of forces or "children" who characterize the two parallel planes of reality.[2] For example, in 1964 religious historian Mircea Eliade reported a Buryat tale wherein the first shaman was purportedly created through the offspring of a human woman and a celestial eagle—or, alternately, the woman herself became the first shaman through the encounter.[3] Religion scholar Stuart Ray Sarbacker points out that important cosmological parallels are "tied to the sexual joining of primordial or archetypal forces [with humans] and are characteristic of religions throughout the world (with numerous examples in Ancient Near Eastern, Greek, Japanese, Chinese, and Indian traditions)." These include "the formulations of Abrahamic theism such as in Christianity, where God the celestial Father, paired with human mother Mary, begets Jesus the Son, Mary being the 'mediatrix of humanity.'"[4]

IN THE MARGINS OF HISTORY

Many spirit marriage traditions have survived over and against socio-religious forces that sought to subdue or erase this practice from such accounts. Traditional research relies heavily on these surviving written and scholarly accounts of spirit marriage practices. The eighteenth century saw the height of the Atlantic slave trade, indentured servitude, and the oppression of indigenous people native to the colonies. Ultimately this diaspora of oppressed and marginalized practitioners led to the hybridized beliefs and practices now known as Vodou, Voodoo, hoodoo, rootwork, conjure, and the like.* These hybrid traditions combined

---

*In this book, I use the spelling *Voodoo* when referring to the New Orleans tradition and *Vodou* when referring to the Haitian tradition.

African Traditional religion, Christianity, and indigenous spirituality under the yoke of slavery, indentured servitude, and colonization and were practiced predominantly by nonwhites, servants, and slaves.

Likewise, Faery Seership is a specific form of eco-spirituality or folk magic that rose out of the Pagan and folkloric Faery beliefs and practices of the Celts who, according to Scotsman and hereditary Faery Seer R. J. Stewart, were forced to protect their lineage during the witch trials of the Middle Ages by hiding it in plain sight.[5] According to oral tradition, Faery magic is considered by some to be the foundational lineage that underpins many forms of Traditional Witchcraft and Earth-based spirituality, Faeries being the prehuman inhabitants and cocreators of Earth.[6]

The Indic Tantra and the Tibetan Buddhist practice of deity yoga includes the practice of visualizing a deity as divine consort. A subset of Tantric practice known as Shakta Tantra emphasizes the relationality of the human to transpersonal or divine forces through the worship of the female principle. This principle is embodied both as the human *yoni* (vulva/womb) and Earth—as the prime mover at the foundation of all Creation. The tradition itself is borne out of the pre-Vedic indigenous North Indic tribal practices of *yogini* worship and veneration of Earth as the physical body of the Goddess—known as *shakti pitha*. It is further informed by the struggle of Indian women to maintain Goddess worship and the agency of women in an increasingly patriarchal system.[7]

In all these traditions, spirit marriage is an encouraged and practiced form of initiation and spiritual development. Subtler forms of spirit marriage may be implied or covertly practiced in other traditions—most notably in the Christian monastic tradition where nuns become the brides of Christ. However, with the exception of the aforementioned practices, very few religions openly encourage and practice a marriage-like union with a spirit.*

---

*Other subtler forms of a bonded union with a spirit may be insinuated in the Pentecostal Christian tradition of being baptized with the Holy Spirit, the New Age and neo-"shamanic" practices of channeling and mediumship, African Diaspora traditions of uniting the practitioner with their patron deity, and the Western esoteric practice of sex magick.

Like the Faery Seership tradition of the Celts, these traditions hid their knowledge and practice in plain sight: in the folkloric and oral histories of their lineage. Their members preserved spirit marriage rites through ritual, song, poetry, magical practice, and esoteric teachings. Therefore, in addition to surveying the academic literature on spirit marriage, I have also looked to both esoteric and mythopoetic sources as well as occult and transpersonal accounts. This could have been a lifetime undertaking, however. Thus I limited myself to investigating accounts that dealt specifically with the bonded marriage relationship between a human and any predominantly incorporeal entity. These included deities (Gods, Goddesses; Lwa/Loa), angels (fallen angels, the Watchers or *Grigori*), Faery (including *Sidhe,* pronounced "Shee," and *djinn*), elementals (gnomes, undines, salamanders, sylphs), ancestors (beloved dead, ghosts and tutelary spirits), as well as daimons (also spelled *daemons*).[8]

The fact remains that literature on spirits dates back to the origin myths of humankind, and it appears that the range and breadth of spirits who may be contacted and betrothed are numerous. Much like various ethnic groups of humans, these extraordinary beings are typically distinguished according to their geographic and cosmological locale. Unfortunately, while general communication with spirits is better documented and researched in academic and parapsychology circles, literature on present-day practices of spirit marriage is scant.

This book, then, offers a transcultural assessment of spirit marriage, piecing together the appearance of this practice in various traditions as well as filling in the knowledge gap on contemporary practice and experience. I seek to situate the current practice of spirit marriage against the cultural and historical backdrop of mythology, folklore, and religion, setting aside the psychological and philosophical considerations of spirit contact and cosmology for another day. That said, to better ground this research in a transpersonal framework, I briefly discuss key scholarly figures who have reported having a bonded relationship with a spirit or daimon who influenced and enhanced their life and work.

My survey of the historical, religious, folkloric, and occult accounts of spirit marriage leads me to believe that, to date, accounts of spirit marriage are predominantly found in mystical and experiential literature written by practitioners of this phenomenon. Very little has been done on the subject by serious academics or religious scholars, particularly from a psycho-spiritual approach. This, I believe, indicates a great opening and a calling for this research. It is my hope that the research contained in this book contributes unique and heretofore undocumented experiences of extraordinary interaction with Otherworldly entities in a variety of traditions, showing the similarities and differences when spirit marriage is surveyed transculturally with an open mind.

2
History, Folklore, and Religion

ANTHROPOLOGY AND HISTORY

When examining the validity of the spirit marriage down through time, scholars have found it helpful to trace evidence of this practice from six different areas of study, as follows: Assyriology (first- and second-millennium love lyrics and rituals); biblical studies (the Song of Songs); Classics (Graeco-Roman philosophies, Chaldean Oracles); gnostic studies; Jewish mysticism (Kabbalah); and Indology (Hindu rites and myths), including ancient Egyptian and Ugaritic evidence.

Although much is known of this practice esoterically, much remains undocumented. This is largely due to a lack of evidence in the written record. As well, a longstanding debate—about whether or not the sacred marriage, or *Hieros Gamos,* was an actual sexual rite between a priestly representative of the God/Goddess and the ruler, or whether it was a metaphorical union—continues to simmer among scholars today.

But what if the scanty and unclear evidence of the sacred marriage ritual is due to the fact that it was a secret rite passed down orally, leaving us with only fragmentary evidence of what actually took place and for what purpose? I argue that most scholars assume that the text on sacred marriage is always referring to a mundane kind of union, whether by two human proxies or on the level of metaphor. But based on the oral histories I have collected from my coresearchers, I offer that the rites of sacred marriage may be just that—sexual unions between an extraordinary entity and a human being. Furthermore, many of the stories I collected bolster the theory that these rites were not exclusive to the priestly or kingly class but were used to support human evolution at a time when humanity needed to take great cultural strides forward.

Given the secret and initiatory nature of most Hieros Gamos rituals, the lack of explicit language describing the ritual doesn't mean that these marriages weren't happening. We should also recall the ancient tendency to use coded language when referring to sexual mysteries in most esoteric traditions, which would make written evidence more inaccessible. To protect the inner mysteries that are shared only with the initiate, coded or *twilight* language is often used, accessible only to those with ears to hear. In my view, instead of continuing to seek written records that may or may not exist, it would behoove us to avail ourselves of the rich information found in oral traditions, practices and folklore that back up our belief that these types of unions between humans and spirits were in fact happening.

An important theme within the sacred marriage tradition is that of gender reflexivity and queerness as exemplified by the transgender devotees of the Goddess Ištar. Feminist scholar and Assyriologist Saana Teppo argues that although devotees did not participate in a "'ritual enactment of the marriage' with Ištar, in their performances they were joined with Ištar in a union comparable to sacred marriage."[1] Notable among these devotees are the gender-variant priests called *Assinnu*, whose cuneiform sign means "man-woman."

It is in this ancient cult of Ištar that we first discover the recurring theme of gender transfiguration and transgender identity development through sacred union with a deity. This same theme—the fluidity of sexual orientation and gender identity—was present in many of my coresearchers' stories as we sought to understand the kinds of agency that spirit marriage offers its practitioners.

Moving on from ancient Assyria, we find evidence of spirit marriages in ancient Greek texts as well. Herodotus in the Histories gives two non-Greek examples, which may offer some of the earliest recorded accounts of spirit marriage–like unions in the West.

First, he reports that Bel, a Babylonian deity akin to Zeus, chooses a Chaldean woman to spend the night with him in his temple—presumably so that they can have sexual intercourse.[2] Second, he reports that in Egyptian Thebes a priestess of Zeus spends the night with the God in his temple, but is forbidden sexual intercourse with men.[3]

On the European continent, Faery lore and practices pointing to the existence of the institution of spirit marriage were in evidence and only seemed to prevail as time went on. Although members of the clerical elite officially did not believe in faeries, at least not as "credible entities," it did not prevent the church from attempting to rationalize, negate, and/or dismiss faery beliefs among the laity. In fact, the fervor with which the medieval church sought to eradicate the Faery faith actually tells us a great deal about both the vigor and prevalence of Faery belief.[4] This is supported by medieval historian Richard Firth Green in his work on the subject, entitled *Elf Queens and Holy Friars: Fairy Beliefs and the Medieval Church*. In his introduction he reports that fundamental to his approach "is the assumption that the beliefs of those for whom fairies were a living presence were sincerely held and that we should do them the courtesy of taking their beliefs seriously."[5]

Coupled with a persistent belief in faeries is the idea of the *Faery lover*, or incubi, as well as offspring of faeries as a result of the faery lover having mated with humans. Indeed, the idea that the famed wizard Merlin, the celebrated British seer and adviser to kings, was the child of faery-human coupling persists in many Merlin tales. In fact, in Geoffrey of Monmouth's *Historia Regum Britannie*, Merlin's parentage—that of a human woman and an incubus—was stated as historical fact.[6] Celtic folklore is rife with tales of faery-human coupling. Medieval writer Walter Map chronicled several stories of love affairs between humans and Otherwordly beings, notably Eadric the Wild—an eleventh-century Anglo-Saxon magnate—and his faery bride, who lived in the forest where they would meet for their trysts. Apparently, the untamed edges of domestic versus wild, the betwixt and between places, is a common location for the faery lover to dwell.[7]

Moving forward in time, written records of early modern European witchcraft and sorcery trials have documented the accused speaking of a familiar spirit not only as a guide but also as a spouse. According to British historian and author Emma Wilby in her book *Cunning Folk and Familiar Spirits,* for some witches, sexual relations with the familiar were part of the marriage. Alleged witch Ellen Driver, a seventeenth-century woman, claimed in her confession that she had lived with her spirit husband (a cloven-footed devil-like figure) for three years and bore him two children.[8] That same year, Rebecca West confessed to having been visited by the devil, who told her he would marry her and be a loving husband until death.[9]

In both instances it is important to understand these confessions were extracted often under duress and colored with the prejudices of the witch-trial prosecutors. The prosecutors, who were informed by the Christian Church, sought to label any form of unorthodox spirit contact as nefarious and evil, hence the repeated identification of the spirit-spouse as a devil figure.[10] It should be noted, however, that folk magic practitioners of early modern Britain did venerate a vegetative horned deity, whom the church sought to demonize and supplant with the Christian God (a subject we will return to later).

According to Emma Wilby, popular belief of that period incorporated the idea that humans had sexual relations with spirits. She makes a connection between the marriage of a witch and her familiar to the relationship between a shaman and their helping spirits.[11] This references Eliade's research on the Siberian Goldi shaman's marriage to his *ayami,* which we will explore momentarily.[12]

In Ireland it was traditionally believed that the successful and prosperous governance of society was due to a sacred marriage. Scholar of medieval Irish history Máire Herbert draws upon the tradition of the Hieros Gamos when she cites various Irish legends that illustrate the belief in this early Celtic practice. Here again, most scholars only view this practice through a ritualized, metamythic context to legitimize the status of current political claims to sovereignty. I argue that the early Irish understood that something much more Otherworldly was going on, namely the sacred, sexual union between the Goddess of the land and its sovereign.[13]

Moving to India, we find tantric yogini cults and temples arising in the ninth century CE. The Yogini Sadhana—a ritual performed to worship the yogini—specifies that if a man worships a yogini—an Indic regional Goddess—as a wife he will become the "king of kings," presumably ensuring the sovereignty and prosperity of his domain.[14] In both instances the conferring of land, power, and community was believed to be a by-product, or perhaps the intended outcome, of the spirit marriage.

In the last hundred years, it is clear that the practice of spirit marriage remains alive and well. This is according to various anthropologists and ethnographers who have uncovered evidence that this is indeed the case. Specific examples include reports on the use of the Yin Ch'u or "ghost" marriage in Singapore. The Yin Ch'u is a marriage in which one or both parties are deceased. This practice is replete with elaborate marriage rites and ceremonies and provides a means for unmarried deceased children to be venerated as ancestors. Alternately, it solves the problem of unmarried daughters by marrying them to a spirit. The practice of the ghost marriage also appears in five other cultures—those of the African Nuer tribe and the African Atout tribe, as well as the cultures of China, Japan, and ancient Greece. The reasons for a ghost marriage can arise from a few different motivations: property, maintenance of the family name; appeasement of the spirit of the deceased, creation of interfamilial bonds, and marriage hierarchy among brothers.[15]

Evidence also exists for the practice of spirit marriage among Siberian shamans and women of the Goldi tribe. According to Mircea Eliade, who gives perhaps the most widely referenced documentation of spirit marriage in *From Primitives to Zen: A Thematic Sourcebook of the History of Religion* in his chapter entitled "Mystical Marriage of a Siberian (Goldi) Shaman," not only is spirit marriage prevalent there but the women of the Goldi tribe also claim they can even be made pregnant by such entities.[16]

However, Eliade gives little mention of this practice in the remainder of his study on shamanism. And apart from explicitly calling out the sexual nature of the relationship between the shaman and his *ayami*—or spirit-spouse—this leaves many open questions about the nature and function of this relationship in the shaman's lived experience. Questions arise as to how the spirit-spouse manifests for the shaman, how the spirit assists in the shaman's work, and how the relationship is integrated into the tribe. These questions were foundational to my inquiry into current practices of spirit marriage transculturally.

Transgender or two-spirited shamans also exist. These are shamans who are called by their spirit-spouse to adopt the dress and behavior of the opposite sex. In *Shamanism,* Eliade cites numerous accounts in which the calling of the shaman involves a gender inversion by the shaman, most often a male to female transition.[17] He reports, "This transvestitism [sic], with all the changes that it involves, is accepted after a supernatural command has been thrice received in dreams; to refuse would be to seek death."[18]

It is also true that transgender people are more frequently called by their tribe to serve as a spiritual leader because in these traditions a transgender or genderqueer person is generally considered to be better suited for performing shamanic duties. They are seen as being naturally capable of the kinds of transformation and metamorphosis required to be a shaman.[19]

This is discussed in the work of queer scholar and Paganism expert Randy P. Conner, who points out that gender-variant or transgender shamans are considered to be more powerful because of their ability to transgress the male-female polarity. Thus they are often seen as supernatural or Godlike. This gives them prestige within their culture due to their intimate contact with the spirit world.[20]

We will revisit the theme of gender identity and spirit marriage in part III, specifically when I discuss how gender identity relates to spirit marriages between a human partner identified with a binary sexual orientation—homosexual or heterosexual—and the request for marriage from an entity representing the inverse of one's ordinary sexual orientation. For example, among my coresearchers are a homosexual male called into a spirit marriage by a female entity and a mostly heterosexual female called into marriage with a female deity.

Anthropologist Karen McCarthy Brown's groundbreaking study of a Haitian Vodou priestess entitled *Mama Lola: A Vodou Priestess in Brooklyn* details her journey toward spirit marriage. Although Brown first approached Mama Lola as a research subject for an ethnography on the Haitian Vodou community in Brooklyn, her relationship with Mama Lola deepened to the point that she initiated into the Vodou tradition—ultimately leading to her marriage to a Vodou spirit. Brown's work is monumental in that she brought attention to the widespread practice and validity of the Vodou religion. This helped to begin to break down ignorant negative associations with Vodou, as well as portraying the complex influences that affect Haitian women's lives.

South Asia yields another variation on the theme of the spirit marriage. There we find the female temple priestess, or *devadasi,* who married the deity Jagannatha, a form of Vishnu.* Although the term *devadasi* is sometimes understood to be synonymous with a dancing girl or prostitute, this is a degeneration from the original role of her service as a temple priestess.[21]

Historical debate continues around the role and position of the devadasi through the lens of feminist scholarship, challenging the traditional academic assumption that the devadasi were simply courtesans. They do not marry any mortal men because their dedication to temple service is regarded as constituting, as we have already stated, a marriage with the deity Jagannatha. They are called "the auspicious women" who sing "the auspicious songs." They are also ritual specialists, the only women allowed to participate in the rituals and festivals of Puri. However, because of their association with sex, the devadasi are also

---

*Ethnographer Frédérique Apffel Marglin traces these rituals and traditions in her book *Wives of the God-King* and explores the world of the devadasi through the lens of Odissi Indian classical dance.

considered to be impure and barred from entering the inner sanctum of the temple. This tradition, that of the temple devadasi, began to die out in the 1980s or thereabouts. Its demise is a complex topic that involves the loss of income due to the state government takeover of the temples in 1955, and the desire of the devadasi to disassociate themselves from the more erotic components of their lineage. As well, the refusal of the daughters of the devadasi to follow in their mothers' footsteps was a significant factor in its eventual demise.[22]*

In South India the God Paandi Muneeswarar—a form of Shiva—is reported to join with barren women and engender virgin births. Similarly, in the Nepalese Kathmandu Valley the Newar people have a tradition called the *ihi* wherein prepubescent girls are married to a *bel* fruit—generally believed to be a gloss either for the God Vishnu Narayana or Shiva's son Survarna Kumara.[23] As a result of the ihi ritual, Newar girls are not forced into child marriage and women in general hold a higher status than other ethnic groups in Nepal. Some Newar believe the purpose of the ihi ceremony, in fact, is to give the young girls a protector spirit that will keep away malicious and unwanted attention. The girl keeps the fruit with her—even when she marries her human husband—thereby reinforcing the primacy of her spirit-spouse.

It might seem like spirit marriage is not as prevalent in cultures of the world that are not discussed here, most notably Africa,† South and Central America, Australia, and the Pacific Islands. In my opinion, this is not because spirit marriage does not appear in these regions—in fact, given the data I've collected I'm fairly certain that this is a global phenomenon. Instead, it's probably due to the lack of research being conducted into traditions that incorporate the practice of spirit marriage. As you can see, the topic of spirit marriage as a viable spiritual practice

---

*For further mention of the devadasi and their role as divine consorts, see David Gordon White's *Kiss of the Yogini: Tantric Sex in Its South Asian Contexts,* and Jalaja Bonheim's *Aphrodite's Daughters: Women's Sexual Stories and the Journey of the Soul.*

†Although anthropological and historical literature on spirit marriage in Africa is lacking, we do dive deeply into the contemporary lived experience of a West African Dagara practitioner who is wed to a spirit in the chapter "The West African Shrine Keeper."

receives scant serious attention in traditional anthropological literature, which often consigns it to the realm of sympathetic magic or metaphor. It is in the field of folklore and mythology that we find a much richer narrative evidence of its presence.

FOLKLORE AND MYTHOLOGY

Let's return to Greece (and the Hieros Gamos) where there is strong evidence of spirit marriage as it was originally practiced within the mystery traditions of ancient Greece. Practitioner-scholar of the ancient Mediterranean mystery traditions Marguerite Rigoglioso takes a literal interpretation of Hieros Gamos in classical mythology. Rigoglioso argues that one stage of Hieros Gamos was the visitation of a male being (God) who possessed the power to impregnate a human woman.[24] Rigoglioso goes on to say that the intended purpose of the Hieros Gamos was the conception of divine beings, destined for the roles of priest/priestess, hero/heroine, demi-God/demi-Goddess, or king/queen.[25]

Later in this work, I will postulate that the use of spirit marriage was and is a theurgic undertaking used by humans as a tool for personal transformation and evolution of consciousness—an assertion rooted in prehistorical hints of the phenomenon of Gods and Goddesses mating with humans. At this point, the Hieros Gamos began to move away from its original purpose of an individual *entheotic* relationship with the ineffable, into what Dutch historian Kees Bolle refers to as a stylized form of royal sexual ritual.[26] Rigoglioso posits the ultimate goal of this practice was divine birth. I offer that we can expand upon this theory by including discussion of the Hermetic undertaking of the Great Work—that is, the evolution of the species through apotheosis of the Self, what I refer to as *entheosis,* which we will discuss at length in part III.

Greek mythology offers up some clues as to the nature of spirit marriage as reflected in the mytho-historical life of Numa Pompilius, the second Sabine king of Rome, and his spirit consort and counselor Egeria, a nymph. Egeria is credited with counseling Numa to establish the original framework of laws and rituals in Rome; giving oracular guidance and divination of omens; assisting as an intermediary with other divinities, namely Jupiter; and perhaps cultivating an intimate relationship with Numa. According to Plutarch, "The Goddess Egeria loved him and bestowed herself upon him, and it was his communion with her that gave him a life of blessedness and a wisdom more than human."[27] This is an example of a committed, cocreative relationship between a human and a spirit-being.

Apuleis's myth of Cupid and Psyche—although often interpreted as a metaphor for the evolution of the soul—can also be viewed through the lens of spirit marriage.[28] In this case, a mortal woman Psyche is wooed by a divine being—Cupid—and through overcoming trial and tribulation is finally united in a sacred marriage with her divine husband and given the gift of immortality. The significance of this myth is that it hits many of the major tropes found in spirit marriage narratives—the initially opaque identity of the spirit-spouse, loss and longing, testing of the human spouse, enactment of the sacred marriage ritual, and ultimately bestowal of some form of suprahuman quality upon the human spouse. (We'll keep all these themes in mind as we explore the contemporary lived experience of this practice in part II.)

Moving to the northwestern European traditions, in the Middle Ages the human-faery marriage was accepted as fact.[29] This might cause us to ponder: How could such couplings go largely undetected? Perhaps the offspring of such unions, unlike ancient Greek heroes and demi-Gods, "differed in no respect from the normal human child, though they were usually very handsome and possessed intelligence above the average."[30] There is also evidence, however, that the bestowing of "faery blood" was not necessarily dependent upon the mating of a human and faery but could also be bestowed as a "gift of powers" from the nonhuman realm to the devout human.

This theme is echoed repeatedly in the fairy tales of mystical power being given to the worthy human, most notably in *Sleeping Beauty* by way of blessing and cursing by thirteen fairies. Later we will expand upon this idea by discussing the nature and form of changes that humans allegedly experience as a result of being wedded to a spirit.

An excellent example of the complexity of the human-faery marriage can be found in the Irish myth of Oisín, son of Irish hero Fionn mac Cumhaill and his faery wife, Niamh Chinn Óir, daughter of the sea God Manannán mac Lir.[31] In this tale Niamh visits Oisín and falls passionately in love with him, whisking him off to the land of the ever-young, Tír na nÓg. There they have children and are presumably happy. However, after what seems to Oisín to be only three years he becomes homesick and asks Niamh if he can return to Ireland to see how his homeland is faring. She agrees and gives him her magical white steed, Embarr, warning him not to dismount under any circumstance.

Unfortunately, when Oisín arrives he discovers three hundred years have passed and his home and country is in disarray. Oisín dismounts—some say by accident, others due to dismay—and he immediately ages three hundred years and dies. This tale is an excellent example of the *geas*, an idiosyncratic taboo or vow often placed upon a human when they enter into union with an extraordinary being.

Echoing the story of Oisín and Niamh is the Scottish initiatory ballad of Thomas Rhymer, or Sir Thomas of Erceldoune, a thirteenth-century Scottish laird who was famous for his prophetic abilities. In *The Ballad of Thomas Rhymer* Thomas encounters the Faery Queen who whisks him away to the land of Faery where he receives initiation into the Faery mysteries and presumably becomes her consort. However, unlike Oisín, after seven years Thomas is returned to the human realm with blessings and gifts, namely the gift of prophecy.[32] Thomas Rhymer's story is significant in that he was a historical figure who was well respected—not only for his prophecy, but also for his poetry and social standing.

Finally, in the Welsh folkloric account of the *Physicians of Myddfai* we find not only evidence of the Faery marriage but also of the by-product of that marriage—offspring who sire a line of famous healers whose descendants practiced medicine well into the eighteenth century. The folktale centers on the story of a young man who supposedly lived in the parish of Myddfai in Carmarthenshire in the twelfth century.

This fellow marries a faery woman and they have a son, Rhiwallon, who is gifted by his faery mother with the secrets of making effective herbal remedies derived from local plants. Rhiwallon became a skilled practitioner, his reputation spreading beyond his immediate locality, and along with his sons Cadwgan, Gruffydd, and Einion, he was appointed court physician to Rhys Grug (1165–1233) of the House of Dinefwr.[33]

The brothers created a collection of treatises on humors, medicinal herbs, and similar topics that were included in the *Red Book of Hergest,* a fourteenth-century manuscript collection under the title *Meddygon Myddfai.* This story is noteworthy not only because of its account of spirit marriage but also because there is generally believed to be a taboo against the creation of human-faery offspring lest they spawn monsters. Yet here we find the establishment of a reputable lineage of healers as a result of this human-faery coupling!

Looking East, we can examine spirit marriage through the lens of Indian culture and specifically through Shaivite mythology.[34] In this we note the humanness of Shiva's consorts, specifically in his marriage ritual to the king's daughter Minakshi, celebrated annually in South India. This is reflected in the work of history of religion professor William Harman, who suggests that the question about whether Minakshi was human or deity is misguided. Instead Hinduism maintains a fluidity in considering the distinction between human and divine and the need to distinguish between the two is a monotheistic proclivity. Hindus, apparently, are much more comfortable with "the simultaneous co-existence of undivided human and divine attributes in a single figure."[35] What is key to our inquiry is, What are the methods by which these humans are contacted by and wedded to a deity, and how was Minakshi eventually deified herself?

In Islamic folklore it is commonly believed that the Queen of Sheba, known as Bilquis in Islam and Makeda in Ethiopia, is the daughter of a djinn mother and a human father.[36] It is noteworthy that Judaism, Christianity, and Islam Solomon is reported to be a great magician who engages legions of djinn in his service. It seems to follow that Solomon would have acquired his great magic through his union with the half-djinn queen. Solomonic magick is, in fact, the basis of many modern occult magic practices that claim to take a majority of their workings from Solomon and the Kabbalah. These practices allegedly went underground during the purging of the Enoch texts in the fourth century and eventually found their way into the mystery schools and esoteric cults arising in Europe in the nineteenth century and later.[37]

I'm certain that if you dig deeply enough you can probably find, in most of the world's mythologies, stories of other marriages that were spirit-wed. For brevity's sake, I've only shared with you the ones that I came across that jumped out as stellar examples. That said, I think further research could be done collecting stories from Africa, the indigenous American traditions in North, Central, and South America, the Norse traditions, and the Pacific Islands, as well as any other areas of the planet that aren't discussed at length herein.

RELIGIOUS LITERATURE AND PRAXIS

Discussions of spirit marriage can also be found within religious texts and in writings by practitioners of those religions. This is actually where, in my opinion, things get really juicy, because in the context of religion we are finally, hopefully, talking about the intimacy of someone's lived experience. Again, I have only included accounts that directly reference spirit marriage or have a strong inference of spirit marriage, rather than taking on the more exhaustive yet relevant discussion of how spirit contact in some form has shaped and informed most of our world religions.

Let's start with two of the biggies for us here in the West: Judaism and Christianity. The discovery of the Dead Sea Scrolls in 1946 brought into the public eye the book of Enoch, a key piece of apocryphal literature on the study of angels, or angelology. It revealed just how much monotheistic religions may have left out in regard to the relationship between angels and humans.[38] The text states: "[A]nd they said to him. . . . We [Fallen Angels] will [not] turn away, any of us, from this plan. . . . They and their lieutenants they took women of all that they chose [. . .] to teach them sorcery [. . .] and the women became pregnant by them and bore [. . .] and giants were being born on the earth" (1 Enoch Col 3: 1–21).

Only a brief mention of the phenomenon described here can be found in the Christian canon. In Genesis we read: "The Sons of God saw the daughters of men that they were fair; and they took to wife such of them as they chose. . . . The Nephilim were on the earth in those days, and also afterward, when the sons of God came in to the daughters of men, and they bore children to them. These were the mighty men that were of old, the men of renown" (Genesis 6:2–4, RSV).

Various accounts of these so-called "fallen" angels, also known as the Watchers or Grigori, prevail in both Hebraic, biblical and postbiblical texts and in commentary on these texts in the form of insights written by Jewish and early church scholars. These accounts refer to the story of the sons of God (the angelic Watchers) coupling with the daughters of men. In another early common era account, the Hellenistic Jewish philosopher Philo of Alexandria (born 25 BCE) examines the morality of other beings, warning that we should not assume demons are evil and angels are good,* but that the terms *angels, demons,* and *souls* refer to the same beings. He goes as far as to say that what Moses (Torah) calls *angels,* the philosophers (Greeks) call *demons.*[39]

Biblical scholar Kevin Sullivan states that the "fundamental problem with the 'sons of God' (angels) coming to earth and taking human wives is their transgression of the boundary set at creation. Their union with human women creates a hybrid, interpreted as 'giants,' that was not meant to exist."[40] In his footnote to this statement Sullivan calls for further study into the issues of gender and sexuality in relationship to beliefs regarding angels, noting that much is made of angelic celibacy in the gospel accounts but the gospels are the only texts that support such an idea. It should be noted that a large body of literature exists suggesting that at least one group of angels was not celibate.[41]

Further evidence of sexual relations between angels and humans

---

*Yes! More on this in my story "The Erotic Mystic."

is described in the Genesis account and the extracanonical books of Enoch, the book of the Watchers, and Jubilees. Although postbiblical tradition cites this mating as the origin of evil, canonized literature views such acts as something simply to be discouraged.[42]

Yet to be explored is the question of exactly why the mating of humans and angels was considered taboo. It is an open question as to whether the original act was a direct violation of God's commandment or simply something frowned upon due to the aftermath of problems it created.

According to paranormal investigator Andrew Collins, whose work centers on questioning the origin myths of Christianity, the early church fathers cultivated a climate of fear around the dangers of "seducing angels"—for the primary purpose of keeping women veiled and silent.[43] Many of the early church leaders from the first to the third centuries CE used and openly quoted from the Enoch texts and generally accepted that the fallen angels possessed corporeal bodies. It was not until the fourth century that these assumptions were questioned, and subsequently the book of Enoch and many teachings on angelology were suppressed. Accounts of Christian mystics and monastics from the Middle Ages still hint at the continuing presence of these fallen angels.

It is also surmised that spirit lover practices may have been hidden in plain sight within Christianity. Specifically, St. Teresa of Avila's autobiography is a primary testament to the ongoing practice of spirit marriage—or at least human-entity eroticism. In her autobiography St. Teresa describes one encounter as follows:

> I saw in his hand a long spear of gold, and at the iron's point there seemed to be a little fire. He appeared to me to be thrusting it at times into my heart, and to pierce my very entrails; when he drew it out, he seemed to draw them out also, and to leave me all on fire with a great love of God. The pain was so great, that it made me moan; and yet so surpassing was the sweetness of this excessive pain, that I could not wish to be rid of it. The soul is satisfied now with nothing less than God. The pain is not bodily, but spiritual;

though the body has its share in it. It is a caressing of love so sweet which now takes place between the soul and God, that I pray God of His goodness to make him experience it who may think that I am lying.[44]

When viewed through the context of monastic vows, wherein a nun espouses herself to be the "bride of Christ," this type of encounter seems a kind of spirit marriage. However, the church has traditionally classified such activity as *congressus cum daemone* (union with demons), and during the Inquisition it went so far as to promote the idea that witches gave birth to children by consorting with Satan and other nefarious spirits. Yet in the case of St. Teresa, it is considered to be a form of communing with God himself and thus a form of sainted activity.

Similarly, San Juan de la Cruz (St. John of the Cross), a close friend of St. Teresa, writes of his ecstatic union with Jesus through highly erotic innuendo. Notably, in his poem "Noche Oscura" (Dark Night), St. John expresses his relationship with Jesus as rendering his maleness female through mystical union.

Feminist and queer scholar Sue-Ellen Case describes this gender inversion:

> Then, in "The Spiritual Canticle," where his love finds full expression in the trope of marriage, John inverts his gender, writing his desire as if he were the bride with the other being as the bridegroom. John, the bride, languishes for her lover, seeks him everywhere, finally reaching him: "Our bed: in roses laid / patrols of lions ranging all around. . . . There I gave all of me; put chariness aside: there I promised to become his bride" (*Poems* 7–9). And the bridegroom says to John: "I took you tenderly hurt virgin, made you well" (15). The wound of love liberates the lover from the boundaries of being the living, dying envelope of the organic. Ontology shifts through gender inversion and is expressed as same-sex desire. This is queer, indeed.[45]

Through the lens of the courtly love tradition, ecstatic accounts of union with the Divine were prevalent in the writings of many Beguine mystics in the thirteenth to sixteenth centuries. When I was in seminary I explored this topic in a paper I wrote entitled "The Beguine Movement: Lovers of God or God's Lovers?" In it I explore the idea that the Beguines were creating a kind of mystico-erotic spirituality as a way to exercise power and autonomy in a highly misogynistic culture. Beguines adopted the monastic practice of marrying Christ and extolling the ecstasies and virtues of this nuptial union. They apparently harbored an intense mystical experience of passionate love for the Divine—understood to be both Christ, the Beloved, and Lady Love, a feminine face of God. Three prominent Beguine mystics—Mechthild of Magdeburg, Beatrijs of Nazareth, and Hadewijch of Brabant—exemplify mystico-erotic contact in their writings and poetry, ultimately describing their spirituality as a passionate love affair between the soul and God.

Echoing de la Cruz's gender inversion, Mechthild of Magdeburg writes of the unitive experience of being possessed by a deity who is decidedly female. She repeatedly beseeches Lady Love to vanquish her. It is through this longing that Magdeburg believes her soul is being perfected. "You should ask God to love you long, often, and intensely so that you may be pure, beautiful and holy."[46] Her poetry reflects a rapturous state of homoerotic and overtly sadomasochistic (BDSM), desire: "O lady love, cast me beneath your feet! / I delight when victorious you vanquish me / And through you my life is destroyed / For in that, O lady, lies my true safety."[47]

Suffering for God's love is a theme repeated in the writings of Beatrice of Nazareth who, like the courtly lover, is at the complete mercy of the whims of the Lady Love and suffers according to her pleasure. Like the story of Psyche, the human lover is compelled to do the bidding of the transcendent and somewhat impossible lover. Through this process of perceived humiliation and degradation, the soul is able to take flight and abandon its selfish motives to the will of the Divine.

Following the theme of utter possession by God, Hadewijch of Brabant extolls a radical experiential theology of love. Anthropology of religion scholar Fiona Bowie in *Beguine Spirituality* observes, "For Hadwijch, Love (*Minne*) becomes her spouse, her Lady mistress, her God, her companion, a mistress who leads Hadwijch through bleak times, moments of isolation and despair, as well as giving her periods of rapture and delight."[48] Hadewijch's desire for mystical experience and her hunger to be visited by visions of Christ fueled her visionary writings with sensual expressions based in the experience of the body, most notably in her work "Visions."

Her account is as follows:

On a certain Pentecost Sunday I had a vision at dawn. . . . My heart and my veins and all my limbs trembled and quivered with eager desire and, as often occurred with me, such madness and fear beset my mind that it seemed to me I did not content my Beloved, and that my Beloved did not fulfill my desire, so that dying I must go mad, and going mad I must die. On that day my mind was beset so fearfully and so painfully by desirous love that all my separate limbs threatened to break, and all my separate veins were in travail. The longing in which I then was cannot be expressed. . . . I desired to have full fruition of my Beloved, and to understand and taste him to the full. I desired that his Humanity should to the fullest extent be one in fruition with my humanity . . . and in all things to content him fully in every virtue . . . and in this way to experience nothing else but sweet love, embraces, and kisses. In this sense I desired that God give himself to me, so that I might content him.[49]

Hadewijch describes an occurrence that follows this account, of her beloved coming in the form and clothing of a man "as he was on the day he gave his body for the first time; looking like a Human Being and a Man, wonderful, beautiful, and with glorious face."[50] She then goes on to describe how she gave herself to him, how she partook of his flesh and was made one with him. All this, she says, was accomplished when she took the sacrament, after which "he came himself to me, took me entirely in his arms, and pressed me to him; and all my members felt him in full felicity, in accordance with the desire of my heart and my humanity."[51]

For Hadewijch, Christ also becomes the Lady Love, the passionate other toward whom the Beguine can project all her yearnings and desires, suffering like Christ did so that she becomes united with him in her love and her suffering for that love. Hadewijch's writings are rich with metaphors of marriage, gender-fluidity, and sexual union. She speaks of the desire and the delight experienced by the joining of the two into one. In "Letters to a Young Beguine," letter 9, she states, "He shall teach you what he is and with that wonderful sweetness the one lover lives in the other and so permeates the other that they do not know themselves from each other. But they possess each other in mutual delight, mouth in mouth, heart in heart, body in body, soul in soul, while a single divine nature flows through them and they both become one through each other, yet remaining themselves."[52]

Here we find an excellent account of the process of being *indwelled* by a spirit, a concept we will discuss later. It is here in the records of the Beguines that I believe we find some of the most explicit accounts of spirit marriage in the Christian tradition.

In contrast, it is apparent that the church developed conflicting views toward such mystical unions. This is illustrated by the life of the late sixteenth-century Italian abbess Benedetta Carlini. Her mysticism, namely a trance-like mediumship in which she claimed to be speaking with Jesus and a host of angels, as well as manifesting stigmata, led to her rapid elevation within the Theatine convent. This encounter culminated in a full-fledged wedding ceremony between Carlini and Jesus that was sanctioned by the church.[53] However, over time and upon deeper investigation by the Catholic authorities, some of Carlini's manifestations, particularly the stigmata, were determined to have been faked.[54] Adding to the accusations were reports of her homosexual relationship with another nun, Bartolomea.[55]

However, Carlini claimed to be possessed by a male angel who engaged in sexual activity via her body. This was activity that she claimed the angel had sanctioned because he wished to marry Bartolomea.[56] This account is an excellent example of the complex and shifting acceptance of spirit marriage within Christianity as it gradually moved away from its medieval focus on miracles and extraordinary experiences. In so doing, it moved toward an emphasis, colored by the Enlightenment, on obedience and good works, eventually categorizing most spirit contacts as demonic possession.

Moving East, deity yoga—a practice on both the Tantric Buddhist and Hindu Tantric paths—actively encourages intimate involvement with a visualized deity. The primary technique employed to cultivate the deity within oneself—a process of seeing the God/dess within—is also used to establish a working rapport with an externally visualized deity.[57] In this, the practitioner works with the process of Tantric inner and outer cultivation to develop an experience of oneself as the deity. The practice is done through the cultivation of one's *ishtadeva/i,* the deity chosen to be one's personal deity—which should not be imposed on us by another but is our individual choice. The chosen deity then becomes the focus of one's devotion, and a relationship is built as if the deity is another person. Eventually, one begins to assume the qualities and habits of the ishtadeva/i by visualizing the external deity as a Tantric partner wherein the deity form built up in oneself interacts with the deity of worship as a consort.[58]

Shifting to the subject of the intersection between shamanic spirit marriage and Tantric tradition, we see that Siberian shamanic practice parallels and illuminates the more transgressive Tantric practice—namely sexual union as a means of attaining spiritual powers, called *siddhis.* The bonded commitment in both traditions is the pact or contract that confers initiation, mediumship, and possession. From this union a "psycho-physiological relationship" between the human and spirit world is forged—one that may produce hybridized offspring or potentially lead to the eventual divinization of the human partner.[59]

However, there is also a shadow side of spirit marriage wherein the possibility of sexual possessiveness and the disruption of human relationships sometimes accompany wooing by the spirit. Research by ethnographer I. M. Lewis has shown that the worldly relationships of female shamans were also prone to suppression by their spiritual suitors.[60] Indic religion scholar Stuart Ray Sarbacker surmises that "some sexual relationships may be desired; others not, and in both cases shamanic practices aim at the control of such spirits,"[61] lending credence to the idea that *a practitioner's ability to skillfully negotiate with the spirits may be what gives them sovereignty and protection in nonordinary states*—a subject we will discuss at greater length in the sovereignty section in part III.

It is in the African Diaspora religions of Haitian Vodou and New Orleans Voodoo that we find some of the most vital and unbroken lineages of spirit marriage in the West. Born out of the slave arrivals from the Middle Passage, these traditions hold vestiges of African Earth-based spirituality, indigenous folkloric magic, and Christianity.[62] In their efforts to survive, the various African tribes that were brought together under the yoke of slavery—often with disparate spiritual practices—mixed together, learned from their surroundings, and masked their beliefs with the icons and trappings of Christianity.

These practitioners brought their spirit-spouses to the so-called New World and enshrined them in the land and culture of the Americas. Although their deities may carry the names and behaviors of those found in a mainstream religion, these deities arise from a distinct spiritual tradition unto themselves. We see this distinction clearly in the well-preserved hybridic centers of New Orleans, Haiti, Brazil, Mexico, and the Caribbean. The practice of union with a spirit stands front and center in these traditions, whether in the form of a marriage rite or divine embodiment.

The *New York Times* journalist Gergana Koleva reports on the practices of Haitian Vodou immigrants in New York City: "Joining hearts with a . . . Spirit is like signing a contract with an invisible protector to bring good luck, dispel loneliness and ease financial woes. . . .

A spiritual marriage offers something for everyone. The Spirit gains entry to the human world, where in dreams or visions it makes its proposal of marriage to the person. If the proposal is accepted, the Spirit is honored and celebrated, in exchange for which its earthly spouse is promised divine protection from life's misfortunes."[63]

There appears to be a long-standing protocol for spirit marriage.[64] Its formula can be summarized as follows:

1. Contact is initiated by a spirit in a dream or visionary state.
2. A relationship is built.
3. The spirit proposes marriage and the human accepts.
4. A ceremony or ritual is performed during which a human stand-in is possessed by the spirit to be married.
5. Marriage vows are taken and rings are exchanged; this includes a substantial dowry or offering to the spirit.
6. The human spouse is then expected to set aside a specific time, anywhere from one night a month to three nights a week, where they will "commune" with their spirit-spouse. On that evening the individual is visited by the spirit husband/wife in dreams that may have sexual content or that may involve more platonic counsel and advice.
7. Violation of the wedding vows is seen as dangerous, and spirit partners often show their displeasure if one ignores them, just like a real spouse would. This union is a lifelong commitment.

This formula, with some variance, was cited repeatedly by my coresearchers as their initiation into a spirit marriage. It seems that a discernable transcultural protocol is emerging—one that I believe may help to elucidate a process for fostering, developing, and concretizing an interdenominational form of spirit marriage.

The cultural historian Marilyn Houlberg interviewed Vodou practitioner George René about his marriage to the two Ezilis in "My Double Mystic Marriages to Two Goddesses of Love," which is included in Cosentino's seminal *Sacred Arts of Haitian Vodou*. George René's marriage to the lesbian Loa Ezili Dantò again raises the theme of gender identity and flexible sexual orientation among both the practitioners of spirit marriage and the spirits themselves. According to René, "She loves men, yeah, but she's a lesbian. . . . She's marrying me, but she sleeps with women."[65]

This idea is echoed by Conner, Sparks, and Sparks in regard to African and African Diasporic traditions. In *Cassell's Encyclopedia of Queer Myth, Symbol, and Spirit,* they state: "The relationship between priest and God is thought to be characterized in feminine-masculine terms because the Yorùbá, like other peoples we have encountered, think of the state of possession as a receptive, hence traditionally feminine, state (i.e., to be possessed or "ridden" by the God is to be penetrated by the God)."[66]

In the case of René, we see a heterosexual human male marrying a female lesbian deity that, according to the definition above, places René in the female receptive position to Ezili Dantò's male penetration—a dizzying gender-bending if ever there was one. Again, the ideas of gender inversion and sexual flexibility have repeatedly surfaced as core themes in my research. As a result, I have sought to unlock the ways in which human-entity relations perhaps transcend and include a variety of human sexualities, potentially offering a much queerer view of the spirit-world than orthodox tradition would have it.

In summary, I searched for current examples of spirit marriage in Judaism, Islam, and other less mainstream religions, as well as any alternative spirituality that had even a whiff of relevance. And as I mentioned previously, there is definitely a long-standing practice in the West African Traditional religion of the Dagara people of Burkina Faso, which I imagine isn't unique to just that region of Africa. However, it's not something that has, to my knowledge, ever been put into print. And we know from historical accounts that spirit marriage is also an important, albeit often hush-hush, aspect of Witchcraft and Shamanism.

That's where this book comes in. I hope that by weaving all of these threads together, more stories will surface within both mainstream and marginalized religious traditions, which will help to give us the biggest possible picture just how pervasive spirit marriage actually is. To that end, if you have a lineage-based practice or personal account that you think I should know about, please visit my website spiritmarriage.com and share your story.

3
The Occult and
Psycho-Spiritual Practice

$\int$pirit marriage began to make its way into the public imagination as a result of the growing popular interest in all things paranormal that hit a peak in the late 1800s. This was due to the emergence of various movements such as Spiritualism, whose members held séances and readily communed with unseen forces. At this time, the revelation of Hermetic (mystery school) knowledge made its way into the mainstream through groups like the Theosophists, Anthroposophists,* and the Golden Dawn.[1]

In 1894 an erudite East Coast woman named Ida Craddock claimed to be married to an angel named Soph, an account of which was later published under the title "Heavenly Bridegrooms." In this account, more remarkably, she painstakingly traced the history and psychology of spirit marriage from the Pagan traditions through the advent of Christian civilization and into her experiences of Spiritualist

---

*Theosophy is a religion established in the United States during the late nineteenth century by Russian immigrant Helena Blavatsky. It draws upon European philosophies such as Neoplatonism as well as Asian religions such as Hinduism and Buddhism. Drawing upon his study of Theosophy, the twentieth-century esotericist Rudolf Steiner (1861–1925) founded Anthroposophy, a philosophy that posits that an objective, intellectually comprehensible spiritual world—a world that humans can access—exists.

and mediumship practices within the Theosophical Society.[2] Craddock was a staunch advocate of women's sexual pleasure, the art of which she claimed she learned from her angelic spirit-spouse. Her courage in sharing her spirit-sex story and advocating for women's sexual autonomy would inspire and influence the sex magick practices of the twentieth century developed by renown occultist Aleister Crowley and his contemporaries.

Craddock's accounts are indispensable because although she was not recognized among the educated elite of her time—a privilege held by few women in that day and age—she is greatly revered and recognized among occult scholars as an American mystic, sexologist, and expert practitioner of this phenomenon. Tragically, Craddock would pay a high price for her openly mystico-erotic relationship and advocacy of women's sexual rights. Ultimately, this led to her being persecuted by U.S. Postal Inspector Anthony Comstock. She was imprisoned at Blackwell's Island workhouse (on what is today Roosevelt Island in the East River of New York), the result of which drove her to commit suicide.

Other accounts of spirit marriages began to emerge at this time as well. Contemporary to Craddock was the Scottish faery author William Sharp (1855–1905), who wrote on behalf of his purported faery wife, Fiona Macleod. During his lifetime Sharp did not publicize that his relationship with Macleod was a spirit marriage. Instead he chose to produce writings under her identity, going so far as to make up a false residence and backstory for her.[3]

Fiona Macleod was extremely popular among the Victorian public, and her fairy tales, poetry, and prose were in high demand. It was only after Sharp's passing that it came to be known that Sharp had channeled the writings of the spiritual entity that is Fiona Macleod. Sharp's letters and journals demonstrate the deeply intimate, wedded nature that Sharp and Macleod held in a human-faery co-created authorship. It is also clear that Sharp-Macleod knew of other faery marriages. In her essay "Iona" she tells of a woman who falls in love with a faery man, becomes pregnant by him, and comes to the point of death during the delivery. She must choose between going with him into the realm of Faery or staying with the child and facing death. She chooses to stay with the child in order to give it a Christian baptism, and her faery husband leaves her.[4]

In her 1904 essay "Winged Destiny," Macleod retells the Watchers myth through a Faery lens, describing the mating of a Faery God with a mortal woman who gives birth to half-human, half-faery descendants. Macleod explains that there are prohibitions commonly associated with this kind of coupling. The offspring "may not" have any contact with humans; however, rather than being evil and condemned, these offspring simply must remain separate. In the case of the human-faery child born to the woman who was abandoned by her faery husband, the child lived among humans but had difficulty integrating into society and eventually left the human realm to be with his faery kin.[5]

The mixing of the blood was a taboo, but one that was often transgressed.[6] The *Carmina Gadelica* is a nineteenth-century folkloric text that warns of "the grave dangers of taking a Faery lover and of having children by this lover. It was clearly a situation that was much on the minds of the people, and one they knew, like the Faeries knew, should not be permitted."[7] However, there seems to be a snarl in the fabric of the prohibition, showing us that prohibitions were often ignored and violation of them did not cause the transgressor to suffer catastrophic consequences.

The Hermetic practitioner and lay analyst Dion Fortune (1890–1946), acknowledged, in her day, as one of the foremost experts of the occult, takes these prohibitions even farther. In *Psychic Self-Defense,* Fortune cautions the reader against entering into these kinds of unions, warning that they lead to a deterioration in the human participant and can also lead to offspring that she describes as "soulless." She references the Giants and Nephilim of biblical tradition who are "characterized by a marked callousness, which in one case developed into deliberate cruelty."[8] Yet she seems to soften her position when she reports that two human-faery hybrids she had met, "although very peculiar to look at, neither of them was in the least defective, both being, in fact, possessed of considerably more than the average share of brains."[9] Fortune describes the conception of these beings as resulting from the psychic impregnation of the mother by an entity while she was under the influence of a substance.[10]

Fortune also details the psychic conception of such beings via the sexual union of a human man and woman wherein the entity superimposes himself upon the sexual union and impregnates the female with his own energy. This is a process that is very similar to what Rigoglioso described as union by "surrogate" in her work on divine birth.[11]

Fortune, however, seems to reverse her prohibitive stance later. In *The Esoteric Philosophy of Love and Marriage,* she claims: "A mate may be found who has passed the phase of evolution during which incarnation takes place, and that strange partnership between the unseen and seen may be built up. It is by such a partnership that much of the work of the Masters is carried on."[12] It can be inferred then that Fortune is in support of certain *kinds* of spirit marriage, those that are with "elevated" beings, but not with "lower" entities.

Fortune's work seems to be deeply influenced by Christian beliefs, with her teachings focused on the notion of purity; upon making oneself "pure" and maintaining that purity. Her Christian, colonialist leanings tend to discredit and discount anything not associated with the upper, or heavenly, world. As such, she relegates shamanism and other pre-Christian traditions to what she and other Western researchers rooted in a colonialist mindset derisively call "primitive" consciousness. However, it is notable that she claims firsthand knowledge of what she refers to as "changelings," the offspring of human-spirit union. As well, she is clearly a treasure trove of information on occult practices and techniques. Therefore, her work bears attention, although it's important to read it with a critical eye.

As previously mentioned, throughout the twentieth century in the West the phenomena of spirit marriage began to be developed as a form of sex magick. The ultimate goal of sex magick is to transmute sexual energy into spiritual energy. This is done via the use of meditation and practices done initially by oneself and then with a physical partner, and ultimately with a spirit. Some contemporary sex magick practitioners, notably Ceremonial Magician Donald Tyson, argue that a loving relationship with a spiritual being can be one of the most rewarding relationships in life. Tyson claims that denial or demonization of this type of spiritual practice is akin to sticking one's head in the sand. Distaste for the idea of sex with spirits does not equate to the impossibility of it.[13]

In the folkloric Faery tradition of Faery Seership, the practice of spirit marriage is much rarer and more complex. The Faery Seer and British Traditional Witch Orion Foxwood has one of the most publicly recognized Faery marriages in contemporary practice. He describes the Fae as a prehuman race more akin to angelic or Godlike beings than they are to sprites with wings.[14]

According to Foxwood, true Faery marriage requires immense work and transformation of the Self on every level and usually takes seven to nine years, at a minimum, to achieve.[15] Most seekers are not suited to the marriage level of relationship with a Faery, and very few ever make it to this stage.

Foxwood categorizes six stages of Faery contact.[16]

Stage 1, the Contact phase, involves the Fae making itself known to the human through dreams, visions, and/or magical ritual. This contact can often feel sexual in nature, but sex is not the intended result. Fae energy simply has an erotic effect on the human nervous system, arousing one's life force or vital center.

In Stage 2, called the Cousin phase, the individual cultivates familiarity with the Fae. In this stage, resonance and consistency are built between the human and the spirit.

Stage 3, the Co-Walker phase, brings greater collaboration between the two beings, as the Fae becomes a constant presence in the human's life—as if he or she is walking together with the individual.*

Stage 4, the Companion/Lover phase, involves the building of a

---

*Notably, the term *walk with* is a common expression in Vodou and in Regla de Ocha (Santería) for this type of phenomenon.

"ring of light" around the two beings, resulting in a deepening affinity whereby sharing of the upper and under world cultures happens. Energetic shifts take place in the human and the Fae to readjust and imprint both beings to each other.

Stage 5, the Consort/Marriage phase, is rarely reached by a Faery Seership practitioner. This stage involves a folk rite in which the two beings are wedded in ceremony. The ceremony takes place through an "overshadowing," a kind of channeling in which a host who already holds a spirit marriage is possessed by the spirit of the Faery intended to be married. The host then stands as a proxy for the Faery so that the marriage rite can take place on the physical plane. The human is then believed to be indwelled, or holding dual consciousness, with the Faery spouse.

Stage 6, the final stage known as the Cocreation of "Other," the married couple now becomes a living bridge between the worlds, a hybrid being.

Foxwood, who has achieved the final stage of an indwelled Faery Seer, describes his experience thusly: "[W]hen I close my eyes, I see into her world, when I open them, she (my Faery Queen) sees into mine."[17] Foxwood's work is some of the most complete literature written on this practice in the occult tradition and, as such, invites deeper research. The work also raises the question of why the folkloric Faery marriage practice is considered to be such an exclusive path when other traditions, such as the African Diaspora traditions, marry humans to entities (*Loa/Lwa*) quite regularly.

Spirit marriage is also seen between humans and the plant kingdom. Through the lens of *entheogenic** shamanism, Amazonian plant teachers (and other sacred plant medicines) offer erotic experiences that can transform the quality of the practitioners' sexual and spiritual lives. Plant spirit teachers also often offer a connection with other than human entities in the subtle realms, and can open a pathway to God/dess. These encounters often reveal that viewing our bodies as

---

*An entheogen, also called a *psychedelic,* is a chemical substance, typically of plant origin, that is ingested to produce a nonordinary state of consciousness for religious or spiritual purposes.

sacred temples is essential to becoming spiritually embodied. In fact, interactions that involve sexual union and erotic encounters with plant spirits during sacred medicine ceremonies, like ayahuasca, can help us merge with extraordinary beings.

Psychologist and entheogenic researcher Yalila Espinoza reports on the six-month *dieta* (diet) of one woman, Maia, with the plant *sacha* (wild garlic) during which she claims the plant spirit married her. Maia reports that *ajo sacha* merged with her to the degree that he was present with her in spiritual and mundane activities. When she asked him why he wanted to indwell with her to this degree he responded, "The human body is the most incredible playground ever and if you can maintain an environment without salt or sugar so that I can stay in your body, it's the most fun playground of all—to see things from a human perspective—in a human body—to be able to move in a way that I've never been able to move before."[18]

This account demonstrates how the plant was able to enter the human kingdom, and how Maia, through merging with the spirit of the plant, was then able to enter the plant kingdom—fostering a mutually beneficial cocreative experience for both. The idea of an erotic relationship between a human and a plant spirit is a theme that I will share more about in my own story, "The Erotic Mystic," when I discuss my Faery Beloved who also manifests through a hawthorn tree.

THROUGH A TRANSPERSONAL LENS

To better place this research within a psycho-spiritual context, let's look at two key figures who have contributed to the realm of transpersonal philosophy and psychology and who also claimed an ongoing relationship with tutelary spirits or extraordinary guides. Although these relationships do not qualify as a spirit marriage as previously defined, these sources do report on the kinds of relationships that may be cultivated between humans and Otherworldly entities. They include well-known scholarly figures who have ascribed their ideas and inspirations to a relationship with a spirit guide or inner teacher.

First, the Austrian philosopher, social reformer, and esotericist Rudolph Steiner attributed much of his spiritual knowledge and practical philosophy to guidance by a group of nonphysical beings he called "the Masters."* In a Berlin lecture on July 14, 1904, Steiner reports, "The Masters can be regarded by us as Ideal. They have attained what we must attain in the future. We can therefore question them about our future development."[19]

Steiner claimed that his knowledge of plants, the cosmos, and human nature all came to him through his conversations with the Masters. His lectures from 1904 to 1909 often had references to his calling on them to be present and thanking them for participating. And he specifically stated that in some instances the Masters used his body to deliver a lecture.[20] The Anthroposophical Society, founded by Steiner, later removed many of these references from the literature on him to distance him from the fake psychics and dubious channelers of the time.

Steiner himself, however, never retracted his claims to having received information and illumination from extraordinary entities. This information would become the cornerstone of the Anthroposophical Society's beliefs and teachings.†

---

*That Steiner was in contact with and at times spoke for the Masters is a matter of record. In an address in Berlin, on October 22, 1906, he told the assembled that "all twelve Masters of the White Lodge have passed through the entire evolution of our Earth. They cannot work directly into the physical plane. We must lift ourselves up to them. Through the school they work upon us, and in us and through us. The mediator, the teacher of the school, is obligated to answer to no one except him in whose name he speaks." The White Lodge that Steiner refers to is considered to be a group of twelve evolved beings who exist in order to guide humanity in its evolution, post-Atlantis. They include individuals who helped mankind progress at critical junctures in its history, as follows: Koot Hoomi, who affected the transition between the third and fourth cultural epochs; Hilarion, who inspired the fourth cultural epoch; Jesus, who aided in the segue between the fourth and fifth cultural epochs; Christian Rosenkreutz, who oversaw the birth of the fifth cultural epoch; and Morya, inspirer of the sixth or Slavic cultural epoch. Steiner apparently had contact with all twelve of these ascended masters.

†Although some of Steiner's teachings have been criticized for containing presumably racist ideology, his influence on contemporary New Age spirituality and occultism cannot be ignored.

In the discipline of psychology, the 2009 release of the Liber Novus, commonly known as the Red Book, written by the Swiss psychiatrist and father of depth psychology Carl Jung (1875–1961), brought to light a little-known aspect of Jung's personal practice. This was, namely, his relationship with inner figures—unconscious intelligences that some might classify as entities. In 1913, at the age of thirty-eight, Jung experienced an unsettling "confrontation with the unconscious" wherein he began to see visions and hear voices.[21] Although initially concerned that this could be a form of psychosis, Jung decided to take this opportunity to plumb the depths of his unconscious by engaging in active imagination, consciously dialoging with the alleged entities that were manifesting to him.

According to Red Book editor and Jung scholar Sonu Shamdasani, "The central premise of the book was that Jung had become disillusioned with scientific rationalism—what he called 'the spirit of the times'—and over the course of many quixotic encounters with his own soul and with other inner figures, he comes to know and appreciate 'the spirit of the depths,' a field that makes room for magic, coincidence and the mythological metaphors delivered by dreams."[22]

A key figure prominent in this work is the personage of Philemon, a kind of tutelary spirit or *Dantesque* guide. For sixteen years, Jung would meticulously draw, paint, and transcribe his encounters with Philemon, ultimately creating an illuminated manuscript of extraordinary relationality. What is most noteworthy is that it was during the period in which he worked on the Red Book that Jung developed his principal theories of archetypes, the collective unconscious, and the process of individuation. Jung was quite clear: "All my works, all my creative activity has come from those initial fantasies and dreams."[23] However, as with Steiner's followers, Jung's family sequestered this material until 2009 for fear that it would cast a suspicious light onto his sanity or "grasp of reality," thereby tarnishing his legacy.*

---

*Although Jung as a person is admittedly problematic—due to some arguably anti-Semitic remarks and his mistreatment of women—the influence of his work on transpersonal psychology cannot be underestimated, and the pivotal role that extraordinary intelligences played in guiding and informing his theories should not be casually dismissed.

In summary, the reach and impact of spirit marriage on human and social development, since the dawn of recorded history, is significant if not foundational to who we have become as a species. Let's now make our way out of the library and into the light of daily lived experience. Here we will be able to view the applicability of what we have learned in these early chapters. We will start off with contemporary stories of spirit marriage. Put on your sunglasses and get ready for some blinding revelations!

PART II

The Present

✱

A Druid chant for entering the depths

Deep into the Earth I go,
Deep into the Earth I know,
Deep into the Earth I go,
Deep into the Earth I know,
Hold my hand, sister, hold my hand,
Hold my hand, brother, hold my hand.

4

Contemporary Stories
of Spirit Marriage

*W*e share our planet with many other species and beings—both seen and unseen—from the bacteria that live as some of the smallest units of measurable life to the celestial forces and powers that shape our solar system. These "invisibles"—although most often unseen, unheard, and untouched—have long been held by many spiritual traditions as integral to human development. Indeed, on occasion they are believed to make themselves known and available to the prepared (and sometimes unprepared!) individual. The wisdom traditions of our planet have long held the practice of spirit marriage to be a powerful means for the cultivation of extraordinary powers, acceleration of evolutionary development, and progression of humanity. These practices are esoteric and often shrouded by mystery cults and shamanistic initiations.

The calling to a spirit marriage comes in many ways and affects each individual differently. As such, the procedure and journey vary from person to person. Whereas one person may self-medicate to shut out this extraordinary experience, another may be compelled to seek this union from an early age. Each person's path to spirit marriage is unique.

I believe it's important to openly share our stories of extraordinary intimate spiritual contact so that we may frankly discuss what appears to be a thriving practice among a not-insignificant portion of the population. To that end, in this section I've chosen to highlight the individual experiences of those who have participated in a spirit marriage, rather than just giving you an overview of the practices. I call this form of extraordinary, experiential storytelling *normalizing the paranormal.*

In the following pages are firsthand testimonials of spirit marriage practitioners whose marriages are an integral part of their spiritual practice. Front and center to their experience is the fact that most of these practitioners sit outside the scope of mainstream religion. They are witches, magicians, mambos, seers, tantrics, and more—all situated within a variety of edge-walking spiritualities. Their stories contribute to and elucidate the contemporary practice of spirit marriage as a potential means for spiritual growth, personal development, and planetary evolution.

These present-day practitioners of spirit marriage have been trained and initiated into a form of ongoing relationship with an entity and as such they illustrate the power and vitality of engaging in intimacy with the Otherworld. These interviewees, in many ways, are sharing intimate and, for some, never-before-revealed details of a form of spirituality that might raise a few eyebrows in more traditional religious circles. I encourage you to set aside any distaste you might feel about the edgier content of these stories and their authors. Give them the respect and honor one would give any holy person—for this is who they are: mystics, visionaries, and ministers in their respective traditions who hold spiritual power and religious influence.

Nothing less than that was required of me.

As I sat with each practitioner and took in their story I was changed in ways that I am in awe of and deeply humbled by to this day. With each interview it was as if an extrasensory energy had been introduced into my nervous system. I left feeling expanded, altered, and sometimes as though my psyche had in some way been reconfigured. It quickly became clear that the interviews were more than just a process of data collection. I was encountering extraordinary beings who were now part of my constellation of spirit contacts.

Frankly, I was wholly unprepared for the intensity of that experience. Stepping into dialogue with the spirit-spouses of my interviewees was consciousness-changing. My sensitivity became heightened to incredible ways of knowing, to perceiving subtle changes in the natural world, and to the nuances of emotion and thought in others. Many things in my life began to shift and arrange themselves in new ways. My health, relationships, and career all underwent significant upheaval. The interviews I collected became more than just stories of spirit-spouses and their relationship to their human partner. They became a kind of psycho-spiritual attunement and reconfiguration of my own mind, body, and spirit. Conducting the interviews altered me and affected how I interacted with beings in both the seen and unseen worlds.

It is my hope that by reading this book you may also experience some degree of that recalibration yourself. There is a mystery here. Perhaps you've experienced something like it before? You're reading a book and suddenly your perspective shifts as the intelligence of the book takes you under its wing and opens new vistas of possibility, new portals of awareness. Nonordinary beings are talented like that. They have a way of attuning us simply by making us aware of them.

It is my hope that the practitioners' stories below will weave with my own to offer an illuminating and transformative experience for you. I have communicated—with great respect and honor—the stories of these sacred relationships that have been entrusted to me. In so doing, I am following the long-standing tradition of Earth-based spiritualities. By telling a story, a series of stories, I hope to illuminate the unity and diversity of these extraordinary intelligences and the intimacy that we humans may enjoy when we are connected with them. I see my role of scribe and coresearcher as a bequest from the spirit of this book to bring greater tolerance and diversity into the discussion of Earth-based spiritual traditions and subaltern spiritualities.

This is but an overview of how much variety and also how much similarity may exist among disparate traditions that perhaps have never been discussed alongside each other before. In so doing, it is my goal to ultimately give these traditions a common voice with which to share their message. It is my wish that as a result of this work, spirit marriage practitioners—and those who feel called to undertake a spirit marriage—develop a greater understanding of their calling. As well, I would like to imbue my readers with a vision for how better to support others who walk this path, in a realm that can sometimes be isolating and confusing. It is also my hope that this book will stand as an exhortation toward more awareness and tolerance of oppressed spiritualities.*

Ultimately, it is my fervent desire that this book will broaden our understanding of what it looks like to live with integrity in a world populated with extraordinary beings that extend far beyond the current anthropocentric worldview. In reading it you may find yourself opened to the possibility that perhaps humanity has had help from interceding entities from the very beginning of civilization, and that perhaps we continue to be guided and loved by these beings today. It is to this end that I hope this research will stimulate a discussion of how and where the continued practice of spirit marriage may take us collectively as a species and as a planet.

TELLING OUR STORIES

Grounded in my own story and initiation into this practice, I have collected and compared the personal stories of ten practitioners of spirit marriage in the traditions of Haitian Vodou, New Orleans Voodoo, African Traditional religion, Faery Seership, Witchcraft, Hermetic Magick, and Shakta Tantra. My goal was to learn more about the practices and experiences associated with spirit marriage and to determine commonalities, variations, purpose, and desirable outcomes among the various practices and practitioners. I invited each person to go "on the

---

*In this work I am also following the call of, and giving voice to, a heretofore unnamed additional guiding *daimon*—the spirit, dare I say, of spirit marriage as a practice and a phenomenon throughout Earthly history. Therefore, this footnote, and in some way the entire experience and outcome of this research, is generated by, borne of, and dedicated to the spirit of spirit marriage.

record" with their story or to maintain anonymity. Two decided to go public, the rest have been given pseudonyms.

I chose to use a method of collection called organic inquiry (OI), which involves the tools of narrative interviews, autoethnography (auto-biography on steroids), and feminist and indigenous praxis. Organic inquiry honors the sacredness of the researcher, participants—whom organic inquiry designates as coresearchers—and subject matter. It also acknowledges the potential for transpersonal forces to guide the research. I consider the coresearchers to be both the human beings interviewed and their spirit-spouses who were involved in the interviews by nature of the dual consciousness believed to be held by those partici-pating in a spirit marriage. I also adopted organic inquiry because the phenomenon of spirit marriage is purported to take place primarily in an altered state of consciousness, via intuitive and somatic means.

I asked my coresearchers open-ended questions in a conversational manner designed to help me understand the following: What is the purpose of this practice? Who is called to this path and why? Why is it predominantly a subaltern practice? What are its benefits? What are the cautions? The guiding question of each interview was always, How do contemporary practitioners of spirit marriage experience their relation-ship with an Otherworldly being?

Organic inquiry also allows for the idea that the innate intelligence of the research—the spirit-being that guides the research, what I refer to as my research daimon—would speak through the researcher. Through this method a cocreative story is told.

5
The Faery Seer

*O*rion Foxwood is a Traditional Witch, Conjure Man, and Faery Seer. He was born with the second sight in the Shenandoah Valley of Virginia, where he was first exposed to faith healing, root doctoring,* Faery lore, and the second-sight practices of Southern and Appalachian cultures. He has been learning and teaching spirit-doctoring practices in workshops, intensives, and lectures in America and other countries for the past twenty years. He is also the founder of House of Brigh Faery Seership Institute where he teaches a multiyear program on the lore, practices, traditions, and skills of Faery Seership. As well, he is the founding elder of Foxwood Temple, a Traditional Witchcraft coven, and holds a master's degree in human services.

I met Orion in February of 2009 at a Pagan convention in San Jose, California, where he was giving a talk on a form of folkloric spirituality called Faery Seership. According to Orion, Faery Seership is an eco-spiritual practice rooted in the indigenous lineages of British Traditional Witchcraft and the folkloric Faery tradition that was handed down

---

*Root doctoring or root working arose in the North American South during the time of slavery. Root doctors had a working knowledge of roots, herbs, and folk remedies, and were the slave community's primary source of medical and spiritual care. This wisdom has been preserved and passed along through the generations as a form of natural medicine and spiritual treatment.

primarily as a secret tradition through families. Orion received the Faery teachings from the hereditary Scottish Faery Seer R. J. Stewart and various traditional practitioners. These practitioners, known as *hedge witches* and *cunning people,* cultivate Faery ways throughout the UK. Based in the ancient lore of the Faery faith, Orion has retooled the Faery teachings for a contemporary audience. The teachings are now centered around the Tree of Enchantment, a teaching glyph for Faery contact and anointing.

The moment I heard Orion speak I felt my spirit leap, as if my soul recognized him. I sensed I had finally found a teacher with whom I could go deep and far. Over the course of 2009 I took various classes with him and in November of 2010 I formally apprenticed to him through the House of Brigh Faery Seership Institute. One of the things that attracted me to Orion's teaching was that he holds a wedded relationship with a Faery being named Brigh. I intuitively felt that he could help me unpack, research, and further explore this burgeoning topic of spirit marriage. Orion agreed to an interview and also very graciously agreed to go on record with his powerful story.

Before we enter into the tale of Orion and his spirit mate, it must be said that in this interview, more than in any other, a serious distortion of time was in play . . . *is* in play. I have made an effort in this text to create coherence through consistent use of past and present tense. In general, I use present tense to make general statements about Orion or Brigh and their outlook on things. I use past tense to relate the specific sequence of the interview or the progression of their relationship. Additionally, when Orion is quoted at length, it's easy to notice the fluidity of tense in his speaking. I sense that this time-bending comes from a numinous or ceremonial sense of timelessness that Brigh makes increasingly available to him.

RITUAL INVOCATION AND GRATITUDE

My interview with Orion took place in the spring of 2014 in the back of a metaphysical bookshop in Santa Cruz, California. It began with each of us lighting a candle and stating our intentions for the interview, as well as doing some energetic exercises and movements that helped us attune to the energies we would be invoking. The energy in the room shifted significantly after this opening ritual; it had a palpable depth and Otherworldliness and our voices deepened in register. Stillness pervaded and I could feel the potency in the room as well as between us, as if a holy presence had joined us.

The interview commenced with much appreciation and gratitude. I thanked Orion for agreeing to the interview and stepping into this holy dance with me. I observed that it felt as if I had prepared for many years and many lifetimes to begin this research. I offered my deepest gratitude and devotion to the work that he does, to the relationship that he holds with Brigh, and to the deep calling of service and ministry that they both bring to this planet. I offered my deep love and appreciation for their roles as changemakers, healers, and reconcilers.

Orion's response was generous and touching: "We are both honored to be part of your work, to uphold your work. Your work is a major change agent in the world, so it's an honor to be here. Thank you, thank you so much."

Orion went on to share a little bit about his mission with Brigh, his Faery wife:

It is our hope to inspire other cocreative relationships. In fact, that is what's going to save our planet, our species, and help us avoid extinction.

I paused for a moment to feel the weight of those words, to really integrate the information, and to feel the vastness and power of Orion and Brigh's work.

You may see me, Orion, the human counterpart, close my eyes from time to time, and often in fact that's to defocus externally and to meet Brigh on the platform of my spirit, which is where we cohabitate.

I realized that I must give this great presence that Orion is hosting all the space and time she needs to speak through him, and I told him so. This is not a process that can be rushed, and I knew that Brigh had certain things she wanted to communicate.

FIRST CONTACT

As a boy, Orion spent a lot of time in the Blue Ridge Mountains where the spirits of the land, often called by the locals "them folk," are still greatly revered. He was raised with a cultural understanding that there are invisible forces of nature, and that these sacred and even capricious powers need to be honored and propitiated.

It was in the early nineties that Orion was first introduced to the specific strain of British folkloric magic known as Faery Seership, which would lead to his eventual marriage to Brigh. Orion attended a workshop with R. J. Stewart, a Scot and a leading authority on Faery lore. At this workshop Stewart was teaching visionary processes based on the old folkloric images in ballads and in the tradition of Faery doctoring,* which originated in Scotland.

Faery Seership teaches that we have a threefold soul: a *Star Walker,* which mediates the forces and influences of the upper world; a *Surface Walker,* which mediates the forces and influences of the surface world; and a *Dream Walker,* which mediates the forces and influences of the under world.

In 1990 Orion was elevated to the high priesthood of British Traditional Witchcraft, also known as "taking the third degree." This initiation began the descent of his Star Walker, the upper world influence of his threefold soul, into his Surface Walker, his mundane human consciousness. It was at this time that he took the craft, or initiatory, name Orion Foxwood. Soon after this initiation, Orion's Dream Walker—the under world influence of his threefold soul—began to ascend through the agency of Brigh. Orion asserts that the descent of

---

*Faery doctoring is a practice that draws from British folk healing, which uses stones, herbs, water, and charms, and combines it with the guidance and support of a Faery ally who helps to diagnose and heal the afflicted.

the Star Walker brought the light of the Old Ones, like the descent of the Godhead, into him. This got Brigh's attention and made it possible for her, as "Lady of the Land," to begin bringing him into sovereignty over his under world, the shadow aspects of the Self.

Initially she introduced herself to Orion as a Faery Queen associated with the under world. Orion was quick to point out that the under world in the Faery tradition is not the Christian hell of demons and punishment. Instead it is the subtle inner world of Earth, the dwelling place of powerful forces that shape this planet.

During this first visitation with Brigh, Orion experienced a somatic confirmation of her presence. During the vision she pressed needles into his fingers, a very dramatic gesture that was physically painful. Upon emerging from the vision Orion noticed that there were little red dots on the tips of each of his fingers where Brigh had pressed the needles.

He describes asking R. J. about this manifestation:

I love what R. J. did. He didn't try to interpret a lot. All he did was pat me on the shoulder and say "That's good! That's good!" I'm thinking "This is good? What's good about this? This is weird!" But he was just gently, as wonderful mentors in any spirit work do, encouraging me. As I say, "I encourage you to follow that thread."

So Orion's earliest knowledge of Brigh was simply as a being, a Faery Queen of the nature spirit realm who appeared intermittently in his visions. She was off on the edge of his perception "like a fleeting shadow at the corner of your eye." However, very quickly he started to realize that Brigh was bringing him back to his original love of the land, which had been instilled in him as a child.

As Orion describes it:

I'm thinking "All right, I've met this spirit, she's very dramatic, and there's something about my relationship to nature. Well, I'm a Pagan witch. I've already got a sacred relationship to nature." I really had no idea it was gonna become that profound.

However, the frequency of the visitations began to increase. Then he began to get what he calls *imprinting,* experiences during which Brigh would flow through his nervous system and he would receive visions. So he began to keep a journal to write down what he was seeing. One day Brigh made it clear that he needed to move out of the urban environment he was living in and move onto a piece of land. She told him that he needed to live on wild land or in the woods. He and his partner at the time packed up and moved the Foxwood Temple, his coven, to a place called Moonridge, just twenty minutes outside Washington, DC.

Moonridge was to become a major influence on the development of the House of Brigh Faery Seership. The land of Moonridge was twelve acres, part of which included relatively untouched wild woods, like a hidden oasis. Another part of the land, however, had been horribly strip-mined. So they divided this land into two sections: the *nature spirit campus,* untouched land with springs and wilds that were left to the nature beings, and the *human campus* where they erected two geodesic domes and where the focus was on humanity.

Orion recounts:

When we went to buy this land, it was funny—a man came out there, a friend of ours. He said, "I don't know why you'd want to buy this land, it's trash land." Brigh and I got furious because where is trash land? You mean land that humanity has waged war on, or parasitically devoured its resources? Brigh made it clear she wanted us to live on this land for a period of time because of the strip-mined piece. That's when our relationship went to a whole new level.

Brigh instructed Orion to build a specific type of cairn, a stone shaping, which became a threshold, a place to meet with her and learn the *force, flow,* and *form* dynamics that would later become foundational to his Faery Seership teachings. Orion would go out to the cairn and pose questions to Brigh, and she would respond. Some of these questions were, How does the vitality from the nearest star to us, which is the star burning at the center of our world, reach out to the physical world? And, How does Earth also take the vitality that descends from the heavens, specifically from the sun and the regulated rhythm from the moon and the stars, and comingle those two to create life?

Orion observed:

It's Earth that does this; the stars don't create life. Earth takes the stars and makes life out of them. She's a pretty cool lady. So I wanted to understand how that worked.

Unlike in other mediumship traditions, Brigh very rarely possessed Orion. Instead, Orion had to make time and space and pause the activities of his regular life to be with her and learn her voice. He had to learn to note the consistent feelings and shifts that became her signature contact.

Over time she helped him to understand how things move from unbound vitality to physical presence and back to unbound vitality again. Every morning at the cairn she would speak to him about how nature works from the inside out and tell him specific things to do with the land. Her guidance dramatically increased the pace of reconstruction of the local land and ecosystem.

Eventually he learned just to sit quietly and reach his spirit to hers. It was often in those moments that she began to flow into his system, inspiring him to write streams of knowledge. He was able to validate some of this knowledge in old folk traditions, where he found that some of the information he received from Brigh had a long history and provenance in folkloric practice. Brigh also gave him other streams of knowledge—knowledge that was later validated by conversations he'd had with astrophysicists, biologists, and scientists. She seemed to be decoding the building blocks of the universe and humanity's place in it.

Although Orion did eventually begin to hear Brigh speak to him audibly, he reports that in those first years her presence primarily felt like she was, again, imprinting herself onto him. And although the relationship had started out with Brigh being simply a very dramatic nature spirit in a historically Celtic practice, she rapidly began to reveal to

Orion what she was and what their relationship was going to be. Bit by bit, over a period of ten years, she shared teachings that would become his first book on Faery Seership, entitled *The Faery Teachings*. All of this was made possible by his living in nature where she could show him that she was real.

Brigh's actions also began to manifest in significant physical ways. Orion reports that February in Maryland could be very cold, with sub-zero temperatures, and yet inside the cairn purple flowers began to come up out of the ground and bloom in the middle of zero-degree weather.

As their relationship evolved, Brigh asked various things of Orion. One was that he stop drinking caffeine. She said that it made him fuzzy and interrupted the imprinting process.

Orion explains:

> I find that with these beings there's prohibitions and promises, things you can't do, sometimes for the rest of your life or a period of time, and things you must do, like a geas. She took caffeine away from me for over seven years, which seven or nine in the Faery Tradition shows up a lot, they call it the tain, or "the tithe to hell"—payment made. Some say it's associated with human or animal sacrifice but my experience is that's not what it means. It means a period that a part of your spirit is in the under world and a piece of their spirit is in you. You're being reshaped.

BRIGH: THE FAERY QUEEN

Orion was quick to point out that Brigh, his Faery Queen, is not to be confused with the Celtic Goddess Bridgit. When he first asked her if she was the Goddess Bridgit, Brigh replied, "I am like that." Brigh seems to have originated in a lineage similar in divine quality to Bridgit in that she is a being of light. She is not a being of starlight; she is a being in the land, inside the planet itself. He described her name *Brigh* as the sound of a breath. He observed that when she initially shared her name with him it sounded like "Breeeeeeee," and that *Brigh* is the closest way to spell it phonetically.

Orion and Brigh are married according to folkloric Faery practices in which the Faery marriage is understood to be a symbiosis. The term *marriage* is used for the sake of human understanding in that it's a union of two beings.

However, Orion is clear to point out that it's more than that:

> *It's not just a union of love, although there is great love between us. If by love one means harmony and the human emotional experience of what that harmony feels like, then we are very much in love. But we are symbiotically, not symbolically, interwoven in our spirits, and there is no divorce. There is no unbinding that.*

Although Brigh is what would be called in folkloric traditions a faery, she is not to be mistaken for some trite, small, winged being that is whimsical or capricious. Instead she is something much more profound. Orion sees her more like an angel of the Earth, an angel being an entity that originally had a stellar nature. Brigh came to Earth in the earliest phases of the creation of this world, in what's often described as "the Fall." However, Brigh says it is erroneous to think of Creation as a "Fall."

Orion clarified:

> *She makes fun of humanity when we talk about the Fall, the great Fall of Lucifer, the Fall of the Lord of Light. She says, "Where did he fall from and where did he fall to? From space to space?" It's a great illusion. So she calls it the "Great Extension."*

This Great Extension was the first emanation of living, stellar nature that emerged out of the breathing mouth of space, or as Orion calls it, "She Who Breathes Forth, the Utterer."

> *This particular stream, this extension of primal light and primal movement, extended itself into the place we now think of as Earth's orbit, and Brigh came with that stream. She is as old as the planet but older than its*

form. She is as old as its stellar nature. That is her origin. That is where she comes from. We are married in a cocreative, coexistent companionship to bring about certain things in this world.

Orion added that Brigh is, in fact, the feminine side of Lucifer. Brigh says of her origins, "I came with the Fall, but I remember the Fall and heaven's vast expanse before the Fall."

She adds:

The use of the concept of light falling out of grace because of false pride is fundamentally incorrect. The only "Fall" was in what you may call vibration from faster and unbound to slower and bound, so as to give the plasmatic origins for Earth's physical or particle-ized state and all life-forms (including humanity) [were] given existence by it. A more correct description would be "the Great Extension from original light and divine breath to a particle-ized expression of the creative power of heaven."

This identification of Brigh with Lucifer has strong resonance with an aspect of Orion's inner craft tradition (normally only taught to the highly initiated), wherein she is known as Diana-Lucifera. Sometimes described as the Ancient One, she is the divine providence of all things. Diana-Lucifera is the bridge that links the light in the heavens to the light in the heart of the world soul. Conversely, Brigh would be the bridge that unites humanity with both the light in the heavens and the light in the heart of the world soul.

As Orion described the vastness of Brigh's ancient origins I could feel the import of the work he is here to do. My skin prickled, and I imagined he must have had to go through quite a journey to wed such a being.

Orion's description of Brigh is as follows:

[Her voice sounds like] where breath, water, and fire all come together at once. She is made of a type of liquid flame. Her language is of pure vitality, with no conflicts about who or what she is, whatsoever. Brigh

is absolute presence. She lives in the original vision of this world, in the ever youthful, ever-becoming presence of this world, what is sometimes referred to as Eden. When she arrives in my awareness, and she is never very absent from my awareness, I feel her in my vitality. I often call it "my summoning," she's summoning me inward to touch where she's imprinting her vital presence on my nervous system. She flows through the nerve endings, the synaptic cleft between neurons, the way honey flows into honeycomb, and in that flowing into there is a completeness of being between us . . . she arrives like a breath, but a breath of light that enters my body. Now I know to stop and wait for the vision to come.

Typically Brigh arrives first in Orion's nervous system. Half-jokingly, Orion said, "Her presence reaches into the drag closet of my mind, hunting for garbs, hunting for context, something to wear that will relate to me human-wise."

One of the most profound things Brigh has spoken to Orion about is the language we use to describe her. She has mixed feelings about the word *spirit*. She says, "If you mean by *spirit* a being that is made out of the essence of things that are unbound, then that is correct. If you mean by *spirit* that I am something that is not alive, that is incorrect."

During the interview I began to notice a pattern to our conversation. Orion's energy and voice shifted when he was quoting or speaking as Brigh. He took on a sovereign, queenly resonance and a commanding voice, distinct from his normal voice and tone. I also found that the hair on the back of my neck stood up when Brigh spoke.

Orion says that Brigh is adamant that people understand the distinction among beings that are prehuman, nonhuman, and/or have never been human:

We as embodied humans understand that there are three levels or dynamics of what it means to be alive: incarnate, nonincarnate, disincarnate. One of the invocations she and I often use is, "By the seen, the unseen, and the thresholds in between." She is able to move along the entire continuum of those levels because of her relationship with me. I'm

the seen, the embodied. I close my eyes and I look into her world through
her eyes. I open my eyes and she looks out my eyes into this one.

Orion uses the folkloric Faery image to describe Brigh because she is the living spirit of nature itself, as the Faery folk or the Fair Ones are often said to be. She is nature in its most vital energetic presence. Her people, her species, are responsible for guiding life, sheer vitality, from the core stellar nature of our world outward into the many embodied states of existence. There are things, places, and events that she can only touch via Orion. Likewise there are forces, energies, and knowledge that he can only access via Brigh. Brigh needs Orion to enact change in the physical world, just as he needs her to tap into that vital force of the planet.

DISMEMBERMENT

As Orion shared his story I began to realize just how profound and potent it must be to hold a symbiotic relationship with a being as vast as Brigh. I realized that this was one reason I had been pulled into this research in the first place. I wanted to understand what it meant to be wooed into a relationship with a being with knowledge, power, and access far beyond human capabilities.

How does sharing consciousness with a being who is not limited by human physicality open one up to the void—to the *prima materia* of all Creation? I wondered aloud how interacting with a being that potent might affect the human body. Could it be confusing to the physical body? Might it cause one to go to pieces at times?

Orion chortled at my question.

Might? What I found in my earliest contact with Brigh is that she didn't reveal the fullness of her nature at first because I didn't have a way to interpret it. She came to me very humanoid at first. It was very clear she was one of the angelic presences in the land, the deeper spirit-beings of the land, associated with its life vitality—what we think of as a nature spirit. But she came as a queen, and it took me a while to understand what a queen really means in Faery tradition. It means that she is an aggregate being, a colonial being, made up of tens of thousands of beings in one being. She often says the difference between her people and our people is they haven't forgotten who they are, whereas we've gotten intoxicated on an illusion of isolation that has caused the need for such things as religion and spiritual practices to help turn our eyes back in the direction of our origins.

Brigh wants us to connect to the memory of our origins as a type of vitality, the visionary directive and inspiration latent within us. Unfortunately, according to Orion, most of humanity does not feel this connection and as a result has moved into a place of fear—fear that we have been abandoned by Creation.

Orion experienced a vast *dismemberment* in the earliest phases of his relationship with Brigh; his career, relationships, and health were taken apart and reassembled into a new order. This recalibration was not expected and he wondered aloud that if he had known what would be required of him, would he have volunteered for it? Part of him said, "No!" while another part said, "If I could have seen what the outcome was going to be, I probably would have." But then a third part said, "Well, the other two are just illusions, because all you were doing was succumbing to who and what your destiny was to be." The ripping apart and the shattering that he experienced were primarily about illusions, what he calls *soul cages* or *false shapes,* which needed to be dismembered. These soul cages constrict our vitality.

He describes vitality as:

The pulse of planetary vitality that pulsed our presence into existence. We all arrived here on a pulse; we all ride here on a river of blood, that's the final pulse, the genetic pulse which connects us to a stream of human ancestry. But human ancestry, the human river of blood, is pulsed here by something older, and that is a quality of the planet's dream or vision of itself. We are Earth when it humani-centrifies itself. We are the human quality of nature.

Brigh doesn't see a difference in quality between humans and Faery beings; humanity is not a lesser quality. Nor is Brigh or Faery a greater quality. Rather, Brigh says that humanity has wandered too far into overdifferentiation and distance, rather than knowing itself as a cocreative participant in this planet's vision of itself. Humanity is what happens when the planet humanizes itself.

Orion points out:

Humanity . . . our destiny, why we were considered needful by the planet's vision, by its stellar pulse, is [that] we were born to live out a balance and to create new balances. We were born to "Boldly go!" We were born because we are Earth being curious about what happens when it pushes its own buttons. Its inherent balance is a beautiful basket that upholds life, but it doesn't always inspire full creativity. That's what humanity is here for.

Brigh has come forward through Orion to deliver this vision to the world so that we can step back into a healthy cocreative relationship with the life pulse of this world.

As Orion reports:

In order to get a human there, especially one—meaning myself—who was tasked to mate with that vital vision, that presence of knowing the original pulse that brought this world here, [it] would mean that everything I had inside of me that would confine that pulse would have to go. Sort of like when you get an old house . . . the old house Orion was wired for say fifty volts. Brigh, and the understanding of what humanity is in its original state, is a hundred volts. I had two options: rewire or house fire! I encountered both. Being rewired and consumed and devoured by the vision and made in its own image.

I asked Orion what the rewiring entailed. He exclaimed, "Well, I almost died! It required every shape in my life that I had poured false identity into—whether that was a major career which I had in the government, or whether it was relationships that were outworn, that were confining, that were untrue to my vital pulse—be shattered. Brigh needed me to be true to my vital pulse the way she is true to her vital pulse."

Orion went on to elaborate on the difference between humans and the Faery people. Humans can step out of congruence with our vital pulses for some time, whereas Brigh can't. She is composed of vitality one hundred percent, and therefore she can never be out of congruence with it. Brigh is a preconditioned state, but the physical state is a conditioned state of being.

Orion contends that we humans are primarily wed to our brains and our nervous systems, and so:

Brigh needed to get me out of the forms of myself and the forms of relationship with life that were girdling and strangling my soul pulse. It felt like I was dying! I remember when I finally gave in to it, I was like, "either I'm going to die or I'm going to become something that is greater than I've ever been."

Although Orion sees divinity as both masculine and feminine, his strongest relationship is to the feminine, the Goddess quality of divinity. During the process of dismemberment he recollects being angry and swearing and being livid at Brigh and at the Goddess, furiously questioning the necessity of what he was going through. He said that at times it felt like he was being punished. However, once he finally surrendered and said, "Okay, Goddess, Mother Spirit, Brigh, whatever's listening, take my heart, make it your heart. Take my soul, make it your soul. Take my body, make it your body. Help me to see me the way you saw me when you made me." That was the moment that the full allowance happened. He let the familiar things he was clinging to flow away, and the ignition of his True Self was finally able to pulse its way out.

However, the sacrifice he made for this process was no small thing. During this dismemberment phase he lost a career of almost two decades leading a major government rehabilitation program in Washington, DC. About that same time half of his immediate blood family died: he lost both his sister and his father within eight months of each other. Orion explains that although this dismemberment was not the cause of their passing, Brigh used the fact that they were dying to calibrate his path of awakening with their path of transitioning. He also lost a relationship with his partner of twenty-five years. He quips, "Because I'm gay, in gay years, which are sort of like dog years, it was like a two-hundred-year relationship!" We laugh at the analogy, and yet he is clear that all of these sacrifices were no laughing matter.

He went on to list more ways in which his life had been transformed. Health issues started manifesting and hastened his descent into a darker period of drug use.

"I don't recommend it," he said laughingly:

> But it worked very well for shattering, and that's what Brigh [was doing]. Brigh was literally taking everything she could get the hands of my experience on and was using that to shatter the bulk of the past that I identified with so I could become a hundred percent present. Anyone who says they have a marriage to a powerful spirit-being or Otherworldly being but their life has been Skittles and rainbows is probably not telling the truth.

At this point a question arose, and I asked Orion if he thought all this shattering had to take place because he was in resistance or was holding tightly to old forms. He confirmed this and went on to say he has always had a strong sense of responsibility.

> I was directing one of the largest witchcraft temples on the Eastern Seaboard. I'd already written a book, was in the middle of [writing] a second book. I was running a government agency where I opened thirty-one drug treatment centers. So my life was poured into helping others. But here's the thing, I was poured into helping others through their hurting voice. But I had not listened to what the deeper part of my soul was crying out for and wanting for itself. So I was definitely in service. Brigh wasn't shattering me because I wasn't in service. Brigh was shattering me because I was hyperextended outwards. I was poured into so

many different roles. She had to undock me from those roles that I had done well, but I didn't know it was time to let go. [There is a] wonderful saying: "Sometimes God does for you what you can't do for yourself." I know in retrospect that I would probably be dead from exhaustion, heart attack, something, at the rate I was going. Brigh was [insistent]: "I don't think so!"

Orion paused as his voice got throaty and he teared up, "She even said to me once, 'I'm going to take everything from you until there is nothing left but you and I, and then you will have everything. You will be sovereign over your kingdom.'"

Orion's response to this statement was not, as he puts it, "Oh holy one, oh lady of light!" It was more like "You *bitch!* You mean, cruel . . ." However, as a result of his outrage, Orion discovered that these powerful spirits really can handle our temper tantrums. In fact, he believes that if we don't push back against their potency then we won't have interior velocity, a force that he describes as "building like a volcano which reshapes the land from its eruption"—a force that we need. He believes that this force gives us the initiatory spark in our spirit. Brigh was not trying to make him into something alien to himself; she was trying to get him to become more fully himself, to embody his fullest destiny.

As I listened to Orion I began to see this process through an evolutionary lens. He had been functioning at a super high level in his life, doing good things, and being successful and happy. But to use a software analogy, he was like Orion 1.0—an outdated version. He needed to become Orion 2.0—the newer version—expanded, updated, overhauled. There was an innate quality inside him that was his evolutionary edge and to get there all the things in his life that had formed his old identity had to be taken away. He was fine as Orion 1.0, even great, but there was something extraordinary that needed to come through him, which he was destined to host.

Orion wholeheartedly agreed with this assessment and added that he had not known how to let those other identities go. He said he had been rationalizing, saying to himself, "Well I've committed this amount of time in this relationship and these identities. . . . I am serving the Department of Health." What Brigh was saying was that he had to undock. He had done all those things and done them well, but there was more. Again, a bigger picture was trying to emerge.

Orion's dear friend and mentor, the occultist and Western mystery school adept Dolores Ashcroft Nowicki, was a major presence in his life during this time. Dolores had been taught by the renowned occultists Israel Regardie, W. E. Butler, and Dion Fortune. Eventually, Dolores inherited the directorship of the Servants of the Light, one of the largest Western Hermetic mystery schools still publicly teaching, which had been founded by Dion Fortune.

Dolores would become a seminal figure in Orion's eventual marriage to Brigh. Orion describes Dolores as someone who "carries a major mantle. She is indwelled by a powerful spirit. This is an adept. She is a holy woman."

When the Tree of Enchantment, the cosmogram of the material that Brigh wanted Orion to teach, came through him as a result of this dismemberment and recalibration, he took it to Dolores. The first thing she said to him was, "I knew it! I knew there was a Western Kabbalah! That there was a Kabbalah of the Dark Goddess, of the Underworld!" And then she said, "I haven't seen a vision like this come forward since Earnest's work [referring to famed occultist W. E. Butler]. I hope you survive this!" At that last statement he thought, "Well, that's a strange thing to say!"

Within a year he understood what she meant.

When these beings come, they often have a specific vision for you, and it's not that they're trying to force you to do something, they're trying to get you to do the thing you were born to do, to unbind, or undock you. But where you're sailing into is going to be unfamiliar waters from where you've been on your human path, at least this lifetime around. But it often does require shattering. What we call the soul cage *has to be shattered.*

THE FAERY MARRIAGE

I asked Orion what had led him to decide to marry Brigh. Had he even been aware that this kind of thing was done? He reported that there had always been folktales and legends about Faery marriage, not just in the Celtic traditions, but also in northern Europe and beyond. This kind of union is also not distinct to Faery beings; Orion is aware of traditions that wed humans to other entities such as the djinn and angels. There are even traditions, like the African traditions, that quite readily talk about marriage between humans and a nonhuman Otherworld. This rite of sacred marriage appears to take place all over the world. However, although Orion knew of such marriages, he had not been seeking one. In fact, one of his teachers had told him that one does not seek a marriage with these beings at all, but instead one's fate will move one into a place of irrefutable relationship. A marriage ritual is often indicated when someone of high regard, like a seer or seeress, has a visitation wherein an extraordinary being proclaims they want to marry a specific person. This is how it happened with Orion.

Being a gay man, he had never considered marrying Brigh. He was enjoying the information she was giving him about nature, and he thought that that was the extent of their relationship—that it was all about ecology and ecospirituality. Little did he realize what the full range of ecospirituality actually meant. Orion thought, "Oh, she's contacting me [so that I can] learn about nature, its cocreative presence and dynamics. Even maybe to get humanity to stop being an asshole, to stop introducing battle and parasitic energy, to get back into cocreative relationship." He thought it was reminiscent of his witchcraft work, helping him deepen a relationship with nature-based deities and the sacred rhythms of the land and nature itself.

As an aside, he suggested that these angels, djinn, and faery presences rarely reveal their full form to us. Our nervous systems are not ready for the massive expanse of their energies. This reservation is out of compassion to us, because in some cases, full manifestation of their presence has been known to cause madness, delirium, or worse. However, when they do fully reveal themselves, they are known for their radiant beauty, and as Fiona Macleod says in her poem "The Immortal Hour": "How beautiful they are, / The lordly ones / Who dwell in the hills, / In the hollow hills. / . . . They laugh and are glad / And are terrible."[1]

Their "terribleness" is due to the greatness of their power, what theologian Rudolph Otto (1869–1937) called the *mysterium tremendum,* the awe-inspiring mystery. The religious studies scholar Andrew P. Wilson describes it as "a primal fear that marks them [these experiences] as encounters with something wondrous and at the same time terrifying: a dread-filled mystery before which one can but tremble. Words fail, faces blanch and limbs quake before the *mysterium tremendum.*"[2]

Orion came to be asked to marry Brigh in the following way. Orion had been doing his work with Brigh at the cairn for a while, and they had developed an understanding with the nature spirits—the forces involved in upholding the vital nature of this planet's natural life. It was when British occult author Dolores Ashcroft Nowicki was staying at Moonridge to teach a workshop that Orion received the directive to marry Brigh.

> One morning she [Dolores] came out, and this is an adept, this is a woman who I swear she calls the angels and they know to cancel whatever is on their schedule. . . . She really understands the dynamics. She also knows old Traditional Witchcraft. Like many of the early serious occultists out of northern Europe, especially England, she has a high regard for the Faery tradition. . . . A lot of the Golden Dawn members were involved in the Faery tradition. Brigh had come to her, but in full form.
>
> Dolores comes out; she's white as a ghost, and she's stuttering. And she goes, "Orion, she loves you, she loves you so much. She's so beautiful! She's so beautiful! She's so beautiful! Why haven't you married her?" And there's a part of me going, "Oh shit, this is like a shotgun wedding! Like up in the hills."
>
> [Dolores asked,] "Why haven't you married her?" and I just said, "I don't know, I don't know, I don't know." I'd never thought of it.

And she said, "She loves you so much! You should marry her! Why don't you marry her?"

And so it happened that a high-level adept brought the proposal to him, independent of his own agenda. Then Dolores started to describe what Brigh looked like, using details that no one knew except Orion. Within a year, the Faery marriage was performed between Orion and Brigh.

At this point in the interview I was curious about the effect this proposal had on Orion, his sexual orientation, and his existing relationship. Was it strange to be a gay man marrying a female entity?

That didn't seem odd for me. Because she would also do things like come to me in visions of really hot-looking men. She would intentionally say, "I'm doing this just for your pleasure because ultimately the vision of me as female is to express how my spirit works. I'm much bigger than your biological gender images." To these kinds of beings, form is a kind of language. Brigh said to me, "The periodic table of elements you look at as elements, we look at as an alphabet, albeit incomplete, but a very good initial attempt at the language of Earth."

I asked Orion to explain the protocol for the marriage, how it was arranged, and what took place. He reported that, according to his understanding and from oral traditions passed down to him, the Faery being, in this case Brigh, would for the period of the wedding come into the physical form of another person. This person also had to be indwelled with their own spirit marriage and had to be the opposite gender of the person being wed.

The opposite gender requirement is somewhat unique to the Faery tradition. Orion postulated that this may be because some of the folk Faery teachings were a bit more rigid about gender polarity. He emphasized that this was more a product of human cultural conditioning than of the actual gender identity of spirit-beings. When spirits contact us they tend to fit into some of our language or metaphors at first until they start to defy that language. Orion refers to Brigh as "my queen" and "her" because that is how she initially manifested to him; however, Brigh is much more than a gendered being.

In some traditions there is also a sexual relationship that occurs between the two humans as part of the marriage rite while the proxy is being indwelled; however, Orion's marriage did not require that. What it did require was that they create vows to each other. Orion said that looking back on this, his vows were sweet and in some ways "pitiful." He said they were well-meaning but he could not get his brain completely around what all this was really going to be. Brigh chose Dolores to be her proxy, so she dictated her vows to Dolores who was incredibly adept at transcribing Brigh's voice. When she wrote her vows Brigh said things like, "And I shall be with you until the stars grow old." This exchange left Orion overcome with emotion and a sense of her powerful presence.

I asked Orion whether he and Dolores had collaborated on the wedding ceremony. He said they had based it on more traditional wedding ceremonies. Because he was aware of the folklore around the Faery marriage, he knew that the Fae (Faery) would use human marriage ceremonies as a protocol to perform the Faery marriage rite. According to Orion, Faery beings consider oaths to be reality; they are unbreakable. Therefore, Faeries, particularly the noble Fae, the deep ones, the ones closely connected to the deep planet, do not lie. Orion believes that this is why the seer often receives what they call "the tongue that cannot lie"—a gift, some might say prohibition, often imparted by the Fae.

Like a traditional marriage ceremony, after the exchange of the vows there was an exchange of rings. Instead of an actual ring, Orion was given a single thread of Dolores's hair, which she wound around his wedding finger as a way of confirming the vow. This ritual took place at Moonridge, the sacred land of his coven, in a circle cast by this coven, with about twenty people in attendance. Brigh wanted Orion's witch family there to witness the rite because the marriage would not only affect Orion as a high priest in witchcraft but also his many initiates and students. As well, Brigh wanted this commitment irrefutably seen by the community. She wanted it clear to the human world that this was not a symbolic gesture, but that it was real.

Orion described the rite thusly:

So when [Brigh] came into the room, and into Dolores . . . first of all, everybody fell on their knees! People were all crying. They said the sacredness was so thick you could cut it with a knife. The room was thick with ectoplasm; it was thick. There was no denying that something profound and Otherworldly was going on. . . . Believe me, everyone knew it. When I say they dropped to their knees, it's not like they got down in this poetic [manner] . . . they were dropped! It's like their heart pulled them down to their knees. People were crying out, they were overcome by sacred presence. It was something!

Afterward Orion felt shaken because he could feel something new was inside him and growing. The hardest part, which Orion expressed pain in sharing, was that after entering into the Faery marriage, his relationship of twenty-five years ended.

Orion began to tear up as he observed:

My ex said it was at that moment that he knew he'd lost me. That was the beginning of the end of my human relationship. I don't know that that always happens, and I don't think that she took him away. I think he couldn't deal with the sharing of intimacy at that point. He said, "I've shared you with the government. I've shared you with the coven. I've shared you with the world. Now this is one more. How do I compete with something that lives in you at that level?" And so the relationship started to fall apart. Of course, I'm in a relationship now, but a relationship with a wonderful man I'm engaged to who has never known me without Brigh. For him, her absence would be odd and strange and bizarre. She loves him. Well, she loved [my ex] too, [and] she blessed him for his sacrifices.

TRANSFORMATION
AND TEACHINGS

After the marriage, Brigh began to reveal the purpose of her union with Orion. As he put it, "She used the platform of my humanity to teach me about humanity." She inspired him to ask specific questions about the human experience, which led him to finally ask, "Brigh, there's a wound in humanity and it's delivering it to the ecology, delivering it to each other. What is it?" Orion was trying to understand the benefit of their relationship to humanity. He sensed it was something beyond our avoiding extinction, or even restoring our relationship with the life of this planet. That is when Brigh revealed what Orion and Brigh call "the dampers on the blue flame of the soul." Brigh said the number one damper, the number one wound in the human experience, is the illusion of isolation. This wound shows up primarily as abandonment pain, and abandonment pain expresses itself as fear, resentment, or shame. All the other dampers, she revealed, are products of this primary one.

It became clear to Orion that humanity has a great need for reconnective remembering practices that were part of the original instructions of our species but have been lost or forgotten. Orion believes that all the medicine and indigenous wisdom practices, as well as the sacred teachings of the ancient world, hold these original instructions. Many of these practices have been destroyed due to persecution and suppression, and must be reclaimed, resurfaced, or repurposed for modern people.

For Orion to understand the illusion of isolation, he had to find it in himself. He had to clean out what he refers to as the "dust bunnies" in his soul—an arduous process that, like all cleaning work, is ongoing. According to Orion, these dust bunnies are the ghosts that haunt the inner house of our being. As he began to record his conversations with Brigh, certain sayings began to take shape to describe this process: "The past is for reference, not resonance"; "The past can be a zombie that can't eat enough of your present to fulfill its insatiable necrotic appetite"; and "A tree that grows too top-heavy without growing deep will topple over."

The process of cleansing and reconfiguring deepened Orion's relationship to the collective soul of humanity and our relationship to this world. It also required him to go inside himself, to unearth and sweep away those inner dust bunnies. He had to face his own very human abandonment pain and lance that wound. However, Brigh did not leave him to figure this out by himself. She taught him techniques and practices and gave him insights on how to work with the pain.

It was essential that Orion do this work initially on himself so that it would have integrity. Only then could he teach others these practices. This is how many of the basic processes he teaches in Faery Seership came about. He had to be the product of his teachings. He had to be shaped by them. Eventually, Brigh unfolded nine vision keys essential to the Faery Seership work. These are nine keys that express the foundational forces of our planet, or what Dolores Ashcroft Nowicki referred to as the Kaballah of the Dark Goddess (the Tree of Enchantment mentioned earlier). Although these keys show up in some form in various Faery traditions, Brigh and Orion put them together in a cohesive system that has become the foundational system studied in the House of Brigh Faery Seership Institute.

Ultimately the result of Orion and Brigh's marriage was a system for healing—not only for Orion's benefit, but for bringing healing out into the world and benefitting all of humanity. Previously his work had been focused mostly on diagnosis and treatment of specific mental health and behavioral conditions, but these new processes offered transformational and transmutational healing for *everyone*.

Orion describes the House of Brigh Faery Seership in this way: "Faery Seership is an integrative, cocreative, and restorative ecospiritual paradigm and practice." Inherent in this process is the mandate to help others discover a relationship with unseen forces, ancestral, human, Faery, and other—forces that helped humanity arrive physically into this world. The task before Orion was to translate the oral traditions received from his elders, the teachings he received from Brigh, and his academic folkloric research into contemporary practices that help us reconnect to our original blueprint as humans.

Orion asserts that folklore and mythology help us remember and awaken the subtle senses, which have gone dormant. These subtle senses were a greater part of our lives when we lived in direct cooperative relationship with the forces of nature.

We're still in nature; there's nowhere to go but nature. But because of our lights, our heaters, our air conditioners, which we love, I love them too . . . there's a distance from the uncontaminated rhythms of nature. All our body needs are practices, rituals, processes like in Faery Seership and ceremonies, to plug back in, to move out of resistance, allow our body to remember. There's nothing the Earth knows that our body doesn't. Our body knows everything the Earth knows. These beings, like the Faery beings, can encourage us in coming out of what I call "the spell of forgetfulness."

Orion's sacred assignment, then, was to distill what Brigh was showing him, what was implied in the Faery tradition, about our sacred relationship with the land. Orion believes that folkloric practices were not just for fertility or food; they were for humans to cultivate a sense of well-being in the natural world.

The thing that drives people to spiritual traditions and religious practices is homesickness. It's all homesickness. People want to feel connected to the family of life. When they're willing to detox the fear . . . get rid of the illusion of isolation that breeds such things, like believing we're exiled from the oneness of life, which we're not. People want to feel home again, and they're driven by this homesickness. Drug abuse, the overuse of alcohol, sex, you name it, is all connected to trying to feel alive, home.

In order for me to teach this and to teach restorative and integrative practices, Brigh had me figuring out with her a way to help awaken those senses in the students that would come [to study with us]. That's where the basic processes of Faery Seership came into being.

DISCERNMENT AND SEXUALITY

When you are part of an initiatory folk magic tradition, a relationship with unseen forces is a common occurrence; indeed, it is an expectation. Orion's relationship with Brigh was ripened by his other spirit contacts, and his relationship with Brigh eventually breathed more life into the other contacts he held. What Brigh uniquely required of him, however, was that he change his perception of himself and his identity. He observes, "I was a decent high priest and witch before Brigh. But after Brigh, you can't even compare it. People that come to my ceremonies wonder how I got that way, and it was the ignition of Brigh's contact." Brigh became what in old witchcraft was called the *familiar spirit*.

There is a common misunderstanding in modern witchcraft that a familiar spirit is an animal, like a cat or dog. Orion explained the older origins of this practice—the witch's familiar was a spirit or Otherworldly being linked to them. This entity taught, informed, and guided the witch. After their marriage, Brigh became Orion's familiar spirit.

However, Orion was quick to point out:

I don't worship Brigh. Brigh doesn't want that. She says it's contrary. I'm devoted to her the way anyone is to a beloved, because the work is sacred and powerful, but not because I fear her, because I don't. Do I think she's powerful? Does she have the ability to affect a broader change than my physical body? Absolutely. But I also know what I bring to the table. I always say if a divine being expects you to become less of yourself, run away! It's not a divine being. It's not a sacred being.

Previously Orion had mentioned Brigh touching into his vitality and had alluded to there being sexual energy between the two of them. However, Orion is also adamant that the Faery marriage is not about having sex with faery beings. In our interview, I expressed curiosity about how the faery beings' relationship with the vital center of the planet perhaps translates into sexual arousal when they contact humanity. Orion's response to my musing was rapturous and moving, as he poetically describes what it is like to be touched by a faery.

Tears welled up as he related:

Brigh and I make love the same way that the roots of a tree make love to the soil, that the stars make love to the night sky, that the clouds make love to the sky. The way that ecosystems, that whole threads of life, make love to each other. In a co-creative existence that does have sensual nature to it, it has deep intimacy. There's a dialogue in ecosystems, like our body, going on between all the cellular structures, molecular structures, fibers, microbes, that is intimate, and they make love to each other. But in the deepest meaning of making love, interpenetrating like honey in a honeycomb, filling and flowing in and out, producing and inspiring creative reflection and expression from each other.

Because Brigh lives in the life pulse of the planet at its earliest phases, older than the lava, the stellar nature, it's a cool light. She describes it as the cool light at the center of the world. That is what pulses out as all the vital processes of this world that become life forms. Just like vitality that flows through our body when we are sexually or sensually aroused. We say, "I'm hot for somebody," that flush that comes on, it is vitality, it's an increase of a vital response. If we go pregenital on that—to what causes the genital and other body reactions of vital flow to happen—that's where she lives. Now do I feel it in those [genital] parts of my body sometimes? Oh my God, yeah. Except the difference is when she flows in that way with me, at the risk of sounding vulgar, it's not just my penis that goes erect, it's like all of my cellular structures go into exaltation, into full life.

[That is] once I got past the terror. Because sometimes for people if a being like this flows in that way into relationship with them, a type of terror can hit them because they feel like they're being consumed, like the burning bush of God. But the truth is, what they don't know is, they're becoming alive. That which was constricting is dying, and they're breathing.

Orion points out that ultimately these beings are not gendered in the way we think of gender, and yet they come to us in the gender that will bring the greatest medicine to our soul. He emphasizes that we are at a point in our human evolution where we need to cultivate sacred relationship to the Divine Feminine.

A dear witch friend said to me, "How is it that we drink the blood of our mothers for nine months and then turn around and curse her and think that we can be happy in life?" What I say is: "You cannot curse the roots and bless the fruits. This concept of the Divine Feminine, which is so much about origins and how we come to this world and even how we're composed of this world, is crucial for our survival."

Orion believes that to truly revere the feminine, in Her deepest and most powerful, we must connect to the chthonic forces of the Sacred Feminine, the under world spirit forces like Brigh, which (and who) call us back to the roots of our origins. From that perspective we can then look upward and see the vastness of life, but first we have to see its depths; that is where life's nutrition is. As Orion says, "The tree grows from the ground up—not from the sky down, but from the ground up."

Brigh describes this concept thusly: "It's not about thee, and it's not about me. It's all about the tree." By this she means that the central theme doesn't concern the individual or the spirit-being, but rather the companionship that inspires others to come back into integration within themselves and with Earth. This relationship is a companionship that helps melt away the soul cages and the false dissections of life that choke out its wholism.

As Brigh explained to Orion:

We pay reverence to the same mother. The only difference between you and me, Orion, is that I've forgotten nothing. So I'm not here to be your divinity. I'm here to midwife you to its awareness—not for you to be consumed, but so you can be expressed as the unique quality of divinity.

Orion once asked Brigh, "Are you dangerous?" and she said, "Well, of course I am! Are you dangerous?" He sat and thought about it for a moment and realized, "Well, of course I am." Brigh followed this by saying, "Am I coming to harm you? Of course I'm not."

It was then that Orion realized he had been projecting things onto her. She also said to him, "I am not your mommy, yet I am of the true essence of what the mother is." Orion thinks we project onto our lovers, our mothers and fathers, the union that our spirit most wants. The spirit partnership is to him "a union with the threefold nature—the under world nature, the universal nature, and the expressed or embodied nature—of our being, and our Otherworldly companions in a cocreative relationship. . . . When we're most whole, we have a companionship on both sides of the threshold."

I postulate that perhaps the very nature of who and what Brigh is and where she comes from necessitates a different kind of spirit marriage than those other more formalized traditions like Vodou. The Loa are deities with well-formed psychological characteristics who have developed as a result of hundreds of years of devotion. There is a sense of solidity and fixedness to their identity, whereas Brigh is not defined by human attributes. In such traditions, it is fairly common to hear that a Loa, especially the more sexually assertive Loa, make love to their spouses.

Orion agreed that Brigh cannot be defined in terms of human attributes. "She defies them," he told me. In Faery Seership terms, Brigh is closest to the concept of the *holy formless fire,* the spark that gave life to our planet. By nature of who she is, she flows in a different way with humanity.

Orion helped me to clarify the difference between contact with the Loa versus contact with the Fae by explaining that he has had a relationship with both. He has had relationships with the African Diaspora religions and was raised in the conjure practices of Southern folk magic—both of which include relationships with powerful ancestral spirits.

However, he clarifies the difference by saying:

Whenever I've touched or been touched by the Loa or Orisha,* I do become aware of the humanlike images we give them. It is a way to have an ancestral point of contact with them, and then they show how much more they are. But Brigh . . . wants to make it clear that any image of her is sort of like notes of music. We write down the notes, but that isn't the music, and it doesn't sound like that diagram. But it is a way to describe how to get to a relationship with it.

I was struck by the thought of an *egregore,* the collective morphic field that accumulates around an idea, or in this case, a being. Thousands, probably millions, of people have relationships with the Loa, whereas Brigh, although she may move and work with other Faery Seers, is married only to Orion. It is a relationship that is unique to the two of them, and she is primarily defined through his experience of her. However, given the vastness of her identity, I imagine there are ways that even Orion is perhaps not aware of her presence.

Orion agrees. He adds that he had been at a museum looking at a piece of ancient history and she had said to him, "Oh yes, I was there when that happened. I was there, but they did not know me in this way." He describes going to an exhibit on Egyptian magic, and a specific image in the exhibit caught his attention; Brigh was prompting him to look at it. The Pharaoh had had a vision of "a new *nefer* emerging from the primordial lake," and Brigh wanted him to see this as she explained to him:

Great profound beings will often show up a certain way out of the primordial lake, the primordial waters of existence. They'll allow us a dial-up, a phone number, a code, a way, a floor to meet them on. It may come out as a deity form, or divine form, meaning they look like this, their symbols are this or that, but understand that profound forces, spirit-beings, divinities, you name it, are always arriving. Some of them [are] just born, some of them [have just been] received in the human awareness, [and]

---

*Orisha is a term for Afro-Caribbean deities.

some of them were re-received in human awareness under a different
garb or form, but [are] the same being.

Brigh had to relearn certain things about human restrictions as
well. She would wake Orion up in the middle of the night just to show
him that the first dandelion of spring was blooming. Orion quips that
this kind of observation is very powerful to Earth and its vitality, but
perhaps not as relevant to a human who needs his sleep. On occasion
she would ask him to do things that were physically dangerous.

> *One day she asked me to jump off a cliff. She said, "Jump!" And I said,*
> *"No!" And she said, "Jump!" And I said, "I can't!" And I'm realizing,*
> *"Okay, we're at a communication gap here." And I said, "Okay, let me*
> *go get my iron blade. Let me lay that upon your presence, hold it, and*
> *then I'll jump." She said, "Well, I can't," because iron distracts their*
> *spirits, it doesn't destroy them, it distracts them. Especially forged iron,*
> *the way forged iron distracts lighting, or electricity—it moves, it's pulled*
> *towards it. And I remember she goes, "Oh you mean like that!" What*
> *she meant is: there are certain things contrary to our life structures.*
> *Although she certainly had me do things that would otherwise be physi-*
> *cally impossible. People have seen me do things like the top of the body is*
> *moving one direction and the bottom is moving in the other, and every-*
> *one knows I have serious arthritis and also that a human body doesn't*
> *do that.*

Brigh also shows off every now and again, effecting major weather
changes when she and Orion are working together. She manifests physical things for Orion, like the purple flowers in the middle of winter.
Brigh says she does this because humans sometimes need this kind of
validation in order to understand that our faith is real.

Orion describes the beginning of their relationship as something
like dating, learning to discern her touch. However, now Orion can distinguish her touch from any other touch—to the point that if he does
not feel it for a few days, things feel strange to him. He starts to long

for her, just like a couple who shares a house together but perhaps due to their work schedules do not see each other every day.

At this point in my life the loss of Brigh would be like not living, because she's showed me the life of life, the wonderment. She said, "The side effect of this work will be absolute wonderment." And wonderment not just of that which feels good, but sometimes of that which doesn't. Where you're actually able to feel, not happiness, but joy even when you're in sorrow—to be fascinated even when you're watching your body age or bleed, and that moves you into a state of nonresistance which allows a time of healing to happen.

THE DAY-TO-DAY RELATIONSHIP

What is it like to live married to a Faery being on a daily basis? Orion reported that it ranges anywhere from the sacred to the humorous. There are times when Brigh says nothing during the course of a day. Brigh has her own life; like any person, she is an independent being. Apparently spirit marriage does not exactly mean being enmeshed. Orion and Brigh are symbiotic and their spirits are linked, but he still has his human life and she has her faery life. There are times where he has to call out to her to get her attention, so that he can be with her and ask her a question, or enter into some spiritual or magical work, like teaching.

Orion performs many of the daily processes and practices that they developed together. These practices keep him aligned and allow him to be a good vessel for their work. This element of serious discipline is balanced by a certain sense of humor, especially as Brigh finds certain human things particularly entertaining.

Orion reports:

One of my favorite ones to share is Walmart. She loves Walmart. She says, "It's so human! The farthest ranges of human!" Every now and again my partner and I will go to Walmart with Brigh, when my awareness is entirely comingled with hers. All I do is physically run my fingers down shelves of things while she gathers data through my substance.

At this point in the interview, I interjected: "Like a barcode scanner!"

Yes! She loves it! She'll show up in things that I'm just doing in the human world. . . . The Faery people love the human arts, human creative expression. Our sciences are boring to them. There's nothing about this human world or this universe that we can tell them they don't already know. They were there at the beginning. And then there's times that she rings my doorbell and I know that she's summoning me to reveal something, or I'll feel she's guiding me to go somewhere or speak to someone about something. Because she runs along the threads of fate—she rides those like roads—she'll intersect me with different people, places, things, or experiences. Little will I know that it's a seed of some "ah-ha," some understanding. Then she'll draw me in closer to her and reveal what that seed was about. That's when I'll see a whole major insight come in through the Faery Seership work.

As with any intimate relationship, there are times where Orion and Brigh want to be alone. At these times Orion goes into the woods and calls out to her, so that their spirits can walk together. Sometimes Brigh walks beside him, sometimes within him, but both experiences are very intimate. Then there are times where he says the equivalent of "Brigh, I need my space." Those are the times he wants to go out and just be, as he puts it, "a silly gay boy, to go out to the clubs and watch drag shows. Well, that doesn't usually work too well, because she thinks drag queens are fabulous because [they're] so artistic . . . so flowery . . . so beautiful. So I usually don't get [to do] that alone." However, there are times when Orion asks for his privacy, like when he is making love to his human partner.

I am struck by how much of what Orion is describing is the activity of boundary-setting and agreement-making that is such a large part of creating successful polyamorous relationships—or any kind of close partnership. I begin to see how spirit marriage may be a more esoteric expression of polyamory. In fact, in Haitian Vodou, polyamory is the rule among the Loa: Erzulie Freda is wife to Damballah, Ogou, and the sea king Met Agwe, and the God Ogou wears the rings of both Erzulie Freda and Erzulie Danto.[3]

What is perhaps unique to Orion and Brigh's marriage is that Brigh is a holy being, although she does not like to be called a Goddess or God. She has told Orion, "I am not a Goddess. I give birth to those!" Brigh is adamant about this. Orion understands this statement to mean that she gave birth to the sacred inspirations of divinity, but not the actual divine flows or streams.

As described above, there are times when Orion and Brigh have their distinctive lives, then there are times when the distinction blurs. Orion has discovered that he no longer suffers with their relationship. Once he stopped resisting and let her *doctor* (transform) *his spirit,* once he was able to "ride the wave of that doctoring and let go what needed to be let go," the struggle in their relationship ceased. It was then that Orion realized his own habits or perceptions had been the biggest obstacle to harmony in their relationship. He says his favorite moment was when Brigh told him, "You agonize too much! You're burning your system up!" while lovingly reminding him that he has only to ask and she will manifest for him whatever it is he needs.

There are times where Brigh is in nature, off somewhere doing her work privately, and Orion can feel that she is distant from him. She has even told Orion, "Never forget I have my own religion. I have my own holy things, and they don't always include you." Brigh has the intimacy of her own presence.

Orion speculates:

Likely even the great Goddess or God has its own . . . a part that it doesn't show [to] its creation. I think there are parts of us that the Divine allows us to have just for ourselves, too. I really do. It's not that the Divine couldn't push into all those areas; it's that the Divine allows us our life.

Ultimately, Orion and Brigh have a very intimate day-to-day life, while at the same time maintaining the privacy of their own individuality.

REQUIREMENTS

At this point I was very curious about how Orion negotiated boundaries with an entity with whom he shares consciousness. Were there any rules or requirements that they have agreed on? Orion reported that part of their relationship agreement is that Brigh must understand and honor his human experience. When it was clear that she wanted him to leave a very high-paying job so that he could bring the vision of the Tree of Enchantment and Faery Seership work out into the world and make their cocreative relationship public, he told Brigh that he needed his basic needs, like food and shelter, provided for. He also told her that she needed to uphold and respect his partner, who should not suffer needlessly because of their relationship. Orion laid all these things out to her in the beginning. He soon discovered that because she is not human, she can't anticipate what he needs. She expects Orion to let her know exactly what it is that he needs and to ask for her assistance. She even asked him: "Why is it you sit in wonder or worry and don't come to me, when I have vast spiritual resources at my disposal?"

As a result of asking Brigh for support, there has been a noticeable difference in how his needs are provided for. While he had experienced synchronicities and magical events before their relationship due to his background in magic, he can now feel the intervention of something very intimate when Brigh steps in to care for him. She leaves an energetic signature behind and lets him know that what transpired was due to her intervention. When something extraordinary happens, he will ask, "Is this Mother Fate, the Goddess, or is this Brigh?" As a result, he has learned to feel the difference between the different forms of providence. Sometimes Brigh simply tells Orion: "What just occurred was a gift."

BENEFITS AND RISKS

Following our discussion on the ways in which Brigh blesses Orion, I also wondered whether there were any dangers involved in being wedded to such a potent force of nature. Orion insists that the greatest risk is that you cannot undo what has been done. There is no divorce court. Once the ceremony is done and the oaths are made, at least in the Faery Seership tradition, you cannot undo it. You have become a symbiote. Although you still have your distinctive life, a part of you has come together with an Otherworldly being and as a result of that union, something new is born from the two of you.

I paused to think about this for a moment from the perspective of reincarnation. I asked Orion how and whether this symbiosis might affect his future incarnations. Orion responded by saying he is not sure that he will reincarnate.

He clarifies:

I'm not saying that because I'm so evolved that I won't come back into form. I'm not sure yet if once I step into the invisible strata of life that we won't completely merge, that then we may resurface in another form of life, another human form. I don't know. Some things we're not meant to know, maybe because it's not done yet, or to prevent us from getting in the way of something sacred and holy that's happening.

Orion also shared a sage warning about the importance of learning to discern a spirit's intent. He wants people to understand that when these powerful Faery beings come to us, our vitality gets stimulated and sometimes overwhelmed by their presence, and we should not automatically interpret this as having sex or as a kind of rape. However, if an entity comes to a person and mandates that the person enter into union with them, this is a telltale sign of an unclean spirit and needs to be dealt with accordingly.

One of the most powerful things Orion did to discern Brigh's intent was to say to her, "May I pray for you?" Orion's litmus test of a spirit's integrity is to ask if he can pray for it. If a spirit is unclean, it will recoil from this request and further contact should be avoided. However, when Orion asked Brigh this question, "She practically threw up her hands and said, 'Have at it! Of course!' What a stupid question, right? Like, may *I* bless *you*? I knew she was clean then." Orion asserts that clean spirits do not overcome us unless it is for our well-being. With regard to the latter, sometimes they need to save us from ourselves and will, without our vote, shatter us. Typically, we find out later that that was the moment they saved our lives.

The benefit of being wedded to a spirit is the gift of a life rich in meaning and purpose. The illusion of isolation, our abandonment pain, falls away, and a type of aliveness takes its place. We begin to see the world in a way that perhaps we have never seen it before. Our perception of the sacred changes. We begin to see everything as sacred, and this sacredness is constant and ever present. For Orion, a big benefit was a sense of legacy—that he would leave behind some positive contribution to the human world.

He became deeply emotional when he said:

Through my union with this profound spirit woman, this profound being, we've given birth to a "child" that will live likely centuries beyond us, and that's this body of work. It's now published, so it's alive in the literary system. They [the Fae] also want us to have a legacy. I've had people say, "That's trite and humanesque." It's not trite. They know some of the things that mean a lot to us as humans, and it's not so trite to them. What they do see as trite are some of the kinds of fear we live by, or the types of greed, or the over-righteous ways we can be. They see those as unhealthy. But the desire to make an impact on the world, and [leave] a legacy of life and creation-promoting work? Oh no, they don't see that as trite! They will help us achieve that. That I know. [Brigh] told me: "I will help you achieve your immortality. That is my love back to you." Isn't that beautiful?

Orion spoke quite a bit about how his relationship with Brigh affects our side of the threshold, the physical side, but he pointed out that their relationship also affects Brigh's side of the threshold.

I was curious whether Orion was aware of the concept of spirit children, a concept reported in Eliade's (1964) work on shamanism; found in the traditional religion of the Dagara people of Burkina Faso; and present in other reports of spirit marriage. Orion said he was aware of this practice, but he thought that people may have spirit children in a variety of different ways. Some people unite with a spirit-being that moves through their physical partner, and as a result the child of that union is touched or seeded by the spirit. Orion says that the result of this kind of union is what are referred to as the Indigo children: children who have special gifts and who are born to transmit something to the world physically. There is also the idea in some shamanic traditions that a spirit-spouse may give birth to spirit children, noncorporeal offspring born of the union between the human and the spirit-spouse. One can even have an entire spirit family with the spirit-spouse. Orion says these spirit children become helping beings, born to become spirit guides for humanity.

Orion and Brigh's spirit child is the House of Brigh Faery Seership tradition, the Tree of Enchantment cosmogram, and the cocreative spirit companionships that this work fosters for Orion's students. Those students continually discover and are discovered by spirit companions, some for the first time and some who have been reaching for each other across generations or lifetimes.

FUNCTION AND PURPOSE OF THE RELATIONSHIP

As our time together drew to a close, I asked Orion to share any final thoughts about the greater purpose of his relationship with Brigh. Orion said that understanding the assignment of their relationship, what Earth wants of Brigh and Orion, was a threshold experience for him, a kind of breakthrough realization. This happened when he realized that Earth is Brigh's mother too. Although Brigh came here with the "Fall," the deepest part of Earth is her origin, her source. Therefore, the prime directive of their relationship is service to this planet and its life, not necessarily to humanity exclusively. He believes that if they keep their focus on serving the wholism of this planet and its vision of itself, humanity will benefit as a result. "What will come out of our union will re-engage humanity with its sacred relationship to life." This vision is a very important part of the paradigm with Brigh and Orion.

Brigh has said: "As long as humanity does religious and spiritual practices so it feels good about itself—and not in sacred relationship with life and this planet—it's drifting farther into the illusion of isolation and will move into extinction." The real drive behind Brigh and Orion's union is helping humans integrate themselves and their three-fold nature into one stream of life. As Brigh says, "Do what the trees do. They breathe from the deep, they draw from the heights, and they comingle and express within."

Orion elaborates:

[Trees] touch the heart of the planet to the heart of the embodied state to the heart of the universe. So our real drive is to get humans to link into that [threefold integration] via these processes, the vision keys, which are a big part of these dynamics of spiritual forces at the under world, over world, and middle world levels of life, which are really just fractals of one stream of life. If we can get people doing what the trees do, working with alignment, it will shift humanity's relationship with itself and with life. And thus, we won't be a cancer anymore. We won't be a consuming parasite, but a cocreative partner.

Integration, cocreation, and restoration are the three primary strands of their work. Now that they have ten years' worth of developed materials, which have become the core teachings within the House of Brigh, the future of their work is to turn these materials into a curriculum that will live beyond Orion. Due to ongoing health issues, Orion realizes that he cannot continue to work at the pace that he has been working these past ten years. Originally his focus was on taking the work that they developed out into the world to demonstrate its utility. Then he realized that he needed to refine the practices so that he could write them down in a way that others could teach them. Now his focus is primarily on ensuring sustainability of the work so that it can continue to expand and grow independently of him.

Orion also believes that we are at a critical moment in history where our species is ripe for this kind of work:

> *Because of the nature of our planet, its executive order to its life-forms is a unified state of life. It's requiring us to come back into the family of life, and it's not putting that up for [a] vote. There are pulses coming from the center of our world . . . that affect the neurobiology of all of life. Life-forms are shifting, species are coming back we thought were extinct, species are showing themselves we never knew existed. We're going to see more of it. The world is recalibrating its own balance. Hopefully, humanity—if it gets to a tipping point of good relationship, if it moves off the battlefield of life and onto the dancing floor with it—will be a part of that shift.*

Orion observes that these pulses are being released by the deep spirit world of this planet, the Faery realms, and as a result, a lot of people are spontaneously being contacted by extraordinary beings and having what is often called their *psychic senses* awaken. Orion prefers to call them our *subtle inner senses,* which he says are quite natural to humans. Suddenly people are aflame with a spirit contact or with subtler modes of perception, and this quickening is waking people up to extraordinary ways of knowing and being. Part of Brigh and Orion's work is to help people integrate this awakening, to translate and integrate it for humanity, and to train more translators and integrators—what we traditionally call shamans, witches, or seers.

The world needs more shamans, more seers, because our species has killed off so many of the keepers of the original instructions. Brigh has led me to a stream of lineage, inwardly, which we call the Wisdom Keepers. They are the ancestral dead who are the very embodiment of the original instructions, teachings of how to live in cocreative life with this planet. They are the very embodiment of it; they transmit it.

One of the most haunting things Brigh has said to Orion about the evolution of our species is: "You are as we have been; we are as you shall be." I've heard him say this before, and each time he says it I feel the vastness of its implication. It's as if there is so much potential that humanity is holding and yet we are only tapping a small fraction if it. At this point in our conversation, I noticed that the hairs on my arm stood up, what Orion calls the *delicious shivers,* and I sensed a question, perhaps a revelation, percolating in the back of my mind, like an itch that I couldn't quite scratch, or an ah-ha moment waiting to happen. It had to do with divine union, the Hieros Gamos between humans and holy spirits. As we mate our essence together, we cocreate a new being, a hybrid consciousness that infuses humanity with the consciousness of the Faery and other spirit realms. In this kind of indwelled cocreative union, perhaps these beings are activating humanity's dormant DNA, helping us to remember, resurrect, and refashion our latent potential to be as *they* are.

To conclude our interview, I asked Orion if there were any closing remarks he would like to make. Orion said that Brigh wanted us to know that her people and many like her people, whether of the upper world, the under world, or anointed human ancestors, are doing what they have always done. They are holding the gate open for our species so that we can become the anointed child of this planet's creation, its *creativity,* which is what we are meant to be. Humanity is meant to be the custodian, the guardian of life here, as well as the innovator on behalf of Earth. Brigh and spirit people like her stand ready to help midwife us back into ourselves again.

6
The Shakta Tantric

*K*ama Devi has been studying the South Asian Tantric traditions for more than twenty-five years. She was an academic
with a Ph.D. in the social sciences before turning fully to the spiritual
path. Kama has been initiated into a variety of South Asian Tantric
lineages. Her practice and teachings focus on the Divine Feminine and
awakening in the body.

I met Kama in the spring of 2014 when I attended her weekend workshop on the traditions of the Kali kula and fire *puja* in the
Oakland Hills of California. I had been practicing Sri Vidya Tantra for
a few years, and one of my puja sisters recommended Kama as a powerful and direct lineage teacher. I was hungry for the Divine Feminine,
for any teaching that honored and cherished my body as a blessing and
a sacrament. Yet as an academic I also longed for a practice rooted in a
direct, historically grounded lineage.

When I met Kama, I felt that she was someone who could perhaps
understand this longing and offer greater insight into the worlds that I
straddled as a religious studies scholar and practitioner of embodied spirituality. Over the course of the weekend I told her about my dissertation
research. She surprised me by telling me that she was, in fact, married to
the Goddess Kali. I felt the rush of synchronicity and immediately asked
if I might interview her for my research. I am grateful that she agreed. In

fall 2014, I conducted an in-person interview with her, during which time I also attended a weekend celebration and puja with her *kula*.

INVOCATION AND ORIENTATION

Our interview took place at the home of one of Kama's students who hosted me for the weekend. I began by laying out tea and cakes as an offering, called *prasad*. I invited us to each light a candle and set an intention, and I lit incense as an offering to the muse (or daimon or deva) of the research and to all the beings—human and other—supporting my inquiry. I also gifted Kama with a candle that I had made and blessed, specifically dedicated to my relationship with the Kali kula.

I was a bit nervous talking with Kama. She is a potent force, and I found I was quickened by her presence, as if everything were magnified. I was aware of not wanting to sound ignorant or inadvertently show disrespect toward her lineage or protocols. I was new to the Kali kula, and there was much I didn't know. I also realized that simply sitting in the presence of one who is wed to Kali Ma is very activating.

I began by thanking Kama for agreeing to meet with me and telling her how I hoped this interview would further not only my dissertation research but my own personal inquiry into the Divine Feminine. The Divine Feminine or "Ma," as I have come to call the energy of the Divine Feminine, shows up in many different forms for me, given that I hold a few different lineages. Kama explained that she had just now begun to share more about the different lineages that she holds with her community and students. This is not because she mixes and matches her traditions, but rather it allows her to give her community the language to better describe and name what they are experiencing.

I told her that I was open to this being a conversation with the three of us—that I was open to Kali speaking through her if she so chose. This statement created a lovely teaching moment wherein Kama shared that in her lineage they don't practice trance and possession. She explained that her lineage acknowledges that possession and channeling happen, and they are fine things, but her practice is to become more wide-eyed, bright, and clear in the world, not to disappear into trance or possession. She reported that in each of the four Tantric lineages that she carries, practitioners are required to become more alive. They teach a very specific practice of "Can you see Goddess now?" Thus, when she has information and contact with Kali, it's not because Kama has disappeared, it is because Kali has made herself present.

I wondered aloud if this might become a key phenomenological distinction in my research, the practice of channeling or possession versus the sharing of consciousness between humans and extraordinary beings, which is a kind of cohabitation or indwelling. Kama agreed that her experience is much more like indwelling. Kali is simultaneously next to her and around her—not separate from her and yet separate. Again Kama asserted that in her lineage she doesn't have the luxury of disappearing into the Divine. She noted that this is often problematic for students who want their spiritual practice to be a refuge, a place into which they might escape. She said it can be a challenge to step into a practice that requires radical presence and accountability.

This is the knife's edge that is often talked about on the Tantric path: the requirement to be more present, to tolerate more of the world's suffering, not less. She admitted that her practice is not pretty and sweet, and not very ecstatic. "Mostly," she said, "it's actually good hard work, and when we're lucky we get a little bit of sweetness to carry us through, but mostly it's good, hard work to be in this relationship."

Honestly, I can't imagine it being any other way in a lineage that is devoted to the fierce primordial Goddess Kali.

WHO IS KAMA'S KALI?

For many, the image of Kali's lolling red tongue, array of weapons, and garland of human skulls evokes fear and resistance. Many understand her solely to be a Goddess of death and dismemberment. To amplify this picture, Kali's devotees are often chosen by her in a wild, unnerving, and unremitting way. She lays claim and then it's up to them to learn how to make room for her in their lives, eventually falling in love with her. However, there is no clear-cut path for most Kali devotees—at least not in the West.

Kali has many faces and many names. One such name is Adya Kali, the primordial Dark Goddess through whom the universe is continually birthed, destroyed, and rebirthed. This is the form of Kali with whom Kama most publicly works. This is the fierce dark esoteric Tantric Goddess who is both death-giving hag and life-giving mother. For Adya Kali is also a healer, protector, and lover. In this aspect she is a totality. She gives the disease but also offers the medicine to heal it. Like many fierce Tantric Goddesses, she is a paradox, and in being so she points the way to freedom.

Adya Kali is nondual union, ultimate reality, *a priori* of gender differentiation. And yet, Adya Kali gives birth to the cosmos through the power of Her own fecundation, so she is seen as feminine, the womb of all Creation. In fact, it could be said that Adya Kali gives birth to all the other forms of Kali that we might know as Mahakali or Dakshinkali. Adya Kali teaches us to come into deeper relationship with all the various aspects of existence, inviting us into the mystery of living fully embodied, nothing rejected. And inside this mystery we discover the mystery of the cosmos and the female energy of Creation, or *shakti,* that creates, preserves, and transforms/dissolves all existence.

Thus Adya Kali moves as consciousness in the primordial womb, as the primordial womb, and takes form so that we might be in relationship with her. As Kama put it, "She is truly the mother of the universe, and thus also the mother of enlightenment. The mother of everything, really."

FIRST CONTACT

Kama's first experience of Kali is something that she doesn't often share publicly because it involves a rather controversial subject for many Westerners, namely animal sacrifice. Kama explained that in the West many of the traditional taboos against things like eating meat, having sex, and drinking alcohol are no longer considered taboo. Tantric practitioners eat meat, have sex, even work with menstrual blood, but animal sacrifice is still an off-limits idea. It is difficult for Westerners to wrap their minds and spirits around what is happening in animal sacrifice as we have a lot of judgment about it.

Kama observed that we could spend the whole interview just talking about what is actually happening in an animal sacrifice. Suffice it to say there is a lot more going on in this ritualized act than most Western-conditioned minds readily comprehend. Regardless, two of the major moments in Kama's spiritual development involved animal sacrifice. First, when she stepped onto her spiritual path, and second, the moment she stepped into her lineage stream. Therefore, she takes animal sacrifice very seriously.

Kama first encountered animal sacrifice when she was living in Nepal from 1990 to 1993 while researching her dissertation. She reminded me that living in Nepal one sees a lot of animal sacrifices, and that these are part of daily life. Kama eventually got used to their common occurrence. She also understood that as a social scientist it was her job to figure out what was going on from the insider's perspective of the practice, and not overlay her judgment or interpretation from an outsider's perspective. In fact, Kama insisted that her training as a social scientist was not all that distinct from her training as a Kali worshipper.

You turn towards. You walk a mile in somebody else's shoes. You try to understand it from their point of view, not from your own. The Kali practices also ask us to do that, to turn towards everything we seem to have an opinion about and to move towards it with openness. So, as a social scientist, I was trained to move towards with openness.

And so, in the interest of her research, Kama had witnessed many animal sacrifices, had attended cremations, and had tried to experience as much as she could of the culture in Nepal. Eventually it was this hunger for discovery and understanding that led her to Kali.

One of my good friends was convinced that I was in Nepal, in Kathmandu, not to do my dissertation research (she said that was the cover story), [that] the real reason I was there was to meet my Goddess. And she had seen some signs that it was clear that I was a Goddess worshipper, not a God worshipper, even though she herself worshiped Shiva. She spent a lot of time taking me to all the different temples in the valley to see if there was [any] resonance. She taught me first how to bow and do worship and make offerings. What a sakhi! What a sister on the path!

One day they went to a Ganesh temple. (Kama reported that you always go to see Ganesh before you go to any other deity.) As Kama placed offerings in the trunk of the statue of Ganesh, she also put her forehead to his feet.

As I put my forehead to his feet, I felt something soften in me, like the moment when butter melts. I felt so vulnerable and very open for no particular reason. I stood up and I actually couldn't look at my friend. She kindly stood behind me and said, "Ah, you felt something, didn't you?" And I said, "Yes." And she said, "Good. Ganesh has cleared the way. Now we can find your deity."

Her friend had received some signs indicating that Kama's Goddess was a fierce Goddess. However, Kama explained that in Kathmandu there's not just one form of a fierce Goddess, there are a thousand. "[My friend] was pretty insistent that she get me in front of the precise form of the Goddess that was mine, not just the neighborhood of my Goddess. So [we visited] every Durga temple, every Talaju temple, all the different lineages . . . she was unrelenting."

One day Kama and her friend went to the Dakshinkali temple in the south of the Kathmandu valley. This is an open-air shrine that is surrounded by the *matrkas* and the *yoginis*. Kama described how Kali's mother lives up on the hill above this shrine, which is rare because there is no mythology around Kali's mother. Mothers and daughters often go on pilgrimage to this hill once the daughter has married and left her mother's house. As a result, the energy of the hill is permeated by a familial sweetness. However, at the main shrine below there is a loud, rushing river, and it is there that animal sacrifices are performed.

Kama had been to the Dakshinkali temple before and had seen the animal sacrifices being performed there, so none of this was new to her. However, on this particular Tuesday, as they were walking toward the main shrine, they stopped to observe the sacrifice.

We hadn't yet gotten into the queue for darshan *and we were probably thirty feet away, quite a distance. They were about to take the head off the next animal in line. We had stopped, and we were watching. Now the goat has to shake its head in a particular way to give its agreement to the sacrifice, but one goat didn't. There was a big hullaballoo, and eventually they had to let that goat go. They had to have a talk with the owner of the goat, the person who brought the goat for sacrifice, because that's a month's salary for these people, a goat. The fact that it hadn't been offered was quite distressing for the people who had brought it. But finally they got that worked out, the goat went free, and the next goat got into line.*

There was a lot of tension because nobody really knew what was going to happen next, now that this one goat had broken the sequence of things. Were we going to get back to business or not? But the next goat agreed and consented, and the moment the head of the goat was severed from its body by the priest, by the executioner, more accurately . . . there is a huge amount of shakti that gets released in the death of the animal, the cutting of the neck and the blood. They actually take the animal, the body, and spray the blood on the murtis, *so there are blood offerings on each of the murtis around.*

Before they got to the spraying part . . . when the head was severed from the body and the blood began to flow, a huge amount of energy came directly from that goat and hit the front . . . of my body. It was so powerful I actually fell over—from thirty feet away. Now my friend is still standing, worried about me because it's a concrete floor and I'm down on my knees and it was very, very painful. I was dizzy and kind of fell over.

She was concerned. She picked me up, brushed me off, and said, "Are you okay?"

I said, "Yeah, I don't know what that just was, but okay." Then we got in line for darshan, had our picnic, and that was the end of that.

A few days later, however, Kama began to realize there was more going on than met the eye. She began to experience a foreign sensation in her chest, and it occurred to her to talk to its energy. She entered into dialogue with it, asking: "Who are you, and what are you doing in there?"

The energy in her chest replied, "I am Kali."

Kama responded by telling Kali, "Well, you know, I didn't really want you in there, and I didn't ask you to come in there. I know I've been visiting and all that, but please go."

Kama elaborates:

I mean if I'm going to propitiate and ask a Goddess to take up residence in my body, it's not going to be Kali. She is the last of the last, and the most dangerous of the dangerous, and there are plenty of pretty Goddesses and sweet ones, and that's not where I would have gone in that moment.

Kali's response to Kama's request to leave was a flat-out "No."

Kama was perturbed by this refusal to leave, saying, "I'm not really sure this is how it works. Don't I get to choose? Don't I have free will?

"But [Kali] says, 'I'm not leaving.'"

Kama called the friend who had taken her to the Kali temple that day and told her, "There's this thing in my chest. Remember when I got hit? There's something in my chest, she says it's Kali, and she won't leave.

"And my friend says, 'Oh shit.'"

It happened that there was a well-respected exorcist in town at that time. Her friend decided they should go see the exorcist to see if she could convince Kali to leave. They entered a giant room full of people; it was filled with smoke and drumming. The exorcist was a woman, and she was performing all kinds of amazing feats like pulling bones out of people's bodies and other wonders. As a social scientist, Kama says she was in heaven watching this giant melee of curiosity and miracles. She was also keenly aware of a deep devotion that was present. People understood that this exorcist was the incarnation of the Deity, that they were in the living presence of the Goddess, of Ma.

At the very end, her friend took Kama up to meet the exorcist. When Kama told the exorcist what had happened, the exorcist said, "So let me get this straight. Whatever it is in your body says that it's Kali, and she won't leave?"

Kama said, "Right."

To which the exorcist replied, "If Kali's not coming out, I'm not going in after her."

At the time, Kama was upset at the exorcist's response. She had hoped that the exorcist would be able to remove Kali and that would be the end of it. However, in retrospect, Kama says she is grateful for what happened because she was given a great lesson in the relationship between deity and devotee, and the kind of permission and power an exorcist is actually granted.

The exorcist demonstrated that it's not about having control over a deity. It's not that we're supplicating a deity for riches and good test scores and all that. There's actually another relationship at stake. She [the exorcist] has got lots of permission to cure people's illness, fix land disputes, and arrange good marriages, but if Kali came into my body and said she's not leaving, then that's not actually her [the exorcist's] realm.

I wondered aloud whether the response of the exorcist was unique to the Goddess Kali. I asked Kama: If Lakshmi, Saraswati, or one of the less fierce Goddesses had claimed you like that, would the exorcist have tried to ask that Goddess to leave? Kama observed that in that moment, it was both about Kali's presence and about the fact that the exorcist didn't have permission to remove a Goddess that had installed herself in a devotee. I asked Kama if being claimed like this by a Goddess was a common occurrence. She explained that deities arrive in people's lives in a variety of ways, but she had never heard of a deity entering the body through an animal sacrifice.

Kama had heard other stories involving animal sacrifice, and even a story of an initiation in which the initiate was in a trance state and a particular deity had come to them in vision. In that case, the deity that appeared wasn't actually their primary deity, also known as the *ishtadevi/a*; it was just the deity that opened the initiatory door for them. This distinction can sometimes be confusing for the devotee as they seek to discern the identity of the ishtadevi/a. Kama considers herself fortunate because there was no confusion about the identity of her ishtadevi (Kali).

Even though she understands and works with other deities, she is most definitely a one-deity practitioner. She suggested that other people may have a path that allows for a relationship with multiple deities and that they sometimes come in and go out like "a revolving set of doors." This kind of impermanence is not what happens in her system. Kali tends to be an all-encompassing ishtadevi; she is not in an "open relationship" with her devotees. I remarked that it felt quite auspicious that she had been chosen like this—unique and important.

Kama agrees:

It wasn't like "Go leave offerings." It was just done. It was done. I sometimes laugh and say that it took me a decade to come to terms with that. What's that mean? How do I worship her? I didn't even know how to make a shrine. But it wasn't even the beginning of my path. It was just the beginning of my coming to terms with her. Once I came to terms with her, really accepted that she was it, and that it wasn't a passing fancy, or this year's phase, or that I would move on to whatever else. . . . Once I got really anchored into that, then she opened up the path, the actual formal path with sadhana *and teachers and lineages. But I had to come to terms with her first.*

DEVELOPING THE RELATIONSHIP

Coming to terms with Kali was no quick or small feat. Kama had no support for the journey of being claimed by a fierce Tantric Goddess. This was 1994—before the Internet, before email. She was living in Nepal at the time and she had the care of her friends in the temples, but no formal lineage teachers. There were no adepts to help her navigate a devotional practice to Kali. One friend showed her how to make a very basic altar with some incense, lights, and a picture, but she didn't have a *murti,* (icon) an instructor, or any formal sadhana guidance. When she came back to the United States, there were no resources, no books written about Kali at that time. One day she went into a New Age bookstore in her town and found a tiny clay statue of Kali. This statue became her first murti, and she carried it around for ten years trying to make sense of it all.

Even as a scholar going through the library stacks, Kama had only found books on Nepal or Goddess worship ritual, but nothing on Kali. She suggested that this was both a blessing and a curse. Because she was alone on the path, she didn't have any preconceptions about what should be happening, which was quite freeing and beautiful. Although it was hard not to have a guide, it was also easier. Because she didn't know what to expect, she didn't try to make the relationship into anything it was not.

All I could do was refer back to her. "What do you want? What am I supposed to do here? Do I have to?" And she taught me enough. She gave me my first sadhana instructions directly. Then things began to happen. . . . I would have dreams about spiritual teachers I had never met and didn't even know existed. And then someone would say, "Oh you should go visit Ammachi," and so I'd go. Then I'd go, "Oh! She was the one in the dream, and I didn't know!"

The first time I ever received a mantra—I'd done a lot of research on mantras, and I'd done some basic mantra practice, but I didn't really have sadhana—I had a dream that Ammachi gave me a very complicated

Kali mantra I'd never heard anywhere before and couldn't find reference
to. Then I discovered [Ammachi] was an actual being and went to visit
her for darshan. But not until I saw her did I know that she was the being
in the dream who had given me the complicated mantra. [Then I went]
up for my very first hug and she whispered that complicated mantra back
into my ear, which is not one of the mantras that she normally gives out.

The internal realms were alive, and then slowly the external
realms began to mirror the interior realms. It was the interior land-
scape that she was developing in me, that the external landscape was
coming to meet.

Kama received sadhana instructions from Ammachi, and although she loved Amma very much, she knew that she was not her root guru, the *sat guru*. She revered Ammachi as a loving manifestation of Kali and learned a lot being with her, worshipping with her, and using the forms that she offered. Being an Ammachi devotee, however, was not intended as her final destination. Slowly, after a decade of searching, Kama's practice began to ripen.

One summer, on a return trip to India, a friend told Kama about the menstrual festival to the Goddess Kamakhya in Assam. "Through the blessings of the yoginis," Kama was able to attend the festival that year and had many powerful experiences there. She began to return to the Kamakhya temple regularly, which in the early years was as often as three to five times a year. She would go for spring break, be there for seven days, and then come back to the United States. As a result of these pilgrimages to Kamakhya, Kama met what would become her lineage family, a North Indian priestly lineage devoted to the worship of Kamakhya. "Then," she explains, "the real sadhana began."[1] It had been twelve years since Kali had first claimed her; by the time she received her first initiation into their lineage, Kama was already well-developed on the path.

My lineage family had thought they were going to give me the first ini-
tiation and start me at the beginning of the path. Instead what came

through was the initiation you get after twelve years of practice. They didn't want to have to, but there it was, and it happened. And I was just like, "Whoa! What just happened?" They were confused, and I was confused. But there it was. We were just going through the motions of something that was already happening.

THE MARRIAGE

Earlier in the interview, when I read the interview question, "What led you to decide to marry?" Kama laughed out loud and remarked, "As if you have a choice!" I was curious about how Kama had gone from discovering that Kali is her ishtadevi to marrying Kali. The fact that Kama's ishtadevi (what I call the Divine Self) is also her spirit-spouse is unique from all of the other accounts I'd collected. In fact, in some traditions it is unheard of to marry the Divine Self. So how did Kama differentiate between these two seemingly related but different concepts?

As Kama previously noted, in her Kali lineage they have what are called *ishtadevis,* the cherished central Goddess of the devotee. Another way of understanding this is that the ishtadevi is the Goddess that owns you. Kama admitted that she didn't talk about this concept in public very often. To people who don't have a sense of surrender and understand the primacy of the Deity, it can sound like enslavement. Regardless, everyone has an ishtadevi (female deity) or ishtadeva (male deity), but not everyone with an ishtadevi/a has a spirit-spouse. The distinction between an ishtadevi and a marriage is the level of dedication and commitment in the deity-devotee relationship.

When describing the ishtadevi relationship, Kama explained that one's spiritual practice orients around one's ishtadevi. This is the deity whom you rely upon, whom you lean back into. In contrast, marriage to a deity is much more about whom you serve. "The relationship with the ishta, in my own experience, is more like a love affair. I get to be in this grand love affair with Goddess. Marriage is obligation and duty, similar to the difference between having a lover who is for our pleasure and the social obligations that come with a legal marriage." This statement struck me as an interesting perspective on a relationship with Deity, and I wondered how her transition had evolved from lover to spouse.

She elaborated:

I met Kali twenty-five years ago in Nepal. I was authorized to teach about a decade ago and I only began to teach about two and a half years ago. The spousal relationship with Kali came much later, and it arose when she determined that it was time for me to take on a level of responsibility with what she had given me and what I had trained in. There was actually the shift from being a student and in a relationship with my beloved to being a teacher and having a spouse.

Kama considers that her official engagement to Kali happened when she was in Assam near the Kamakhya Temple. At that point she had been visiting the temple quite often and had developed a friendship with a family there. One day there was a *mendhi* artist at her friend's house for a wedding, and the women had gathered to adorn the bride. For some reason the women decided not only to dress up and adorn the bride, they also adorned Kama as a bride. "I told them, 'I'm way too old to be a bride! I'm divorced! I'm grey!'" But they insisted on adorning her alongside the bride. In a synchronistic fashion, just a few days later, Kama would meet her lineage family for the first time at the Kamakhya Temple.

One challenge that Kama would discover with her lineage family is that her relationship to Deity had always been primary for her—more primary than her relationship to guru. Kama explained that most lineages exist because of the guru-student relationship, not because of the deity-devotee relationship. Lineage is the movement of the wisdom stream from teacher to student. Deity is involved in this process, but in a lineage, from the standpoint of the practitioner, the guru *becomes* the deity.

Kama goes on to elaborate:

There are five ways to enter the path: You can meet your teacher. You can meet your ishtadevi. You can meet the teachings. You can meet your community. You can meet the practices. We all find one of those doors to entering the path, but we still have to account for and come into relationship with all the other forms. We have to actually come to terms with guru, come to terms with teachings, come to terms with sadhana, come to terms with community. But most of us don't want to. We want to stick with whatever our doorway is. But a well-rounded practitioner who can make progress on the path has to come to terms with all of those. And my lineage taught me how to come to terms with guru. Which was not pretty—at fucking all! Because of my commitment to Kali we had some rough-and-tumbles. It's not that I don't recognize and submit to the lineage teacher, who is actually a mahasiddha, *because I do. But the ultimate teacher for me is Kali.*

The engagement party had given Kama a sense of what she was truly committed to. Once she met her lineage family, she then had to go through the struggle of making sense of this commitment in the context of the world of guru devotion. There had been moments when her lineage family thought they were going to have to send her away, when Kama was pretty sure that could happen and she would be asked not to return. Still, she persisted. It wasn't easy for either party. It is quite uncommon for a high-caste Brahmin family to adopt a single white Western woman into their lineage stream, but it was clear that karmic destiny was involved. They all had seen the signs. Nevertheless, it was not a simple path or relationship for any of them.

I was really a pain in the ass! I wouldn't give over my center of gravity to the guru. They needed me [to] in order to encompass me in the wisdom stream. Yet things began to happen where they recognized that they weren't wrong, but neither was I. We figured it out together, through practice, through the dance of the arising of auspicious signs, through what was actually happening during empowerments and teachings. All of us were like, "Oh great, we're being shown how all of this can work together." But it's not how they knew to teach me.

Kama went on to explain that in her Tantric lineages—she is a lineage holder in both Tantric Buddhism and Tantric Hinduism—sometimes you are given teachings not because you are ready for them, but because the teacher knows that they may never see you again. Certain teachings may be bestowed upon you, and then as a practitioner it becomes your job to ripen them. "Just because I was authorized to teach didn't mean I was ready, and I got that clearly. Even after I had been authorized to teach, I still apprenticed with another teacher quite deeply after that. The marriage arose after that apprenticeship ended." It was after Kama left her apprenticeship in 2011 and returned to the secular world that the marriage process resumed. For Kama it was very much a process. Signs and portents demarcated distinct phases along the way to the marriage.

Kama emphasizes that in each of her lineages, a teacher is only empowered to teach when students seek them out.

> We teach only at the bequest of our students. That is really, really important: It tells us that the student makes the teacher, right? It's the students who are the ones, in my lineages, giving us the titles. My students called me "Ma," therefore I am Ma. It's because they did it, not because I thought I was ready. In all my lineages, just because we're authorized to teach doesn't mean we do so.

Interestingly, as Kama found herself with an increasing number of requests to teach, she found that the process of ripening into her teaching role was also accompanied by a process of deepening toward the spousal relationship with Kali.

> When I finally parted from the last teacher I served in person, Kali then came back and actually once again formally wed me or wed me to her. I was given in arranged marriage to her in a temple on some ordinary Tuesday morning in India. I had just gone in for darshan and I came out a bride. That kind of thing just happens with her. I didn't get prep, and I didn't have choice. I stepped into the sacred space of the temple—which

is her body, by the way. I stepped into the interior landscape of her body, and I was at that point no longer in control of what happened. The same way a bride steps into the carriage that takes her out of her mother's house: She is no longer in charge of anything that happens after that. All she can do is fight or submit. And things just arose . . . I walked out [of the temple] and I was like, "Well, I guess that just takes care of that, then, doesn't it?"

I asked Kama whether there had been an officiant that performed the rite. She reflected that there had been a priest at the temple that day, but it hadn't been a prearranged ceremony. Instead, something numinous had arisen.

In Delhi, there is a beautiful little temple for Kali that has deep links to the temples I'm connected to in other parts of India. There's another one nearby linked to the Adya Kali lineage, but I'm not as happy there. So I usually go to this little one that has Kamakhya inside. The Dasha-Mahavidya are there, and the transgender people come on the holidays. It was built around a tree; it had originally just been a tree shrine in the middle of the city. I know the priests there. They are very kind when I come to visit, and they let me get away with things that normally they don't let people get away with. . . . There was a kindness about how they let me worship there.

One day I had just gone in for normal Tuesday morning darshan— Tuesday is one of Kali's days—it was as if [the priest] knew exactly who I was, and I knew exactly who he was. He clearly had his marching orders. He marked the part in my hair with the sindur. *Someone had earlier brought in an offering for Kali, and they turn those offerings back into* prasad. *People bring in clothing, saris, food, and fruit, and it goes back to the next person who comes in line, or someone that day. They recycle it all: it gets blessed at her feet, and then gets sent out as prasad. [The priest] handed me a wedding sari, and I was just like, "Okay, okay. Never did that before."*

As Kama described this process I was struck by a feeling of profound synchronicity. We may simply be going through the routine of our lives, and yet She, the Goddess, takes those common moments and transforms them to something extraordinary—not when we plan it, but when She determines we are ready.

IMPACT ON OTHER RELATIONSHIPS

I ask Kama whether she had been in a human relationship at the time, and how the marriage had impacted her romantic life. She observed that for years there had been moments when it was clear that she belonged to Kali and that the relationship was leading to deeper and deeper commitment. As a result, partnering with a human had been problematic. Although Kali does have consorts, unlike most other Hindu Goddesses, Kali is not in a divine coupling. This seems to be reflected in the relationship Kama has developed with Kali. Kali has laid a primary claim on Kama, and everything else comes second.

Kama acknowledged that the marriage to Kali was somewhat scary for her because it was an undeniable solidification of their relationship. "I ended up having to work through a lot of fear around not being able to have a human relationship as a result. Those things did not seem to be able to coexist very well for me. That's not been one of the graces that I've had with this."

Since the marriage, Kama has done her best to partner in a romantic relationship with another person, but she says it mostly doesn't work. She came to realize that one reason for the challenge she encountered in conventional partnerships was that she was trying to hide the depth of her relationship to Kali in order to have intimacy with a human beloved. Kama has to be clear—with someone she might consider dating—that there is already a primary relationship in her life. She has non-negotiables.

There are non-negotiables. Those don't work very well in conventional relationships. One of my non-negotiables is that every Saturday night, no matter where I am, I do Kali puja, either publicly or privately, and that's non-negotiable. That doesn't work very well when your partner wants you to go home to meet their family and on Saturday night they're all going to go out for dinner. I can no longer leave sacred context to enter into conventional context for the sake of relationship. It mostly means I don't have a lot of relationship with my partner's social world. I know their friends and their family and all that, but it's not about joining families anymore, it's not about raising kids anymore. It takes a pretty unique individual to have room for this kind of woman in their lives. The potential for physical human partnership decreases once we do this, in my own experience, because I already have a primary relationship, and that's not negotiable.

Eventually, one of her partners named what was going on. He observed that it felt like there was someone else in the relationship with them, and that he was the third person in their relationship. Something else was alive in Kama that he could not touch, get in the way of, or extricate her from. She had already given herself to something that no ordinary partner could ever compete with. Kama was grateful for his calling it out in this way.

The gift of his naming this dynamic meant that Kama could now begin to learn how to live with this knowledge, giving it more space in her psyche. Kama learned that if she did not look at her relationship with Kali head-on, she could avoid experiencing the full force of the dismantling effect Kali's claim had on her life. She needed to soften this dismantling somewhat, so she could give herself the needed time and space to make the transition from being a full-time professor to being a full-time spiritual teacher.

It was so intense. If I looked at it clearly, I knew my life as I knew it would fall apart. The truth also is, of course, that my life was already coming apart at the seams. But if I only looked at it with half of my gaze, I could go through the dissolving with grace, as opposed to catastrophe. I wanted to be able to take care of everything that I needed to take care of.

I needed to get rid of all my stuff. I needed to take care of my finances. I needed to leave gradually from my job instead of getting fired. I needed to have these really good endings.

Some people find a partner with whom they can practice their spirituality together. Other couples have different but perhaps complementary spiritual practices. Kama explains that there are those of us with single-wide *asana karma* and those of us with double-wide asana karma, one seat on one mat or two seats on one mat. Kama has single-wide asana karma. She has her seat, and her consort or beloved might have his seat, but they're not sitting on the same mat—they're next to each other but separate. This separation means that a partner might share in her lineage or might have a lineage that is complementary. However, her karma is the unfolding of her personal devotional relationship with Kali as opposed to other Tantric practices where one might find the Deity through their beloved.

As Kama is talking about the struggle to be in partnership, there is a pregnant pause. She admits that fewer and fewer acceptable partners have come into her life as a result of her commitment to Kali. I am struck by the *sacrifice* (a word evolved from the Latin for "making sacred") this has required: making her relationship with Kali sacred has meant sacrificing other forms of romantic partnership. To be married to a Goddess like Kali is an all-or-nothing endeavor; there are no half-measures. I have wondered whether this would be different if Kama had been a man. During our interview I marveled at how hard it must be for a woman devoted to a Goddess of vitality and passion, like Kali, not to be able to express that vitality and passion with a physical partner.

Kama reported that submission, surrender, and constraint are required of her. Yet alongside that comes a huge amount of grace, possibility, and love. Because of this love, she has never fought Kali's claim on her. Instead she has sought ways to come to terms with what was happening. She admitted that she's had temper tantrums and also shared that it's odd for someone who has as much will, stubbornness, and persistence as she does to be in such a submissive position. Kama explained that some of this is due in part to the fact that she is a Western woman. There are Indian and Nepali women devoted to Kali who also have a human spouse. The Indian tradition of arranged marriages as well as the Hindu devotional worldview somehow make it easier for spouses to accept the requirements Kali places on her devotees.

Kama also admits that she has a snippet of karmic memory in her memory bank. That snippet says that she has been with Kali for lifetimes. It's clear to Kama that she has belonged to Kali for a long time and that she had no other option in this lifetime than to submit to her again.

GENDER AND SEXUALITY

The conversation around relationship brings us to the topic of sexuality and gender. Kama says she is "strangely straight, or as all my good lesbian friends say, 'mostly straight.' And most of my good friends are lesbians." She goes on to elaborate that here in the West many people who have an "outside of the box" sexuality, or a nontraditional gender identity, often find their way to Tantra because Tantra is a radical alternative spiritual path. This radical inclusivity is part of the blessing of Kali. Everyone is welcome in her lap. Kali holds space for people in LGBTQI+ community and embraces them with open arms. Kama elaborates on how her relationship with Kali caused her to question her sexual orientation:

If you look at my life, my best girlfriends are queer, and that's been the case for years and years. As an academic I studied queer theory and taught gender, kinship, and sexuality. In the midst of it all, in looking at the teachings I've been given, it's never about becoming something we're not. We are becoming more of who we actually are. I've been inside of women's culture and women's community deeply for years. That's my primary orientation—it's not towards straight culture. But I happen to be straight and monogamous (well, mostly straight and monogamous).

I once asked one of my queer friends on the path, "What the hell am I doing here? I'm this mostly straight, monogamous white woman." She laughed and said, "It's because you love the yoni as much as we do!"

And yet I'm married to a female deity. I'm not married to Shiva, which is more traditional. People who are married to deities tend to marry the deity of their gender sexual orientation. So lesbians tend to marry a female deity, and straight women tend to marry males. . . . Most women aren't married to Kali. There are men who are married to Kali, and women who become Kali, but they're not married to her.

Somehow the complexity of Kama's multifaceted orientation—being a heterosexual woman married to a female deity—seems totally in keeping with the radically nonconformist ethos of Kali worship. As Kama puts it: "It's amazing to me how much room Kali makes for this ragtag group of scrabbling, trash-picking, beautiful beings who have gathered."

I asked Kama to elaborate on the tradition of spirit marriage as it relates to her lineages. She reported that usually marriage to a deity happens with celibate non-householders—monastics, ascetics, and the like—because spirit marriage gets in the way of conventional social and family life. While spirit marriage does not happen often, it does happen.

Laughingly, Kama says:

In my own life I thought for a while that this relationship with Kali meant that I was probably a repressed lesbian, and I just didn't know it yet. I figured I should find out. Our minds hold all kinds of bullshit. Our psyches are powerful things! I knew enough about the power of the psyche to know that I could probably be faking it, and I could really have messed that one up! . . . I eventually did meet a woman and fell in love, but I actually wasn't in love with her because she was a woman. I fell in love with the person, not the body. So I wasn't actually a lesbian. My primary desire, the way that polarity runs in my body, is with a masculine-feminine polarity. I'm straight, mostly, although I can run polarity with women. But it's usually because one of us is taking on the masculine polarity and the other is running the feminine. I need that masculine-feminine polarity in my system.

Kama claims that to her, it is sexual polarity that generates shakti. She reports that many Tantric teachings state that women with women generates an energy akin to water with water, but in a traditional Tantric context this does not generate shakti. She is quick to add that there is nothing wrong with this energetic, which has its own purpose, but the focus of the Kali kula, her lineage stream, is the generation of shakti. "I am absolutely fascinated by the fact that I am mostly straight, that I have a tendency to fall in love with men and want to be with men, but my entire landscape is so gynocentric that you would think that I was queer."

For a long time Kama worried about this apparent inconsistency. She feared she was subconsciously hiding something from herself. When she was indoctrinated into her lineage family at Kamakhya and began to spend a lot of time at the menstrual festivals, she finally understood how gynocentric the Kali kula universe really is. She noticed many queer and transgender people there, in Kali's lap, alongside many powerful practitioners in traditional, straight marriages. Eventually, she was able to exhale into herself and stop worrying. It finally occurred to her that her purpose in this lifetime is to deeply love women, to teach women how to deeply love themselves, and to discover what it means to wake up in a female body.

Most of Kama's students are women. However, even though there is a focus on generating the masculine-feminine polarity in her teachings, her student community is not heteronormative by any means. As a result, one gift of her teaching is the translation of traditionally heterosexual Tantric concepts for a queer audience.

There are two levels. One is: "What is it for me to wake up in a female body in this lifetime?" Then there's the question of: "What is it for me to provide a context for all these people to wake up in their body, whatever form it is, in this lifetime, no matter what anybody else has told them is possible?" My own partnering with men and being monogamous may or may not be a choice that most of my students make, and I don't need them to. That may not be the way the way they live, and it may be the way they live, but nobody's going to live that way because they think they have to. I'm also not going to let people get away with being something that they're not. Community for me is not about looking like anybody else. You just look like you. My work as a teacher is to actually use the *relationship that I have with Kali, or that Kali has designated with me, to meet each person where they are and to support them in their sadhana towards answering that same question.*

PURPOSE OF THE MARRIAGE

This idea of waking up in a female body and meeting people where they are feels like an important insight into the purpose of Kama and Kali's marriage. Why did Kali choose to marry a highly educated white woman from a Western culture at this particular time in history? Kama reports that Kali's agenda is that "nobody is left behind." Within that "nobody left behind" agenda is a "just as you are" principle. You don't have to fake it to make it with Kali.

> *The only actual chance we have for awakening is to be what we are, not what we're pretending to be. So we are dropping shell after shell after shell. . . . There's the work that Kali does with me as my beloved, which is to teach me through identification with her what is it to wake up in the female body in this lifetime. That's the question of my existence. That's my life's question. What is it to wake up in the female body in this lifetime?*
>
> *First, [Kali's] out there: we see her externally, and we work with her. Then slowly, over time, we bring her [closer] until we have identification with her. Then there's the question: How do I support my students in awakening in the bodies that they come in . . . and the sexualities that they come in, in this lifetime? Because a basic tenet of our lineage is that no one is left behind. . . . It's very rare to abide by this tenet. People say, "nobody left behind," and then turn people away. "We can't talk to them. You shouldn't do that." There's all this posturing and exclusion. The point of the Tantric path is that nobody is separate from her.*

Kama considers herself blessed to be able to facilitate such a community, which she points out really could only happen in the West. According to Kama, Tantric teachings are on the decline in the East due to two main factors: the usurpation of the temples by the government and refusal of the young people to carry on their parents' lineage. She discloses that the circumstances in India, similar to the Sinicization of Tibet, are becoming such that people can no longer practice Tantric spiritualities there. At the temples in India, the priestly families who have carried the lineages for generations are now being forced out in exchange for those who are there to make money and give a cut to the government. These priestly families had lived at the temples for thousands of years carrying their wisdom streams, but now there is no one carrying forward these lineages.

One of the biggest conversations among the men in Kama's Indian community is how to keep their lineages alive when their own children refuse to pick them up. As Kama described the destruction of the wisdom streams, shivers ran through my body. I felt pain, grief, and anger that these holy lineages are being lost and starved out by a capitalist agenda, and I realized that perhaps the rise of Tantra in the West is one way these traditions have found to survive.

Kama knew that the power held by the temples was shifting when her student body began to include more and more Indian students. She explained that at first her students had been only Westerners. Then she began to get a wave of first-generation Indians whose parents were still living in India. She had originally thought that this was perhaps because English was their first language, and the students were more identified with Western culture. However, when an entire wave of Indian women living in India, in traditional Indian households, began to come to her online community, she could no longer ignore what was happening.

This gave her pause. She asked these women why they didn't just go to their family priest, to the temples near them? They replied, "You don't understand. No one will teach us. We have a right to these teachings; our husbands are practicing. But no one will teach us the teachings." Perhaps not so coincidentally, Kama had been trained by her lineage family as if she were a man. Although she was trained in the women's mysteries, they also trained her the way they would have trained their sons, because they didn't know what else to do with her. Kama carries both the women's internal mysteries as well as the men's external mysteries.

I don't know all of the men's mysteries. Let me just be clear: there are men's mysteries, and there are men's mysteries. But I can do puja. I can do ritual. I now know it's because here [in the West], I'm holding both the masculine and the feminine in my community. We have to know how to do the external rituals. I have to know how to train men at least at the basic levels and have enough discernment to know where to send them for training before they come back to us. I have to know what the women's mysteries are in order to take women all the way . . . and to have the refinement to know what's the patriarchal overlay and what's actually authentic wisdom here. That is a piece I bring that even my lineage family doesn't quite get. Because there's this great saying in India about how patriarchy works. They say, "The fish don't talk about the water." They're just swimming in it. They know it's happening, and they love women, but my academic training has given me a space to step through and to see what's happening.

I'm beginning to understand just how important Kama's work is. It feels truly auspicious to have access to her as a teacher. The mantle she carries is powerful and rare. There is something unique about all the various pieces she holds and how they constellate in her teachings. Kama holds very traditional training and yet she has been given the permission and bequest to adapt that training for her Western students, to translate it to a largely nontraditional audience. Kama admits that only a few of her students have a capacity for the rigor of traditional lineage teachings and discipline. She often finds herself asking, What is this translation project about, building a bridge from the traditional teachings that have really anchored something in me, conveying them to my students in a way they can actually connect to?

I asked Kama to elaborate on her statement: "I'm here to wake up in the female body, and then help my students do that." I asked her to define what "waking up" means to her in her tradition.

When I use the [term] wake up, it's the least controversial [term] I can think of to talk about enlightenment. I'm not talking about awakening;

we have many, many awakening moments on the path. I'm talking about full-blown nondual union with the Deity, so that my wisdom stream is not separate from nondual wisdom stream. For some people, one moment they're carrying water from the river and the next they have full realization. Most of us aren't on that path. Most of us are on the gradual path to realization and are trying to create the auspicious circumstances whereby that realization can happen quickly. So when I talk about waking up in the female body, what I mean is gaining full enlightenment, full realization in a female body, which is rare. We talk about it. . . . The teachings say women and men technically have equal ability. In the Tantric path they even say that women have a slight lead on the game, but that's not how it gets played out in monasteries, nunneries, or social life. Most of the practitioners are men; most of the awakened beings that you will meet are men. Not that women don't wake up, but they have fewer opportunities for it in our life and in our world.

Kama went on to say that most of us have experienced a moment of union, a moment where you turn the corner and there's a "hallelujah sunset," as she puts it. Suddenly you are no longer separate from the oneness of nature or being. In those moments we transcend the limitations of the personality and ego.

Most of us have these little moments . . . we could string them together on a rosary, on a mala. *The idea is to gather the circumstances and practice enough so we get more and more of those. First there will be a moment, and then five years later a moment, and then two years later a moment. We practice to bring the possibility of those moments into closer and closer proximity so that there are more. Eventually there will be some moment when the moments of union slightly outweigh the moments of nonunion. All we're doing is tipping the scale from nonunion—living a conventional life of no union, except when you maybe have sex or get drunk or something. Then we're building capacity to hold more, more, more, more union. We're on the gradual path, most of us, and it's a multiple-lifetime proposition.*

Kama's discussion of the idea of nondual union with a deity made me wonder aloud how Kama would differentiate between holding this kind of nondual consciousness with a deity and channeling a deity. I asked her to explain how she distinguishes between the two. She shared that non-dual "waking up" to divine consciousness is a mind stream between the deity and the devotee. Channeling, as she understands it, does not leave a lasting aftereffect on your awareness. The love-bliss field, what Kama refers to as the "mind stream," is not permanently adjusted by the entity when you channel, whereas "waking up" involves the total union of con-sciousness with the deity. This merging may begin as partial union but over time it evolves into a complete cohabitation of consciousness, some-times referred to as indwelling, a concept discussed in chapter 3.

> *For example, we rarely do purification practices. We talk about "open" and "closed," but not "pure" and "polluted." It [pure versus polluted] does, however, get enacted all around us in terms of caste hierarchy and [gender hierarchy]. But because it's all Her, anything in me is also Her, so there is no reason to get it out of the way. There's no reason to purify. There are occasions where we do purification practices, but they're very rare and usually around illness. I don't fast most of the time. I don't have a special diet. We eat meat.*
>
> *Awakened beings still have a personality. Ammachi operates dif-ferently from the Dalai Lama, for example, just to use two well-known [awakened beings]. The shape of the personality is still there. We're each very unique in that way, even if the ego clinging has loosened. . . . Open is union, awakening. Closed is separation. We have a decided pref-erence for open. But you can be open and angry, or closed and happy. So we don't care about the emotion itself, or the way my personality dances. We just care about whether I'm clenched or unclenched. . . . There is a brightness and an uncompromising nature to it. . . . I've seen the Dalai Lama be fierce, but he is open. I've seen Ammachi throw dishes and be open. But we're used to "open equals happy" and relaxed or peaceful, so that must mean someone is awakened. But what we actually know is that chaotic is also awakened.*

What I think happens, in my experience of awakened beings, is that there is no separation between conventional and nondual. It just all is, simultaneously. So there's still going to the bathroom, eating cornflakes for breakfast, washing the dishes, taking the kids to school, but their awareness is not separating out: "that's divine, but this isn't." Pleasure, pain, and preference have no bearing on any of that.

Kama went on to explain that even when we get to the point of realizing everything is Her, Divinity, there is still something beyond that. Suddenly, there is no longer anyone out there to have a conversation with. The practices of the Kali kula are not about having a better life, making more money, getting a better partner, or having things the way you prefer them. It is an uncompromising path, which all nondual paths tend to be—which is why they are so radical.

As we began talking about the uncompromising nature of the path, a pause opened within our conversation. Again, I found myself challenged to allow the power of Kama's story to settle within me. I felt the intensity of Kama's own uncompromising nature working on me. Because I had recently begun practicing sadhana with Kama's kula, I noticed my ego beginning to worry, What will be asked of me? What will I have to give up as part of my path? I found myself wanting to make my path as fluid as possible through the practices of surrender, devotion, and awakening. I wondered: Perhaps it can't be painless, but maybe I can move through it with more grace, open to more without causing needless suffering to myself or others?

During this pause Kama became still, quiet, introspective. When she began to speak again her voice was deep, soft, solemn. "To be married to an uncompromising nondual Goddess with a sharp sword in Her hand is a bit of a conundrum most days. What's required of me is not for the faint of heart. I'll say that. Not for the faint of heart."

I felt the sacredness of this statement. During the pause I sensed that she was searching for ways to articulate it all; the sacrifices she has made to be married to Kali and the way our humanness still has wants, needs, desires, even though we are on a divine path. When Kama talked about the uncompromising nature of a nondual Goddess, I felt something deeper stirring within me. I realized the depth to which Kama has had to surrender, even though I don't know all the details—and that depth brought me to stillness as well.

REQUIREMENTS OF THE MARRIAGE

With all this talk of sacrifice and surrender, I asked Kama whether there was anything she has requested of Kali in exchange for her devotion. Kama pointed to a moment when the work of her teaching was radically increasing, but she was struggling to make ends meet. Kama has a behest that she teaches by donation only. She can only teach when she has been requested to teach, and she doesn't promote her teaching. Unfortunately, here in the West, students don't understand how to support a spiritual teacher in the traditional Eastern ways. Westerners are accustomed to a teacher putting a ticket price on their teaching. Because Kama has a lineage mandate to only teach what her students ask her for and accept what they offer via a donation basket and a sliding scale, Western students often misinterpret this to mean that her teaching is not of great value.

Kama acknowledged that there is an ongoing debate about how spiritual teachers should be supported in the West—citing that there are some who believe that if you put a high price on your teachings, people will value them. She understood the rationale behind this kind of pricing but said that she does not have the option of doing that. She found herself in the precarious position of having her teaching demands increase while at the same time not being able to find paying work.

As the pressure mounted, she finally appealed to Kali:

"Look, I'm here. It's clear you want me to do this work and the students are arriving, but I actually need you to make sure that I have a thousand dollars a month, and here's why: I need to pay my rent. I need to pay my utilities. I need this much for gas." I said, "A thousand bucks a month would be the bare minimum in this economy here, and fifteen hundred dollars would mean I could get a massage once a month and go out to

dinner." And I just yelled. I was so mad, because I was just like, "Fuck, the rent is due and I don't have it, but if I figure out how to make money then I'm not going to be translating this text and doing these other things that She's asked me to do."

Since that moment, She has taken care of me very well. I don't have money; it's not like I've got a bank account. I don't have a car. I don't have a lot of stuff. I live in someone else's house for free. I can't even really afford rent. I'm about to go on pilgrimage and someone else paid for the plane ticket. So there's a lot of grace and goodness in my landscape, but it's not based on a traditional monetary economy. It allows me to continue to put out an offering basket and to live by whatever arrives in the offering basket. There are fat times and there are thin times. I'm okay with that.

Kama's life is surrendered to not making much happen and letting the grace arise. There is a dance to it. If Kali, through her students, makes sure she has a roof over her head and enough food, then Kama says, she can bear everything else. She asserted that living this way makes the goodness sweeter, more rarified and sublime. However, this also means that the awfulness is rougher. Life does not necessarily get any easier. In fact, it often gets harder.

Because of this, the work of the Tantric path becomes the art of finding pleasure in every single moment of life. The work is not about delayed reward or gratification in the afterlife.

There is no tradeoff. This is it. Right here in this moment, this is exactly what it looks like. That also brings a level of sparkling intensity and depth, if I can bear to live there. I don't know how long I have. I may have twenty years. I may have twenty minutes. Part of living into this depth relationship with Kali is trusting that too. Hoping that I live long because the longer I live the more chance I have of awakening in this body in this lifetime. Getting together this set of karmic circumstances again for some other lifetime is unknown. It's not necessarily guaranteed that I'll have all of the same circumstances that I generated in this lifetime for the next lifetime. I have a real sense of applying myself here and now to this in order to actualize what I've been given. Through these deities and these lineages, I've been given far more than I could ever potentiate in a single lifetime. It is my work to pay that back consciously. . . . I can never pay back what's been given to me thus far, and it's my work as an individual practitioner, as a woman on the path, to potentiate that.

THE SHAPE OF THE DEITY

As our time together came to a close, we realized that we hadn't talked about Kama's phenomenological experience of Kali—that is, how Kali makes contact with Kama. Kama observed that she first developed her relationship to Kali through Kali's voice. Kali tends to communicate with her more through direct voice contact than any other means. Sometimes Kama has a glimmer of a visual, but Kali primarily interacts with her through the auditory sense. Kama is quick to clarify that Kali is not a big conversationalist.

Normally, I get one-word answers or no answer at all. Or the ever-frustrating "Wait." I get a lot of "Wait." Then I also have a feeling sensation at the back and side of my body. She's kind of back there. She'll grab my shoulder, or grab my neck, or push at me. But I don't have the visual stuff that a lot of people get, which isn't surprising given my lineages. There is visionary activity in our lineage but that's not the way she speaks to me. . . . [I know] the shape, the feeling of the shape of her fingers at the back of my neck. So I'm being held by the scruff of my neck on a very short leash.

I was struck by how Kama described the feeling of Kali's touch, a somatic knowing that does not rely on visuals. Our body can know what is true. Kama's discussion of her somatic sensitivity led me to bring a lot of my own quest into question. I began to wonder if I'd spent too much time trying to ascertain a name or an image of my spirit contact. Perhaps all we can ever really know is their imprint on us; how we physically respond to their presence.

Kama went on to explain that at one point she was even doubting whether Kali was actually her ishtadevi or whether she was just the gatekeeper for yet another deity. She explained that on the Tantric path, practitioners tend to elaborate form exhaustively, and there can be myriads of expressions of a single deity. Finding the identity of one's ishtadevi is an extensive process designed to emphasize duality. Similarly, Tantric rituals are elaborate, structured, and also emphasize duality. This is because it is believed that until you go all the way into duality, you cannot go into nonduality. Instead of escaping to the cave or monastery to absorb oneself into Deity, in Tantra you have to come into sensory engagement with all of life and the many ways Deity manifests.

> As we do that, our suffering actually increases. It doesn't decrease. But our puja, our sadhana, increases our capacity. Then there comes some shift in our sadhana. . . . We recognize that there's formlessness under the form. Then it's like going backwards off the cliffs in Acapulco. There may or may not be other beings jumping off the cliffs with us. We don't know where we're going to land, or if we ever land. We don't know what it means. And yet, because I've had twenty-five years of relationship with Kali, I'm willing to do that.

I shared with Kama that I felt much resonance in what she said as it relates to my own exploration. My search for the identity of my spirit lover had prompted this inquiry in the first place. I had also been trying to understand this primordial energy that I had a felt-sense of, which almost defies a name. Thus I had begun to refer to this contact as "Her." I have learned to dance with Her in many different names. I dance with different forms, but when I really tune into my relationship with Her, she has no name. She is a breath. She shows up for me as a certain way in which I breathe, which has a specific sound vibration but is not a formal name. It's like space, like the void. It is almost a priori to a name.

Kama cautioned me that without form we can never address the mystery of the formless. This is one of the challenges on the Tantric path: We focus on form/duality to reach the formless/unity, and in so doing we must encounter suffering, separation, minutiae. The Tantric practice requires one to get, as Kama puts it, "so highly attuned to detail that you can feel the dust motes in the next room."

CLOSING REMARKS

In closing, I asked Kama if Kali ever interacted with her through other people or things. Kama said that occasionally things happen, and she knows it's Kali at work.

> The cashier at the supermarket will say some bizarre, weird thing [that has a lot of relevance for me vis-à-vis Kali] and I'll be like, "Whoa, how did you know?" They didn't even know that they said it. I'm always scanning the landscape energetically and visually for auspicious circumstances and Her signs to me, signs on the side of city buses and posters on walls. I'm always watching to see what's being communicated. [One of my lineages discusses] how awakening arises when auspicious circumstances have been arranged in the body. That doesn't mean "purity" versus "pollution." Part of what we do in our ritual and why we learn physical puja is to learn how to arrange auspicious circumstances. And that's why we do feast practice and the other things that we do, so we get actual practice in arranging auspicious circumstances. That doesn't mean "pretty," and it doesn't mean I'll like it. Then [we must recognize] that [auspicious circumstances] disappear as quickly as they arrive. We can't keep a grip on it, as nice as it is to [enjoy them in the fleeting moment].

We ended by my thanking Kama for her time. I said, "May it serve others to be guided by your candor and depth, and to find inspiration in your devotion." She replied, "May it benefit someone, somewhere."

7

The West African
Shrine Keeper

*M*adrone is an initiate in the African indigenous tradition of the Dagara people of Burkina Faso brought to the West by elder, author, and teacher Dr. Malidoma Somé. She serves her spiritual community as a *Tingan sob,* a tree shaman, and is married to an elder and diviner in the Dagara tradition. Together they are cultivating a Dagara-based spiritual community in the San Francisco Bay Area. Madrone is a successful investment advisor, financial planner, and holds a master's degree in psychology.

Madrone and I had met socially a few times, and I knew of her work in the world helping people find a spiritual and heart-centered relationship to money. I was thrilled to discover she had recently entered into a spirit marriage through the Dagara lineage, and that she was willing to talk to me about this initiation. We sat down in her home to discuss the protocol and process for spirit marriage in Dagaraland. I brought traditional Dagara offerings of milk and honey for her and her spirit-spouse, and she generously invited me to accompany her to visit the tree shrine for her spirit-spouse, Tingan, and give him the offerings.

DAGARA COSMOLOGY

Madrone is married to Tingan, the father-Earth spirit in the Dagara cosmology. She was introduced to Tingan through her husband's teacher, Dr. Malidoma Somé, whom she met some seven years ago. Somé has been working to establish the spiritual technologies of Dagaraland on the West Coast of the United States for the past ten years.

Madrone explained that in Dagara culture, developing a community or village requires installing specific shrines, and the first is the Tingan shrine. A Tingan shrine is established by initiating a Tingan sob, a priest or priestess who marries Tingan through his manifestation as a tree. This is because a tree represents the vertical access around which the community can revolve. In Madrone's case, Tingan is a giant redwood tree living on public land in the Oakland/Berkeley hills, where she has installed a shrine to him.

Madrone clarified that the word *sob* means "job," so the title *Tingan sob* means "the person whose job it is to tend and feed the Tingan shrine." There are different types of sob in Dagaraland. Calling Madrone a Tingan sob is basically designating that her role within her community is to keep that shrine and mediate its energies for the group.

Tingan connects the community to the masculine energy of Earth as father via the vertical axis of the tree. This masculine energy is the natural complement to Timbalu, who makes available the feminine energy of Earth as mother through the horizontal. Timbalu is Earth, which is abundant and easily accessible, whereas connecting with Tingan requires an intermediary. Madrone says that to contact Timbalu, "You just need to put a pile of dirt in a mound, put your hand on it, pour some milk, and you are in contact with Timbalu. Anyone can go to Timbalu; it's like the mother's womb . . . the unconditional love of the mother."

However, to speak with Tingan one needs an intermediary to help navigate his powerful energy. Tingan is like a discerning father figure that helps keep the balance in the community, specifically maintaining that balance around wealth, health, and well-being. Timbalu as mother is unconditionally nurturing and accepting, whereas Tingan as father is more concerned with justice and discernment.

I tell Madrone that in my research, a balance between justice and mercy, boundaries and compassion, has proved to be an important theme in many systems of personal transformation. I find the ritualized way that the Dagara engage this dynamic to be both embodied and practical. She reports that community members go to Tingan when a baby is born, to be registered as part of the community or if there are problems in their life that seem to be repeating.

It's like your birth certificate: you go to register and say, "I'm here in this physical form." For the Dagara people, a baby is just an ancestor who has decided to incarnate. They come and they register, and the parent or the godparents tell Tingan what the [baby's] mission is. They've done a baby hearing [in which] they've gathered information about why this baby came—information which the baby then will forget. Tingan holds that energetic imprint for that child and for that person as they circulate in life.

After the initial registration, community members don't routinely come back to Tingan unless a divination reveals that a trip to him is deemed necessary. Usually this is because the person is out of balance somewhere in their lives and require a balancing visit. A community member might feel naturally called to visit the Tingan shrine, particularly if they are experiencing a series of recurring events. In the case of inherited family trauma or repeating life or family patterns, like a similar accident, a similar disease, or something that has been passed down unbroken through the lineage, a trip to the Tingan sob might also be in order. All things cyclical and recurring are related to Tingan.

THE PROPOSAL

Madrone points out that she is only one of two Tingan sobs in the Bay Area. The other is a male elder in the tradition who received guidance to become a Tingan sob intuitively after a fourteen-day advanced initiation. Madrone was specifically invited into her role by Dr. Somé.

I was actually presented with the invitation to become a Tingan sob. Partly because Malidoma felt that in the Bay Area there needed to be both a masculine and feminine energy. Normally, the Tingan sob is a man. I'm the first female Tingan sob to ever exist, especially outside of Africa. . . . We've been doing a three-year intensive training with Malidoma: the Indigenous African Spiritual Technology training. Last October [2013], I was given the invitation to step into this role and told that it would require marrying Tingan. Coming back to your question, "How did this come into my life?" It was kind of dropped into my lap. [My human husband] thought I was going to be overwhelmed by it, but really it didn't feel any different to what I was already doing in my community. At least that was my initial feeling, so it was easy to say "yes."

Once Madrone accepted the invitation to marry Tingan, the marriage ritual followed swiftly thereafter.

I understood arranged marriages after this. . . . I'm at the wedding and I'm thinking, "Oh my gosh, I don't fully know you! I hope this is going to work, but I don't fully know you. Let's give it a try!" . . . I was saying yes to a role that my community was asking me to play. I've had my own special relationship with trees for many, many years. I remember back in the day, when I was a grad student in 2007, writing the trees a contract and saying, "I actually work for you. If we get people to go through less of you [consume less paper products], then my work is done in the world." I've had that relationship with trees for a long time, and I said this at my wedding. I felt that what had been very private was being made public. That was a big difference. Now I have a public role in my community. There is a certain expectation that I will follow through, that I'm available, that I can guide that process.

I ask Madrone whether Tingan is the same spirit that manifests through all Tingan trees, or if her version of Tingan is unique to her. She elaborates:

When we knew we were going to become Tingan sobs, one of the first things we needed to do is go choose a tree. But that doesn't just make it Tingan if you choose a tree. You have to have the actual marriage that brings that tree spirit alive, that brings the Tingan spirit alive in that particular tree. So all Tingan sobs are interacting with the same energy, but it's a different physical entity that demarks a certain community. In Dagaraland every community would have their own Tingan. That's the vertical axis. . . . It doesn't become the Tingan shrine until the actual marriage ceremony happens.

I'm curious whether Tingan ever expresses himself to her through other trees; whether other trees can represent Tingan to her. She explains that not every tree can be a Tingan tree. His energy is unique to Madrone through the tree that has become his shrine. Just like every man does not express the energy of justice, so every tree does not express Tingan. Not every tree has that particular strength.

THE MARRIAGE CEREMONY

The marriage ceremony required several components. First, several village members must be present. Community is of the utmost importance in the Dagara tradition; the spiritual technologies cannot be used in a vacuum. Madrone stresses: "Tingan requires a community, and a community requires Tingan."

Second, an animal offering is required. Animal sacrifice is very important in the Dagaraland practices; offerings of four-legged animals and chickens are often mandated by the tradition. These offerings are made to the ancestors and various spirits that inhabit the Dagara cosmology. Only when Tingan is fed by a sacrificial offering is the tree shrine officially installed.

Madrone admits that in our culture the concept of animal sacrifice is not always easy to accept. She observes that the other Tingan sob established his shrine in his backyard, making it much easier to make offerings. Madrone's Tingan shrine is on public land. I asked her how she managed to establish it with the required offerings.

> I had to drive all the way up to our Tingan shrine, climb the tree to get a branch—I don't even know how I climbed that tree to get a branch, but I got a branch—and brought it to the Tingan in Fremont [a neighboring community] to do the animal sacrifice there. It was private land. We were able to put up tarps and [screen the area] from the neighbors, and then having my branch there, we did it by proxy. On the next day we had the wedding ceremony at my Tingan shrine with the offerings already done.

I am struck by the importance of animal sacrifice. Based on my interviews, I notice that it is a key element in many of the traditions that practice spirit marriage. I share this with Madrone and observe that the animal sacrifice is never frivolous, but it's truly a sacrifice, a making sacred of the animal offering. The animal's life is handled in a much more ethical way than it would be in, say, a slaughterhouse. The animal's life is revered, and all the parts of the animal are used. To me, this approach indicates a more integral relationship with the animal than buying sterilized meat in a plastic container from the grocery store.

Madrone agrees:

> My daughter, who is four, knows how to skin a chicken. We would be eating a lot less meat if that's how we got our meat—if it was through ceremony. It's a lot of work, and so you don't take it for granted. You consume all of it and you're grateful for its life.

The marriage ritual itself closely resembles a human wedding. The Tingan sob is dressed in white, and there is music and feasting. Vows are exchanged, but because Somé is not himself a Tingan sob, he could not tell Madrone exactly what kind of vows to make. Instead she had to base her vows on her own personal commitment to Tingan. This was informed by another important aspect of the marriage ritual: surrender. The Tingan sob is asked to lie facedown on the Earth in front of the Tingan tree, and then a Dagara chant is incanted above them. The sob is surrendering to that entity, surrendering to their energy, and opening themselves up to be guided as to how the shrine will need to be cared for.

Another important part of the marriage is the celebration. After the offerings are made and the ritual has taken place, the community has a potluck and the meat of the animal that has been sacrificed is consumed. The focus is on gratitude for the animal's life and the auspicious event that has brought the community together once again.

THE COMMUNITY

Community is such an important part of the Dagara spiritual technology that its whole system has been designed to work best in the context of relationships. Madrone underscores this fact by describing how she has been deeply supported by her community in her role as a Tingan sob, even though she has been required to navigate much of that role intuitively.

There is tremendous support in the sense that Malidoma brings the Dagara cosmology, and it holds me. My husband is an initiated elder, so I know that he holds me. . . . I felt very much held by the elders of that community, but none of them are Tingan sobs. . . . I've had to figure a lot of it out by myself. I had another elder visit us. We sat down and had a conversation about what a Tingan sob in New York is like, and what are some things that he's developed. So I do have that person to reach out to, but a lot of it is just connecting to my intuitive guidance: "What is this energy, and what does our community need?" Because that's the one thing that the Dagara people [in Africa] don't know: "What is this Bay Area community, this West Coast village that is birthing?"

The Dagara village in Burkina Faso energetically supports their US communities. There is a bridge between the two cultures, and the elders in Africa are aware of the goings-on in the United States. When people come to visit Tingan, they are asked to come with offerings that match the intensity of what they are asking for. A portion of these offerings are then sent back to the village in Burkina Faso. There is an ongoing financial connection between the communities and an understanding that what is being created in the United States is also meant to help support the Dagara village in Africa. Thus, the non-African communities can honor and uphold the lineage stream from which they are benefiting—by making sure the people from whom they receive their teachings are well cared for.

THE FUNCTION OF A TINGAN SOB

After Madrone's wedding ceremony she extended an invitation to the community to come and register with her at Tingan. That entails sitting together at her Tingan tree, sharing why they have come to register, and stating what they want to establish as their purpose in the community. Tingan is a place of community wealth, so the intentions registered with Tingan are held and witnessed not only by Madrone but ultimately by the larger community as well. Madrone records the intention, then together she and the person make an offering to Tingan. Madrone presents the person to Tingan and opens herself to intuitively receive any messages for them from Tingan. Registering like this means they are committing to a formal role in the community.

Madrone offers the first Friday of each month as open time for community members to come to her to visit Tingan. Generally, at least once a month, the space is open for her community to interact with Tingan. If someone needs an extra visit, they can contact her directly to arrange a time to go to Tingan together. This is an arrangement that allows a certain balance between her personal life, human marriage, parenting duties of a four-year-old, the requirements of a full-time job, and the needs of the community. She points out that the other Tingan sob is available more readily since his Tingan is in his backyard. She reports, however, that he lives farther away from the core of the community, so some people prefer to come to her because she is close by. Ideally, there would be a Tingan sob installed in each town so that people could simply go to the one that is closest to where they live. However, this may take some time, as the Bay Area core community is currently only about twenty people.

Many people have worked with Dr. Somé over the years, but he has yet to bridge the various generations of his students. Madrone believes that once the core group has finished their intensive training, they will begin to offer what they have learned to the greater community.

EXPERIENCING TINGAN

Because it is not possible for Madrone to visit Tingan daily in his form as a tree, she has a statue of him that sits on her altar. She begins each morning by greeting Tingan and meditating with him.

It's the first thing I do in the morning. I'll wake up still groggy, light a candle, and sit there for fifteen to twenty minutes, just starting my day with Tingan. . . . He's just up here [gesturing to the mountain on which Tingan lives], so I'm sitting at my window knowing we're not far away.

Madrone's primary sensory experience of Tingan is somatic, just as her primary experience with the world and with spirit entities in general is somatic. It seems natural, then, that her communication with Tingan tends to be conveyed via a felt-sense, sometimes along with internal visuals.

It's like sitting down and speaking to your partner or spouse. You just bare your heart. So a lot of my morning meditations are saying, "Tingan, this is what's on my heart today," and just seeing where it unfolds. I take a meditative journey with him and receive the guidance. It really is like a morning check-in with a spouse who can listen to me and maybe help me see something that I hadn't seen before. It's a great complement to my human husband. Because my human husband is dealing more with human problems with me, and Tingan is not human, he can give me a different perspective on my human problems.

So that's my daily practice with Tingan. My nuclear family, [my husband] and my daughter, will go up and visit [the Tingan shrine] once every two weeks at a minimum. Sometimes I'll escape and go by myself—it's on my way to work. [For the family visit] we'll bring offerings; my daughter likes to bring him honey sticks. She gets one, and he gets one. I'll bring any community messages, or if someone's asked me something that I'm pondering, I'll go sit and meditate.

IMPACT OF THE RELATIONSHIP

The mention of her family leads us to the question: How does being married to a spirit impact her human marriage? Madrone says the integration has been quite easy, partly because her husband is also immersed in the Dagara community and tradition. He intimately understands what it means to hold this sacred community position and relationship to the spirit realms. In fact, Madrone was asked to wed Tingan in part because her husband needed to install a shrine to another Dagara deity and could not do so until the Tingan shrine was installed. In some ways Madrone did him a favor by marrying Tingan, because now he can move forward with his own spiritual work.

He didn't necessarily know it was going to be me. He was sitting with Malidoma, saying, "Gosh, we need another Tingan shrine." Malidoma looked at him and said, "Don't you know who that is? It's your wife. She will be the other Tingan sob here." So I think it surprised him just as much [as it did me], but it's been extremely easeful.

Madrone says, however, that they had to deviate from protocol somewhat by establishing that her husband could go to Tingan on his own. "I didn't want to be the intermediary. If these are my two husbands, I want them to talk to each other." This negotiation made a big difference in the health and balance of their relationship.

Tingan plays an important role in the Bay Area community as the entity responsible for helping the community work through their somatic experience of scarcity. Tingan's benevolence is a huge aspect of his identity and is deeply tied to Madrone's work in the world as a financial advisor, wealth manager, and teacher of inner economics. It's why her marriage to Tingan has felt so seamless for her. It made spiritual what she was doing practically.

When Madrone is facing her own fears around scarcity or when members of her community come to her with financial worries, she goes to Tingan.

> I just sit, and he continues to teach me how I can help others go through that similar process. When my husband's scarcity comes, I can't be his financial advisor. I'm too intertwined with the scarcity. In being able to say, "You go to Tingan," it's taken a lot of that pressure off of my shoulders to have to be everything to everyone and also to my two husbands. Tingan is really just a part of our family.

MARRIAGE REQUIREMENTS

Madrone is required to perform a yearly community celebration at Tingan to honor their anniversary. Her biggest requirement is to ensure Tingan is fed; how, when, and what he gets fed is up to her intuition. For example, when the drought was happening in California, she felt led to bring a lot of water to Tingan. Other times she simply has a feeling that he needs an offering, so she goes to him with her husband to make an offering. Offerings are also sometimes prescribed in a divination, but primarily she experiences Tingan's needs manifesting organically:

> There are things we do on a ritual, daily basis that make us feel balanced, and for me that's every morning lighting my candle and sitting with Tingan. My day hasn't started until I've done that. [Sometimes I get a sense of something happening in Dagaraland and will] see if is there a ritual that needs to happen . . . to get you back in balance. Then it's the pouring of the milk for twenty days in a row. That's been my experience; "Follow the flow of life in the moment."

DIVINATION

In Dagaraland there are different types of divination. Some, like *kontomblé* voice divination, or channeling, and bone and shell reading, sound very familiar to me from my study of American folk magic, specifically Conjure. Kontomblé voice divination is done through the merging of the practitioner with the kontomblé, the playful "little people" of the Dagara cosmology, and the delivering of messages in the kontomblé's voice. Bone and shell reading is a process of divining messages through the patterns that objects make in relation to the five elements.

Given the many different spirits and types of divination for approaching the spirit realms, I was curious about how one decides whom to ask for divination. Madrone explains that the various diviners in the community are the first to be contacted when something is "off" in one's life and one needs clarity. Madrone is also quick to point out that her role as Tingan sob is not a divination role, even though she speaks for Tingan.

> If someone comes to register, they'll tell me their name and their physical location. Then I'll ask them questions: "What is it that you're requesting in terms of wealth, health, well-being, community?" One of the first questions I'll feel prompted to ask on behalf of Tingan is, "What do you take responsibility for? Of all this that you're asking, if I were to flip it, what do you take responsibility for?" Part of what I do through Tingan is to balance that justice. So it's not just asking—it's stepping into and stepping forth.
>
> A lot of what I do is through question and answer more than divining. I'm not channeling the divining energy. To some extent when I'm listening to Tingan's messages I'm channeling divination, but they don't come to me for a divination per se. They come to me to set things in balance.

Madrone says her husband is both a bone and shell diviner and a kontomblé voice diviner. Often in his divinations he prescribes a sweep—a ritual performed to clear the energy field using a fertilized egg. People who need a sweep often go together and do the ritual at the foot of Tingan. The Tingan shrine has now become an important place for various community gatherings and rites to take place.

I note that egg sweeping is also an important ritual used in Conjure practice. Madrone asserts that the reason Malidoma calls his workshops "Indigenous African Spiritual Technology" is that these are not just folklore practices; they are a technology integral to African tribal culture. Although different from the kind of Western technology we are accustomed to, it cannot simply be discarded or discredited. Madrone points out that many of the same technologies are used in traditional religion, though by different names and means. In the Catholic Church, for example, incense is used to "sweep" the practitioner's field of awareness, and holy water to cleanse and purify the practitioner. Also, I shared that in my thirties I had realized that my Pentecostal Christian childhood had been very psycho-magical. Anointing with oil, laying on of hands, speaking in tongues—all these rituals have their counterparts in African Traditional religion and in indigenous spirituality in general, although I imagine most Pentecostals would cringe at the comparison.

BENEFITS

The first benefit that came to Madrone as a result of marrying Tingan was a deeply grounded sense of belonging.

I've always struggled with that in my life because I was bicultural. My family is from South America—Colombia. I grew up in New Orleans. I always had this feeling: "I'm not from here, I'm not from there." I went to high school in Colombia, but I was "la gringa" in Colombia. I lived in Oaxaca for several years, and I spent journal after journal writing about this. But I don't feel that anymore. I feel that with Tingan I've totally found my home. I totally belong here. This is my land, and it doesn't discard any of my other lands, but I'm not searching. That feeling of searching for a sense of belonging is gone, which I never anticipated.

Madrone's search for belonging has now been replaced by a sense of being rooted and connected to the community she serves. She explains that now when she travels, she can't leave for too long or she begins to feel homesick. "I couldn't imagine living abroad for six months now, without having a very serious conversation with Tingan. When I do leave, oftentimes I feel like Tingan is extending his branches to me where I'm landing. There's never really a disconnect."

Madrone says Tingan has given her "a sheath of protection, a sense of belonging, a ground to surrender to." Madrone's work in the world is focused on helping her clients develop a sense of wealth, enough-ness, and abundance. Therefore, Tingan, as the embodiment of wealth in Dagaraland, has become one of her biggest teachers and allies. She is never alone in the journey of exploring these themes with her clients, for herself, and her community. Tingan is the axis that holds her, as well as everyone else in her community, in balance.

RISKS

Madrone identifies the biggest risk in her marriage to Tingan as the impact on her life and identity outside her spiritual community.

My parents and my other extended family don't know I'm a Tingan sob. I don't think they'd be able to understand it. So there's still that risk of separation, misunderstanding, or just being persecuted for the role that you play. That's why I requested the confidentiality [for our interview]. I work in a different world; I'm a financial advisor and investment manager. Ultimately I will become a certified financial planner, which in my day-to-day experience has absolutely no separation from being a Tingan sob. I bring that into my work with my clients, and I bring my clients' work into Tingan. There's no separation, but I don't think that the world could understand that. I do think that in my lifetime, that will become more public, but I don't think it's quite there yet. It's so new to me. When I'm sixty-five years old, I will have been Tingan sob for thirty years. That will be very different from where I'm at right now. There will be a moment to speak more publicly and bridge the two worlds, but that time's not now.

With regard to going public with her relationship to Tingan, Madrone has often sat with the questions, How can I better serve? Where is my energy best used? She realizes that her role as a Tingan sob is best used in a way that does not cause stress to her career or relationships. Rather than having to defend or explain herself to people who do not understand, she believes her energy is best applied to serving her community who know, love, and appreciate the role she plays for them.

COMMUNITY IMPACT

I comment that being upheld by the love and support of a community, as well as the support of a well-established lineage that holds a spiritual technology and system of divination for spirit marriages, also makes a huge difference. Madrone is recognized and embraced in her role and has a context for her service. She also acknowledges that because her work in the world requires her to interface with a traditionally nonspiritual community, she has access to people that she would not otherwise meet. This allows her to impact a group of people who might never attend a community event or seek out the more esoteric aspects of her work. Nevertheless, all those spiritual energies are contained in the service she provides to the world, whether she chooses to articulate them in the terminology of Dagaraland or of Wall Street.

When I come back [from work] and communicate with Tingan, I don't do it in a vacuum. I don't do it by myself, so it's very fulfilling. I come back and I interact with humans where I can be Tingan sob. . . . I can bridge different communities here, so it allows me to go back into the financial planning world and not be so dependent on those human interactions [since] I have [other] human interactions that are more fulfilling and spiritual [at home].

What strikes me at this point in our conversation is how important community can be to a spirit marriage. I postulate that someone trying to navigate this process without a community to support them might find it unnerving and confusing. Practitioners need a context for the spirit contact and a supportive container of some kind of tradition or guide, so that they can relax into the relationship. I suggest that a marriage with an entity is so life-altering—there's such potency there—that the human partner needs other people around to help hold the energy of the relationship. Even though one person is holding the marriage, everyone else in the community is, in a sense, also in the relationship.

Madrone agrees. She insists that when we live in isolated family units, we can't fully meet our own needs or even the needs of a spouse. This is why she and her husband decided to raise their daughter in community; they live with seven other adults. Living in community or deeply connected to community helps to create balance in their lives. Although their needs can sometimes get lost when dealing with the demands of other people, more avenues of support become available.

I pointed out that the core of what we were talking about was how to cultivate a healthy relationship, whether that relationship is with a physical being, a spirit-being, or a community, and how to manage the many relationships we have in our lives. Ultimately, relationships cannot function in a vacuum. Healthy relationships need community around them to thrive, to flow, and to be balanced. I offer that here in the West we are starving for authentic community, even though most people don't realize it. We long to be held, seen, and witnessed deeply. We yearn for an experience of real belonging amid a culture where we divide up into nuclear families or insular groups and close ourselves off from everyone else. I ponder the idea that for a spirit marriage, and really any kind of relationship, to be generative and of service it needs to function within the context of a community.

CHALLENGES

Madrone observed that I had asked her about the benefits and the risks of her work, but not the challenges. She offered:

I'm thirty-six. I'm the mother of a four-year-old. I live in community, so I'm in relationship with seven adults. I'm in my own personal relationship [with my husband], and I'm in a spirit relationship. And there's community. I often feel torn in all these different directions. People say, "I need to go to Tingan," and I don't want to give up my weekend 'cause that's when I'm off, when I'm a mom, when I unplug. There are a lot of urban constraints that I have to keep coming back to.

That's why choosing one day a month where I naturally open my schedule has been a really good start for me. Friday mornings. We're doing this interview right now because I would normally be offering this time to Tingan and to the community. I have to deal with my own feelings of, Is that enough? I should be available every week for people. Eventually that would be my hope. It's just my work in the world, in the same way that I have my financial planning career and give so much time to my clients. I need to eventually get to that place, but I'm not there yet. So my own guilt, my own judgment, and coming back to, "No, you're doing what you can." . . . That's the challenge.

I see this as the challenge of trying to live an Earth-based spiritual lifestyle within a Western urban context. Unfortunately, the West doesn't offer ample opportunities to live in an actual village, on the land, surrounded by a spiritual community—particularly for those who need to work in urban environments. Although increasing numbers of Westerners are turning to Earth-based spirituality in its myriad manifestations, to then translate that individual spiritual journey into a cohesive spiritual community can pose a serious challenge for many multilineage Pagans. The gift of having a smorgasbord of many spiritual lineages and traditions to study here in the West can also become an obstacle to fostering a grounded, coherent community. Even if we choose to follow a single spiritual lineage, as with the American Dagara communities, we are still faced with the task of translating that lineage into the context of life in the West.

A VISIT TO TINGAN

I ask Madrone whether she is familiar with the concept that her union with Tingan could create spirit children as their progeny. I have heard that this is a common belief in the Dagara tradition, but Madrone says she is not familiar with it. She does point out that her human child would be expected to take on the role of Tingan sob when she comes of age. It's a role that is passed down through the lineage, although her daughter is too young to understand this now. I observe that it is a blessing that she has been raised in the Dagara tradition and that she will grow up with inside knowledge and experience of how to perform the role. Madrone agrees.

> *She's not the only child in our community. One of her best friends, who is six, goes to all the Malidoma retreats, and we go camping with that family. And they're doing "ritual offs," like who can do the better ritual. "Now we're gonna go stand in the tree and touch it. Now we're gonna go in this circle and throw leaves." I mean, this is how they play. It's beautiful to watch. And we're like, "Can we take a break now?" and they're like, "No! Let's play ritual!" instead of playing house.*

I am struck by the beauty, the gift of meaning that Dr. Somé has given to the West by bringing his culture and teachings here. He has given a group of disparate seekers not only a technology but a thriving community within which they can deepen and express their connection to Earth-based spirituality. Madrone is one of many practitioners deeply committed through spirit marriage to what Chalquist and others are calling a "re-enchantment of the world."[1]

We end our time together with a trip up to Tingan, a few miles away from her home. I take my offerings of milk and honey and pour them on his roots. Madrone has asked me to assist her with completing a ritual she is in the process of doing for her community, which now requires that we grieve at the foot of Tingan for a recent death. I am honored and humbled to be included in this practice and feel the power and potency of Madrone's role as we keen together.

After we part, I'm struck by a sense of coming full circle in my research inquiry. When I first began researching spirit marriage, a friend introduced me to the Dagara teachings. This was long before I began a formal Ph.D. on the subject. There is something very potent about our interview, almost as if I'm coming home. I deeply resonate with the Dagara practice of being integrally connected to Earth and intuition. It's not about a set form or a prescribed way of doing things.

I feel a strong connection to the energy of Tingan, the Divine Masculine Earth energy of the trees. In fact, long before I began this research, I worked with a Dagara diviner who had given me a Tingan ritual. I had been instructed to find a Tingan tree and make offerings there. I had immediately known exactly which tree to go to, a tree that I grew up climbing and in whose branches I would often sit and sing. There was no question in my mind that this tree represented Tingan's energy.

Reflecting upon the various lineages I have studied that have led to the culmination of this research, I feel as if I am receiving knowledge of the Divine Masculine through the Dagara lineage, knowledge of the Divine Feminine through the Shakta Tantric lineage, and an understanding of the Divine Lover through the Faery Seership lineage. All have their own important pieces to add to my inquiry.

Madrone commented that perhaps my research inquiry suggests a possible polyamorous marriage for me with more than one lineage. I am curious and intrigued by this idea. I was completely at home as a Faery Seer supporting Madrone doing this work in the Dagara context; I did not feel at all conflicted. Rather, it felt very natural and easy. After our interview, I noticed a renewed sense of hope and anticipation that this research inquiry might ultimately lead me to an illuminated and embodied experience of my own spirit marriage or marriages.

8

The Washington, DC, Witchdoctor

*C*aroline Kenner was born in Washington, DC, where she was a shamanic practitioner, Witch, and Pagan community organizer for thirty years. She has been initiated into a variety of religions, including Tibetan Buddhism, Cuban Santería, Wicca, and Norse Heathenry (a belief system of the Germanic peoples of the Iron Age and early medieval Europe and a form of modern Pagan religion). Having been involved in the East Coast Pagan community since 1987, she is an outspoken activist working for Pagan rights, women's rights, and the environment. Caroline was instrumental in getting the Pagan Pentagram (five-pointed star) included as an accepted symbol by the Veterans Administration to be used on federally funded military grave markers and plaques. Caroline holds a master's degree in political broadcasting communications.

I was introduced to Caroline through a mutual friend who thought Caroline's unique story would make her an excellent research participant. Caroline calls herself a Witchdoctor, drawing upon the Old English definitions of "a professional worker of magic" and "one who heals through magical powers." She is not only married to varying deities across differing pantheons, she has also divorced a spirit-spouse—a practice that many of my other coresearchers said was impossible.

Therefore I was eager to include Caroline's story to demonstrate both the diversity and also the transcultural potential of spirit marriage for practitioners who work within a variety of traditions. Caroline was eager to be interviewed and her spirit-spouses were adamant that their story be included in my research. She very generously shared her story with me during a period in her life when she was dealing with some health issues. As a result, we had two phone interviews, spaced approximately six months apart.

I began our interview by invoking the spirit of the research and the spirits guiding and informing our conversation. I lit a candle and took us into a short resonance-building meditation, inviting us to settle in and open the doors of our perception. I invited her to receive the sacred questions that would help us and all those who witness this story, to hear the power, medicine, and beauty of her relationship. I explained to Caroline that even though I had not met her in person, I trusted that the people who had agreed to be interviewed would be exactly those I was meant to include in my research. I emphasized that the nature of organic inquiry encourages her own inquiry into the topic of spirit marriage as part of our discussion. Our conversation quickly evolved into a shared collaboration of stories, musings, and questions that we probed together.

Caroline is animated, articulate, and well-versed in a variety of Earth-based spiritualties. She has such a deep passion and intensity for the topic that talking to her is a bit like getting on the back of a wild stallion; she is full of Spirit. As we spoke, I sensed that the entities she works with had a definite message they wanted to share through her.

BACKGROUND FOR SPIRIT MARRIAGE

Caroline reported that she had been involved in the Pagan community since the early 1980s, but that the knowledge and practice of spirit marriage is still on the fringe of Paganism, which is itself at the very fringe of religious practice today. Pagans are traditionally willing to explore some of the strangest and most unorthodox spiritual practices and beliefs. And yet spirit marriage is still relatively unheard of in discussions of Paganism. She elaborated: "The more we can open the door to other forms of religious experience, the better. [Spirit marriage] is something that has been known in human history for generations, but was suppressed by monotheism."

I agreed and interjected my belief that perhaps spirit marriage was at the root of all religions and spiritual traditions, even though it had been largely suppressed. Caroline concurred and noted that she believes this suppression is due to the sexual repression within mainstream religions. The erotic energy that the spirits often stimulate in their devotees is seen as dangerous and frightening by traditional religions, and therefore has prevented people from receiving the love the spirits have to give. Opening oneself to being passionately loved by the spirit world requires an unorthodox understanding of sexuality, its purpose, and the esoteric nature of the energy exchanged during sexual contact. Caroline goes on to say that the practice of spirit marriage is a challenge for humans but not for the spirits: "The spirits are the ones who practice spirit marriage, and the traditions are the ones who struggle to encompass it."

I was eager to interview Caroline in part because her story differs from, and in some instances contradicts, information I'd received from other interviewees. Unlike other practitioners I interviewed, Caroline is married to multiple beings in multiple pantheons. Additionally, Caroline is the only interviewee who reported divorcing a spirit-spouse, which again is practically unheard of in most of the other lineages practicing spirit marriage. As a result, our conversation tended to jump around, touching on discussions of the various relationships she holds and her multiple marriages.

ANCESTRAL TIES

Caroline situates her story by reporting that her ancestors were some of the first European settlers in America, emigrating to Jamestown,

Virginia, in the 1630s from England. As a result, she has a strong genetic tie to the Anglo-Saxon Gods and Goddesses of northern Europe. This ancestral connection is important to Caroline because humans "are less distinct as individuals to [the Gods] than we realize, and the ones that vibrate to us genetically are the closest to us of all." Connecting to the deities of our ancestors makes it easier for the Gods and Goddesses to reach us and for us to hear them.

That being said, Caroline emphatically states that she loves and honors all the pantheons and is also dedicated to a variety of non-European deities. In fact, she first dedicated herself to the Egyptian Goddess Nephthys at the age of nine, and her first encounters were with the pantheons of Greek, Egyptian, and African Diaspora deities. Although Caroline was baptized Episcopalian at the parish church of the National Cathedral and married to her first husband by an Episcopalian priest in the cathedral itself, she never joined the church. At a very early age, the spirits of a variety of pantheons reached out and began talking to her. This multi-pantheon path, Caroline admits, has made her experience as a Pagan a bit more complicated.

> I look like a nice suburban lady. [But] my mom took me to all these places full of death in Rome when I was seven, and to Pompeii where I saw the death agony rictuses of all the people with plaster casts. . . . She took me to the catacombs and to a church with the monks' bones on the walls. I have a collection of skulls, carved from stone mostly. I really like Samhain. I just resonate with divinities of death. I also belong to the Morrigan. So at all times, I'm balancing the Orishas, the Morrigan, Freyja, and Nephthys at minimum. I hear them all. It's why I was afraid to tell anyone what was going on with me as a kid. Because I knew what people who heard voices . . . what kind of treatment they got. I wasn't going to let on what was going on inside my head!

Caroline observes that her spirituality is also based on growing up in the highly cosmopolitan and multicultural Washington, DC, area, where virtually every country in the world comes to do business. However, DC is also a temporary transplant community; almost no one lives their entire life there. Caroline considers it to be an extremely "unmagical" town. She reports that Caroline Casey, a DC-based astrologer, refers to Washington, DC, as a "hardship post" for a spiritual person, because DC is not very supportive of eccentricity. To be one of the rare people born and raised in DC and to be as psychically gifted as Caroline has meant that she fosters relationships across many different traditions and pantheons, often trailblazing the connections without much support.

> *The Gods and Goddesses that I resonate with have a few common threads. One common thread is what their avatar's job is . . . like Durga, Athena, Oya, Freyja, and the Morrigan all vibrate very similarly. . . . The idea that the Gods created us is just ridiculous. The Gods were created by us, by the mythical resonance of thousands of human minds over thousands of years, because we needed spirits to work with. The different archetypal energies of the spirits are expressed very similarly in many different cultures and have a similar flavor if you look for the common threads. Freyja resonates very closely with the Morrigan, and because of the interbreeding of the Anglo-Saxon and Celtic strains, they're sister Goddesses.*

It is not much of a stretch to imagine Caroline as a highly placed member of some deific-human diplomatic corps . . . that she might as well be talking about having dinner with various heads of state from around the globe instead of juggling the vicissitudes and scheduling challenges of simultaneous marriages to several deities from Africa, Egypt, Norway, and other regions.

PRIMARY DEITY

I was interested to understand Caroline's relationship with her spirit husbands. Caroline clarifies that before we can talk about her marriage to Odin, we must first talk about Freyja. She reports that her primary spiritual (nonmarital) relationship is with the Norse Goddess Freyja. Freyja is the Goddess in charge of her life and is so close to Caroline that she is almost indistinguishable from Caroline's experience of herself. Because of this close resonance, for many years Caroline missed Freyja's presence. However, ten years ago, after Caroline was initiated by Janet Farrar and Gavin Bone—longtime prominent authors on Wicca and devotees of Freyja—the connection became clear. Janet and Gavin work with the Norse divination system called *Seidr* and teach this type of trance-possession work internationally. With their help, and also the assistance of Diana Paxson—a prominent novelist and metaphysical writer—Caroline was able to have a full-body spirit possession by Freyja. Afterward, Freyja's presence in Caroline's life began to manifest more clearly.

Caroline points out that Freyja is a Goddess of the Witches and the Fae; she calls her a "high Fae Goddess of the land." She also describes the mythology surrounding Freyja and her conquest by Odin as paramount to her own story, particularly as it relates to how Caroline was wooed by and finally wed Odin after many years of resistance.

Caroline explains that Freyja and her people had been invaded by Odin's forces, and that Freyja had been held hostage by Odin until she agreed to submit to his authority. She says that this story reflects the ongoing drama of her spiritual life and manifests in her own rebellious nature. In spite of being connected to many Pagan communities on the East Coast, Caroline has never been initiated into any of the most conveniently local witchcraft traditions because she is not willing to submit to their regulations and strictures.

Resistance to conformity is a recurring theme of Caroline's spiritual path. She sees her own resistance to Odin's advances, which began over twenty years ago, as mirroring Freyja's struggle to maintain her personal sovereignty. Freyja does not like to be controlled. She is the Lady of the Land. She has sexual freedom to choose whomever she wishes. This struggle between Freyja and Odin played out again when Odin began making contact with Caroline.

FIRST CONTACT

When I first read the question, "What led you to decide to marry your spirit-spouse?" Caroline bursts out laughing and echoes Kama when she says, "As if I ever had a choice in marrying any of them!" This is an important distinction in Caroline's story, for each marriage she has undertaken, up until her marriage to Odin, was a *fait accompli* by the spirit; she simply found herself being married to the entity. Only with Odin did Caroline have more agency in the process.

Caroline recounts that Odin started courting her in 1988, but she resisted marrying him for twenty-three years because of her penchant for independence—and Odin can be bossy. Although according to modern interpretation Odin is commonly understood to be a war leader, according to Caroline he's not innately a war leader—he's a strategist, a divinity of communications. In ancient interpretation, he is more like Odysseus, crafty and wise. Odin is the God of ideas and communication, and his seduction of Caroline was characteristically strategic. He even went so far as to place a wager that he would wed Caroline by the time she hit menopause.

> Odin first appeared in my bedroom when I had left my first husband. I had basically made a life change [away] from being not very truthful . . . to myself about what I really wanted in life. I was in a very conventional marriage. My first husband was the son of a prominent American diplomat, and I could never have been a public Witch if I'd remained in that marriage. I was thirty-two, and I had already started working with Andras Corban Arthen of the EarthSpirit community, who now represents us in the International Parliament of World Religions. I had already met Starhawk.* I was on my path.
>
> I woke up very suddenly in the night, and I thought there was an intruder in the room because the energy of [Odin's] manifestation was

---

*Founder of the Reclaiming Witchcraft Tradition and prominent Witch activist and elder.

so palpable. I looked over and he was standing right by the altar, taking the form of a friend of mine who looks just like Odin in real life. Amusingly, he is a physics professor at a local university, and a very brilliant guy. . . . [The Odin in my room was] gigantically tall; he had an unruly gray beard and hair, and in my vision he was naked. . . . I could tell it was Odin because he was holding the staff and he had . . . both of the ravens on his shoulders. He was just looking at me intently. It was extremely intense.

Although Caroline began to work with Odin after that first encounter, she resisted his marriage proposals because she didn't have a good framework for maintaining a relationship with him. The fact that she found Odin notoriously bossy was a turnoff for many years. Initially she tried to connect to the Heathenry groups in her area, but she didn't feel accepted by them.

Instead, her work with Odin evolved alongside her shamanic training and initiations, wherein she discovered that Odin has increasingly been working with people outside of the Heathen tradition. In fact, her work as a powerful shamanic healer is due in part to her ability to enter into intense relationships with spirits, of which her marriage to Odin is only one example. In time, Caroline discovered that although Odin is picky about who he works with, he does not limit his interaction to a strictly Heathen audience.*

Caroline points out that she came to Witchcraft because of her love for the Goddesses and Freyja, not because she was seeking magical power. However, she learned that the spirits often give the most power to those who do not seek it: "They have given [me] so much more magical power than I could have ever dreamed I could possibly have, because I never sought it out. And one of the ways spirits empower people is through sexual intercourse between [your] astral body and the spirit's manifested divine form."

---

*In Heathenry, and other Norse traditions, the term for spirit marriage is *Godspouse* or *Godwed*.

Sex with spirit(s) is a key point that comes up again and again in our conversation. An important way Caroline interacts with the spirits is through sexual union. In fact, she asserts that from the spirit's perspective, sex with humans is *primarily* about empowering us, with most of those empowerments being for healing and longevity. Sexuality with spirits involves eroticism because humans are more open to direct divine empowerments when they are experiencing intimacy. Unfortunately, for many people in the West, this kind of interaction with the spirit realms can be unsettling at best, and for some, downright frightening. Even in decidedly Pagan circles, Caroline has been told over and over again that "the spirits won't work with you in that way," only to have the spirits' behavior prove the humans wrong. Fortunately, Caroline's open-minded sexuality and sense of personal empowerment have enabled her to enjoy the love and gifts of many spirit lovers.

SENSORY EXPERIENCE

Caroline is a full-spectrum visionary. During visions and visitations she leaves her body but retains all her senses: sight, sound, touch, smell, and taste—with the exception of being able to feel weight. Everything else, she feels and sees quite clearly. Her primary method of communication is through trance. Often she goes into trance just as she is falling asleep and has a complete experience during that time, one that she remembers perfectly. Other times, she enters trance through shamanic ritual or by simply walking in nature.

Caroline reports that she has houses, or astral temples, set up in the spirit realm in which she meets her different spouses. The house where she meets Odin resembles the domain of the Rohan in *The Lord of the Rings*. "It's a beautiful place, basically a longhouse with a central fire and openness. There's a loft where we have a bedroom, and sometimes there are other beings there, but mostly not. It's a beautiful space with giant columns made of tree trunks."

Caroline also does divination by watching birds. She points out that all the Gods she works with have birds associated with them. As well, she has learned to interview spirits by using tarot cards. She asks them a question like, "How do you feel about me?" or "What is your role in my life?" and then pulls a card for the answer. Through this method, she has divined, repeatedly, that her spirits think of her as etherically tied to them. She goes on to say that working with so many different spirits who have different ideas and who make their wishes clearly known to her is a balancing act, all the time.

AGREEING TO MARRY

Caroline finally accepted Odin's marriage proposal after she received the same guidance from two different elders in two different Pagan traditions who were independent of each other. Both talked to her about commitment; about needing to get serious about her lineage path.

> [These conversations] convinced [me] that I really did need to go into this with my whole heart and to understand that on some level I needed to submit and take Odin's advice, at least most of the time. That's when I got [Odin's two ravens] Huginn and Muninn tattooed on my shoulders. . . . That's when I fully accepted what Odin wants for me. Before then, he had incrementally asked me for more and more commitment, even though I've been making love with him for a long time. But I also was married to other Gods.

Caroline observes that when the Gods approach humans as powerfully as Odin does to her, they are not accustomed to a mortal saying, "I'm having a fine time with my Goddesses here. I like the Orishas." I wonder if part of Caroline's strong will and stubborn Taurus nature is one of the things Odin likes best about her. She is a force to be reckoned with, which seems like a perfect match for a powerful, opinionated deity like Odin.

I ask Caroline whether there had been a formal ceremony for her marriage to Odin or whether the taking of the tattoos had been the totality of the rite. She says that there was much less ceremony with

Odin than there had been with her other spirit marriages. The marriage took place in trance, just between the two of them.

> *Odin took Freyja as a hostage before he won her heart. . . . He won her heart by making her people his people. They became one people . . . and it was a long, bloody, and violent transition before the two peoples became one. When all of Freya's people and Odin's people were one, that is when Freyja stopped resisting Odin's love. It took me a while, but eventually I understood Freyja differently, and that made me feel less uncomfortable with Odin's bossiness. It's all been really, really good, but there was much less ceremony with him.*

Caroline made that commitment manifest when, as mentioned earlier, she had Odin's ravens tattooed on her shoulders. The tattoos she chose of the ravens, Huginn and Muninn, have two runes in them that are very important to Odin. The runes represent aspects of the ravens: one who is able to see through space, and the other who is able to see through time. For the raven that is able to see through space and is associated with Odin's magic, she chose the rune for "communication." And for the raven who can see through time, she chose the rune for "homeland." She chose to use these specific runes in her tattoos in part to reclaim them, as they have been negatively co-opted by white supremacists.[1]

MARRIAGE REQUIREMENTS

I ask Caroline whether any requirements came along with this marriage. She asserts that Odin is very possessive of her.

She elaborates as follows:

> *First of all, he just wanted me to be his, to the point where he and Freyja both gave me the Devil card in the tarot because they want me chained to them. They apparently like to think they are like puppet masters of me, to some extent. . . . Odin didn't really want to share me, as much as*

I wanted to be in contact with lots of different pantheons. He is particularly jealous of a handful of Gods. He really doesn't want me talking to Thor at all. I mustn't wear a hammer, and I like a hammer . . . so I have the ravens. And he's jealous of Manannan mac Lir, whom I absolutely adore, and he's jealous of Lugh . . . and he is jealous of Zeus. He doesn't like Zeus very much. [Zeus] is very handsome, and Odin really, really doesn't like him. It's comical, because it mirrors humanity, you know? Odin is possessive of me, and if that's how he feels, it's kind of flattering in a way, and kind of silly because, you know, I don't resonate with the other Gods as much as I do with Odin.

Since Caroline married Odin, he has relaxed some of his almost overwhelming possessiveness toward her. However, because Caroline is a visionary, she constantly receives marching orders from Odin, Freyja, and her other spirit contacts. Sometimes she is given instructions for major undertakings such as instigating a political action to get the pentagram included on military burial headstones; other times she receives instructions regarding minor matters, such as what color of clothing she should and shouldn't wear.

I'm very argumentative with him. He knows how much I like to fight: I practice depossession for my clients—the removal of parasitic spirit entities from people's energy fields. I don't want to go into despair, or [give] up. It seems to me that agreeing to be on his Ragnarök* team is tantamount to saying I despair over the epoch. And I don't want to do that. I really think if we can evolve beyond war, we can maybe evolve beyond Ragnarök. Those are the kinds of arguments that I have with him. That's the kind of thing that makes him a little cross with me sometimes. He made me witness Ragnarök, which was perfectly dreadful, and fortunately most of it's been erased from my memory, because that's how bad it was. But it was very geologic. I don't think it's about nuclear destruction, which at one time I worried about.

---

*Ragnarök is the climactic, apocalyptic event in Norse eschatology.

Odin hasn't ever asked Caroline to be sexually faithful the way a human husband might. She also points out that Odin seems much less jealous of the African Orishas than he is of the northern European deities. I'm curious if there is anything Caroline has requested of Odin. She explains that she asked him to change his appearance when he appeared to her: "I told him I didn't like it when he came to me all scraggly and unkempt, with such wild hair and beard. I preferred him to look more closely trimmed. So he usually manifests to me more closely trimmed than he's generally seen, because he knows that I prefer it."

I am curious about this request, because other interviewees shared how their spirit contacts often manifest in a variety of different forms according to what they want to communicate. Caroline reports that her standard operating procedure for the spirits she works with is to ask that they work with her in an appearance that they consider to be their true form, but that all of them have multiple true forms.

> The longer you work with spirits, the more accustomed you become to them having multiple true forms. . . . I appreciate them giving me a degree of choice and autonomy insofar as they do . . . but they also know that I am not going to do the thing that a lot of people do. . . . I am not going to treat them like they are so, so, so high far above me, because they are not. They are not as high, far above me as a lot of people who approach them in a ritual seem to fall into the error of thinking.

I find this a fascinating and complex distinction. Although Caroline has used terms like *puppet master* and *chained* to describe her relationship with Odin, she also is in full possession of her own personal sovereignty and choice in the relationship. She is both in service to her marriage, and yet lives in self-possession.

> Odin has been a wonderful spirit husband to be with. He's a very good, I hesitate to say master, but they would uphold that, the spirits would. When I've interviewed them on the subject—this is something that really irritates me, but they all do it; Freyja has given me this answer as well as Odin and other spirits—they give me the Devil card as being

metaphoric of our relationship. The Devil card, in a more negative sense, is considered to describe something like an addiction or something you're chained to in a negative way. But the truth of the matter is that if you take out the pejorative-ness—instead of seeing the demonic unpleasant figure there, you substitute it with a loving figure—it certainly does change the paradigm, doesn't it?

I am encouraged by Caroline's twilight interpretation of the Devil card. Through the Pagan lens, the figure of the Devil in tarot definitely takes on an entirely different meaning—one we will return to and reconsider in greater depth in my own story chapters.

BENEFITS OF THE MARRIAGE

Given Caroline's description of being tied to the spirits, I wonder what might be the benefits for her of such an intense relationship. Caroline insists that Odin serves as a strong protector and benefactor. After two devastating late-term miscarriages, Odin foretold her daughter's conception. Odin came to Caroline on December 15 in a vision and told her that a baby was coming. Her daughter was conceived that Yule, and she successfully delivered the baby nine months later. She feels like Odin helped her heal enough to carry a baby to term.

Having my daughter was a huge shamanic victory for me, because I had lost two children previously in advanced stages of pregnancy. . . . My babies died within hours after their births, and it was very, very difficult. Having my daughter, who is going to college next month, was a huge shamanic victory to me, one I think Odin helped with. That's one of the things I'm supposed to be doing: showing people that the energy of the old Gods [is] very potent still, very potent. . . . They want their power to be made manifest through healing as well as through prophecy.

Caroline suggests that one of the main ambitions in the Norse Pagan community is to revive Norse-style oracular work, Seidr. Caroline contends that her work with Odin is to demonstrate that the Gods are able to share many other types of sacred gifts and abilities beyond prophecy. They can also help people with powerful physical, mental, and emotional healings.

Because Caroline spent a lot of time talking about her resistance to marrying Odin, I was curious about what it's like for her now that she's committed to him. Caroline describes how a few years ago she had become quite sick and Odin had been with her throughout it, supporting her and helping her heal.

> I had a giant health crash starting in 2008, and Odin was with me the whole time. He's been so supportive and helpful. . . . I've been happier since I committed to him. He was just fantastic. He could reach me when I was sick, and it was hard to reach me because I was so poisoned. That's what I mean about the genetic component [enabling a stronger connection].

Caroline noted that because she has Norwegian ancestry, Odin was able to reach her in a way that the other spirits she works with could not because they do not share a genetic bond. Having genetic ties to the pantheon a practitioner is working with seems to make the access and ritual all the more powerful.

Caroline went on to elaborate on how her relationship with Odin goes back many lifetimes.

> Quite recently when I went to visit Odin, and before I moved into the journey fully, I heard this sound that was like, "creak, creak, creak, creak." When I came more fully into the journey, it was the sound of an old-fashioned rope. I was hanging upside-down in a big ash tree. I was freezing cold, and I was naked. I felt this terrible blow to my mouth. My whole mouth exploded with blood, and my teeth were knocked out. . . . And then the next blow to my head sent me out of my body. And I watched, I sat in the tree up above where this was happening, and I watched this beautiful blonde, naked woman get beaten to death while she was swinging from her feet hanging in this ash tree.

It looked like a primitive European village. We know from archeology that adultery was a capital offense in ancient times. The backstory I was told was that I had been married as a very young, beautiful, and horny woman to an old smelly man who basically bought me from my parents like a goat. I committed adultery and was then considered a criminal. By that culture's mores, I had cheated my husband out of the money he paid for me, for my value as sex partner and brood mare. We also know that criminals were executed on Odin's trees.

What I've gathered from this is that Odin feels proprietary towards me partly because of that experience. . . . He felt terrible and thought it was amazingly stupid . . . [because] I was expressing Freyja's sexually free energy in that lifetime, just like [I do in] this one.

Caroline reports that Freyja, according to ancient matrilineal lore, is not sexually faithful. She is a sexually independent Goddess. However, in later myth, patriarchal ideas creep in and devalue her sexuality, casting her sexual nature in a negative light and dirtying Freyja's nature by describing it as shameful. Having Freyja as her primary deity supports Caroline's relationships in the spirit realm. Since Caroline is sexually independent, she is able to enter fully into sexual union with her spirit lovers.

The primary reason that we have sexual contact, or what I prefer to think of as metaphoric sexual contact, is because [the spirits are] empowering me this way. They're doing healing for me, and they're empowering me this way. Fortunately, my third husband is an experienced shamanic practitioner, and he understands these practices perfectly well. . . . Some of my friends in shamanism, people I've been trained with, especially people who had happier relationships within monotheism, don't operate this way, because they have too much instilled guilt and shame to accept this type of empowerment. . . . They can't take in the kind of love that I can take in from the spirits, that I work with in the way I'm able to, because they still feel guilty and ashamed of their own sexual desires.

For Caroline, then, spirit sex is less about "good" or "bad," and more about how much you are able to open yourself—body, mind, and spirit—to receive the blessing that working intimately with a spirit has to offer.

OUTCOME OF THE MARRIAGE

The idea that humans can be healed and empowered by spirits, and sharing that possibility with others, is part of the larger purpose of Caroline's marriage to Odin. The Gods care about the fate of humanity. According to Caroline, we face certain challenges in reviving Pagan practices because Pagan deities have not been worshipped in a long time, so their connection to the mortal world has become more tenuous. Caroline says that once worship of the old Gods and Goddesses resumes on a wider scale, our ability to receive their blessings will once again flow more freely.

> That's why it's so important what we're doing. The stakes couldn't be higher. It's the survival of humanity. . . . Here's what I've been told for the past twenty-five years. This is really depressing, but it's what they say. They say there's going to be a tremendous contraction of the human population. The humans will regard that as a type of End of the World, a type of Ragnarök, but I've seen what happens during the actual Ragnarök. It's geologic, and it's not any time soon. . . . This is what they told me; this is really important. . . . This is what [Odin] says: "The ability to be psychic will be just as determinative of who goes forward in evolution as the ability to speak was when the species began."

Caroline stresses that the development of our psychic abilities is of paramount importance for the evolution of our species. It will be like moving from *Homo neanderthalensis* to *Homo sapiens*. Our psychic development, of which spirit communication and marriage is one aspect, is one of the means by which we'll be able to evolve as a species. She says it is how we'll become transdimensional. Because she believes this, Caroline and her husband, an MIT graduate, have developed an interactive tarot app for mobile devices, licensed more than one hundred individual oracular decks of cards—mostly tarot—and offered them for sale on iTunes and Google Play. Caroline describes the apps as "oracular wisdom tools disguised as games."

Caroline goes on to emphasize that the worship of the Gods is not and should not be limited to strictly genetic affinity, because otherwise the Gods are considered property of the descendants of the people who first conceived them, which is a type of nativism. Almost everyone in the modern world is not a pure-blood genetic example of any one region. Thus Caroline believes it reduces the Gods to human property to claim that only the genetic descendants of the people who first imagined that God-form into manifestation can ethically work with those spirits. Therefore, although an ancestral tie makes it easier to reach a certain pantheon, it is by no means a requirement.

> [The Gods] need us too, to go into the future. They need us just as much as they need the traditional forms. . . . It is sad to me that the people who practice the reconstructionist forms of Paganism often seem to believe that they literally own the spirits from their tradition. Similarly, many Roman Catholics don't want Pagans worshipping the saints, and this holds true for some Hellenic Pagans, for some people who work with the Gods of the African Diaspora religions, and many others as well. If you don't have the right ethnicity, some folks don't want you worshipping their Gods.. . . .. I'm catholic with a small c. I despise parochialism [based on] a bunch of religious rules that were made up by humans. It's just ridiculous.

Caroline stresses that the Gods and Goddesses themselves don't live by distinguishing lines of racial identity; this is a human construct. The Gods and Goddesses are usually open to whoever will revive their worship. Because of Caroline's devotion to a variety of pantheons, part of her mission appears to be embodying and modeling what living at the crossroads of spirit marriage can look like.

OTHER SPIRIT MARRIAGES

Throughout our conversation Caroline has alluded to the other spirit marriages she holds. I ask Caroline to describe these other unions and I ask her whether the marriage protocol was any different than her marriage to Odin. They were.

> *The first one was unexpected because I literally never got his name. I used to call him the "wrong thing," and he would hold my chin and say "Don't call me that. Call me Ellegua," and I never knew what avatar [of Ellegua] he was. He was so handsome, and his palace was very beautiful, but it just didn't work out well. The next one was Papa Legba, and [then] Anubis and Ogun.*

All of these marriages took place when she was in trance, and they all were more or less spontaneous in that Caroline found herself being married to these deities without much input on her part. Caroline also explains that none of her spirit-spouses until Odin ever asked her to focus entirely on them, so it doesn't seem surprising that she has a variety of spouses.

The Orishas

Her first contact with the Afro-Caribbean Santería deities called the Orishas dates back to a trip she took to London in the 1970s.

> *I was first introduced to the Orishas back in the seventies. I met them in the Museum of Mankind in London in either 1973 or 1974. The Orishas literally saw me when I saw them. I was looking at an exhibit of consecrated shrines that had been stolen from Yorùbáland in Nigeria under British colonialism. Eventually I initiated into Santería. . . . The Orishas have traditional initiatory paths, unlike the emerging northern European Paganisms.*
>
> *I love the Orishas dearly, but I just can't do all the rules of the religions devoted to them. I don't think it would be appropriate for me to*

receive more initiatory ceremonies and make Ocha* with my paint job, frankly. . . . Obatala† owns my head, in the terms of Santería. One of my Wiccan priests, a man born in Cuba, suggested that Obatala is my head owner‡ because the Orishas knew that they were going to have to share me in this lifetime. . . . I'm truly devoted to them.

I've loved the Orishas since the seventies, and I've spent countless thousands of dollars on traditional initiations and on worship, and never regretted spending a penny of that. I also love the Gods of Vodou, the Loa, but still I am the wrong color. . . . One thing that [the Orishas] are interested in doing is putting forth the idea that they too are having unsanctioned relationships that the priests don't approve of. The truth of the matter is [that] the Gods do what they want and the priests do what is convenient for humans.

I'm reminded of a comment that a Dagara diviner once made to me about how some Gods and Goddesses will open themselves to whoever can see them. Their worship has had so many obstacles (due to monotheism) that they really don't care who you are; if you can see them, they want to work with you. Caroline's experience of the Orishas seems to corroborate this.

Unfortunately, the Santería houses Caroline was able to find were unwilling to accept her unorthodox ways, so she has mostly worshipped the Orishas alone and developed her own methods of celebrating them. This seems to be another example of the balancing act required in Pagan spiritual practice. How do we honor and serve the Gods of another culture while still being mindful and respectful of that culture? This is a key inquiry of my research and practice as I navigate my own complex spiritual path through a variety of traditions. It's a topic that we will discuss further in the New Orleans Voodoo Mambo's story.

---

*Ocha is an initiation similar to the *couché* ritual in Vodou/Voodoo, which we will discuss later. Caroline is a white woman and Santería is an Afro-Caribbean tradition, so she is respectful of not taking liberties with Santería rites.

†Obatala is the eldest of the Orishas and the father of all Orishas and humanity.

‡Like an ishtadevi/a or Divine Self.

Caroline's marriage to Ogun was unsanctioned and disapproved of by her *Madrina,* her Santería priestess. Unlike some African Diaspora religions like Vodou, according to Caroline spirit marriage is a forbidden practice in Santería. Nevertheless, the spirits didn't seem to care whether their priests approved of Caroline's marriages; they married her anyway.

Frankly, Ogun didn't offer me a choice either. . . . This is the kind of alleged "choice" that people get offered when spirits decide to marry them: One night I was at someone else's house and journeying as part of the group. I went to a further journey, and Ogun was there. He waved his hand, and suddenly I was wearing this beautiful black and green dress. . . . It looked like something that was all the rage in about 1865. He took me before Obatala and married me. I had very-little-to-no say. Every single time I'd meet Ogun, for at least a year, I would express anxiety and nervousness that I was doing the wrong thing, because that's what my human teachers were saying. I felt like I had to hide my relationship with Ogun from my teachers.

Finally, he got tired of hearing it. I have anxiety, and I've had this experience more than once where the spirits are like, "Give it a rest. Don't talk about this anymore. We are tired of it." Here's what he did. I went to meet him and he took me to a bluff, a high cliff above the sea in the Caribbean. There's this beautiful scene with this high fossil coral promontory, trees, and all this beautiful verdant grass. We walked right up to the edge of this point. Ogun had in his hand a suitcase, one of those old leather suitcases from the 1940s with two straps of leather around it, and a zipper, a primitive one. All over it, it had stickers that said "The Casino of Havana" and things like that, brightly colored hotel stickers from the forties. He held it up by its handle, and he shook it to emphasize it. He said, "Do you see this suitcase? This suitcase represents all the rules in Cuban Santería." And then he threw it into the sea.

After that I stopped questioning whether I was doing the right thing. My teachers continued to tell me I was doing the wrong thing, but the truth of the matter is if you're a shamanic person, you have spirit relationships. If you look at the Tibetan material, the kind of avatars that they work with are different, but the way they work Tantrically with spirits is the same. There's just no more mystery about it. All the Pagan Gods and Goddesses worked this way in the way-back.

Caroline feels a sense of being guarded and protected by the Orishas. She believes they are stronger than some of the other spirits because they receive blood offerings regularly, a practice that gives them more force in this world. She contends that the Orishas and other deities who receive regular sacrifices will continue to be more accessible to humans until the egregores of other Pagan Gods and Goddesses expand and are fed by regular devotional worship.

Egyptian Gods

After she had been married to Ogun for three or four years, Caroline began taking workshops once a year with the leading occultist Dolores Ashcroft Nowicki, who was mentioned earlier in Orion Foxwood's story. Dolores formally introduced her to the Egyptian pantheon. Traditionally, the Egyptian Gods do not work with humans in the capacity of spirit lover or marriage partner, and Caroline was told that she should not expect them to engage with her sexually. However, as Caroline began working with the God Anubis, son of her devotional Goddess Nephthys, he told her that he would interact with her in a sexual way because that was what she needed, which she says is often true for people who are shamanic. At first Anubis requested that they both shape-shift into the form of jackals and have intercourse that way. However, over time, he began to manifest in an anthropomorphic form in their encounters, which were often set in an oasis. Then, just as suddenly as happened with her other spirit-spouses, Anubis married her.

I often go into a trance when I'm on a dog walk. In my practice, Anubis's colors are black with some gold, and the bird that represents him best is the Baltimore oriole. The Baltimore oriole is vanishingly rare. I've seen the Baltimore oriole in Maryland twice in my life. It's one of the birds that, despite being our state bird, has been really badly affected by climate change and deforestation in Central America. So . . . I was walking in the forest near our house, and I started having visions in which Anubis was marrying me with the same degree of lack of notice or choice that the Orishas had given me. And as I was walking, suddenly I saw a Baltimore oriole.

I was just like, "Oh wow!" That is so rare that I knew that it was a sign that the vision I was having right then [was legitimate]. . . . Then, on the ground before me was an orange plastic bottle cap with the initials AB on it.

You just never know what kind of tokens they're going to give you.

. . . This is the weird part: I went home and told my husband what happened. At the same time that I was in the forest seeing the Baltimore oriole, he says to me, "Well this bright orange bird with black on it came here too!" . . . He saw a Baltimore oriole the same time I saw one. That's technically a minor miracle! I knew I had married Anubis, and it wasn't just some strange fantasy of my own.

Bird divination, also known as ornithomancy or augury, is an important piece of Caroline's relationship to the spirit world. The birds are one of the ways her contacts reveal themselves. Anubis and the other Egyptian Gods and Goddesses are generally considered to be beyond the stage of having sexual relationships with humans (apparently it is not a common form of relationship for them). However, Caroline's relationship to Anubis demonstrates that such sexual relationships are not entirely outside the realm of possibility. She believes that shamanic people are like coyotes: They are most comfortable on the fringe of accepted practice; on the fringe in communities that are more devoted to ritual observances than seeking individual visionary experiences. In keeping with the trickster nature of coyote from the Native American worldview, they often do the exact opposite of what is acceptable and sanctioned. They regularly transgress the boundaries that humans have constructed for what is and is not possible with the Gods and Goddesses.

DIVORCING A SPIRIT

Earlier in our conversation Caroline mentioned that she had actually divorced one of her spirit-spouses. Divorce is practically unheard of among the other practitioners I spoke with, so I was eager to understand the circumstances and how this took place. Caroline reports that she never received a name for the particular avatar that she divorced, and that it all began with the purchase of a sacred item.

I was in Louisiana. I saw a Louisiana folk rendition of an Ellegua and I was really attracted to it. It was a head, and Gods only know what had been done to it. It did not appear to be a consecrated head, but it was inhabited by a spirit just the same, and the spirit talked to me in the store. So I bought it, and then it started talking to me in ways that made me a little uncomfortable and were definitely on sort of the stalky side of being happy with the ways things were going. I didn't know that this was a possibility, because the Orishas aren't supposed to have relationships like this, according to the babas. . . . That's a really bad thing. It's a really bad feeling to be not in accord with what you're being told is the right way. But it's also really, really hard to say no to a spirit that big. It was very overwhelming, so I started interacting with him. I could see his palace really clearly, and he was so handsome. He was unbelievably, divinely handsome, and I could see him quite well.

But sometimes he acted like a spoiled child, which is true of many men, and tragically, famously, true of Ellegua in many of his manifestations. I got progressively less comfortable. I finally went before Obatala and officially asked him for a divorce. So I think I'm the only person I've ever met who's gotten a divorce from a spirit that they married, but I wasn't offered a choice when he married me in the first place, as usual.

A REJECTION OF SPIRIT MARRIAGE

Given Caroline's emphasis on her not having had a choice in any of her spirit marriages, I wondered aloud what the repercussions are of resisting or refusing a spirit marriage. Caroline says she has seen many people reject spirit advances, with a variety of outcomes. However, the one that stands out for her as perhaps the most dramatic was the account of a very sick person with whom she was doing shamanic work.

The person was so sick, I had to come to their home. When I sang my songs and [then] woke up from my trance and all the possessions that the songs [had] called to me, what I saw was this black cloud where I normally would see the aura and the spirit body. I could not believe it, because I'd never seen anything like that before. This was someone who had [many] medical problems. I went behind the person, and at the back of their neck, there was what looked like a plug, like a bath plug. I unplugged it, and that's when a horrible gooey black fluid started to drain off.

The fairies loved this person so much. The person was amazing. Then the fairies came on to the person. [This person was] Catholic, so [they had] totally rejected the fairies' advances, and the fairies got mad. . . . The fairies came during the session to explain it to me. It's not like the fairies were punishing this person. It's like monotheism made that person punish themselves, and then physical illness followed.

Working in harmony with the spirits is the way to physical, mental, and emotional health, in my experience, with the spirits being the senior partner of the union. I truly believe our spiritual bodies precede the level of our physical bodies. Our physical bodies take their cue, at least in part, from our spirit bodies. If you're constantly being healed on a physical level because you're being healed on a spirit level, this is part of the gift spirit marriages bring people. It's not just additional magical power; it's physical healing, well-being, and the feeling of being loved. And everything that intimacy on a human level brings, intimacy on a divine level also brings.

One of the most important points Caroline emphasizes repeatedly in our conversation is how healing and regenerative a spirit marriage can be. She emphasizes how our fear of sexuality and intimacy often leads to disease in our bodies, minds, and spirits, and how opening to the spirits can help us heal this. One of Caroline's key motivators for agreeing to be interviewed was her desire to set the record straight on this front: The spirits don't make us sick. We make ourselves sick with our own fear and repression, by rejecting the gifts they have for us.

CLOSING REMARKS

In closing, I asked Caroline a few follow-up questions. I was curious whether she has heard of the concept of conceiving spirit children with one's spirit spouse. She said that she has two children in the spirit realm who show up as bear cubs. These are the spirits of the two babies she miscarried. While she knows other practitioners who have spirit children with their spirit lovers, she herself does not.

I asked her what it was like to keep all these different beings and relationships straight? How does she differentiate among their various voices, needs, and attitudes from her own Self? She claimed that having so many spirit companions has made her much less interested in her fellow humans, because she finds humans boring, immature, and self-focused. She also observed that when she is in a shamanic journey, she always knows who she is talking to, but when she is out of a trance state, she isn't always sure exactly who is talking.

Freyja is hard to discern, because she feels so much like me that it's hard to tell us apart. Nephthys is hard to discern because she's subtle, indirect, and mysterious. . . . Of the three Goddesses I work with most closely, the Morrigan is in some ways the easiest to hear. . . . I don't always know who is talking, but a lot of times I do.

[One time] I was about to pack for Conjure Dance, and they all talked to me. Everyone is excited about going to it; it's a very fun ritual. Everyone is invited, all of the spirits I work with. I do it annually,

and it's my big annual blowout trance ritual. People enjoy it. I have elaborate altar setups. I have a statue of Santissima Muerte; I really like deities of death, so I am definitely happy to have her, but she's not everybody's cup of tea. I was packing her and some of the other Gods didn't want her statue in with them. And I heard Osiris say, "Bring her to us! We love the dead in Egypt. No problem, Santissima Muerte can come hang with us!"

Caroline reports that in Santería her head owner is one of the female paths of Obatala. She is an old lady, a crone form of Obatala instead of a grandfather form. Obatala and Anubis help organize things in her head. Caroline laughs as she describes how busy her head can get with all the various deities. "I have four Elleguas that I work with, four avatars of Ellegua, and sometimes they quarrel. And I've heard Anubis say, 'Do you really think the human is edified by hearing you lot quarrel in her head?'"

Caroline admits that the conversations the Gods and Goddesses have in her head keep her quite entertained, and she laughingly explains that their company is oftentimes preferable to human company. She reports that she is currently writing a book and that her spirits are often dictating the book to her, which she finds helpful. Caroline goes on to say that some of her teachers find it unsettling that she merges with more than one spirit at a time. However, as someone who is trained in shamanism she does not find this overwhelming at all.

It seems that being a crosspantheon shamanic practitioner has suited Caroline quite well for the task that has been laid before her. She is working in and embracing many different traditions, and that is a very "coyote" thing to do. Caroline elaborates: "It's a way that shamanic people have worked from time immemorial. If you look at the information from the witchcraft trials, a lot of it was about spirit lovers, which made [the church] really uncomfortable."

One of the most important insights to come out of our conversation is how Caroline's experience illustrates that there is no final say as to exactly how spirit marriages can or must be conducted. That is one reason her perspective is so important to my research. Whenever I hear a lineage or tradition dogmatically assert, "This is the way it happens, and nobody ever divorces, and nobody ever marries more than one spirit, and nobody ever . . . ," I immediately wonder whether there are exceptions. This is Caroline's story—the story of the exception, and at the same time, perhaps, the future of the practice.

POSTSCRIPT

After we conducted the original two interviews, Caroline's shamanic practice and marital life with spirits continued to evolve. Approximately two years after our initial interview, I spoke with her again to finalize her story. During our conversation she reported that since we had last spoken she had married Loki—under outright duress—in March of 2016.* Loki had promptly healed her of a dire psychological problem that had plagued her since college.

Then, in late 2016, Caroline realized that the spirit-spouse who had ultimately been wooing her through all these various marriages was the divinity Abraxas, the gnostic Christian God-form considered to be an Archon or an Aeon—the source of all being and the ground of material reality. Caroline now understands that her spirit husbands are all individuated forms that Abraxas has taken as he has manifested in different human cultures down through time. As a result she now feels more comfortable having marriages with so many God-forms. She says she responded to this degree of relaxation by also marrying the Finnish blacksmith God Volund, also known as Weyland.

---

*Loki is the trickster God in Norse mythology.

9

The New Orleans
Voodoo Mambo

*S*uzette is a native of New Orleans and an initiated *mambo* in the
Haitian Vodou and New Orleans Voodoo lineages. She is a spirit
medium and leads cemetery tours in New Orleans where her focus is
on helping clients develop greater sensitivity and respect for the unseen
realms of ancestors and spirits.

AN EXTRAORDINARY DREAM

The circumstances by which I was led to interview Suzette are extraordinary and bear sharing as an introduction to her story. I wanted to
interview a practitioner of either Haitian Vodou or New Orleans
Voodoo, because spirit marriage features prominently in the practice of
these religions. Because of the sensitive and unconventional subject matter of my research, I preferred to interview people with whom I already
had an established connection or who came highly recommended by a
trusted source. Unfortunately, since I had little connection to Voodoo,
I found myself at a loss for an introduction to a practitioner.* Months

---

*Again, for simplicity's sake, throughout the remainder of this story, I have chosen to use
the spelling *Voodoo* as it is used in New Orleans, unless I am specifically referring to the
Haitian tradition, which is spelled *Vodou*.

passed, and I began to wonder how I was going to manifest an interview in a tradition that can be very guarded with outsiders due to the prejudice and vilification Vodouisants (practitioners of Voodoo) receive by mainstream religions and the media.

Then I had a dream.

I am in a place that looks like New Orleans. I am drawn to a white house with wrought iron railings. As I enter the house, I meet an old African American woman who is a mambo. She is dressed all in white and is wearing a pair of sunglasses. She says to me, "I've been waiting for you. I want to be one of your interviewees." She tells me that her spirit-spouse is San Jak, a manifestation of the Voodoo Loa Ogun. She says, "San Jak wants to talk to you. He wants you to interview me, so that he can talk to you."

We sit down together, and when San Jak possesses her, she starts speaking to me in a nasally, high-pitched voice. I am surprised by the falsetto register of his voice given that Ogun San Jak is a powerful warrior Ogun of great masculinity. Nevertheless, he gives me an illuminating and powerful interview, which includes specific information he wants to impart to me. I am overjoyed with the degree of clarity and connection that we have. It feels destined.

Unfortunately, once I woke up from this dream, I couldn't remember the details of the interview, other than that he insisted I write down his name as San Jak, so I could see it spelled out and would remember it once I woke up. However, I did feel very excited and optimistic. Even though I did not know how it was going to happen, I knew that the roads were being opened for me to collect an interview with a Vodouisant.

The next day I emailed a few friends who organize a folk magic festival in New Orleans each year. I shared my dream with them and asked if they were familiar with anyone in New Orleans who might fit the description of the woman in my dream. They put me in contact with a prominent New Orleans mambo, Voodoo Queen Bloody Mary, who graciously agreed to speak with me on the phone. She patiently listened to my dream and then quizzed me about the specific details of my dream. "Was the name you heard specifically 'San Jak'?" she wanted to know.

"Yes."

"Did the old mambo have one lens missing from her sunglasses?"

"No."

After she was satisfied with the details of my dream, she explained that she believed the mambo in my dream was a Ghede, a spirit of the dead, and told me that if I came to New Orleans she would do an interview with me, and also put me in contact with others in her lineage who might want to be interviewed. She instructed me to create an altar for San Jak and to put out offerings to him and to Papa Legba to help open the roads for my trip to New Orleans. My ritual to San Jak and Papa Legba worked above and beyond my expectations. I went from having no one to interview in the Vodou/Voodoo traditions to having four interviewees. A few months later, I traveled to New Orleans to interview Bloody Mary and her colleague Suzette, a New Orleans mambo who is married to a Ghede named Baron Samedi and whose *met tet* (patron deity) is San Jak.

MEETING BARON SAMEDI

Suzette and I met in an upstairs attic apartment in the French Quarter of New Orleans during the Traditional Folk Magic Festival. The night before our interview, I had attended a Voodoo ritual where I met Suzette for the first time and witnessed her skillful work as a mambo. For our interview, I brought offerings of rum and incense, and lit a candle that had been dedicated to Marie Laveau, Voodoo Queen of New Orleans. I explained my personal journey with this research, and we invoked and thanked the helping spirits that had brought us together.

A friend of mine had left a large papier-maché skeleton head wearing a top hat in the apartment from the night before, and Suzette remarked that this felt appropriate for our interview because she is married to a

Ghede, Baron Samedi. Suzette reports that the Ghede in New Orleans Voodoo are the spirits who rule the afterlife, the spirits of the dead. They are usually depicted as skeletons in formal attire like top hats and tuxedos, and Baron Samedi is the chief of the Ghede.

> There's the [Ghede] Barons: Baron Lacroix, Baron Cemetaire, Baron Criminale. Maman Brigette and him [Baron Samedi] rule the Ghedes. He's like the king and she's the queen. . . . I work with Maman (Mother) Brigette; I don't really work with too many of the other Ghedes, but I can feel them. When we're working in the cemeteries or doing Ghede ceremonies, I can feel the other Ghedes and I sense they're around, and I know they're there. But I'm not as close with them as I am with Maman Brigette and especially Baron Samedi.

Suzette explained that the Ghede are powerful spirits, but they are not technically considered Loa. Therefore, they do not obey the same ceremonial protocol that Loa tend to follow. Typically, in a Voodoo ceremony one must invoke Papa Legba, the guardian of the crossroads, before any other spirit can come through. Papa Legba is honored so that he will discern which spirits are allowed through into the ritual. However, Ghede, being ancestral spirits, can come through anytime they please during a ceremony.

Suzette describes how she first got involved in Voodoo and met the Baron:

> When I was a little child, I always heard who Marie Laveau was. You grow up knowing. Your mother threatens you when you're bad that she's gonna come and put the gris-gris on you. And since we weren't that good, we heard about Marie Laveau just about every day. That she was gonna come with the gris-gris if we didn't behave! When I went to the Voodoo museum and I saw her wax figure, it was like she smacked me on the shoulder and said to me, "Little girl, you belong to me! I'm yours." I felt an instant maternal connection with her. That made me wanna grow up in the Voodoo tradition, made me wanna do Voodoo, made me wanna be

like her. . . . So [as an adult] I started going to Voodoo ceremonies, and in Voodoo ceremonies normally what you strive for is that one of the Loa, the spirits, possesses a person. It makes it able for you to communicate, ask advice or insight, help you with a problem. . . . So, through the course Baron Samedi would pop out and he would always find me straightaway. He would pick me up and throw me in the air, and he would hug me and tell me I was his beautiful blonde, and he was always flirtatious. Of course, the Ghede are always known to be very sexual creatures, and very fun loving, gluttonous, drinking and all this good stuff. And, of course, when you have the human element in it every now and then, you do wonder if somebody's really possessed or not. But when I saw the guy drink a bottle of rum loaded down three inches thick-worth of hot peppers in it, and he drank it and didn't bat an eye? Well, that's gotta be real!

She described how for five years she would attend ceremonies during which the Baron would often come out to flirt, play around, and have fun with her. Then in 2005, he asked her to marry him. The Voodoo community was a bit stunned by this, as Baron Samedi doesn't normally ask people to marry him. But he was adamant that Suzette was to be his bride.

THE MARIAGE LOA

The *mariage Loa* is the Vodou/Voodoo term for the ritual marriage to a Loa. Suzette explained that normally in Voodoo the *houngan* (Voodoo priest) or mambo determines when and whether a celebrant should marry. Typically, this is done to bring balance and stability into a person's life, as the Loa that they marry will normally govern an area in their life in which they are lacking or need assistance. However, in Suzette's case it was the spirit himself who asked for the marriage.

In Baron Samedi's case he really never asks anybody to marry him. But that night he did ask me to marry him, and he wanted the ceremony to be on Day of the Dead, November 1, which is their day. He described exactly what I had to wear. . . . He described an outfit I had hanging in my closet for ten years, [one] that I'd never worn to Voodoo [ceremonies] because it was black, and in ceremony you normally don't wear black, and he described it to a T. It happened to be the same dress that a santero *had a dream about me wearing—that exact same dress! [He] told me I was supposed to be working with the dead. And I'm like, "How the hell do you 'work with the dead'? What am I supposed to be, a funeral director?" I didn't know exactly what "working with the dead" meant. . . .*

[So] I had my outfit. And I had to have a cake, but it had to be chocolate, since the Ghede are notorious for liking spices and peppers. I made a dark chocolate cake and I had my own little recipe, and I put a little cinnamon and cayenne in it. I had a bridesmaid. I wore that dress. All he wanted was a black vest with a boutonnière that had the colors red, white, and purple. So I had that made for him. And we had the wedding ceremony.

The ceremony took place within a few months of the proposal and was conducted in a Haitian Vodou temple, a *hounfou,* on the Day of the Dead. Suzette observed that she was fortunate that everything aligned perfectly to make it possible for her to marry the Baron right away. Not everyone who is asked to marry can afford the wedding. Like a human wedding, a spirit wedding requires a dress or suit, cake, food, clothes, and wedding gifts. Many practitioners cannot afford the marriage right away, and years may pass before they can afford to marry.

He didn't want anything fancy that I couldn't manifest. I didn't have to go out and buy a dress. He described a person with a leather vest, and the person owned it and gave it to me. All I had to pay for was some cake mix, ingredients, and a flower. I had everything else. He made a way for me to do that. Now had he said, "You need a Vera Wang dress. . . . " Okay, maybe for ten years I'll have to save and then we can get married. But I don't think he would expect me to sell my house, car, jewelry to get a Vera Wang dress.

Suzette suggests that if the spirits begin to make unreasonable requests or demands that would cause hardship, you should begin to wonder whether the requests are really coming from the spirit or from the human the spirit is possessing. I find that the potential for human agendas to creep into spirit possession is a noteworthy consideration. Having a community that can provide checks and balances to a spirit's demands seems helpful.

During the ritual, the Baron possessed one of the practitioners and the marriage was conducted with the exchanging of rings and vows similar to the way human marriages are conducted. After the ceremony, the Baron accompanied Suzette to the cemetery with the rest of the celebrants. As the evening came to a close, he started to withdraw his spirit from the person he was possessing, and he told Suzette that it was time for him to leave. He gave her a kiss and said he'd be back soon.

Suzette said he pops in to visit with her here and there outside of ritual and ceremony. She reports that day-to-day she mostly has a felt-sense of him, although sometimes he visits in her dreams, and she also sometimes hears him in her head. He has a very distinct accent and pronounces her name in a specific way that gets her attention and lets her know it is him.

Suzette set up an altar to the Baron and she likes to buy him little gifts of skeletons and skulls. She clarified that Baron Samedi is married to Maman Brigette, the Queen of the Dead. He told Suzette that Maman Brigette is a tad jealous of their relationship, and so Suzette includes Maman Brigette on her altar and puts out extra offerings to her. Maman Brigette had been the first Voodoo spirit to contact Suzette, so it feels natural for Suzette to honor her alongside the Baron.

Normally in Voodoo on that spirit's day—and Samedi *means "Saturday"—you honor that spirit. Even if you are married or engaged, you don't have sex on that night. You don't even sleep in the same bed in some traditions. But he told me he wasn't holding me to anything, that I could do exactly what I wanted when I wanted as long as when I*

was having sex, once in a while, I would think of him. He laughed, and I
laughed. It was so Ghede! It was so Baron Samedi.

I wondered if Suzette had any doubts about agreeing to marry the Baron. She insisted that she feels as at home with Baron Samedi as she did with Marie Laveau. She wanted to belong to him.

The afterworld seemed more appealing to me more than any other world, anyway. And that's [where] he rules. To me it was like coming home, my full circle. I knew where I was guided, where I was supposed to be. And now I'm not worried about what happens to me when I die, because I know where I'm going. [Our marriage] gave me a little more reassurance of the afterlife in my head. Psychologically it was more of a comfort.

AFTERMATH OF THE MARRIAGE

Since their marriage, Suzette has a deeper connection to the afterlife and all the various spirits associated with it. She reports regularly seeing ghosts of both humans and animals, and her ability to hear, see, and communicate with them have amplified since her marriage.

Suzette has a strong connection with animals, having spent twenty years working in a veterinary clinic, as well as training horses. Her marriage to the Baron opened a connection to the afterlife of animals as well as humans. She explains that animals are just like us: they have souls, and when they die their spirits can contact us. She can see and hear them, and she finds it very comforting to know that her beloved animals are still around.

Not long after her marriage to the Baron, Suzette was invited by a fellow mambo to help lead cemetery tours in New Orleans, during which they perform small Voodoo rituals to the dead, inviting the spirits to manifest. Suzette began to notice that it was not just the spirits of the dead that showed up for her. Fairy spirits, animal spirits, and other nonhuman spirits also came. Again, her marriage to the Baron opened the doors for her contact with a whole new pantheon of beings.

I noticed that once I started doing the tours, something shifted. . . . [I worked for] this animal emergency hospital that had existed since 1972. All of a sudden, [the owners] wanted to sell it. I was already doing tours, brought home some spirits to the vet clinic occasionally and freaked out some vets. One of them actually ran and hid and locked herself in the [exam] room one night. She goes, "What kind of freaky shit are you bringing in here?" And I was like, "They follow you sometimes!"

The clock would spin backwards until 4:00 a.m. . . . I saw a couple out there [in the waiting room] and had them fill out paperwork, but there was no couple out there, no paperwork was filled out. I was obviously talking to a little old ghost couple with a little old shih tzu, and they didn't exist. They were looking at [the security] cameras, but they weren't there. . . . The clinic cat, who loved me—I was the only one he wouldn't hiss, scratch, and bite—I sat down next to him. His eyes got so wide and he cracked me so hard in the face he bruised my eye. He saw something on me.

Not long after this, the veterinary hospital went up for sale, and she found herself naturally pulled into full-time work as a New Orleans cemetery tour guide and mambo. Suzette exclaims, "I'm like the Santería priest [said I would be]. I am working with the dead now, and it's on a nightly basis!"

IMPACT ON
HUMAN RELATIONSHIPS

Becoming a Voodoo mambo was a significant departure from Suzette's Roman Catholic upbringing. Many of her relationships shifted after her ordination and spirit marriage. Suzette reports that her conservative Catholic mother was horrified to hear of her ordination.

She did tell me, when she found out I was an ordained Voodoo priestess, that I was going to go to Hell when I died. I asked her to save me a seat, and she doesn't say that anymore. Sometimes you gotta fight fire with fire, or else they're going to continue to point and aim. I eliminated that problem.

At the time Suzette started formally practicing Voodoo, she was in an eight-year relationship. Her partner told her he thought that practicing Voodoo was making her stupid. Suzette quips, "But you gotta consider the source. This is coming from somebody who couldn't go three minutes without a drink." She goes on to say that the source of his derisive attitude was the fact that she had finally found a tradition within which she felt at home. Voodoo gave her confidence. Suzette asserts that she had found her community and was therefore no longer sitting at home waiting for him to come home after a night of drinking. Voodoo made her more independent and gave her a purpose. Once she started focusing on that, she became less and less interested in supporting his alcoholism.

One of the Voodoo deities, Erzulie Dantor, ultimately helped Suzette in making the transition away from this unhealthy relationship. Erzulie Dantor is a fierce, dark-skinned female Loa who protects women, children, and single mothers. She was Suzette's first *met tet,* and she empowered Suzette to end that relationship. "I was a single mom, so I think that's one of my deep connections with her. She pops up in dreams a lot, too. I actually paint images of her. . . . For my initiation for Dantor, 'cause you bring them a gift, I did a portrait of her."

I mention that I've heard to use caution when working with Erzulie Dantor because she is seen as "dangerous."

Suzette offers a different perspective:

I don't consider her to be that fearful. To me, she's my mommy. I love her. You're not gonna be fierce with your own children or your own kind. You're gonna be that way with an enemy. . . . I think that if you ask [her] to help you because someone is really hurting you, like a woman in an abusive relationship, Dantor's gonna kick his ass! He's the one that needs to be worried about her fierceness, not the person working with her.

Since she ended her human relationship, Suzette has chosen to remain single. She reports, "He [her former partner] kinda did me in. I wanted to take a break, and I started focusing on other things. I really haven't had time [for a relationship]." We talk about what it would be like for Suzette to get involved in another relationship, now that she is married to the Baron. Suzette observes that she thinks part of the reason she hasn't found another partner is that the Baron is very picky and doesn't want her involved with just anyone. Suzette elaborates, "He did tell me, 'You're gonna be set when you die because you're gonna be a baroness!' So maybe he thinks somebody has to be baron-worthy." She goes on to explain that she had a lover at one point, but after a few months, apropos of nothing, she found herself completely repulsed by him. Suzette says, "I think that it was him [the Baron] stepping in and saying, 'This guy ain't right for you. This guy has nothing to offer you.' And he was right—he didn't."

I ask Suzette whether she has ever asked the Baron to bring someone into her life. It seems to me that if there are specific requests that he can make of her in their relationship, this might be the kind of thing she can ask his help with. She admits that she has been focusing on other things in her life and has not really wanted a relationship. She ponders the question a bit, though, and then adds, "Maybe I'm here doing this interview because that's something I didn't even think of, and maybe that'll help me manifest, or help something unfold that I want."

I next wanted to know whether Suzette's relationship with the Baron is ever erotic. She says it is, and that he primarily shows up for her that way in dreams. However, he also has a way of warding off unwanted men in her life.

I don't really feel him around me if there's a man around me. I think he kinda backs off a little bit. But, then again, with certain men I can feel. . . . You know how sometimes you can feel a magnetic connection with somebody? And then when you put the wrong ends of the magnet together, they [move] apart? That's how I feel with some men that are trying to get too close. And I think that's kind of him stepping in, [saying] this guy's not right.

REQUIREMENTS AND BENEFITS

I was curious about the requirements and benefits of Suzette's marriage to the Baron. Suzette underscored the importance of leaving offerings for the spirits; how important this is in developing a relationship with them. Suzette said she leaves offerings for both the Baron and Maman Brigette daily. She puts out alcohol, food offerings, and other small objects she thinks the Baron and her other spirits would like.

I asked Suzette whether there are things that she has asked for, or that the Baron has given her as a result of her devotion to him. She said that many traditions teach that different spirits are to be appealed to for different things. Some spirits provide money, some love, some luck, some protection. However, what Suzette found is that Baron Samedi can provide all these, and so she does not have to appeal to other spirits for her needs. "Whenever I want something, or something's happening to my life, I ask him to help me, and he usually pulls through. Whether it's a financial crisis, an emotional crisis, my pet got lost, whatever, he always comes through."

During Hurricane Katrina, for example, Suzette stayed in her home and didn't evacuate. She had known that where she lived, she was not in any imminent danger, and the Baron had told her she was going to be okay. Her boyfriend at the time did not have the same faith, and as a result he panicked and drove his car into deep water where it sank. Suzette and her menagerie of pets came through the crisis just fine: no one was hurt and nothing was lost. She attributed this to the Baron's protection and guidance. She elaborates: "I knew my spirits. I had no doubt in my mind that I was going to be okay. And I know that when it's my time to cross over he's gonna be there waiting. Baron's gonna be there to take my hand and walk me through with him."

In addition to guidance and protection, Suzette said marriage to a spirit gives her a deeper connection with the spirit world in general.

One of the benefits of being married to a spirit is to know they do have your back and they're gonna watch out for you. If you ask them for something—I mean, of course you can't ask them for silly, superficial, unreasonable things like "Can I win the three-million-dollar Lotto?" They're gonna go, "What the hell's wrong with you? No." But whenever I wanna connect, I know I can connect with him. Whenever I wanna work with the dead I know I can ask him to help me strengthen that bond. I don't fear them, and a lot of people do. People who don't work with the dead are like, "Oh God, I'll die if I see a ghost!" It's like, "Why? Why are you so scared of them? If it's your own family, why would you be afraid to see your grandmother again? Would she hurt you in your real life? No. Then why would she hurt you now?" Of course, if it was an abusive parent or something, then you wouldn't want to talk with them.

Suzette suggested that being married to a spirit is not all that different from being married to a human. You are in a relationship with a *someone*. You are married to a person, a consciousness, except they are not in a physical body. You cultivate a relationship with your spirit-spouse just like you would a relationship with a physical spouse. You talk to them every day, not just once a week on a "special" day. You carry out a daily ongoing dialogue in which you share your hopes, dreams, fears, and concerns.

I shared with Suzette my belief that we season ourselves with the relationships we develop in life, and spirit relationships are no different. We bring things to them; they bring things to us. We become more of who we truly are by being in relationship with someone else, and we are given greater access to the realms of spirit and expanded consciousness by seasoning ourselves with spirit marriage.

Considering Suzette's confidence in the middle of the Katrina crisis, I wondered how she learned discernment. How does she balance feeling empowered and protected in her spirit marriage while also not taking unnecessary risks? I imagined that some people may seek a spirit marriage to escape life's challenges or difficulties, thinking that if they are married to a protector spirit, nothing bad can happen to them. Suzette insisted that this is simply not the case. One does not enter into a spirit marriage to avoid the bad things in life. We must still go through the usual challenges of human life, as well as the ordinary day-to-day living, all in service to our growth and evolution as humans. Her marriage to the Baron has given her confidence that no matter what she faces, she will be okay, but that does not mean she will not face challenges. Spirit marriage does not take away the job of being human and doing human things.

We still have to go through the trials and tribulations of being a human, so that way maybe we can be more of an elevated spirit. Everybody's got to pay their dues, you know? . . . I know I'll make it through, but there might be hot coals to walk on. In the long run, I'll be okay. . . . It's an ebb and a tide, like the waters. We come from the water. There's gonna be a tsunami now and then. There's gonna be an ebb and a tide, nothing's even even-keeled. So maybe they need to strengthen me by making me go through this first [to] open my eyes about something and make me more aware. But they're gonna pull me out of it in the long run, even though I have to work. They're not going to give me a cakewalk, and nothing's a free ride.

That said, Loa are known to be helpful intercessors in their devotees' lives. Suzette describes how her friend, the maid of honor at her wedding to the Baron, had some family members with serious health issues. Because the Ghede also rule the realm of healing, Suzette asked the Baron if he would help them.

A friend of mine came to the Day of the Dead ceremony with her mother. Her mother has major health issues, was facing knee surgery, and could barely walk. She came to the ceremony and I was like, "Are you sure? We have to walk eight blocks to a cemetery." And Baron Samedi came through that night, and I said, "Baron, she's having issues with her health," and so was her brother. He had had a heart attack at twenty-three and had something else wrong that wouldn't heal. And I said, "I need some help for my friends." He kissed me and said, "You know you're the one I can't deny anything to!" So he went and did a little somethin'-somethin.' Her brother got a clean bill of health, and her mother walked to and from the cemetery, and she didn't even limp.

RISKS

I asked Suzette whether she feels there is any risk in marrying a spirit. She astutely remarked: "There are risks in any relationship, but I don't feel that this is a normal relationship. You're with a divine being, so what's the risk?" I pressed the question, citing that I've heard the rumor in Voodoo circles that if a spirit proposes marriage and you do not accept the proposal, they may make life difficult for you until you acquiesce.

Suzette responded with certitude:

I don't believe that. They know sometimes that we're incapable of doing things [such as producing a wedding] because of lack of income or because lack of means. . . . [If you feel worried about this], [t]hat's your own guilt coming out. I think it's a manifestation of your own guilt that [you feel] you're not doing this fast enough. I don't believe the spirits are going to smack you on the wrist and say, "You didn't do exactly what I say!" They know that everything's gotta be a journey for you, and it's gonna happen when you can make it happen and when you're ready. You wouldn't want to meet at fifteen and get married. No. You need to be prepared to be married. Even if you meet the love of your life at fifteen, you're not gonna get married until maybe twenty-one.

I don't think the Loa would do that [make life difficult for one who does not marry them right away]. I think that's a manifestation of your own anxiousness and guilt. It's the human aspect coming out of it. . . . It's almost like the Greek Gods. The Greeks blamed everything on them [being] petty or jealous. . . . It's a fear factor, a fear control. "This is what's gonna happen if you don't do this." But that's a human aspect in there. That's not the Divine. . . . Like [the idea that] if you don't get baptized, you'll never get to heaven, and all this kind of BS that goes along with it. That's a human aspect.

That's not a divine creature who is supposed to be embracing and loving.

I think that sometimes you cause your own bad luck. Sometimes you cause your own misery. And if you were asked to marry, and people think that it's gotta happen today? People today are always in a rush! So unless the Loa give you a specific date, like mine did, it has to be this Day of the Dead. . . . One year for us is a minute for them. Or ten years for us is a minute for them, you know? Unless they put a time frame on it, people are just manifesting and saying it's the Loa. . . . [Then] you gotta wonder if this is really the actual spirit that's asking you to marry. It might be a hoax.

I am struck by how similar this pattern is in many religions—of using fear of punishment or being ostracized to ensure submission. Suzette agreed: "If you don't do this, they're gonna smack you down. If you do this, they're coming to get you."

This topic of motivation for marrying a spirit felt like a key part of our inquiry together and it caused me to lean into the question of the practitioner's reasons for wedding a spirit. Is the purpose of marrying a spirit to make demands for something you want, such as petitioning God, "Please, make my life better! Please, give me a house, a car, a partner, a million dollars!" Or are you stepping into a spirit marriage to be more empowered, to be full of the Spirit (literally), and to bring that energy forth into your life and into the world? To me the latter seems a more empowering and cocreative way to understand this practice. One does not marry a spirit to improve one's physical world, although that may be a side effect of a spirit marriage. One marries a spirit to expand and enhance one's consciousness and spiritual growth.

Suzette agreed:

Everybody's got their own path and their own rate, and it's up to you, a lot of it. If you get a little divine intervention here and there, somebody to pick you up when you fall and brush off your knees and put a Band-Aid on the boo-boo, then that's great. . . . When you're a baby and you're first learning to walk, Mama couldn't stand there and hold you or you'd never learn to walk. She had to let you fall down and scrape your knee or bust your head on the sofa. As long as you weren't walking off the second story of a balcony, you know?!

Perhaps due to the constant vilification of Voodoo in movies and the media, I was still left with a question about the alleged dangers of serving a Voodoo spirit. I had heard tell of spirits that are called *rada*, gentle spirits, and *petwo*, fierce spirits. These labels seemed to contradict what Suzette was describing, so I was curious about where these distinctions have come from and whether they factored into her experience at all. Suzette explained that the terms *rada* and *petwo* are unique to Haitian Vodou and are not really used in New Orleans.

Petwo [is a term that came from] the Congo, which is where the Ghedes are from. The Haitians made a more modern aspect to that and called [some Loa] the petwo, and those have some revolutionary warriors. Of course, they're fierce, because they were fighting wars for the oppressed people! So they are considered fiery spirits. But they're actually being kind to the poor by trying to free them.

You play with matches, you're not careful, you're gonna get burned. I don't believe they are any less nurturing. . . . They're protective, and they'll do what it takes to protect you. They will protect you and take care of you and they will not let somebody hurt you. They're taking care of your own. Why would you be that fearsome to people if you're fighting for the oppressed? . . . A general in the army whose town has been obliterated. . . . Is he gonna turn around and stab somebody in his own community in the chest because they didn't honor them properly? That doesn't make sense to me.

Suzette contends that the key is approaching these fierce protector deities with respect and humility. You must develop a relationship with them, show them your authenticity and reverence, before you can approach them for assistance.

You and I don't know each other that well, but you wouldn't come up to me and say, "Give me five dollars, I need it." You would say, "If you don't mind, could you please lend me five dollars? I left my purse, and I'm really hungry." And I would give it to you. But if you come up to me and say, "Give me five dollars!" I'm gonna look at you and go, "I ain't got it." You gotta show them a little respect, of course. It's earned. That's common sense and courtesy. It's also that old thing that religion is instilling fear to maintain a certain type of behavior. I think that's where that comes from.

I was struck by this last sentence for it confirmed what I had been thinking as Suzette was describing how to interact with the fierce deities. I found myself thinking, "Well, of course some religious leaders are going to say that these are dangerous deities! Because they are the powerful ones, the fierce ones, the ones that give you backbone and *cojones,* and that get shit done for you!" I told Suzette this, and she laughed and agreed, adding, "And who in their community wants everybody to have cojones? What leaders really want 'em to have that? Have their own empowerment? Then you don't need them [the leaders] anymore!"

I realized that this is one of my key findings. It has surfaced in almost every interview. *Spirit marriage makes us autonomous, powerful— our own spiritual authority.* This is an idea that is rapidly becoming one of the strongest arguments for why I believe spirit marriage was demonized and eradicated by mainstream organized religions. *Spirit marriages lead to a kind of self-sovereignty and self-governance, which require that you know yourself, claim your power, and then act in full agency for yourself and your community, regardless of what hegemonic forces may tell you. Spirit marriages can lead to audacity of spirit, spiritual transformation, and even social revolution.*

Suzette wholeheartedly agreed with my assessment:

Just like the Catholic Church doesn't want that little phrase getting out "the church is within you." Because it's about control, power, and money. And if you eliminate those three elements, you're gonna have a lot less angry spirits and ones that are fearful and ones you gotta watch out for, be careful with. If anybody's been elevated to the level of being a deity, they're an example that you follow. Why would you follow a petty, self-serving, antagonistic, step-on-you-if-you-step-one-fraction-out-of-the-line [deity]? . . . Why would you want to be a part of that pantheon? I don't.

Most of it is a control thing. It's to enlist a certain behavior of the group members, and this is why organized church sucks. . . . You get a group of five people and everything's hunky-dory, everybody feels the Spirit and is doing their service. You make it twenty people and it starts getting a little more about the ego, the ranks, and the power. And then, here it comes, you got leaders, and they don't want anybody filling their shoes. They don't like threats, so they eliminate them by making up all these frikin'-ass rules. And if you don't [follow the rules] and this spirit finds out? Beware! Then of course everybody's gonna fear that spirit.

Suzette's passion for poking holes in patriarchal, homogenized dogma, be it Catholicism or stricter forms of Vodou, is inspiring. I found myself wanting to jump up, cheer, and add a volley of new ideas that arose as she spoke. Yet I realized that to truly do justice to practitioners of subaltern spirituality, I needed to slow down and remain quiet, listening more carefully as she spoke from inside her own tradition.

We need to hear these voices. We need to learn from their years of experience working in the shadow of hegemonic religions. We need to allow them to tell us how best to undertake a dialogue of inclusivity and cocreation.

HAITIAN VODOU VERSUS NEW ORLEANS VOODOO

Because Suzette had initiated into both Haitian Vodou and New Orleans Voodoo, I was curious about their similarities and differences. Do the practices and beliefs differ greatly? Suzette explained that originally she had initiated into the Haitian Vodou temple in New Orleans, which was the only official temple in the city at that time. However, now she and another mambo practice New Orleans Voodoo and have started their own temple.

She reports that the New Orleans tradition intermingles greatly with the Haitian tradition; many of the practices and beliefs are the same. During the Haitian Revolution (1794–1804), an influx of Haitians poured into New Orleans, bringing Vodou with them. New Orleans was already what Suzette refers to as a "gumbo pot" of Spanish, French, and Creole culture, and the Middle Passage and the Haitian Revolution added a West African influence to that mix. Therefore, New Orleans Voodoo is a mixture of African Diaspora religion, Catholicism, and indigenous spirituality.

Some spirits served in New Orleans are not served by Haitian practitioners; other spirits, while having different names in the two traditions, are basically the same entity. Finally, some spirits are the same regardless of their provenance. However, where Haitian Vodou has more of a strict set of protocols and procedures that must be followed, New Orleans practitioners have more of a laissez-faire attitude toward their practices. This laxity is largely due to the multicultural influence that is a hallmark of New Orleans culture. As I understand it, New Orleans Voodoo is focused less on the right or wrong way to do something, and more on what works—that is, whether what is done brings about results.

GENDER IDENTITY
AND SPIRIT MARRIAGE

One of the most notable differences between Haitian Vodou and New Orleans Voodoo is the gender identity of the spirits that a practitioner can marry. As I understand it, in Haitian Vodou one can only marry a spirit that is the opposite gender of one's gender identity. However, in New Orleans Voodoo, Suzette said that marrying a same-sex spirit is not a big issue. However, she admitted, she did not know anyone who is married to a same-sex spirit. Given the increasing aware-ness being brought to the transgender and nonbinary community, I am curious about how this would play out for someone who is more gender-fluid.

> *It's always been male-on-female, because some people look at a marriage as [a means] to procreate. But that's not all the marriage entails; it's a spiritual connection. It's melding with another. . . . If a spirit asks you to marry them, I don't think they're considering your gender. They're con-sidering your connection to them, what they feel about you, and creating something out of this relationship. It's not just sexual, and if it is a sexual relationship maybe it's like [for] transgender [people], [the spirit is] pro-moting their sexuality within them.*

I think back to our discussion about spirit marriage as "seasoning." I am beginning to realize how traditionally heteronormative many spirit marriage practices have been due in large part to the belief that marry-ing a spirit is about balancing your polarity. That is, if you're a woman, you need the masculine polarity to balance you out—or vice versa. But this seems to oversimplify the concept of gender identity, as well as leave out an entire population of gender-queer and gender-questioning indi-viduals. Further, gender identity is not necessarily an indicator of gen-der expression. For example, there are women who identify as women, and yet their gender expression is very masculine. It seems to me that it is the practitioners themselves who are placing restrictions upon gender dynamics in spirit marriage based on outdated ideas of marriage, gender identity, and sexuality.

I share my thoughts with Suzette and add that for a long time I had held a very strong, fierce feminine persona, my "business Megan" energy, as one partner called it. I was often referred to as a "Medusa," a "ballbuster," and a "bulldog" by friends and colleagues. Then, when I was in my mid-thirties, the love Goddesses began to show up in my life—Lakshmi, Aphrodite, Erzulie Freda (Dantor's rada sister)—and they helped connect me to a different kind of femininity. They balanced my fierceness with compassion and achievement with pleasure. Suzette said this makes perfect sense to her. The spirits tend to manifest when you need them most.

INITIATION AND THE MET TET

As part of my background research into New Orleans Voodoo while I was in New Orleans interviewing Suzette, I also interviewed the Voodoo Queen Bloody Mary. Mary is the Vodouisant who had initially spoken with me on the phone about my dream and is an expert on Voodoo in New Orleans. Mary does not herself hold a spirit marriage, but she has been proposed to by two different spirits, and she performs spirit marriages.

She explained to me that Voodoo possession is not necessarily just about a spirit entering into someone; it is perhaps more accurate to think of it as the spirit coming *out* of someone. Possession might be understood as an aspect of who someone already is, expressing through the personality of a Loa. That is, while one is possessed, the Loa comes out more fully to be seen and recognized as who one already is or could be, perhaps indicating certain aspects that the individual needs to express more fully in life. Ideally, the practitioner is bringing forth an archetypal quality that has perhaps lain dormant or subdued within until the person is ready to open more fully to its expression. I understand this kind of Voodoo possession to be one method the Divine Self, the archetypal blueprint of our most empowered Self, makes its way into embodiment. We will discuss this later in the book where we talk about *entheosis* (chapter 14), which is any kind of spiritual technique that allows an individual to access their divinity.

Mary's conceptualization of spirit possession is a different concept from the more conventional idea that spirit possession is a matter of giving over control of oneself to an outside entity. However, Mary was quick to point out that both practices are present in Voodoo ritual and in dream possession.

Mary elaborates:

A Voodoo crisis is a term for the process of this change—the in-between states of rejection and acceptance as the spirit and the flesh balance into harmony or disharmony in the Loa. Does the "horse" [human participant] want to be "ridden" [possessed]? Does he or she buck and fight or protest too much? Or is there grace and trust in the surrender? This is the internal and external gist of it. Each encounter is unique.

Although the divine archetypes are within all of us, and we are a part of them, Mary made it clear that it is also an external spirit that takes possession of us. She describes possession as a two-way street.

When the spirits enter, they use your body and "ride the horse." You are the horse. They then enjoy the physical pleasures of food, dance, liquor, etc. You may do superhuman or unusual things during the possession, that you do not usually remember. You could give divinations and healings and such to the group. And when the spirits exit, they leave a little divine spark in you and lift you up.

To me it seems that there is a similarity between the relationship one has with the met tet and the relationship one might have in a spirit marriage. Both involve a sort of hosting in one's body, as well as an extrasensory sharing of consciousness. The differences are subtle and yet important—between expressing an innate archetypal quality that emerges from inside oneself as the met tet, and seasoning oneself with marriage to a Loa.

When I brought this up with Suzette, she elaborated more fully on the difference between the way she experiences her met tet and the way she experiences the mariage Loa. She says that she has never been possessed by the Baron: he has always interacted with her through "riding" someone else.

The met tets, however, are different:

[The met tets are] the spirits that live in your head, the ones that claim you as their child. You are part of them, too. But the marriage is a little

different for me. My met tets, I feel they're aspects of my personality. With the marriage I was chosen by somebody to share and to be part of them.

Suzette has three met tets: Erzulie Dantor, Ayizon, and Ogou San Jak. These are the spirits that were placed in her head during her initiation.

When you're initiated, it's to open your head, and that's how the met tet gets in. You pick godparents. . . . It's treated as a death, and then you're reborn. Well, one of my godparents was a priest in the temple, and I had a dream that me and my friend were outside, and we were laughing, and we wouldn't stop laughing. So he took his ason *[ceremonial rattle] and he hit me in the head with it, right on top of the head, and it broke. But all these little asons, like baby asons fully developed, came falling out. . . . He picked one up and put it in my hand, and he closed it. He said, "Plant this, and you can grow your own."*

When my dream was interpreted, I was told, "Oh, you're definitely gonna be a mambo, then." And then I was, a couple of years later. So it was about cracking. And she said, "That's what you do. You open your head."

The idea of initiation as death and rebirth is a widely recognized concept in many initiatory mystery traditions, both ancient and modern. Initiation rites the world over include the mythos of dying to a prior identity and being reborn as something new, something that is in greater connection and integration with realms beyond the ego or the mundane human personality. Through initiation one is given an opportunity to transform one's previous consciousness and transcend one's previous identity, which then gives one access and contact with extrasensory and perhaps supernatural forces.

The concept of the met tet reminds me of the Tantric ishtadevi, the idea that you have a patron deity, or a deity that you are most like. I shared with Suzette something I had noticed: when a deity calls to me from a specific pantheon, say Lakshmi in my Tantric practice, her counterparts in other traditions will also begin to call to me, in this case Erzulie Freda, Aphrodite, Mary Magdalene, and Oshun. Still, it's important to me to consider each Goddess as being distinct unto herself. For example, just because a Goddess is a Goddess of love or abundance we should not assume that all deities of love are the same entity across all traditions. These deities may have similar functions, but the expression of those functions is unique to their lineage and community.

Consider the example of a police officer: an officer in New Orleans or Dubai or Tokyo may function as someone who upholds and enforces the law, but the laws they are subject to and the ways in which they enforce the law differ from country to country. Suzette agreed and added that she believes there is a common good, a common thread, in all religions—if we look closely enough.

> *Okay, so maybe [in] one tradition they use salt, [and in] another tradition they don't because it will drive their spirits away. So when you're going to this one person's tradition, don't bring the salt! You know? Respect that you're trying to do the same thing. But [regrettably] nobody learns to work together.*

For me Suzette's reflections raise the topic of rivalries and infighting among the Loa. This concept is not unique to the Voodoo tradition; the Greek Gods and Goddesses were notoriously competitive. In Voodoo, however, the competitiveness of the Loa seems amplified, particularly in the relationship between the sisters Erzulie Dantor and Erzulie Freda. Interestingly, competitiveness is not considered to be as much of an issue between male Loa. The female deities are the ones who are said to squabble, with some practitioners going so far as to say the two Erzulies must not be honored on the same altar together. I wonder about this "catfighting" idea and whether it is perhaps a patriarchal overlay to diminish women's power in Voodoo, reinforcing negative stereotypes of women.

Suzette offered her insight:

That's supposedly how Dantor got the scratches on her face. Even if you're best friends with somebody, you're going to have a conflict once in a while. I know they say you can't put 'em on the same altar. They don't like each other, so there might be a jealousy there. But if they can't get along with each other, why would they be deities? . . . If the spirits and the Loa can't get along with each other, then how the hell do they expect humans to do it?

In response, I shared that when I first began to feel contact from the Erzulies and learned of their conflict, I had said to them both:

I feel like you're like the Madonna and the Magdalene, two sides of the same coin. So I'm going to talk to you both as such. I'll be in the middle as the intermediary if you want, and we'll all have a conversation about not only what I can bring to the table, but how I can help bridge this healing for women through being an intermediary of sorts between the light and the dark.

As a result, my research and my practice have focused on balancing the Madonna and the Whore, the Freda and the Dantor, the light and the dark.

Suzette explains that La Siren sits in between the two Erzulies and helps to balance those polarities. I am struck by this correspondence: La Siren, the mermaid, is a magical archetype that I have identified with since I was a young girl. I am starting to realize I may have more of an innate resonance with Voodoo than I'd initially anticipated.

CULTURAL APPROPRIATION VERSUS CULTURAL APPRECIATION

This realization brings up an important question for me, and a piece of the cultural shadow. Despite the fact that the Voodoo pantheon was one of the first groups of deities to begin calling to me, and one of the best documented sources on spirit marriage, I had not felt comfortable seeking out the path of Voodoo for initiation or practice because I am white. I had felt that even though these deities were calling to me, I needed to research my own ancestral lineage and traditions first. That led me to Orion Foxwood and the British traditions. However, the Loa have never really left me alone.

I shared this with Suzette: I have not wanted to adopt a tradition without first looking at the issues of white privilege, which can easily get sidestepped when one is seeking to practice a tradition that is not part of one's own cultural heritage. And yet it seems that the spirits themselves do not really care what race their servitors are, so long as spirits are being honored.

Suzette agreed:

I think they're getting fed up with it. I think they're all just stepping in now and saying, "You know what? You all have been on your own a little bit, and we see you can't handle it. You all have fucked everything up, and now we gotta step in." . . . *Show me a tradition on this planet that isn't an appropriation of something else.*

I told Suzette about a similar conversation I'd had with a friend who owns a metaphysical shop. She told me that a white woman had recently come into her shop and asked whether there was a deity named Oshun. She had been having recurring dreams about an African woman named Oshun. Similarly, an African American woman had come into the shop and asked whether there was a deity named "Bridgit." She had been having dreams about a white woman named Bridgit.* My friend believes that the deities are fed up with our isolation and separation, and are calling to people across ethnicity, race, and pantheons for more inclusivity and cross-pollination. When people are being contacted by these spirits and are asked for intimate relationships, whether marriage or another kind of deeply bonded relationship, perhaps this is the way in

---

*Oshun is the Yoruba Goddess of love; Bridgit, the Celtic Goddess of creativity and inspiration.

which the spirits are moving us toward a more cross-cultural dialogue.

That being said, the issue of cultural appropriation is just that, a cultural issue, not a spiritual one. The spirits might be fine with working with a variety of people, however humans are the ones who have to deal with the repercussions of their tradition being co-opted and hijacked by people seeking to profit off of it.

Writer and publisher Lauren Panepinto puts it this way:

> Cultures adopt aspects of each other all the time. This is fine when both cultures are exchanging equally—called "Cultural Exchange"—but if there is a power imbalance between the cultures then it is not an equal exchange. If a minority culture is adopting aspects of a dominant or colonizing culture in order to fit in or survive oppression then it's called "Cultural Assimilation." If it is a dominant or majority culture taking aspects of the minority culture and taking them out of context of that culture and profiting by them in some way the original culture is not free to do, then it's called "Cultural Appropriation."[1]

Therefore, when one begins to work with spirits from a subaltern, or minority, culture—really any culture that is not one's own—it's a good idea to assess your motivation for the work. Are the spirits calling you for a personal relationship that you will practice privately? Or are you seeking an initiatory path in a tradition that you may someday practice publicly? As in Caroline's story, she knew that public practice was out of the question for her relationship with some deities, given the complex cultural and religious issues surrounding them. However, seeking training or even initiation in a subaltern tradition is also a way of honoring and serving those communities. This is provided, however, that one enters with an attitude of respect, humility, and service, not seeking to profit from what is learned at the expense of the originating community. Giving back to the community equal to or even more than one gets is key. As Madrone shared in her story, it's important to keep a close connection with the originating culture, in her case Burkina Faso, where part of the proceeds from the work they do in the United States goes back to the African Dagara community.

In a sense, the spirits are reaching out across race and religious lines to season humanity with more tolerance and open-mindedness, as well as courage and self-authority. The blending of traditions is something that the New Orleans community has quite a bit of experience with and has seemingly done very well. And yet, these successes do not diminish or negate the fact that racism and white privilege persist in our culture, causing deep trauma in nonwhite and subaltern communities. I ask Suzette what she thinks can be done to address the trauma as well as the issue of cultural appropriation as we work toward inter-religious dialogue and inclusivity.

> *What you can do is have a healing ceremony for healing for 'em and invite 'em. That way you merge the two, and they see that not everybody's out to freakin' get 'em. [And you would say:] "This is something that needs to be done. It's come to our attention that there's an enormous amount of healing that needs to happen, and we'd like to take the first step by having a ceremony in our culture. [We] invite you to join it and focus on our common ground." Maybe it won't solve the problem [altogether], but for today it will, just for these few hours it will.*

It seems that cross-cultural conversation is also what the spirits are calling for; part of the reason that they are showing up to people of different races. This observation feels like another important theme arising out of Suzette's interview: by showing up to humans who do not carry ancestral blood ties to their lineage, the Loa and other pantheons are urging us toward greater transcultural understanding, advocacy, and tolerance. Alongside the powerful work of social justice and restitution, we must also cultivate a broader dialogue among various spiritual traditions so that we may better hear the voices of marginalized religions and groups.

SERVICE TO THE COMMUNITY

As we finished up, I asked Suzette how she sees her role in relationship to her community. How does her role as a mambo impact her work in the world? Suzette observed that as a cemetery tour guide, she is constantly on the lookout for spirits. She takes her groups into the forest, opens the gates, and invites the spirits to visit. The dead are around her constantly in her work. She said that because she feels so at home with the dead, in a way, it is as if she's working from home.

Suzette said that her temple is very small, just herself and one other ordained priestess, but they hold ceremonies with a little group of regular attendees. The other practitioners she knows are primarily in the Haitian tradition. Unfortunately, she has had some discouraging experiences with that community, so she tends to steer clear of other temples.

I was curious about this and asked her whether the Loa keep their practitioners' egos in check. Suzette said she wonders about that as well. It seemed to her that sometimes the Loa do not seem to care what their servitors are doing, so long as the Loa themselves are getting fed. In those cases she also questions whether the Loa are actually being contacted, or whether the practitioner is simply "riding their own luck," using their own energy and power to manifest something and crediting it to the Loa. Suzette concludes: "I always feel that something will happen and they'll get hit with a reality check. Maybe not for a while, but you know, give a person enough rope . . . "

I believe that even though Suzette is not necessarily bringing her tour groups into an official ritual, she is still serving as a mambo on her tours. People go on a tour thinking that they are just coming to learn about New Orleans or Voodoo, but what she in fact offers them is authentic contact with the dead.

We do a little bit of ritualistic type things to invite the spirits. If anything, we make them aware that it's not anything they need to be scared of anymore. . . . It teaches them, and they go home with some kind of an

education and experience. . . . We're feeding the dead [too], and actu-
ally connecting with other realms as well, not just the dead people, but
ancestral spirits.

Ultimately, Suzette hopes that the people attending her tours realize that the dead are easy to reach out to. If someone never thought they could have a relationship with their ancestors, perhaps Suzette's cemetery tours create an opening, a moment of possibility, where they are invited to consider that the dead are not so far away from us after all. I feel the power and the importance of this work. Even if she is just planting seeds in the form of fun and play, the opening is nevertheless created.

Mainstream Western religion offers very little to train or guide us in how to connect with and heal our ancestors and beloved dead, and yet we are increasingly finding epigenetic evidence that we need to do just that. We carry forward both the trauma and the brilliance of our ancestors, whether we are aware of their influences or not. To paraphrase the Iroquois Great Law of Peace, when we heal ourselves, we heal seven generations into the future. I would add that this healing happens multidimensionally, effectively healing seven generations into the past as well.

Suzette's service as a guide and mambo is one way that she is demystifying and normalizing the sometimes daunting world of the afterlife. Suzette's work also helps to bring healing to the ancestors, by listening to what they need and helping them settle their affairs. Our ancestors are waiting alongside a host of other welcoming beings to let us know that they want a relationship with us.

Suzette agreed, and added a closing thought:

When you're working with spirits, it's very personal. Because I say it
works this way for me, it's not necessarily somebody else's journey. They
don't have the same things to work on, or to do, or accomplish that I do.
It's just very personal. I don't think the spirits are that rules[-based] and
regulated. That's a human concept, ways of interpretation and teach-
ing that were passed down. They're kinda free spirited, pardon the pun.

'Cause I've always been a free spirit, that's my take on it. I'm not as worried about rules or pleasing. . . . I just know that when I do my best to serve them and to work with them, and I do that in daily life, even [in] my job. . . . I think they're happy. And if I hit a bump, it's not because I displeased them; it's because I need more seasoning.

I find Suzette's approach to Voodoo truly refreshing. She uses the tools it gives her for self-empowerment, and she accepts total personal responsibility for her path in life. Her marriage is one that teaches her to listen to the voices of the dead, look for opportunities to serve and heal, and ultimately teach others to stand in their own agency and sovereignty to do the same. Suzette's marriage to Baron Samedi has made her an empowered, independent woman and a sensitive and effective mambo.

10
The Haitian Vodou Practitioners

*T*he interview I did with Suzette turned out to be the most thorough and extensive interview regarding spirit marriage in the Vodou/Voodoo traditions that I conducted. Given that she is an initiate in both the Haitian and New Orleans traditions, it made the most sense to include her story as my primary resource on Vodou/Voodoo. However, in this section I include outstanding and unique aspects from the three other Haitian-initiated practitioners' stories, insomuch as they add further elucidation and clarification of the experience and practice of the mariage Loa.

THE LOUISIANA ARTIST AND HOUNGAN

Henri is an initiated *houngan asogwe* (Vodou priest) in the Haitian Tradition, a writer, filmmaker, and community college professor of sociology in Baton Rouge, Louisiana. Our interview took place during my trip to New Orleans.

Henri's story is unique in that not only is he married to two Loa—Erzulie Freda and Erzulie Dantor—but also to a beloved ancestor, the celebrated experimental filmmaker Maya Deren, who died in 1961.

Henri did not know Maya in life, but her spirit made contact with him while he was working on a documentary film about Vodou. Maya herself had made a groundbreaking documentary film about Haitian Vodou, *Divine Horsemen: The Living Gods of Haiti.* In it, she was allowed rare access to film Vodou ritual and possession. Henri explains that because Maya was an artist, she was given access to the Vodou community in ways that anthropologists are never allowed, stating: "There's that Haitian proverb that says, 'When the anthropologist arrives the Loa leave.' . . . Artists get access where scientists never will."

Maya quickly became a guiding influence on Henri's art and writing, showing up in Henri's dreams and in other numinous encounters. Eventually, under the guidance of his teacher and mentor, mambo Sallie Ann Glassman, Henri was able to deepen his relationship with Maya through the mariage Loa. I find their marriage noteworthy insomuch as Henri is married to someone who is not only an ancestor but was also a public figure. According to my research, this seems out of the norm for Vodou practitioners who typically marry Loa, although perhaps not all that different from Suzette's marriage to a Ghede.

I asked Henri what he's noticed about his work as an artist and writer since having gone through the marriage with Maya. His response was matter-of-fact: "How does your spouse in any relationship effect your art?" Henri reported that being married to Maya has given him greater clarity and intentionality in his art. His work has taken on a new sense of purpose and drive as a result of their marriage.

Before the marriages happened, I didn't have direction, so it was very sloppy and a little bit more ego driven. Good intentions, perhaps, but that doesn't really get you too far. . . . [Now] I write about the things that I write about because there's a bigger picture. . . . For Maya it was about art and artistry, because I'm an artist, I'm a writer, and I was making a film. It was about partnership and growing as an artist. It certainly is a symbiotic relationship. I don't think that's specific to what I do because I think that all art, especially good art, is infused with Spirit. It's a walk with divinity, whether the artist chooses to recognize that or not. It's just with what I do, it's recognized and it's intentional. Too many artists, it seems—and I say too many because we're so despiritualized as a people—too many tap into that flow of energy by mistake and aren't really sure what the hell they're doing. They're just like, "Oh good, I had a lucky day." There's nothing wrong with that; I just think there's a difference. One is about longevity and a bigger picture, and the other is about a flash in the pan.

Henri's marriage to Maya bridged a huge gap for him in his art, so much so that he never finished the documentary film but went on to create other works inspired by this new relationship. Years later, Henri would also marry the Vodou Loa Erzulie Freda and Erzulie Dantor, the archetypal Goddesses of love and protection. "So that's what I write about," he explains: "Love is the only correct response to everything. So therefore it's probably the most difficult response, most times. But it's the only right response."

Henri also observed that the Vodou community in Haiti is traditionally not very open and accepting of homosexuality. Likewise, the American South is notoriously closed-minded.

In Haiti it's a little more complex with gay men who practice, because I don't think that gay men are looked on that well, just culturally. Then you have a gay man who follows the calling of the Loa and eventually takes up the ason, and at that point there's a degree of respect in the community that they never had before. As a gay man chosen by Erzulie—she has a special place in her heart for gay men—part of that whole process is marriage. . . . Gay men aren't really accepted until they take the ason, and then the marriage is with Freda and Dantor. . . . Being a gay houngan in the South can be a challenge socially, because the South in general struggles with acceptance of both Vodou and homosexuality—but the [wider] Vodou community in the US does not have these issues.

In addition to artistic inspiration, his marriages have also given Henri the opportunity to demystify Vodou for his community through his work as a professor. Henri regularly teaches a module on Vodou in his sociology classes, seeking to debunk common misconceptions about Vodou. Henri claimed that he has his work cut out for him, as many of his students grew up in the Baptist Church and often come to class with preconceived ideas about Vodou as demonic and evil. These views are largely shaped by television shows like *American Horror Story,* a popular horror show that sensationalized New Orleans Voodoo and magic. Nonetheless, Henri's position as artist and teacher gives him a unique platform to reach audiences that would not normally be exposed to Vodou or its practices.

I asked Henri if there is anything that he asks of his Loa wives. He quipped that he probably asks too much of them, particularly after Hurricane Katrina.

Since Katrina my worldview has changed dramatically. The way I oper-ate in my life and my relationship to [New Orleans and to this country] has changed dramatically. Everything. It's been a complete 360. Since then, my relationship with the Loa, especially with Maya and Freda and Dantor, has grown exponentially, because I can count on them. I can't count on my friends or my family, and I can't count on all the agencies that are set up to help us out. I know that from experience, very inti-mately, and they [the Loa] have never let me down.

I feel the potency of this statement. There is a kind of liberation spirituality that seems integral to Vodou practice and belief. There is a way in which, as Suzette and I explored in our interview, the accessibil-ity of personal sovereignty and power is innately a part of the Vodou experience, at least for Suzette and Henri. When the structures around us fail or are actively oppressing us, appealing to spirits or energies that feel bigger than the dominating culture, which we believe have more force and power than human structures, can be a radical act of life-affirming sanity.

In closing, Henri shared a poignant piece of how his marriage to the Loa and his work as a houngan and artist serves the greater good.

My art is how I serve my community. The art that the Loa and I do together is how I serve the community. I write about the Southern gay experience. I write about a population of gay men that are the products of genocide. I write about religious bigotry. I write about men who think other men are disposable because they're operating out of fear. Those are all important things that I navigate and put in the work that the Loa and I do.

I find Henri's perspective on cocreation with the Divine through the medium of art truly inspiring; it is also an ancient concept. Harkening back to the cultures and moments in history wherein all art was sacred art, Henri's experience seems to be an excellent example of the deep and profound potential for conscious, ritualized relationship with one's spirit-spouse as tutelary spirit and muse.

THE BROOKLYN HEREDITARY MAMBOS

Nanette and Monique are third- and fourth-generation Haitian mambos who live in Brooklyn, New York. Nanette was born in Haiti and moved to the United States with her mother—a prominent Haitian mambo—when she was a child. Monique is her daughter. Monique and Nanette are females in their thirties and sixties, respectively, of Haitian descent. I traveled to Brooklyn to interview both of them in person. The interviews took place in their home, which was filled with people coming and going, including neighbors, family members, and lots of children.

Monique, a fourth-generation mambo, was born into Vodou. From the moment she came into the world, the Loa were waiting for her. In fact, at her birth the Vodou Loa Papa Ogou possessed her grandmother, pushed the doctor out of the way, and delivered the baby. Not long after, Papa Ghede stepped in and announced to the delivery room, "That's my wife!" Monique says that every time she hears this story of her birth, she thinks to herself, "I can't believe what the poor doctors were thinking!"

By the time Monique was a teenager she had gone through her first mariage Loa.

Monique reports that she is married to three spirits: Papa Ogou, a Ghede, and Papa Damballah. Her husband, a houngan, is married to Erzulie Dantor and Erzulie Freda. Traditionally it's required to reserve one night a week for a spirit-spouse. This would mean that Monique and her husband would only be able to sleep in the same bed two nights a week, an arrangement that they were not happy about. So they went to the spirits and negotiated. They agreed that they would set aside the first week of the month for their spirit-spouses and spend the remaining time together. This arrangement seems to keep everyone happy. However, it is not always that easy. Sometimes the spirits get jealous.

My husband, he plays the drums. One day he went to a party, and I guess he must have taken his [spirit wedding] rings off, put them in his pocket, and lost the rings. But we always said, "We'll get 'em, we'll buy them [replacements]." Never got a chance to. Now every time we go to the ceremony when one of the ladies [Freda or Dantor] come, they're, "Where's my ring?" They don't even want to talk to him. They're very upset. Dantor even tried to cut off his finger one day. . . . Then I noticed that me and him started to have problems. Started arguing more. We argued over a gallon of milk one day! And then I sat down, and I thought about it, and I said, "You know what? There's friction for no reason. It has to be the spirits." Got a reading. That's exactly what happened. Bought his rings, now we just have to get them blessed. I guess he has to do his ceremony all over again. So I notice that it causes friction, and sometimes on Thursdays I just tell him, "Listen, I don't want your wife to come and beat me up. You stay on your side [of the bed], I'll stay on my side."

Given the fact that being married to one spirit, let alone three, seems like a lot of work, I asked Monique if she finds being married to a houngan easier or more complex for her spirit marriages. It seems to me that, aside from the dizzying scheduling task, being married to a fellow Vodouisant might make spiritual practice much easier, given that they both understand the requirements and general terrain of the mariage Loa.

Monique agreed:

> I've dated other people, and it was always [a] conflict, it was always a problem. I've known my husband for over twenty years. . . . He's been in the tradition longer than me, and he understands more. He knows a lot more than I do. I guess we have some type of great understanding. . . . I can go, like, "Tomas, I had this dream." But I can't do that with some-one who is not a practitioner. Or some days I wake up and I say, "I'm just gonna stay in my prayers today. I'm gonna speak to my Loa." And he understands, and he does the same thing too sometimes. So it's actually awesome that we're both [practitioners]. I think I was meant to marry someone that was in the tradition.

Monique and her husband also came to their human marriage with all their Loa marriages already having been performed. And so they brought their various spirits with them, which Monique said makes a huge difference. I was curious: Given that the mariage Loa is a common Vodou practice, and many Vodouisants marry the same spirit, does jealousy ever arise between practitioners and their spirit-spouses? Do people try to lay claim to the spirits or try to cause friction between spirit-spouses?

Monique said it depends:

> There's not jealousy or anything. We can go to a party where there's ten different people who have [the Loa] Ogou, you know. Between me and my friends we joke around. Like some of my friends that are mambos, and I'm like, "Hey, leave my [spirit] husband alone!" Last year my husband played at a party and [the Haitian Loa] Cousin was there. He came, showed up, and my friend is married to Cousin, so he was going around showing everybody, like, "See, that's my wife!" And I said, "What about me?" And he said, "Where's your ring?" And I was like,

*"Oh my God, you broke my heart!" Just joking around. So . . . I guess it
depends on who it is. [But] me and my friends, we joke about it: "Stop
stealing my husband!"*

Monique observed that typically the human partners are so happy
to see their spirit-spouse that the various spouses feel a sense of camara-
derie when the Loa shows up. I asked Monique how the Loa typically
show up for her. She described how they may appear in a dream or as a
possession. Or she can simply be sitting in a room with her mother or
grandmother, and the spirit will come in and speak to her. Sometimes
the spirits even show up in vision. Often, if Monique wants to cultivate a specific contact before bed, she will set up a white sheet on the
floor, place a candle and a bottle of rum on it, and speak to them before
she goes to sleep. They will then come to her in a dream that night.
However, even when the Loa visit, it is up to the Vodouisant to interpret the dream, which sometimes is not a straightforward task.

Monique illustrated this with a story:

*My husband's dad is a houngan. Every year I throw a huge party for the
Loa, and this was two years ago. I wanted to have a party [for the Loa],
but I told everyone I didn't have money to buy refreshments, to buy certain stuff. So I'm sitting here scratching my head: "What am I going to
do? I don't know what to do." So, stress. I sat down and I had a dream.
I had a dream that I was at a restaurant that had a bar. I was having
dinner with someone, and I didn't know who it was. I looked at the bar,
and I saw [my husband's] dad sitting at the bar. I was like, "Papa, why
you over there? Come over here and sit with us." And he says, "I'm not
talking to you." And I'm like, "Why aren't you talking to me?"*

*He goes, "Every time you ask for me, every time I come see you, you
don't pay me any mind." And I was like, "What are you talking about?"
And I woke up.*

*So when I woke up from the dream, I know my husband's dad, I
always associate him with the Ghede because anytime he does work and
stuff, most of the time, he calls the Ghede to do the work for him. So I*

said, "Oh, maybe it's his Ghede that are trying to tell me something." Because I do have a lot of dreams. Sometimes I have five, six, seven dreams a night. I'll wake up and I won't remember. I said, "Well, if it's the Ghede trying to tell me something, he needs to explain to me what he's trying to say, 'cause I probably won't even remember this dream in the morning!"

I went back to sleep, and [his Ghede] stood up in front of me. He gave me a number, four digits, and I jumped up out of my sleep! I said, "I have to write it down 'cause I'm not going to remember." I got a pen and paper, I wrote down the number, and I said, "Listen" ('cause you know I tend to forget my dreams, I tend to forget everything), "if this is a number you're giving me, let me know." . . . I closed my eyes, lay back down, and heard him in my ear. He gave me the same four digits again. And I jumped up again, and I felt his presence in the room.

I got nervous. I woke up my husband and said, "Oh my gosh, this is what just happened!" And he said, "Well, play the number." I played the [lottery] number. I think that was a Friday. I played it Saturday, Sunday, Monday, Tuesday, Wednesday, Thursday, never came out. That Friday I went to go play the number, I don't know what happened, I ended up not playing the number. It came out straight. Straight! I sat there, and I just cried, "Oh my goodness!"

My party was the following Saturday, and his dad flew in from Haiti to come, and when the party's going on the spirit came, and he says, "What is wrong with you? I just wanna beat you!"

I said, "No, I wanna beat myself!"

He says, "You know I'm a Ghede, and I'm a spirit of death, I'm a mort, and I gave you the number. You know the two days, Monday and Friday, are the day of the dead. Why didn't you play it on Friday? I'm done with you. I just wanna beat you!" So, you know, they do stuff for you; you just have to understand.

I find this story somehow comforting. To know that even someone who has been raised from the moment of birth to cultivate a relationship with the spirits—to hear them, know them, love them, and honor them—can still miss major messages from beyond makes me feel a little bit better about my resistances, insecurities, and sometimes plain old thick-headedness when it comes to hearing and interpreting the subtle signs of spirit contact. Developing one's subtle senses is an art that is evolved over one's entire life.

Monique's mother, Nanette, came into the room and told Monique she needed to attend to some leaky plumbing, so I asked Nanette my same set of questions. Not surprisingly, her answers were not all that different from Monique's. These women have been raised in a household of strong female spiritual leadership, and although at times they may have both resisted that calling, each in her own way, the mantle of succession is not easily avoided.

Nanette explained that when she was younger, she didn't want to be a mambo. She wanted to be an educator, a nurse. For years she avoided the call of the spirits and pursued her education, telling them she would eventually come back to them. Then one day she became very sick, so sick she was hospitalized. During this illness Nanette realized that she was avoiding her calling, that she had made promises to the spirits that she needed to keep, and that her life was going to continue to get more difficult the longer she avoided her calling. It was at this point that Nanette began to woo the spirits. She felt that because she had avoided serving them for such a long time, she needed to work extra hard to prove to them that she loved them and was going to be loyal and steadfast.

Nanette went through all the traditional preparations for becoming an initiate, and during her met tet ceremony, the snake God, Damballah, came to her and asked her to marry him. Nanette, who does not like snakes, was nonplussed. Laughing, she describes the negotiation she went through with Damballah before the marriage.

I had to marry him, [but] I told him to give me a promise. "I love you. I marry you. You my husband. [But] if you coming to see me, you don't come in snake to see me!" . . . There is two of them. There is a black [one] and a white one. So whenever he's coming to me, it always the black boy coming. Beautiful eyes, but you could see snake eyes. And he never come in snake, 'cause I say, "The day you come in snake, we divorce!" You can't marry, to divorce; it's for life. As they say, "death do us part." So he come to see me with curly hair, like an Indian boy. Good-looking. He come talk to me. Whatever I want to ask, he gives me.

Nanette went on to exclaim that at this point she has many marriages and many rings. Too many rings to fit on just ten fingers. She has worked out a system where she carries the rings on certain days, and then specifically honors each spouse during the month associated with them. In the case of Damballah, she wears his snake ring on Thursday, Wednesday, and Friday, as well as the whole month of March, Damballah's month. Nanette has snake rings, snake earrings, and a snake necklace, and throughout the entire month of March she wears her snake jewelry. Then in May, she honors her marriage to Cousin, and so on.

Both Nanette and Monique's experience of multiple marriages and the expert way in which they have negotiated to make them work for everyone, reinforce the idea that even in a highly ritualized form of spirit marriage, like Haitian Vodou, there is room for flexibility, for human needs and desires. Both Monique and Nanette have stressed how much the spirits love us. We are their children, and they want us to live happy, successful, healthy lives. Marriage to the Loa not only feeds the spirits and contributes to their worship. It also forges an unshakeable bond between human and divinity, a connection that empowers and shapes the human spouse to express greater aspects of their Self than they would be able to achieve on their own.

11

The Ceremonial Magician

*F*rater Lux[1] is a high-level initiate in the Hermetic Order of the Golden Dawn, a magical order devoted to the cultivation and study of the occult, metaphysics, and spiritual development. He has been a member of the Golden Dawn for twenty-two years and has been leading his order as *Adeptus Exemptus* for eleven. His lodge was originally founded by the respected author and occultist Israel Regardie in 1983.

I had been introduced to Frater Lux through a mutual friend several years before I formally began this research. When I began this project I reached out to him to ask whether he knew anyone who had successfully performed a ritual called the Abramelin Operation. This is a ritual designed to develop the knowledge of and conversation with a practitioner's Holy Guardian Angel (HGA) and understood as a kind of union with one's Divine Self. Based on my understanding of this ritual, I had a sense it might be a kind of spirit marriage with one's Divine Self instead of with an external entity. I wanted to pursue this inquiry, and so I went looking for people who had successfully completed the operation. When I shared my intention with Frater Lux, he confided that, in fact, he had successfully performed the ritual. He graciously agreed to tell me his story and provided greater nuance to my theory about what constitutes a spirit marriage and the art of embodying one's Divine Self.

A TECHNOLOGY FOR
SPIRITUAL AWAKENING

According to Frater Lux, most people are driven by an attempt to assuage or avoid feelings of isolation and disconnection. Humans feel disconnected from the Divine, from nature, and from each other, and so they seek relief in a variety of short-term solutions: addictive substances, distracting entertainment, even peak experiences. The search for this missing experience of connection and meaning is, in fact, a deep longing for connection to Spirit.

Frater Lux reported that in his experience, once knowledge of and conversation with the HGA is achieved, the feelings of isolation and disconnection go away, as does one's search for meaning. The goal of this process is that one has a direct and lasting experience of one's own immortal soul, after which everything else in life seems to pale in comparison.

The Western tradition is laid out right there in the Magician card [of the tarot]: one hand reaching up, one hand reaching down, and to be right at the middle of the tree. . . . What's supposed to happen at the middle of the tree is that you get the contact and . . . you will become more than human, by your own efforts. . . . But getting communication going takes a lot of effort, skill, and discipline.

The success of this undertaking begins with the cultivation of desire. You must have the fervent desire for communication with the HGA, as well as the faith that it is possible to achieve contact. Once desire is established, the next key is imagination, imagining what it will be like to have this relationship manifest. Desire and imagination set the foundation for the work that follows, which is lengthy and challenging.

Frater Lux stressed the fact that although one might begin the undertaking with the transformation of Self as the initial goal, the ultimate goal of the contact is to fully awaken not just oneself but the whole of humanity. Like cultivating a garden, this is a daily practice that takes effort and discipline.

If you were to peel back what's behind the things that are presented [in Western Hermeticism]—the ideas about ascending the Tree of Life, the ideas about alchemical transformation, the ideas about crossing the abyss—what you're really talking about is expanding your consciousness enough to experience Godhead, while at the same time maintaining your identity. . . . [Both of] which can't really happen in the same moment. How do you hang on to your marbles and stare into infinity? That's the goal, to be able to do that—and in kind of useful slices, where you can see things and bring them back into the world for everybody else.

In the Hermetic tradition, such a profound experience of the divinity of one's Self takes years of preparation. One begins by developing clarity and discernment so as to hone one's ability to differentiate between what manifests internally and what manifests externally. The Golden Dawn practices are designed to help both those with high sensitivity and those with low sensitivity develop this skill. All the foundational practices and teachings of the Golden Dawn and its various offshoots are designed to teach the initiate discernment.

If you're overwhelmed by all the stuff impinging from the outside, we can help you with that. Or if you can't get any visions, if you can't make yourself into a prophet, we can help you with that too. . . . You need a good deal of clarity and control over your perceptions, so that you're not confused about what comes from the inside and what comes from the outside. . . . This involves getting a handle on what's on the inside and what's on the outside. It's what "banishing" is. This space, right here— everything here is mine and I control what goes from the inside outside and what comes from the outside inside. That's kind of the whole of Ceremonial Magic in a nutshell.

Frater Lux explained that these foundational practices are essential in developing a core mastery within one's consciousness, namely the ability to name and identify the quality of contact one is having both within and without. He is critical of the ways in which we here in the West have mixed Eastern mysticism with Western esotericism, diluting and confusing both traditions. He believes our tendency is to syncretize everything, or to cherry-pick practices here and there, which dilutes their potency and outcome. In his opinion, practices in the West have sought to reach a unitive or peak experience without first cultivating the individual consciousness, the container, within which that experience can be contextualized and grounded. The gift of Western magic is that it trains the initiate to identify and contend with the various aspects of the ego or personality by creating a kind of map of one's own psyche as well as the collective, or morphogenetic, group mind in which one lives.

> A lot of the published material floating around today is absolutely terrible for the simple reason that we have gone and muddled up Western teachings with Eastern teachings. . . . [T]hey've removed all the discipline from magical practice. And so, of course, people can't tell what's going on. But if you were to study as people were taught a hundred years ago, you began with concentration. You began with banishing, until you could really banish, and then you moved on to divination. Divination is all about telling the difference between this and that, and what is and isn't going to happen. . . . If you don't work at that stuff and then you go for this big peak shattering experience where the personality sort of dissolves and you merge with this bigger thing, then of course you can't tell what's going on.
>
> You have to build up the strength first. . . . [Traditionally] you didn't just accept everything you saw. You banished the first thing you saw, because the first thing you see can't be what you called. There was a lot of discipline, and a lot of this has just been sort of tossed out the window in the last number of decades. People don't talk about it much anymore.

Frater Lux pointed out that many religious systems focus on transcendence, that is, on escaping the pain and suffering of the material world by practicing detachment or austerities. Contrariwise, in the Hermetic tradition one cultivates an experience of ascending the worlds via the Tree of Life, so that one can then come back down into the material world and affect change. This is the difference between being a mystic and being a magician. The magus (magician) seeks to change the conditions of the material plane by mastering the unseen forces of Creation, whereas the mystic typically seeks to simply make contact with the numinous.

In the Hermetic tradition, long before someone attempts to connect to the HGA, they are encouraged to engage in lesser kinds of astral work. As Frater Lux alluded to earlier, when one attempts to contact unseen forces, one should banish the first thing that shows up—the assumption being that until one develops skill as a magician, one does not have the ability to control what comes in. This ritual is done to help the magician develop sensitivity and control over their ritual space and visionary tools. Unfortunately, this skill has been all but lost in most mainstream schools of psychic and divinatory development.

This is so different from what's taught today. Today, you light a candle, you close your eyes, and whatever happens is good. But in the old days if something showed up that you didn't ask for you [would] say, "Look, I didn't call you, go away!"

It begins with the simplest things taught to a Neophyte. It begins with the Lesser Banishing Ritual of the Pentagram, and it begins with saying, "This is the boundary, and I control what crosses the boundary from the outside or from the inside out, I decide." . . .

Most of the system is for discernment and for crafting the experience. We all know that if you sit someone down, and you make them stop telling themselves their story about where they came from and who they are, if they can really stop, all kinds of things will happen. You want to craft what happens after the crisis, right? That's what most of this system is for.

As I listened to Frater Lux explain the concepts of banishing and discernment, I realized that the tools he was describing are essentially foundational spiritual technologies that assist any seeker in cultivating spirit contact and the indwelling of divinity. These spiritual technologies can be used to orient the human personality, the mundane consciousness, to its Divine Self, so that the ego can be permeated by expanded consciousness.

Frater Lux reported that throughout the Hermetic literature of the late nineteenth century, this process was the primary goal of the magician. Most of the work laid out in the upper levels of the Golden Dawn is all about refining this contact. Far from being the culmination of the journey, however, this achievement is simply the beginning of much deeper work as a magician. And yet, according to my research, the embodiment of one's divine consciousness is not necessarily the goal of every spirit marriage practitioner. Herein the purpose and outcome of the two spiritual technologies seem to differ.

IDENTITY OF THE HOLY GUARDIAN ANGEL

Frater Lux observes that according to MacGregor Mathers, cofounder of the Hermetic Order of the Golden Dawn, the identity of the HGA is distinct from the mundane consciousness, or ego, and what is often referred to as the Higher Self, or superego.[2] As he explains it, the ordinary, everyday "ego" personality is the part of a person that drives to work, answers the phone, pays the bills. The highest part of this mundane self overlaps with the lowest part of the Higher Self—the Higher Self being the part of a person that searches for meaning, longs to connect with something bigger than oneself, or has moments of insight or wisdom. Similarly, the highest part of the Higher Self overlaps with the lowest part of the HGA. Frater Lux also points out that Mathers made use of the term *Holy Guardian Angel,* taken from the traditional Catholic morning prayer, to designate the Divine Self, whereas newer and more accurate translations of the text use a more general, albeit gendered, term of *Sir* or *Adonai* (Lord).[3] Gender, however, does not seem to play a significant role in determining the identity of one's HGA. Frater

Lux suggests that ultimately the HGA may in fact be gender-neutral, and that in his experience it is often hard to distinguish or determine gender.

Apparently, the foundational papers of the Golden Dawn make it plain that in the minds of Mathers and his teachers the HGA is not the Higher Self, but a consciousness that transcends it. Using the language of the Kabbalah, Frater Lux describes: "The Kether of the personality touches the Malkuth of the Higher Self, and the Kether of the Higher Self touches the Malkuth of the Angel." Mathers is quite clear that we humans have a hierarchy within our consciousness and that we need this hierarchy because human beings can only confront infinity in usable chunks. According to Frater Lux, if one touches too much infinity unprepared, one ceases to be human and has difficulty functioning in the mundane world.

> The Egyptians and the Hebrews had [imagined] these different parts of the soul.* There's a part that can manifest emotions, and other people can feel it. Sometimes you can feel it even when a person is gone. I'm sure that was much more obvious centuries ago. When you lived near the desert you could come upon a place where people had died, and nobody had been there in decades; you could walk in and feel it. I bet it was much more obvious than it is now, when we're just so saturated [with input] all the time. Their thinking was that these pieces [of the soul] separate at death. The highest part would dissolve back into the Godhead, and you'd have this flotsam and jetsam of the lower parts. But if you could become an Adept, then you would take more of you with you when you go.

It should be noted that although Mathers's description of the HGA has been the accepted one for the past hundred years, among today's Hermetic magicians there is increasingly more discussion and a variety

---

*The ancient Egyptians believed the soul had many parts: the *ka* (vital spark), the *ba* (personality), the *ib* (heart), the *sheut* (shadow), and the *akh* (Divine Self). The ancient Hebrews also believed that human consciousness is separated into two parts called the *nephesh* (soul) and the *ruach* (spirit).

of differing opinions on the topic. Most of the debate seems to center on whether the HGA is actually an externalized being or whether it is, in fact, some aspect of the Higher Self.

Frater Lux was insistent that one's relationship with the HGA, unlike some practices of spirit marriage, is not an erotic one. Although he is aware of erotic contact with spirits, he holds that this should not be confused with the practice of indwelling one's own HGA, which is, in fact, more like a part of one's own Self than a separate entity.

The Golden Dawn teaches that to obtain consistent conversation with the HGA, one must first learn its name. Therefore, the main objective in the Abramelin Operation is the task of finding the name of one's Angel. There are no prescribed set of names or identities one can use to locate the HGA. The magician must find those answers for themselves. Whereas in other traditions, a senior practitioner might divine the identity for the practitioner, within the Hermetic tradition it's up to the practitioner to wrestle through the ambiguity—to develop confidence and discernment on their own.

I am struck by just how much autonomy and responsibility is placed upon the practitioner in the Hermetic tradition. It feels both liberating and overwhelming.

It took me a while to realize that, in the beginning, you get a great deal of help, and then you have to ascend [the rest of the way on your own]. That's what comes next. There was a lot of work involved. It's not enough just to reach up anymore; you have to actually climb. . . . You have to find the name. That's a big deal . . . and it [the name] could be unpronounceable. On the one hand, there's a thousand pages of occult material. It's all technical intellectual stuff that you've got to take in, that's all sort of a framework for this one thing. But it is very, very broad, and there is a lot put on the individual.

In a way that's heretical in and of itself. It's all about you. What do you see? What did you hear? What does it mean to you? For a lot of people that's a huge leap, because it's the opposite of what they've been told all their lives.

THE ABRAMELIN OPERATION

Frater Lux claims that many of the gifted people who have heavily influenced history had a force of personality or charisma that enabled them to influence humanity on a vast scale. Oftentimes, they were not particularly talented or gifted as individuals, and yet they seemed to have something extra, a *pneuma,* that others around them did not display. He goes on to muse that they may already have been very bright individuals, and yet everyone around them may also have been bright. What was their extra ingredient? He postulates that it was the presence of the HGA. Like Plato's daimon, the HGA amplifies the potential of the individual, making him or her into an exceptional being.

Frater Lux is quick to add that this kind of a relationship does not just fall into your lap because you perform certain austerities until you achieve a peak experience. One must work at building up the contact. The Abramelin Operation is one method to achieve this contact. The basic Abramelin method is thus: Over an extended period of time one withdraws from ordinary things and performs daily rituals and prayers. This process goes on for months, sometimes years, until one enters into an intense three-day magical retreat wherein a kind of peak experience is achieved, one that will forever change the aspirant. However, if the retreat is not performed correctly, or the aspirant is not properly prepared, it can fail. Failure can be a shattering experience, after all the effort and time one has invested. If the magician is successful, however, then another kind of shattering occurs, because the life of the magician is forever altered.

The journey to knowledge and conversation with the HGA theoretically begins when one takes initiation into a Hermetic order. As Frater Lux previously stated, all the techniques taught to the initiate are designed to be used in the achievement of the Great Work, the knowledge and conversation of the HGA. He explained that if the methods are internalized strongly enough, when the aspirant steps into the ritual space with its associated implements, tools, and symbols, then the discipline cultivated over time will take over and automatically quiet the mundane consciousness so that contact can be made.

Being an individual, you must find the name [of your Angel]. It's one of the tasks. . . . There's a point in the Golden Dawn grades where you kind of have to give up a certain part of your identity ritually, and that's the point in which the contact is supposed to begin. . . . At that point you begin to look for the name; knowing the name, you can call it. This can vary: You may have to get it to tell you, which means you have to get some kind of contact. And you can't get there unless you're very experienced. It's not the easiest thing to get going. Having made contact, getting some kind of ongoing relationship shouldn't be really hard. It's all very personal and depends on the way somebody's mind works, what their habits are, and what has to change . . . because things will have to change.

Although in the Abramelin text the recommended preparatory time line is eighteen months, Frater Lux prepared for his Abramelin for three years. During that time, he increasingly withdrew from the outside world, limiting his contact to the necessities of work and minimal social contact. He came home from work, performed his rituals, and didn't do much else. Then, two months before he entered the final phase of the working, he went through a structured regime of physical and psychological cleansing wherein he tried to "clear the decks" as much as possible for the three-day magical retreat. What was revealed to him during this time of cleansing was the overall framework for what he should be doing during his retreat. Once the preparatory work was complete, and he had a plan for the ritual, he was finally ready for the deeper operation.

Frater Lux says that the idea of a three-day magical ritual is that you put a pause on the normal, mundane, day-to-day consciousness, and are guided to replace that with the indwelling of this higher consciousness. He was fortunate enough to have a friend with an established temple in their home. This friend was willing to have him perform the ritual there, as well as function as his gatekeeper.

To begin the ritual, Frater Lux had to ask for what he wanted, in his own words. After that, how much of the formal Abramelin ritual he actually used depended on him, because a lot of the ritual came straight out of his own intuitive self and the preparatory work he had done.

The technique that I was taught is this: You get an alarm clock, you open up your temple, you perform some preliminary stuff and [declare] a statement of purpose, and then you go to sleep. . . . Do some ritual, sleep for an hour, get up, and do more ritual. . . . I was prepared enough that things got very interesting very early. I did a standard Golden Dawn-style opening with a statement of purpose, which I made up on the spot.

The statement of purpose alone produced all kinds of results. . . . I actually felt the lightning flash down the tree, hit me right at the base of the neck. I proceeded along, and it got really difficult, and it got frightening. And then it got absolutely amazing. . . . Part of the way into this I started having some pretty intense visions, and I'm not a person who has these kinds of things, really, very rational and all that. But before long, I began to see the things one is expected to see in this situation. I saw the Angel. We traded places. Certain symbols that one would expect to be there were there. I later saw some of the infernal beings that you're challenged by in the Abramelin Operation. This is the whole formula of Western magic. . . .

Most of the way through this, about eighty percent of the way through this, I started seeing what I thought at the time was the face of God in the smoke of the incense. It was just unbelievable. I was hearing words in the mode of the King James Bible. Some of this stuff is clearly preprogrammed. I realized a few minutes into this that I wasn't actually breathing, and I should probably start breathing. Towards the end of it, when I thought it was all over—I had completed the series of rituals I had laid out, and I had had some pretty profound experiences, I had gotten the name, and I was basically closing the temple— then the real thing happened. "Wham!" It was like a reverse kundalini experience from the top down. . . . It was this top-down cosmic orgasm that literally knocked me to the floor. . . . I was curled up on the floor in the fetal position. I had no idea that was going to happen. . . . That was thirty-six hours in. I wasn't trying to do it. It wasn't something I was trying to do; it just happened. . . . I was really not the same after that for a long time. And I really couldn't do any ritual after that for a long time.

Frater Lux pointed out that the way in which one seeks this relationship is in no way limited to the way he did it, or the way that is outlined in Abramelin. His decision to take on the work as described by the Golden Dawn and laid out in Abramelin was based on the fact that the method offers a fairly complete map, one to which he had access. He was quick to point out that it certainly is not the only map. He also added that he does not believe one needs to belong to a specific group or lineage to do this; nor do all Hermetic magicians choose to undertake the Abramelin Operation.

What appears to be key to a magician's success in this ritual is the groundwork they have laid before they attempt to connect. He cautions that one does not attempt the three-day magical retreat without a significant amount of preparation. He stressed that it is the amount of preparatory work done before the retreat that truly determines the success of the ritual. Whether the indwelling of the HGA is done symbolically at the culmination of the ritual or whether it takes place over the next months, years, or perhaps lifetimes depends on the practitioner, their fate or karma. Frater Lux postulates that perhaps the magical foundation some lay now will come to fruition in the next life: "Some people are going to get there," he suggests, "and some people are not this time around."

It seems to me that ultimately the success of the Abramelin working is not so much determined by whether one achieves knowledge and conversation with the HGA, but how much one is able to clear out the "dust bunnies of the soul," to borrow Orion Foxwood's term, and invest the time and energy into making oneself an available vehicle for the indwelling of the Divine. Divine embodiment then becomes a natural outpouring into the prepared consciousness.

BENEFITS AND RISKS

For Frater Lux, one of the benefits of contact with his HGA is the way it seemed to clear out and reprogram his needs. Habits and desires in which he had been heavily invested prior to the contact practically fell away. He reported that this experience gave him a glimpse of the fact that he is not his body, and it also stimulated his memory of events that happened before this incarnation. This contact profoundly changed his interaction with and understanding of the world.

> *There's the part of you that's going to live, and there's the part of you that's going to die. They have completely different agendas. Harmonizing the two is a big task. Until you stop fearing it, death rules everything. Most people feel very isolated. Until you have the experience of divine intimacy, that feeling drives almost everything you do. And when you don't feel it [isolation and fear of death] anymore, certain things just aren't necessary anymore.*

Frater Lux observes that in his experience another outcome of the successful Abramelin Operation is that there is no longer any way to hide things from yourself. There is nothing you can do that your HGA is not going to know; denial and self-delusion are no longer available coping strategies. For some this may be considered a benefit; for others, a risk. Frater Lux notes that the bigger risk seems to be that if you succeed at this operation, your life will never be the same. One must be prepared to let go of identities, habits, and relationships that one may have been deeply invested in. Another risk he cites is that if one does not achieve the contact, after having put perhaps years into the operation, one could potentially develop a psychological disorder from the shattering effect.

> *If you prepare enough and then jump off the cliff like that, it's not unlike the Sundance: You stop being you. You stop watching TV and running around in your head with all these stories. "I'm so-and-so, and I own all these things." You stop. When you really stop, other things take over. If you take the framework away you need to be able to replace it with a new and better framework.*

OUTCOMES

"You've just seen the face of God/dess. Now what?" For Frater Lux, the ongoing relationship with his HGA is *not* like having an invisible friend who's constantly giving a play-by-play analysis of his life. He described it more like downloads of rapid-fire information ticker taping through his head.

This does not work like Harvey sitting on the seat next to you while you're driving. But there are times that I suddenly know I have to deal with something now, or I should not leave the house today, or I definitely get information that turns out to be true, and I have no idea how it got there. I'll be wondering about something or trying to solve something, and information comes in . . . a whole bunch of things I couldn't possibly have known, and I have a head like a rock. . . . These things usually come like that, faster than I can think. . . . I did the big operation along the Abramelin lines, and after that I gradually withdrew from participating in the [Golden Dawn] group work because it just wasn't going anywhere, and nothing compared to my experience. . . . Five years later, the opportunity came to take more responsibility [in the order], but I was very on the fence about getting involved [again] with the Golden Dawn, taking a leadership position, and all that.

I asked, "Should I do this?" And the answer was not, "Yeah, you are the guy," but "You could do this, this, this, this, this, and this." The answer I got was a pile of material that took me about three months to externalize. All this work to do. Well, that's a pretty good answer. . . . I had a one-bedroom apartment at the time, and I slept in the living room because my bedroom was my temple. There was nothing in there but an altar and some this and that [paraphernalia] that one uses. After this one intense ritual, I would just walk in there and walk around the altar, and more things would come to me. This went on for months. So it took years to build up to that. It took years [of] building up to the initial contact, and then it took a bunch more work to where I was getting information, lots of it. . . . That was actually five years after the initial [Abramelin Operation].

I asked Frater Lux whether this experience changed his relationships with other people, or his interaction with the world in general. He described how the isolation he had previously felt simply went away. Having had a numinous encounter with the Divine, he stopped looking to other people, or other things, to fill that void.

> Once you've actually had this face-to-face with the Divine, you stop expecting it from other people. You kind of relax about that. Of course, there are times when I'm the same difficult child I always was, but then I get this finger in my back: "Go do this. You have to solve this problem. You have to make sure somebody understands this. It's time to start initiating people." . . . And that becomes more important than the things I would normally be chewing on, like where to find a really good brownie. Sometimes it's very difficult, because . . . I'm more qualified than some of the other people doing [this work], but I don't really feel qualified to occupy this position.

Because Frater Lux is one of the most knowledgeable Ceremonial Magicians I've met, and I've met quite a few, to hear him claim he doesn't feel qualified gives me pause. I am reminded of the Reverend Michael Beckwith's statement about Moses, who told God he could not be his prophet because he had a speech impediment. Beckwith asserts: "God doesn't call the qualified. He qualifies the called." Perhaps, similarly, our Divine Self does not call to us, does not plant the desire for this relationship because we are ready for full embodiment in that moment. Perhaps the desire is planted *so that* we will step onto the path of self-actualization, roll up our sleeves, and get to work.

Frater Lux agreed:

> There's a rabbinical joke where this rabbi is talking to God, saying, "Would you look at all this mess in the world! Why don't you send some help?" And God says, "I did—I sent you!" Seeing the problem is always part of the gig, and I can always see the problem. I got that part down.

It took Frater Lux several years to return to the Golden Dawn group ritual after the Abramelin Operation, partly because the rituals he was doing afterward were not having any effect. It was as if the power of contacting his HGA took him back to square one. He stopped trying to recreate the contact and simply went back to the basics.

This seems to be what always happens. Somebody goes to karate school. They think they're pretty tough; they advance quickly through the grades. Then they meet somebody who is really good, and they go back and do the "chop wood, carry water" again. "Daniel-san, show me sand floor. Wax on, wax off." . . . I was back to that for a couple of years. That was maybe the hardest thing. I guess this is very common. You take up something new and it's wonderful. You go through it for a while, and then it becomes very difficult. And it's not until you push through all that that you get to the real thing.

Eventually Frater Lux realized that as a magician one develops one's magical skills to create order out of chaos. Now, because of those skills, he can create purpose and meaning for both himself and others. Ultimately, his work as a Ceremonial Magician is focused on helping others navigate the journey toward self-awakening and meaning-making. "There is a sense of purpose in holding the door open for people . . . which is the most I can claim, really."

Frater Lux's humility and matter-of-fact approach to the work of divine embodiment is quite refreshing. He does this work neither for self-aggrandizement nor notoriety. In fact, when I was searching for practitioners to interview about knowledge of and conversation with the HGA, I was told that those who achieve contact do not typically divulge this information publicly, and that anyone who does publicly claim success in this regard probably has not achieved contact. The change that is wrought by authentic contact with the HGA apparently instills an attitude of humility and quiet service, of which Frater Lux is a glowing example.

12
The Erotic Mystic:
Journey to My Divine Self

*U*p to this point, you've just caught snippets of my story, nuances of my quest to understand spirit marriage and how it applies to my own spiritual journey. I've given you the broad brushstrokes of how I got *assigned* the topic of spirit marriage as a research project. I say "assigned" because this topic chose me; it basically seduced me into a relationship. But my particular story, the story of how a former Pentecostal Christian winds up embodying the Dark Goddess and married to a God of the Underworld, remains to be shared. So drink the little bottle and down the rabbit hole we go!

We'll start off with some wisdom from Orion Foxwood:

The physical body is a soul unto itself. It is the living Crossroads that mediate the lunar tides of the Dream Walker from below and the stellar powers of the Star Walker from above, and bears these forces into the surface world. It is imprinted with powerful ancestral and Faery forces and ancient stellar intelligence. These forces move through your body in your breath, electrical currents, and blood, and are recorded in your flesh and bone. I call these potent forces the Gods of Flesh. They lay sleeping in your Surface Walker until they are intentionally awakened, opened up through trauma, or awakened through other experiences or altered states. . . . The body itself is the temple of ancestral wisdom and the gateway to the path of spiritual truth.[1]

I have always had an embodied, erotic spirituality. My sense of God/dess has primarily been through the medium of my body and somatic experience. Likewise, I have also always had a highly sensitive disposition—some might say I am psychically gifted. For as far back as I can remember, I have often intuitively known what others are feeling, sometimes thinking, without their having to say anything.

These two essential aspects of my personality, the eros of my spirit and my permeable psyche, were often at odds. The eros of my spirit longed for ecstatic union and embodied practice, however, when I was in close proximity to other people my psyche was often overloaded with information. The solution for me was to develop a kind of spiritual practice and personal cultivation that brought me into ecstatic union with nonhuman or nonphysical reality—plants, spirits, and cosmos.

I use the terms *eros/erotic* to represent the vitality, creativity, and desire within humanity, sometimes referred to as *orgone, jing chi,* or *shakti.* I define *erotic spirituality* as an experience of indwelled divine *ecstasis* (similar to the Shakta Tantric concept of Kundalini Shakti) and/or an experience of union with nonhuman or extraordinary beings. This concept is distinct from the more neo-Tantric definition of erotic spirituality wherein one explores altered states of consciousness through high degrees of sexual stimulation and/or erotic cultivation with others. Both are forms of erotic spirituality, but the form most relevant to my story is the endogenously produced, extrasensory arousal of ecstatic spiritual states.

The term *highly sensitive* I define as having a highly attuned intero- and extero-ception of stimuli. Experiences like ESP or visionary states are beginning to be understood as the extreme reaches of a spectrum of highly attuned sensitivities ranging from having heightened capacity with one's five physical sense organs, to empathic or precognitive perception, to full-blown mystico-psychic encounters. Being a highly sensitive person (HSP) on any range of the spectrum can cause subtle shifts and cues in one's environment to blare as strongly as a loudspeaker announcement, and often lead the HSP to interpret and interact with the world around them in a manner that buffers them from the onslaught of external inputs. These two psycho-spiritual aspects of my personality bear a tremendous amount of weight and influence on my story.

Finally, I offer a note on the term *magic*. In renowned parapsychologist Dean Radin's groundbreaking work *Real Magic: Ancient Wisdom, Modern Science, and a Guide to the Secret Power of the Universe,* he explores the intersection of science and magic, stating: "Real magic falls into three categories: mental influence of the physical world, perception of events distant in space or time, and interactions with nonphysical entities. . . . [M]agic can be reframed as the academic study of the full capacities of consciousness in light of the rising interest in informational descriptions of reality."[2]

Following his definition, I define magic as a consciousness-based technology—that utilizes the emotions, thoughts, and vital/erotic energy of the human body in collaboration with the vibration, magnetism, and regenerative qualities of Earth and her morphogenetic field—to affect change. These two physical systems, human body and nature body, are not limited to the surface world. My training as a Faery Seer has taught me that we also collect and circulate the energy of the cosmos and the under world throughout both our human and natural systems. However, for the purposes of this definition, magic is the end result of all three levels—upper, middle, and lower—working together through demonstrable manifestation.

THE HOLY SPIRIT AS WISDOM SOPHIA

My inquiry into spirit marriage is inextricably connected to the unfolding and evolutionary stages of my devotional life: growing up a spirit-filled Pentecostal, communicating and praying with and to trees, being dissatisfied with a sexless Christian God and his disembodied practices, attending seminary and feeling a profound yet confusing call to public ministry, longing for a tradition that held reverence for and primacy of women and the Divine Feminine—and finally seeking a path that embraces both light and dark as co-equal and indivisible. My choices in life have almost invariably been guided by what Orion Foxwood refers to as "sacred longing and divine discontent."

As a child, I often felt the presence and fullness of the Holy Spirit as a palpable sensation in my body. Even though I did not understand exactly how, I knew it was a different sensation from the ones I felt when I prayed to Jesus or his Father God. This Holiest of Spirits often felt most alive to me in and through nature. Later I would come to understand that the experiences I had been having were the indwelling contact of the Goddess, the Divine Feminine, but as a child I simply knew that this contact awakened me in a vital and primal way and left me feeling ablaze.

Also, as a child, I remember hearing the Bible story of God offering King Solomon anything he wanted as a reward for his devotion— any riches, glory, or achievements. Solomon simply asked for wisdom. Traditionally the story states that from Solomon's great wisdom he was able to obtain all the riches and glory he desired, and more. I thought this was an excellent plan, and I decided that I, too, would make this request. I remember praying fervently that God would make me wise, gift me with wisdom, so that no matter what I faced in life I would have the knowledge, discernment, and understanding to face it. Intuitively, I believed that being filled with the Holy Spirit was closely aligned with having wisdom, so I cultivated greater and greater capacity to channel the Holy Spirit.

Reflecting back, I wonder: "What if what Solomon was truly asking for was not the quality of wisdom, but a relationship with the embodiment of the Goddess of Wisdom, Sophia? What if he understood that an intimate relationship with the feminine face of God was more important than all other achievements?" Solomon would go on to not only write some of the most erotically spiritual verses in the Bible but also to cultivate a direct-knowledge relationship with the Divine Feminine through his relationship with the fabled half-djinn Queen of Sheba, Bilquis/Makeda.

And so for most of my life I have been unwittingly calling to the Goddess, inviting Her into my body through my desire for the cultivation and embodiment of wisdom. And through this search for wisdom, for Sophia, for Her, I have been pulled into the orbit of awakening the divinity inside of myself and inside of others.

DEEP LONGING:
THE EROTIC NATURE OF BEING
"SPIRIT FILLED"

For as far back as I can remember I have had the feeling that some part of me was missing, that I was somehow incomplete. I felt as if just behind my mundane perception there was a whole vista of experience just out of my reach. For years I sought ways to *lift the veil,* pierce the membrane between this world and the Otherworld, for it was in connection to the numinous reality of Spirit that I felt most whole, validated, and complete. Suffice it to say, despite my conservative Christian upbringing, my essential nature and practice has always been Pagan.

My relationship with what Orion calls "the Gods of Flesh"—the body as interface for numinous contact—began at an early age. At less than a year old, I was diagnosed with a birth defect in my kidneys, and after repeated illnesses and rounds of medication, I was scheduled to have surgery to attempt to correct this defect.* My family, being Pentecostal faith healers, all laid hands on me, anointed me with oil, and prayed the Holy Spirit fire into my body. As result, the illness disappeared and I was healed.

This encounter left me altered, quickened. I was filled with the Holy Spirit before I could speak, and this spirit, alive inside me, was

---

*Notably, in Traditional Chinese Medicine, the kidneys regulate and house our *jing chi,* the sexual and ancestral energies.

a wild force—a blazing fire that came most alive when I was alone in nature. I grew up with an innate knowledge of the spirit realms and a tremendous amount of energy. It was as if the anointing of oil and laying of hands onto my infant body by a group of adults had opened up a channel inside me, awakened something supranuminous. I spent my childhood and youth with one foot in the human world and the other in the world of Spirit.

My first conscious recollection of having perception beyond my mundane senses was when I was in nursery school. I could not have been more than four years old. One warm afternoon on the playground a young boy named Benjamin held a cardboard tube up to the sky and invited me to look at the sun. As I stood close to him, close enough to smell his earthy scent, I felt an unfamiliar tingling, an altogether delicious sensation in my belly. It was a quaking warmth that seemed to radiate out from my abdomen, down into my legs, and up into my chest. Like a small bird my heart fluttered, and I felt a quickening, a melting and flowing into union. Something told me that this was my true state, and I wanted more.

Because this erotic sensation manifested as sexual attraction, I assumed that I would find my fulfillment in a romantic relationship. I began to search for someone who could permanently awaken this state inside me. Unfortunately, instead of finding awakening, more often than not I found myself longing, reaching, hoping—and always unfulfilled. Eventually I discovered that I could achieve a close approximation to the ecstatic state during the praise and worship service at my Pentecostal church. There I could close my eyes, raise my little arms heavenward and surrender to the delicious nectar of union with the Holy Spirit in my body. My charismatic spirituality manifested in a religious devotion and fervor that often had me telling every child on the playground about the power of the Holy Spirit.

Church became the safe place where I could release my body to be completely immersed in the arousing unitive energy of Spirit without being judged or shamed. In fact, I became the poster child for the model Christian daughter—obedient, respectful, and devout. Little did the church and my parents know that this was because being filled with the Holy Spirit every Sunday felt a lot like having an orgasm—although I would not make this connection until my adult years. Because sexual expression was considered taboo, I learned to channel all the erotic energy awakened inside me by the Gods of Flesh into my Holy Spirit experiences at church.

Unfortunately, outside of church I felt disconnected and empty. Although I found my spiritual practice fruitful, I also longed for an embodied experience of this unitive state. I just was not satisfied with everything staying above the neck, so to speak. Eventually, I discovered that being alone in nature quickened me, and at times I even found my way through the veil and into union while I was deeply immersed in a natural setting.

SINGING TO THE TREES

The Northern California Bay Area is replete with powerful, ancient tree species: redwood, live oak, pine, cypress—all beings of an order and magnitude that dwarf humanity's blip on the evolutionary map in comparison. In my Faery Seership tradition we talk about the trees being our elders, the ones who remember the original blueprint of this Edenic blue-and-green planet and who can perhaps guide us back into cocreative relationship with Her. Recent breakthroughs in forestry research underscore the harmony and interdependence of the forest ecosystem, revealing the cooperative wisdom of the trees and modeling a path for humanity to perhaps step back into right relationship with each other and Earth.[3] Frankly, I've never met a tree that I didn't instinctively want to rub up against and love.

My love affair with trees began when I was in grade school. At the time, living in a suburb of a suburb of the San Francisco Bay Area, there were still quite a few old oaks left standing in my neighborhood. The street that I lived on, although a newer development, still had significant swatches of undeveloped land. On one of these plots stood a live oak tree that was approximately two hundred years old. Its branches reached over two stories high, its root system was vast and complex. Years later, after the land on that lot was purchased for development, they would have to build the house around the tree, so enmeshed was it in the landscape. This was *my* tree—the tree that initiated me into the mysteries of ecospirituality.

We had moved onto that street between my fourth- and fifth-grade years, during a time of painful transition for my family. We had just lost our family home and my parents were bankrupt and unemployed. Somehow, miraculously, fate intervened and found a home for us to live in rent free for a time.

Up to that point I had loved school, my classmates, my home, and my life. But upon starting a new school I found myself ostracized, alienated, and bullied (more on this later). No matter what I did, I couldn't find my way into a group of friends within which I felt held and safe. It was during this period that I discovered my tree friend.

At some point someone had hammered wooden planks up the side of the tree so that one could climb the trunk easily. This tree had a heart center where the branches extended out on either side, like arms open to embrace you. After school, and especially on rough days, I would tell my mom I was going for a bike ride (she was a worrywart), and then sneak off and climb the tree and nestle in its branches. The dappled light as it touched my skin made me feel both soft and secure. It felt like the only true nonjudgmental friend I had.

Sitting in the tree I could listen to the Otherworldly voices of nature. In it I heard deeper than I've ever heard before. I spoke to the tree as if it were God—telling it of all my sadness, all my dreams, all my hopes and fears. As an offering I'd sing it songs, mostly just little ditties that I made up, but sometimes songs that I liked or songs that I remembered from church.

Years later while seeking guidance around spirit marriage from an African Dagara diviner I would be given a ritual to find a Tingan tree, a tree that embodies the masculine element of nature. I knew immediately which tree this was going to be for me—my live oak. I took it milk, honey, and spring water and made offerings to the tree stating my intention for us to reconnect. Sadly, that would be the last time I had access to my tree as the lot finally sold, and the house built upon it made my access to the tree impossible.

However, after that visit I began to revive my practice of singing to the trees and would go on to establish relationships with a variety of trees on public lands, guaranteeing my continued access to tree loving. Eventually I would discover that the trees had been listening.

THE WEIRD KID

That same fifth-grade year I discovered that I was weird. Up to that point my parents had done a pretty good job of sequestering me from the non-Christian world. I only had friends from our Pentecostal church, and I went to private Christian schools. Playing with the non-Christian kids on the block was frowned upon. I wasn't really exposed to anything much outside of Pentecostalism. However, lack of exposure didn't discourage me from trying to transmit my Holy Spirit, pants-on-fire *shaktipat* to every kid I met on the public playground, in the grocery store, or in line waiting to ride the Pirates of the Caribbean ride at Disneyland. But it never occurred to me that this was strange behavior. I had so much energy running through my body, which I had been taught was the Holy Spirit, that it seemed natural to want to share this blessing with others. Laying healing-hands on random strangers became kind of my thing.

Starting a new school in fifth grade had seemed exciting. I would encounter a whole vista of potential new friends, friends that were sanctioned by my parents because I was going to another private Christian school. At first, I was welcomed. The "cool kids," the academic overachievers of the school, took a liking to me because I was brainy. But I soon discovered that theirs was a specific brand of competitive one-upsmanship, which I recoiled from instinctively. Why couldn't we all encourage each other to be our personal best, rather than try to outdo one another? I gave them a wide berth.

Things came to a head one day when at recess I found a sixth grader,

Margaret, sobbing in the girl's bathroom. Margaret was a favorite object of derision at school for no reason other than she was bigger than most of the other kids her age. On this day, Margaret had holed up in a stall in the girl's bathroom and was weeping profusely. I couldn't stand to hear her hurting, so I asked her if I could pray with her in an attempt to soothe her. You know, lay some hands on her and do my spiritual transmission thing. She agreed, and I proceeded to hold her hands and give her as much love and compassion and tenderness as I could muster. I told her that there was something inside of her bigger and stronger and more powerful than these heartless bullies.

Unfortunately, in the middle of this little ministry session those "cool kid" bullies came in. You see where this story is going, right? Isn't it always the kids who think they're special, exceptional, privileged, that feel it's their God-given duty to remind the "other" kids that they're not? They overheard what I was saying to her and immediately began to make fun of me. They spread the word far and wide that I was a freak— a weirdo who liked to pray over people. I became persona non grata.

Now let me pause here and explain something, I was on scholarship at this private Christian school. As I mentioned previously, my parents had just declared bankruptcy, and we were digging in couches and underneath car seats to scrape together enough money to buy Burger King meals for dinner many nights. As anyone who has attended private school can tell you, private school kids tend to brandish a particular brand of entitlement mixed with some heavy othering skills. This new school with its label-conscious, performance-obsessed bullies was devastating to this highly sensitive new kid. Elementary school quickly became a hellscape for me. Whereas previously I had loved learning and academics, now I just wanted to be home with my trees.

I began to retreat deep into myself, self-isolating at school to protect myself from their toxic bullying. This drove me deeper into my inner forest—a safe place filled with luminous spirits and deep devotion. It was also around this time that I decided being weird was probably okay if it meant not being a bully. Being weird meant that I had a connection to a reality, a way of seeing and experiencing the world, that most people would never discover. Ultimately, I felt sorry for my bullies, for they would probably never experience the profound and blessed states that came so easily to me. It was then that I also found my determination, some might say calling, to be a standard-bearer for the weird ones, the fringe dwellers, the mystics, pariahs, and freaks. I would claim this title proudly. Years later I would discover that the word *weird* is actually defined as "supernatural, otherworldly," and is derived from the Old English word *wyrd* meaning "having the power to control destiny." Perfect. That fit me just fine.

LOSING MY RELIGION: A DESCENT INTO THE UNDERWORLD

As I went through puberty and my erotic nature blossomed, suddenly spiritual practice and nature seemed poor substitutes for a soulmate, a lover of my spirit, who I believed would make me whole. This deep longing seemed to magnetize me and charge me psycho-sexually. Like many young women of my generation, I had a vital sexuality that had been given no room for healthy exploration and expression. And because I was religiously devout, I spent a tremendous amount of time and energy longing for the day I would find the perfect partner with whom I could explore the connection between spirituality and sexuality.

This desire persisted into my college years where, at a Pentecostal bible college, sadly I found neither erotic spiritual partner nor support for my unique brand of ecosexual* spirituality. Again, I sublimated this desire into my studies of literature, art, nature, and music—all panaceas for my deep longing. Although I felt a strong pull to the role of minister—what I would eventually understand as the priestess path—I had yet to find a tradition that could honor the fullness of that calling.

---

*Ecosexuality is a term coined by erotic activists Annie Sprinkle and Beth Stephens. It roots in the idea that Earth can be our lover and we can have an erotic relationship with nature as a way to heal ourselves and our planet. For further reading see *Assuming the Ecosexual Position: The Earth as Lover* by Sprinkle and Stephens.

After college, and as mentioned earlier, I decided to attend seminary at the Graduate Theological Union in Berkeley, California—primarily to study the phenomenology of my own spiritual experience, but also secretly hoping that I would finally meet someone who could match my erotically spiritual nature. To my chagrin, most of the seminarians seemed disconnected from their bodies. They seemed to lack a sense of embodied spirituality, choosing to live more in theory than in practice. I became disillusioned and convinced myself that sex was not really sacred or mystical, that it was just an action that I could engage in with anyone, without attachment. I earned a master's degree in ethics and social theory/religion in society, but at the cost of my erotic spirituality.

Until that point, I had been a virgin with a highly sensitized subtle body from years of spiritual practice and discipline. When I had sex for the first time in my early twenties, I was unprepared for how much subtle body information it would introduce into my system. I was flooded not only with my own sensations but also with the sensations, thoughts, and emotions of my partner. It overwhelmed and confused me. I did the only thing I could think of to do to stabilize myself—I got married. This decision proved to be disastrous. My husband, whom I did not know very well, turned out to be a violent and abusive person. As a result, I lost my faith and my erotic spiritual practice. For three years, I struggled to make our marriage work. However, after he directed his violence toward my sister—in a harrowing confrontation that in retrospect reads like a scene out of a thriller—I got in my car and drove across the country to escape his threats. Because of his aggression toward me and my family, I went into hiding and eventually filed for divorce.

At this point, I was desperate for healing and support but I didn't know where to turn. I began working with a therapist to help me heal from the post-traumatic stress of the abuse. Unfortunately, because I knew little about therapeutic methods, I went to the first person I found, a Freudian analyst. The therapy did little to alleviate my suffering, and I found my way into a romantic relationship with another abusive man. Something was clearly amiss, and I realized that the kind of therapy I was receiving was not helping. Apparently, the trauma patterns were not going to dissipate by simply talking about them. I needed to disentangle myself from the underlying patterns and subtle body entanglements that seemed to exist at a deeper psycho-spiritual level.

I ended the second abusive relationship and found a transpersonal depth psychologist, who was also an astrologer. With her, I began to explore the psycho-spiritual influences behind this pattern of abuse. She helped me unpack the nature of my highly sensitive nervous system, and through the lens of my natal chart, offered a vision of me and my way of being in the world that for the first time in my life validated my erotically spiritual nature. Finally I had permission to be the fullness of myself without shaming, hiding, or diminishing who I was and who I was becoming.

After surviving two physically and psychologically abusive relationships, I had lost hope in finding a spiritual partner who would bring me into divine union. Instead, I developed the bad habit of nihilistically rushing headlong into a sexual relationship with whomever was available at the moment. I rationalized that if I could not have the deeply meaningful emotional relationship I longed for, I could at least find sexual fulfillment. Sadly, these sexual encounters were not very fulfilling. I perpetually felt dissatisfied and unmet in relationships.

No matter whom I was with, the deep longing for divine union never left me, but no human seemed to measure up. I began to wonder whether a human could ever truly match my desire. My deep longing became deep despair.

EROTIC AWAKENING AND SPIRITUAL DISCIPLINE: STEPPING ONTO THE PATH OF SELF-CULTIVATION

By my twenty-ninth birthday, coinciding with the Saturn return in my natal chart, I decided I needed to address the unconscious subtle-body patterns that kept magnetizing abusive or unavailable partners. With the support of my therapist, I undertook a deep psychological and spiritual quest, which eventually led me to the practice of yoga and the study of a variety of subtle-body healing modalities. Through yoga, I was introduced to the concept of the chakras, the subtle energy centers of the body, and the flow of energy through the body known as *prana*. Although the yogic system within which these concepts are traditionally taught was new to me, the felt-sense of prana and the experience of energy centers in my body were quite familiar. I had already encountered them when I was a child as the movement and indwelling of the Holy Spirit. I enthusiastically dove into yogic practice and study, searching for a new way to frame my deep longing and erotic spirituality outside of the confines of Christian doctrine.

The year I turned thirty, I began a prolonged period of yogic discipline and celibacy. Up to that point, I had been focusing my energy outward, trying to find a relationship that would bring about an experience of erotic spirituality. The externalization of my longing had been dissipating and scattered my focus and direction in life. I began to turn my focus inward and intuitively to cultivate practices wherein I experimented with contacting and stimulating my vital force, sometimes called shakti, through my energy centers, also known as chakras. I learned to move and clarify the flow of energy in and through my body with breath and movement. These exercises were enhanced by my study and training as an energy healer and massage therapist. This time of open, intuitive exploration helped me to decouple my deep longing for ecstatic union from the years of conservative Christian programming. Through my yogic studies, I soon discovered the concept of Kundalini Shakti—the erotic life-force believed to be the indwelling of the Goddess, which lies coiled like a snake at the base of the spine. I began to see that Kundalini Shakti had been very active inside me for my entire life; I simply experienced Her by another name—the Holy Spirit.

During this time, I had also undertaken a year-long self-initiation into the Anderson Feri tradition, a form of Witchcraft. After initiation, I ended my vow of celibacy and took a lover. The first time we made love, I felt Kundalini uncoil at the base of my sacrum and shoot up my spinal column, piercing each of my chakras as it went up. It felt like light bulbs on a wire were exploding inside me, one after another, as they rose up my spine. The energy was so intense that I passed out. I had no idea what had happened, and was sore and achy for days afterward, almost like I had the flu. Fortunately, I had also been working with a holistic healer, and when I described to her what had happened to me, she explained that I had experienced a Kundalini Awakening. A whole new vista opened before me, one that finally gave me a solid connection between sexuality and spirituality through the medium of Tantra.

I continued to practice the energy experiments of consciously moving prana through my body, now adding in a self-arousal component. Using a phallus-shaped crystal, I practiced circulating Kundalini Shakti throughout my body, drawing it up through my chakras and back down. However, I was still confusing sex with shakti. I thought that to experience my kundalini, to cultivate shakti, I needed to be having sex. I became attached to the idea that I needed to be in a relationship with someone to really cultivate this erotic Kundalini Shakti within myself.

At the time I didn't realize that that according to Tantric teaching working with a partner, depending on their level of cultivation, can also confuse one's practice and disperse the energy one is attempting to build. The potency one cultivates in a solo practice can easily be drained and muddied by a lover's energy, particularly when that person is not themselves a practitioner. For so many years, I had longed for a soulmate, an erotic spiritual partner with whom I could grow. However, I was beginning to discover that perhaps a spiritual partnership—as beautiful and holy as it is—is not the culmination of erotic spirituality for me. A deeper longing for union with the Divine Masculine arose.

THE FIRST PROPOSAL

During this time, I also began to have dreams and visionary experiences of being contacted by spirit-beings, often with an erotic component. In the hypnagogic or hypnopompic states, and sometimes while completely asleep, I would perceive a presence making love to me. At first this was disturbing and frightening, and I sought ways to protect myself from unwanted encounters. And yet I began to wonder: "Was my longing for deep union with a human perhaps leading me to union with a divinity?"

Eventually the entity that visited me in my dreams asked me to marry him. There was something very compelling about his proposal—it felt fated. Yet there was no way I was going to agree to marry anyone, let alone an entity, without knowing him better. I would not make that mistake again! I began to seek any information I could on erotic spiritual contact with nonphysical beings, anything that would give me a context for the somnambulant experiences I was having—other than labeling it as insane or hallucinatory. Eventually, I found the writings of Ida Craddock. Her research helped me to contextualize this experience within the larger context of erotic spirituality.

Unfortunately, very little else had been written about the spirit lover phenomenon at that time. Thus much of what I learned was from my own intuitive experiments with my Kundalini Shakti, and my growing contact with my spirit lover, the one I would later understand as my Faery Beloved. Subsequently, I met and married my second husband, with whom I had a deep spiritual and creative bond. However, we did not have a strongly sexual relationship. Instead, my sexual energy seemed to be directed into the cultivation of inner Tantric practices and technologies. Although the deep longing had never left me, now I was learning to shift the expectation from being met by a physical person to being met by a spirit-being. The identity of this spirit-being, however, was inconsistent, confusing, and sometimes contradictory.

I redoubled my efforts to find a system that could teach me about this form of extraordinary experience, one that was grounded in a lineage, and one that could also protect me from unwanted spirit contacts—neither of which I was receiving from my neo-Tantric studies. Because of Ida Craddock's connection to Ceremonial Magic, I decided to initiate into the path of Ceremonial or Hermetic Magic. Ceremonial Magic taught me how to protect myself in the astral realms and develop greater discernment vis-à-vis spirits. Unfortunately, it did not offer me much understanding or guidance on how to work with a spirit lover.

Not until my late thirties did I finally find a robust teaching lineage, Faery Seership, which would help me better understand what I had been experiencing with my spirit lover. Looking back, I now realize that the bulk of my thirties was spent preparing the soil of my consciousness so that I would be ready for the right teacher to arrive.

EMBODYING THE DIVINE SELF
WITHIN AND WITHOUT

At this point, Kundalini Shakti and the Holy Spirit had become synonymous for me.* For most of my thirties I absorbed as many psycho-spiritual practices and mind-body-spirit trainings as I could find, all in an attempt to understand the subtle realms as they relate to the human body. As I look back on it now, I was trying to understand Her, the Divine Feminine, through understanding myself. By my mid-thirties I had accumulated over two thousand hours of certifications, trainings, and skills in a variety of alternative healing modalities, all driven by my insatiable curiosity about the erotic, the subtle body, and spirit contact. In 2005, I opened a healing arts practice in San Francisco to share my skills as a bodyworker, energy healer, hypnotherapist, and intuitive guide.

In addition to helping me protect myself in the subtle realms, Ceremonial Magic had also given me a series of rituals that could be used to invoke divinity into oneself. I decided that the best way to serve my clients would be to attempt to embody my highest and most Divine Self as my primary way of being in the world. I reasoned that if I were allowing my Divine Self to move through me, then healing would be the inevitable result. I also made a commitment to clear out any impediments that my mundane self might hold to obstruct the hosting of this Divine Self. This included deep psychotherapeutic work with a

---

*Just to be clear, I'm not conflating these two culturally distinct Goddesses. I'm just saying that at that point I didn't feel a discernable somatic difference between their energies.

trusted counselor; extensive physical transformation in the areas of diet, exercise, and cleansing; and intense psycho-spiritual rituals and exercises to heal personal and ancestral wounds. I fasted, prayed, chanted, dreamed, danced, drummed, sang, stripped (both literally and figuratively), and undertook austerities—not only to make more space for this Divine Self, but to learn about and familiarize myself with who She is.

At first I began to call upon Isis as the focal deity with whom I would unite. I had been having dreams and visionary encounters with Isis wherein She of Ten Thousand Names represented the all-encompassing nature of the Divine Feminine. Every day, whether I was seeing clients or not, I would use a Hermetic ritual known as Calling Upon to draw Isis down into my body—asking her to see through my eyes, hear through my ears, speak through my mouth, touch through my hands, and feel through my heart. This invocation also served to protect my psyche from other forms of subtle-realm contact that I did not want encroaching on my consciousness.

MEETING THE GODDESS IN MY BODY

In 2006, I went to a retreat called Evolutionary Women, sponsored by the futurist and conscious evolution thought leader Barbara Marx Hubbard, to network with other women who had a vision and passion for being agents of change. At the end of the retreat, we stood in a circle of forty to fifty women and held hands. As we went around the circle, we each spoke into the center of the circle what we wanted to manifest in the world. I loudly proclaimed, "I want to manifest financial abundance and a new money paradigm"—a world where everyone's essential needs are met, where there is enough for everyone. The woman next to me, a Unitarian minister, turned to me and said into my ear, "*Om Sri Maha Lakshmiye Swaha.*"

Although I had no idea what she had just said, the power, authority, and resonance with which she said it cracked open my crown chakra. Golden light energy poured down through me like honey, cascading from the top of my head down into my womb. My womb grew full and then contracted as my yoni opened. Out flooded the golden energy down into Earth like I was giving birth to that which I had just called in. I knew at that moment that what I had just asked for was now planted in Earth and would manifest. Something ineffable had just transpired, something that I could not describe in words. I felt deeply altered, as if I had been claimed by a deity whom I knew very little about.

Later, the woman who had spoken the mantra to me would tell me that the words she had recited was a mantra of the Goddess Lakshmi. I began to learn about Lakshmi and discovered she had much in common with Isis as well as with other Goddesses of love, vitality, and abundance. A personal deity constellation began to take shape for me that included Isis, Lakshmi, Sophia, and Mary Magdalene. For many years thereafter, I called upon these deities daily in devotional ritual and spiritual practice.

Two years later, I met my mentor and spiritual teacher Orion Foxwood. As I have described elsewhere, it felt like my soul leapt when I met him, and I knew that he was the teacher I had been seeking. A significant piece of Orion's work is teaching humans how to step back into cocreative alignment with the primordial "wild" Faery forces that shape our world. It was my apprenticeship to Orion that showed me how to cultivate and deepen the contact with my spirit lover, as well as to claim my ancestral magic of seership. I began to understand that it was no coincidence that my path of self-cultivation was running concurrently with my search for understanding spirit marriage.

After a few years of doing the daily practice of calling down Isis-Sophia-Magdalene into my body, I began to feel Her energy move and speak through me when I was with clients. My sessions began to evolve from a bodywork focus to a kind of channeling or embodied-presence experience. Physical shifts also began to take place. Many nights I woke up at three in the morning, my head ringing like a crystalline chamber. I could feel my pineal gland in the very center of my head pulsing with energy. Waking visions and extraordinary encounters with nonphysical beings soon followed, which I recorded meticulously in my journals. Because of these extraordinary encounters, eventually I had a dream that guided me to return to school to undertake a Ph.D. and write the dissertation that would become the foundation for this book.

EMBODYING THE GODDESS OR HOW I FOUND MYSELF ONSTAGE, NAKED, AND CHANNELING THE GODDESS OF LOVE

You just never know where the Goddess will decide to rear her tawny head. It was 2011 and my mother was dying. After a four-year struggle with cancer it was clear she wasn't going to survive much longer. Week by week as I watched her slip deeper into the gap between here and there a strange and bewildering phenomenon began to happen. The farther she receded, the nearer my sense of Self drew. It was as if her years of religious conservatism had built up a briar patch around me, a thicket of thorns so impenetrable that my own self-expression was trapped by her fear.

Now don't get me wrong. I love my mom, dearly. But she was the epitome of overprotective. She told me, on more than one occasion, that every single day she prayed a hedge of protection around my sister and me, so fearful she was that we might become tainted by the world. Well that hedge had grown thick and gnarly, and I had been nicking, sometimes impaling, myself upon it for years trying to escape.

I was thirty-nine and I was finally seeing the hedge part—Briar Rose awakening to the dissolution of the spell. It was exhilarating and devastating. Mixed with the grief of her dying was the thrill of newfound freedom, the ability to finally be fully myself without the repercussions of her judgment and obsessive protection. When she finally passed, in February 2011, I made two big life decisions. I asked my husband of four years to open up our relationship to other people, and I became a burlesque performer.

Burlesque had burst back onto the cultural map in the early twenty-first century as women (and men . . . and others!) of all ages, colors, sizes, genders, and sexual orientations found the power and freedom of the striptease. San Francisco's particular flavor of burlesque was rowdy, raunchy, and often offered important social critique. It was performance art at its most dazzling. Taking your clothes off in front of a cheering crowd became a rite of passage as you shifted from who your mom (or dad, or ex, or kids, or career, or social circle) wanted you to be, to who you were choosing to become. And I wanted in!

Within a few months of my mother's passing, I had joined the ranks of San Francisco's sparkly naked ladies, and I was hooked. I burst onto the burlesque stage like an animal only let out of its cage a few times a month. Ideas for acts came swift and fast and I could barely book myself enough gigs to explore them all.

Now let me stop and explain something. This fever pitch, this urgency to perform, it wasn't just about unfettering myself from years of religious repression—although it did just that. I also had a perhaps not-so-subtle agenda hidden in my performances. You see, by that time I was also a Ceremonial Magician, an Adept, and before each show I summoned up the Goddess from my core to come out and dance me. The Vodou traditions call this being *ridden* by the spirits, and I was giving Her the reins. So in many ways I, Megan, wasn't on that stage, but a rarified aspect of me, my Divine Self.

Burlesque performers take a stage name. Perhaps at one time it was to protect their muggle identity, but now it has become, like a drag name, a way to shape your alter ego, your new identity. For me it was a way to fashion the vehicle for who and what I would channel. I chose the name Erzulie Rose. Erzulie is the Vodou Goddess of love and a spirit who frequently possessed me on the dance floor, and Rose is part of my magical initiatory name. And that's who I became.

Each night as the lights dimmed and the intro music arose, while ten or so dancers huddled in a tiny backstage dressing room awash in glitter, feathers, and pheromones, I crept off to a dark corner and performed a clandestine Calling Upon ritual to bring the Goddess front and center into my performance. Then with eyes ablaze and hair on fire, I climbed on stage and shakti-bombed the audience with Her presence.

Needless to say, I tended to leave my audiences a little slack-jawed and bleary-eyed, wondering what had just hit them. And that is how we do deity yoga here on the Left Coast, y'all.

Sacred Medicine Work

Entheogenic Journey Account ✳ *December 15, 2011*

My sacred medicine journey began in the early afternoon, long before I took the 5-MeO-DMT medicine. Something inside me, like a black hole, began to swallow me up, turn me inside upon myself. And as I began to travel inward, I began to understand that the journey I was about to take would devour me—the parts of me that I thought of as me—and leave me forever changed. This medicine had the power to activate the strands of "junk" DNA that after years of activations, initiations, and healing modalities had been holding out inside of me. And this made me incredibly sad.

As we sped to the circle, late due to a number of incidents, my temper flared. It wanted to lash out and blame someone for our tardiness. But no one was to blame but me. I seethed. As we got closer to our destination, I found myself grieving in anticipation of what would die. I knew that whatever was going to shift inside of me would be life-altering. I knew that so much had already shifted inside of me from the work I'd been doing that I was sad to think that I might be "too much," that my world, my relationships might not be able to sustain or integrate the change that I knew was coming.

My beloveds asked me how I was feeling going into the journey. I told them I was deeply disconsolate; that I was afraid that who and what would come out on the other side would take up even more space, and that I was already a lot for them to handle. I feared that we would have to part ways. And so I went in knowing that a kind of death was inevitable, yet ultimately desirable.

That night as we arrived at the temple I found myself incredibly withdrawn. All of my energy, consciousness, and psyche pulled inward to prepare myself for the medicine. As we began the ritual invocations, I found myself willingly offering up myself to the medicine. I was ready to die. I let go of everything I could think of to let go of. I laid it all out on the altar of the temple and let go. Even the fear that this medicine might kill me, I offered up. I was ready to die, if that was the next step for me, I would die. This was my khandamanda, *my manic dismemberment in service to the Goddess. I was ready.*

When the priest asked who would go first, I had no hesitation. I would go. I was ready for the next step. As I took the medicine in and lay back, I launched into infinity.

A star field portal, a fractal dimension like a star gate, opened before me and I catapulted outward into the wormhole of time beyond time. My body dissolved into a radiant glow of nothingness. As I inhaled I knew that I was the cosmos inhaling its first divine breath of Creation, and as I exhaled I was differentiating consciousness from oneness. It was the big bang—which was really more like a deep exhale or orgasm, the first breath of life, an orgasmic sigh of delight. I lay with my eyes closed and yet my inner eyes were wide-open, opening wider and wider with each subsequent breath, as if I were finally seeing for the first time. This sensation was familiar, I had dreamed this before, eyes wide-open while asleep.

As I traveled through the fractalized portals, I began to feel my body undulate, the cosmic serpent uncoiling herself inside of me. And I became the serpent Goddess, cobra hood extended, as she danced her dance through me of life and ecstasy and death and rebirth. It was like being fucked by God Herself. My spine activated in full Kundalini ecstasy as wave upon wave of shakti coursed upward through my body from the bubbling spring at my feet upward through my yoni, opening my heart and flowering at the lotus crown on top of my head. I know these path-ways well as a Tantric practitioner, but no practice, no meditation, no ritual compared to the depth and fullness, the complete perfection, of this release. I literally melted into the Goddess and allowed her to come forth in my cells.

It wasn't a possession, not like when I dance as Erzulie Rose. It was a becoming, an allowing, a dissolving into Her presence inside of me, into a complete, more expanded me. The I AM THAT I AM. And as I danced, all the pain of being human rose to the surface. All the separateness, all the fear, all the solitude and isolation came up to be washed away. As I danced, I regressed back into the womb, covered myself with the blanket, and wept—wept for our separation from this state, wept for the ways in which we have forgotten this moment. And then I emerged from the cosmic womb, I was reborn back into a body, back into this dimension, back now to remember and serve.

I danced on, moving with serpentine undulations flowing through my spine. I could feel the shakti energy rising up, up my legs, up my yoni, up my spine, into my medulla, the mouth of the Goddess, now fully awakened and speaking through me. The snake goddess danced me into a fully extended cobra head of awakening, hissing and growling and fluttering of tongue and uvula. And as I made sounds, I watched the universe form and shape from the sounds I made. I watched as life and Creation shifted based on the intentions I held while I made sound. Primal, first sound, uttered from the Utterer at the beginning of time.

And then Isis danced through me, was *me. I danced the French painter George Lacombe's image of Isis with the breasts flowing blood like milk to create life, one foot on the skull conquering death, her hair forming trees. She who nurses the planet began spurting energetic milk from my breasts to feed all those present there that night. Giving and giving and giving, to the point of exhaustion, to the point of depletion. And again weeping for the pain of the planet, for the pain of Her children, lost, afraid, lonely, asleep. And from Isis rose Kali, snake-tongued Goddess of creation and destruction—Kali's raw power and force, fierce and filled with awe. A force to be reckoned with. Kali and Isis rotated and danced back and forth a play of serpent and mother, creator and destroyer, oscillating as one.*

Then the sign language began. Symbols of the great mystery, the Great Work. The sign of the Neophyte, the Zelator, *and on and on. And I turned to the priest and gave the sign of silence followed by the sign of the V and then through that the tongue of Kali, piercing the cosmic yoni, the* vesica piscis, *the greatest mystery, which cannot be spoken.*

And from this symbology I moved into lotus pose, the realm of the Christos-Magdalene, the position of the teacher. And I heard the words "Come. Come unto me," and I saw that I was to fully embrace my role as a teacher and mentor and priestess. It was time to step into this role and to lead. And then I was the Goddess looking at her children, shaking her head, rubbing her chin, thinking to herself, "Oh my beloveds, what am I to do with you?" Like a mother watching her child continue to make the choices that she knows will cause pain and suffering and wanting so badly to prevent them from hurting, yet knowing they have to learn at their own pace. I was Binah, she who sorrows and weeps.

At that point the mudras began. The positions of the hands moving and transmitting energy. And I began to transmit, to emanate shaktipat energy and look at each person in the room and send them this transmission, this energy, this becoming. And all the while deep inside of me was the eternal "Yes!" This was who I was born to be, this is what I am here to do, this is my Truest Self. I had felt Her there for years, but the layers of doubt, fear, and resistance had clouded Her.

That night the veil was rent, dissolved, and She was able, I was able, to fully allow, embrace, and surrender to Her fullest presence. I was finally able to let go into Her. No more doubt about my visions, my calling, my guidance. No more uncertainty about being "too much."

Yes, let me be too much! Let me be taller than the tallest redwood, deeper that the deepest ocean, vaster than the cosmos itself.

There is a belief that there is too little in this world. Too little patience, too little love, too little time, money, resources, space, and so on and so forth. Let us now be too much!

Let us allow the overflowing abundance of the largess of our souls to envelop the planet in the fecund ripeness of our being and our own greatness. Let it flow out of us like sweet honey from the rock. Let it pour from us like a torrent of rivers finally unleashed by freedom from the dam. Let us all aspire to be too much. And maybe, just maybe, we will touch into the source of our being and fully become our Divine Self.

I returned from my journey by reciting the Kabbalistic prayer, as well as the set of affirmations known as "The Pattern on the Trestleboard."

This brought those energies back down and consecrated my body, puri-fied it, and prepared it for greater service and ministry. After my journey ended, the priest told me that I was the great ocean of darkness reflecting back upon itself, like a mirror. He said that the process I went through was that of embodying my Holy Guardian Angel (HGA). I was the aspi-rant surrendering to the presence of my Angel, inviting Her in.

Days later, I told him that I could still feel the "medicine" in me, teaching me. And he suggested that the "medicine" was in fact me, my Angel, my Divine Self, which was now deeply integrated into me. I like this idea. That the intelligence, the living eucharist of the medicine, is now alive in me, is a part of me, is me. And all I need to do to call upon Her, to be Her, is to surrender and breathe.

Orion once told me that a part of us is always unavailable, on hold so to speak, until our parents cross over. When a parent dies, we receive our spiritual inheritance from that parent's bloodline. My mother came from a long line of seers who had, unfortunately, shut down or hid-den their gifts for many generations. The denial of our psychic gifts had led to oversensitivity and mental illness in my family. As part of my commitment to self-healing, I determined to not only cultivate the inherited spiritual gifts from my mother's line but to also work with my ancestors to heal the broken lineage of matrilineal seership within our family. When my mother passed, I received what I can best describe as an influx of spiritual power, what I identify now as the beginning of the indwelling of my HGA. Many things in my life suddenly became clear, new relationships immediately blossomed, and I was opened to previ-ously inconceivable avenues of cultivation. One such opening was my initiation into working with sacred entheogenic medicines.

As I have just shared, in December of 2011 I participated in a hermetically sealed gnostic temple that uses the sacred entheogen 5-MeO-DMT as its sacrament. This sacramental medicine put me in direct contact and conversation with my Divine Self in an embodied and undeniable way. Although prior to working with this medicine I had been cultivating a relationship with my Divine Self through the

Calling Upon and other rituals, it was the medicine that grounded a multisensory knowledge of this presence and confirmed the contact that I had been cultivating.

During this medicine journey, I felt all my resistance to knowing and experiencing myself as a fractal of Her consciousness dissolve away and be replaced with a sense of permission to be more fully who I am and who I am becoming. This journey was life-changing for me. I felt that I went in as one person and came out another, an upgraded version of myself. All the fear, limitation, and worry about being my Divine Self fell away, and I surrendered to the numinous, potent experience of facing the Goddess within and without.

The medicine journey was multifaith in scope, although notably the primordial Tantric Goddess Adya Kali was one of the first deities to manifest through me. It was She, this ineffable one, who began to deepen my connection to other Goddesses. She confirmed the contact I had been having with various forms of the Divine Feminine, as I felt Her move through me with her many faces: the Utterer, Adya Kali, Kundalini Shakti, Isis, Sophia, Mary Magdalene. I became more intimately united with Her consciousness as my Divine Self, an experience that I believe may have some similarities with the ishtadevi and met tet rituals I describe elsewhere. The priest who conducted the temple, a highly initiated Ceremonial Magician, confirmed that this ritual had brought me into the knowledge of and conversation with my HGA. Her divine awareness was now placed in my body in such a way that I left that ritual forever altered.

Interestingly, this journey did not provide new information. It was as if the medicine simply unequivocally confirmed the work I had been doing to call upon the Goddess both inside and outside myself. The journey put my ego on pause long enough for this aspect of me to present Herself in an undeniable way. It invited me to more consciously embody Her energy. Before the journey, my conversation with Deity, my HGA, had been fuzzy and abstract. I had experienced my HGA as an external entity that I was petitioning, reaching out to. The medicine journey brought Her consciousness directly into my body, fused Her with my reality, and placed Her in conscious relationship with myself and as myself. It was as if Deity was now embedded in my cells and alive in my DNA. This revelation convinced me once again to seek out teachings that would help me experience Her more deeply in and through the interface of my body.

FINDING A FEMALE TEACHER AND SHAKTA TANTRIC SADHANA

Hindu historian Nilima Chitgopekar states, "Initiation given by a woman is considered to be more efficacious than initiation given by a man. . . . The texts claim that women are the purest source of transmission of the sacred revelation. Even to be valid as a revelation a doctrine must be revealed from the Yogini. The presence of women and women's teachings, as well as affirmations of female energy and spiritual capacities, are distinctive features of Tantric religiosity."[4] Although I loved and respected the path of Ceremonial Magic, I also longed to receive teaching from the female perspective. Ceremonial Magic honors women and the Goddess; however, most Ceremonial Magic seems to orient around the male perspective and focuses on being in a male body. I needed to find a path that would help me to understand and navigate the Divine Feminine through the experience of my female body.

Not long after my mother died, I had begun study with my first formal Tantra teacher, Elizabeth Bast. I had completed Bast's Vajrayogini Awakening training, rooted in Shaivite and Tibetan Tantra, and began receiving mantra transmission from her. Bast eventually introduced me to the Sri Vidya Shakta Tantric *pujarini,* or priestess, Janice Craig. In the rituals and teachings of Shakta Tantra, I finally found a path that celebrated the embodiment of Devi, the Goddess, in all women, *as* all women.

Seeing myself and others around me as Devi became my way of moving through the world, making everything sacred. When I shared my encounter with Lakshmi with Janice, she invited me to sit as the murti, the Goddess embodiment, for a water puja called a tarpana that she was performing to honor the Goddess Lakshmi. During this ritual

I became an embodiment of Lakshmi. My "Megan consciousness" was present but muted as the Goddess Lakshmi stepped forward and moved through me, radiating out of me in such a profound way that I felt permanently altered by her touch. The other women there also witnessed this, and we were all filled with grace, gratitude, and humility at the arrival of Deity through one of us.

After the puja, however, the experience led to confusion and overwhelm for my ego. I worried: "What does it mean that these energies are manifesting through me and as me? Who am I?" I went through an intense time of asking myself, "Who am I if I am the Goddess, but I'm still Megan? How do I hold both these energies? What does this mean for my life, my relationships? How do I translate the extraordinary experience I've just had into my mundane life?"

Working with a depth psychotherapist became of primary importance, as well as having spiritual mentors like Orion Foxwood. They encouraged me to let go of trying to figure it all out and to simply allow the innate, divine intelligence to cultivate and transform me in Her own time.

To be frank, this time of integration was neither pretty nor easy. Having my ego dismantled and reprogrammed so that more Goddess consciousness could come forward was not an easy task. It required tremendous self-sacrifice and shadow work. All the parts of me that were attached to self—relationship, agenda, even to my mission of being a priestess, a healer, a minister—had to be disentangled. Ultimately, I found that even my attachment to the Goddess Herself, my longing for her beauty and grace, had to be offered up, as I learned to revere and honor the fiercer faces of the Goddess in her darker aspects.

As I worked with my Tantra teachers, I continued to be blessed with the movement of Lakshmi through my system. In our circle, doing mantra recitation or puja, Lakshmi would often spontaneously come forward in me and look through my eyes or speak through my mouth. It was then that I learned to negotiate with Deity, for it wasn't always appropriate to completely surrender to Lakshmi's presence. I learned how to invite her to sit softly inside me, looking and experiencing through my eyes, but without making a spectacle. Other times, I received permission from the group to embody her energy, and Lakshmi would bless us all with darshan.

The witnessing of this phenomenon by my community as well as their normalizing of it was essential. This was not about me being special. I was just a way-shower, one example of how we can allow Her to manifest in us in a more tangible way. It was important to me and to the group that I was not being worshipped or thought special. I was an example, saying, "This is one way this might look, and it's possible for everyone to do this in their own way." This teaching is a crucial aspect of Tantric practice. Everyone participates, and everyone gets to be worshipped as the Goddess.

LEARNING THE SOUND OF MY SOUL

Up to that point, I had gravitated to working almost exclusively with female deities. I had sought an understanding of spirit grounded in the female perspective, the *yoni-verse* as it is sometimes called in Tantric circles. I seemed to inherently trust female deities—even the darker, chthonic ones—more than I did any of the male deities. To this end, I had intentionally deepened my relationship to the primordial Divine Feminine, the Dark Goddess manifesting through divinities like Mary Magdalene, Adya Kali, Ereshkigal, and Erzulie Dantor. Over time I fell in love with the Dark Goddess, developing a deep devotion to She who manifests as dark, fecund Earth and cosmic womb creatrix. As part of these devotions, I was revisiting what I had been taught about good versus evil and light versus dark—essentially turning those ideas on their heads, as we shall see.

I also began to relate to Earth as the physical body of the Goddess. I realized that the health of Earth correlates to the health of individuals, communities, and society at large. I came to the awareness that how a society treats Earth is reflected in how it treats women, and vice versa. I postulated that the growing attraction to Pagan and Earth-based spiritualities in the mid to late twentieth century was an attempt to heal this disconnect and rediscover the sacred life within ourselves and within the land. Revivifying the Divine Feminine within and without became a key aspect of my personal practice and study. Increasingly, I understood that how we interact with Earth and with our bodies is in direct relationship to how and whether we interact with the Goddess.

Even the way I chose to approach my Ph.D. research was through relationship to my body—via ritualized interactions with nature and inner dialogue with my ancestral bloodlines. My dissertation became a kind of *gestational research* in which I felt pregnant with the seed of the research and sought out the midwife/midwives who would assist me in birthing it into being. My mentorship with Orion was one such midwife, as was the community at the California Institute of Integral Studies (CIIS). I went into the doctoral program pregnant with the idea of this research topic and used the cauldron of academic study to incubate and nourish its growth. Now I find I am in a constant living, unfolding dialogue with the spirit child of my research as it teaches me and shows me what it wants to become, evolving from a dissertation into this book. Ultimately, as Orion put it, "Your dissertation was the love child of you and your Faery contact."

Having spent years practicing the Calling Upon ritual, eventually Isis opened the door to a conversation with my HGA. However, similar to the entity described in Frater Lux's story, that presence had no distinguishable name or cosmological orientation. Her voice and presence had been coming in dreams for a number of years, but she sounded like a breath or a whisper.

Finally I had a breakthrough. After months of nightly Shakta Tantric practice, I had a dream in which the Goddess, appearing as an electric blue snake with my mother's face, pierced my body and revealed the name of my Divine Self. From then onward, this name would come to me spontaneously in rituals and dreams, accompanied by a divine presence that seemed to rise from deep within my body outward, like an orgasm. I began to work with this name inwardly, inviting this presence to take up more space in my psyche.

Since then I have searched for the practices that will help me refine and cultivate this Divine Self contact, synchronistically discovering that these were often from traditions that practiced spirit marriage. Because the presence of my HGA was specifically gynocentric—it was not like *seeing the face* of the Goddess, it was *being the body* of the Goddess—I sought to deepen my study and practice of the oldest Goddess-centered lineages available, namely Shakta Tantra and Witchcraft. These traditions have held intact a yoni-verse or Creatrix understanding of the universe for hundreds of years or more. I realized that because I am a woman, I can have a deeper understanding of my own potential and nature as a woman through the lens of a gynocentric worldview. I can have a fuller conversation with my Divine Self through the forms of spiritual practice that honor women as divine.

Learning the sound of my HGA opened me in such a profound way that my priorities and interests almost immediately shifted. My relationship with Her became paramount; even contact with my Faery Beloved took a back seat for a time. I also became increasingly aware that my practice was not about disappearing into Her presence. I needed to connect with Her in such a way that she would enliven me and move through me to make her presence more grounded on Earth. As a result, the way that I began to approach my work in the world took shape through the questions, How do I serve? How can I embody more of Her, bring Her more fully into the world around me? My Ph.D. research became less about academic curiosity or performance, and more about giving Her space to manifest through my actions, thoughts, and speech—and in particular, through this unique kind of marriage or union with Her as my Divine Self.

The closer I drew to both Her presence and the presence of my Faery Beloved, the more I questioned my purpose in life. I was constantly being reminded that my research is not just about me or my professional career. I have a purpose, a mission to share what I have learned, and this book is a seminal piece of that work. Ultimately, this material is about the ways in which drawing close to Spirit affects not only the individual but also the collective. Like Kama told me, "We're all going to get there together. No one gets left behind, no matter how long it takes."

Along the way, I realized that even if I could earn a spiritual gold medal with my personal practice, if one of my community members is struggling with their practice, then we all suffer. This is a humbling and yet somehow reassuring thought. It allows me to accept people where they are on their path, and to take total personal responsibility for my part in the cocreation of Earth. Instead of focusing on individual personal achievement (which I think has reached epidemic proportions here in the West), I can consider the world from a more holistic perspective. Even as the protocols for Divine Self cultivation and spirit marriage can, on the surface, appear to be a very individual process, ultimately we undertake them in service to the healing and transformation of the whole Earth.

Synchronistically, it was around this time that members of my community began to call me out as a priestess, inviting me to coordinate and facilitate group rituals and sacred gatherings. By reaching inward to cultivate this Divine Self presence, I was unwittingly being tempered by the role of minister/priestess that I had felt called to perform so many years before.

As I was sharing the story of meeting my HGA with Frater Lux, he asked me a useful question: "How do you know [that it is your HGA speaking]? You usually hear something, or you feel it somewhere." Answering him was the first time I had ever put this experience into words and shared it with another person. This elucidation would prove to be an integral step in my self-inquiry, daring to speak aloud to a sacred witness the profound experience of my Divine Self.

I replied:

It's the experience of amrita *(sacred nectar). That kind of energy. I know the feeling and the voice that I hear associated with it—the all-pervasiveness of it. It's the sound of deep space. But it is also the first breath of the first created words of the cosmos. I hear it in dreams a lot. And, I just . . . I don't know. It's like, how do you know the sound of your own soul? You just know it.*

DIVINE SELF, DIVINE OTHER

Eventually it had become clear that the two relationships, Divine Self and Faery Beloved, were feeding each other. The more I took on practices of personal spiritual discipline, the more clearly the Beloved came through. Ultimately, what directed me to the various initiations I've taken over the years was the longing for divine union with the Divine Self *and* the Faery Beloved—a holy longing for both the knowledge of my deep Self and for the spiritual partnership of a Divine Other. At first, I was falling in love with an externalized entity; however, this quickly led to falling in love with the Divine within.

It also became increasingly clear that my dissertation research was more nuanced than focusing solely on the concept of an externalized spirit asking for marriage with a human. On one hand, I was researching the spirit marriage that manifested for me in a male-female dynamic with my Faery Beloved. On the other hand, I was researching the process of finding the Goddess within through the various teachings on divine embodiment like the ishtadevi, the met tet, and the HGA. These undertakings seem comingled in my psycho-spiritual development, embedded within my organic inquiry. I began to wonder: "Is finding one's HGA, met tet, or ishtadevi actually a form of spirit marriage wherein one marries one's Divine Self?" As I interviewed other people about their spirit marriages, I soon discovered that the answer to this question was nuanced depending on the tradition, and that answering it would require even greater and more subtle discernment on my part.

The idea of union with one's Divine Self as a form of spirit marriage, therefore, became increasingly important. This insight led me to question whether perhaps one is most effective when attempted concurrently with the other. Might the spirit-spouse relationship naturally enhance and even require cultivating and claiming one's own spiritual sovereignty? And mirroring this, might stepping into one's spiritual sovereignty activate and awaken the practitioner to the point of attracting a spirit-spouse? This seemingly corresponds to the rituals of the met tet and mariage Loa in the Vodou/Voodoo traditions. One goes through a ritual attunement to what could be understood as the Divine Self (met tet) and is also often asked to wed a deity (mariage Loa). The two spiritual technologies support and inform each other, and yet are distinct.

In hindsight I can see that it was essential for me to do the inner alchemy required in the Divine Self practices of Ceremonial Magic and Shakta Tantra in order to open more fully to the divine union relationship with an extraordinary being. I cannot say exactly which came first—a Divine Self practice or the spirit marriage proposals. It feels like they happened almost simultaneously. It makes sense to me that one practice is enhanced by the other—that being wooed by the spirit realm can put us on the fast-track of self-cultivation work. That was certainly the case for me.

13

The Erotic Mystic:
Encounters with My
Faery Beloved

*W*hen I began this research, I identified a series of questions that I wanted to ask the people I interviewed about spirit marriage. These were questions that, at the time, I was unable to answer about my own spirit lover *cum* Faery Beloved. The questions centered around three primary themes: (1) What is your experience of spirit marriage (initial calling, initiation, practices)? (2) How is it currently being experienced or practiced in your life and tradition? and (3) What is the purpose or end goal of your spirit marriage? As the years progressed, as I asked these questions over and over again, and as I continued to cultivate my own contact, the answers finally began to emerge. Eventually, I realized I was finally able to sit down and answer my own questions.

Reflecting back over the past fifteen years of journals and dreams I had collected I could see a definite progression through the various stages of Faery contact previously described by Orion Foxwood in his work *The Faery Teachings*. The stages, as I experienced them, were: First Contact, Naming and Forming, Searching for Understanding, Deepening, Embodiment, Confirmation,

Requirements, Purpose and Trust. Although my experience did not conform precisely to the Faery Seership stages of contact, there was enough of an overlap to identify a pattern. Here, then, are stories of the specific stages I have encountered in my own journey toward a spirit marriage.

FIRST CONTACT

Twin Flame

Poem ✳ *August 10, 2005*

Twin flame burns brighter
God breath fuels light of pure love
We two are as one
The stars spell your name
Many heavens hold this truth
Luminary love

Tantric Teacher and First Proposal

Dream ✳ *March 2, 2006*

I am sitting on a bed. I see the face of a beautiful man, and I want him to teach me more about sacred sex. He is beautiful, half white and half black, almost seven feet tall, with long braided hair. I beg him to teach me. He takes out a rubber lingam. I tell him, "No! I want you." He asks me if I am sure. Am I really ready for him? I answer, "Yes!" He penetrates me. It feels like fiery joy. I can feel his love rushing into me. I feel us merge. He's gentle and strong, a true teacher. He coaches me, how to grip him, how to breathe, how to circulate the energy, how to sustain him. He tells me to internally grip the tip of his lingam at the tip of my cervix as he moves—to draw breath and light up, and then to use the fire breath, "Ha, Ha, Ha," to fill myself. He is pleased with my ability. I want to please him, to do all he says, to learn from him and be with him. He whispers in my left ear, "Marry me?"

My spirit lover began coming to me back in 2002, when I first stepped onto the path of the healing arts. During my first Reiki attunement, I saw Him appear as twin beings standing on either side of me. Initially I thought they were just my Reiki guides. However, over the years these twin beings appeared to me in dreams and extraordinary encounters, and eventually the relationship developed into an erotic one. At some point the twins began to show up as black and white, or dark and fair.

Then, in 2005, I began to have a series of dreams in which these spirits asked to marry me. The first proposal was from a spirit that had an African-sounding name and appearance, so I sought counsel from a diviner within the Dagara tradition from Burkina Faso, West Africa. Through a series of divinations, it became clear that I was indeed being invited to marry a spirit. However, who and what the spirit was, was not clear to me, for the spirit did not always appear in the same form. Because He alternated his appearance and demeanor, or sometimes showed up as two beings, I was often confused about the identity, name, and cosmological origin of my contact. The only consistency was that the spirit appeared in a male form (or forms). I wrestled with whom I should turn to for counsel, as I had no consistent cosmology within which to place this spirit contact. Was He a deity? An angel? A faery? Something else entirely? Ultimately, I was not willing to enter into a marriage with a spirit I did not fully know. The only consistent element was the way He made me feel—quickened, activated, awakened, whole, and suffused with love.

The African diviner told me that if I married this spirit through the Dagara ritual of spirit marriage, I would be expected to practice their tradition and uphold their ways. As much as I honor and respect the Dagara spiritual technologies, as a white woman it did not feel aligned to become a carrier of an African lineage. When I was undergoing my training in Ceremonial Magic a mentor once told me that there are certain magics that are universal, everyone can work with them, and certain magics that work best within ancestral bloodlines; they just don't work as well for outsiders. Therefore—despite how hungry I was for a teacher and how much I was in need of guidance and support—I sought a lineage that was connected to my ancestral magic, one that could unlock the codes in my blood and bone. All the while, I had to contend with knowing that this might be something of a tall order, given the decimation of European Pagan lineages during the Burning Times.*

When I met Orion, as previously stated, I felt a deep resonance with him and his teachings. I eagerly became a Faery Seership apprentice and undertook intensive training with him two to three times a year for almost ten years. In 2009 I also entered the Ph.D. program in East-West Psychology at CIIS with the specific intention of writing a dissertation about the embodied experience of having a spirit marriage in the twenty-first century.

Apprenticing to Orion and receiving spiritual guidance from him over the years has helped me hone my ability to discern my spirit contact, or what I now refer to as my Faery Beloved. It is through my work as a Faery Seer that I have begun to *re-wild* my soul—a process of diving deep into the chthonic realms of ancestor and Fae to reveal and heal my hereditary lineage of matrilineal seers. Core to the work of Faery Seership is a visionary practice called the River of Blood. In this working, the seer journeys on behalf of their ancestors to disentangle the snarls, or karma, of the dead. Through this work, I have begun to suspect that my Faery Beloved may have been present as a familiar spirit in my mother's line for many generations, but forgotten or outright ignored by the last few generations due to Christian conversion. According to Orion, being in abeyance of a sacred contract like this often gives rise to misfortune and mental health issues in a family line. It sure had in mine. Hence the importance of finding a Pagan lineage connected to my ancestors—although I would not consciously make this connection for many years.

---

*The Burning Times is a reference to the persecution of people in Europe who were alleged to be witches. It extended from the Dark Ages to roughly the nineteenth century. Thousands of those thought to be practicing witchcraft or those accused of heresy were put to death, often by burning.

MEETING THE BELOVED
OR HOW I FOUND DESTINY
IN THE SCHOOL CAFETERIA

The California Institute of Integral Studies, or CIIS, is widely known as a strange attractor for weirdos, misfits, freaks, and heretics. People who come to CIIS often refer to their education there as a cauldron for personal growth and spiritual development—an initiation. The egregore of the school is full of subversive thought leaders and cult icons like Allen Ginsberg, Ram Dass, Joanna Macy, Ralph Metzner, Alice Walker, Robert Thurman, Angela Davis, and others. It boasts first of its kind, cutting-edge programs in Women's Spirituality; Ecology, Spirituality, and Religion; Human Sexuality; Philosophy, Cosmology, and Consciousness, as well as certification in things like Psychedelic Assisted Therapies and Research. It's an edge-walking, paradigm-shifting hothouse of transformative personal and cultural change.

One such thought leader is feminist cultural historian Lucia Chiavola Birnbaum, a specialist on the Dark Madonna. Her research traces the dark, chthonic Goddess from her African origin outward into the populated world. In the spring of 2011, as part of my doctoral curriculum, I took her class on the Dark Madonna in the Women's Spirituality Department at CIIS. It felt like a good way to deepen my devotion to this primordial and often fierce mother. Her class was an initiation of sorts into the Dark Goddess. Alongside this class, I signed up for a course entitled Wise Women, Witches, and Intergalactic Crones with Pagan scholar Randy Connor. It was promising to be a potent and transformative semester.

Little did I know that two weeks into the semester my mother would pass away. My excavation that spring was deep, transformative, and altogether life-altering, and, as we shall see, the Dark Mother had on her agenda some major life transitions for me, beyond just my mother's crossing. "You don't always get your goals, but you do get your destiny," states Tony Robbins. I was to learn this firsthand that semester.

The first day of my Dark Madonna class I was sitting in the school cafeteria on lunch break. A tall, swarthy, beauty of a man whom I'd met in my program the previous semester sat down with me for lunch. He was hard to miss around campus. He always sported a black cowboy hat, had leonine shoulder-length hair, and just a bit of a devil-may-care attitude. It was that day, as we were sitting across from each other, that I noticed the tattoos. On each of his forearms he bore spiraling snakes that wended their way from wrist to elbow. I had read *Mists of Avalon,* so I knew immediately what they meant. He was a Druid.

As we discussed our devotion to the Goddess and to the various Celtic mysteries, a curious phenomenon arose. I watched as the snakes on his arms came alive and began to undulate across his skin. A familiar sensation, one which typically heralded the arrival of my spirit lover, began. There was pulsation in my tailbone, then the feeling of lightning striking upward. Kundalini Shakti. I was left speechless and a bit undone. As I gripped the edge of the table my interlocutor screamed, "FUUUUUCK!"

After lunch, disoriented and confused, I made my way back to class. A classmate and dear friend saw that a shift had occurred in me, and she asked me what had happened. I had no words to explain how this relative stranger had just activated me. How was I, a married woman, to make sense of this?

That night I had a dream. In my dream this Druid appeared to me and I said to him, "You're meant to be my consort." He replied, simply, "Yes." In my dream I then turned to my husband and said to him, "This man is meant to be my consort." And his reply was also, "Yes." I awoke from the dream with chills running through my body. The truth was revealing itself to me, one that I didn't fully have the courage to embrace. I couldn't admit what was happening, not to myself let alone anyone else.

As prophetic dreams go, however, it wouldn't leave me be. I had the same dream two more times that week in exactly the same way. I knew I wasn't going to escape this. A week or so later I attended a large Pagan convention, Pantheacon. I realized I needed some spiritual guidance around this numinous, transgressive phenomenon. So I scheduled a reading with my mentor, Orion, who was a Pantheacon luminary. During our session he confirmed the validity of the contact and encouraged me to talk to both men about what I was experiencing. He pointed out that perhaps the consort work was meant to be more of a spiritual contact rather than play out in the physical. Either way, he said I needed to clue the guys in on what was happening.

I mentioned earlier in my story that although I had been married for four years, my marriage was primarily one of spiritual partnership, bordering on the asexual. When my husband and I had decided to step into marital union we had had a conversation about perhaps opening our relationship up at some point. Nevertheless, the idea of broaching the subject with him (and with the Druid) seemed inconceivable. Mother Fate, however, had a plan.

On my suggestion, the Druid came to Pantheacon. He found me in line for Orion's class and as we were standing chatting, my husband saw us from across the room. I could tell by the look on his face that he was seeing the power between the Druid and me. Later that night I asked my husband what he thought of the Druid. Without hesitation he told me, "If you and I weren't in a relationship, you would be with him." It was the opening I needed.

We sat and discussed this strange phenomena, Orion's advice, and what our next steps should be, and he agreed that I should explore the connection with the Druid. It seemed fated. That was the easy part.

Over the next few weeks we courted a relationship with the Druid. Inviting him over for dinner, unbeknownst to him, was a way for us to feel into the energies between us all. But it took me another three months to work up the courage to tell him about my somatic experience at the school cafe and my dream-visions. Fortunately, by the time I laid my cards on the table we had been spending enough time together that for him it was an obvious yes. He was all in. Then came the arduous work of learning everything I could about polyamory, and the often-perplexing process of discerning the Druid's energy from that of my spirit lover.

NAMING AND FORMING

Beloved

Channeled Poem ✳ *February 11, 2009*

You are my beloved
There is no one else for me but you
You are the spark within me
You are the light that illuminates my soul
The wellspring of my passion finds it source in you
I know you because I see myself in you and we are one
Together we create destiny for
You are my beloved

Scent of the Beloved

Dream ✳ *September 5, 2009*

My spirit lover comes to me as a tall, blond, Viking-like entity, and smells like pine resin, ambergris, and some delicious sweetness, like honey.

Raven's Wings

Dream ✳ *December 8, 2009*

I am with my spirit husband. He is beautiful, perfect; He has huge black angel wings, like raven's wings. They are iridescent with a purple-and-green sheen. I desire him. He carries me, and we fly together. He has to part with me for some special mission, and I beg him to make love to me one more time before He leaves. He takes me to the outdoors, what was supposed to be a bayou, but when we get there all of the trees are cut down, and there is a big Nike store with tons of Tokyo-style billboards animating around it. He is outraged at the desecration of the natural world.

Let's back up a little now. When I had begun my Ph.D. in 2009, I was struggling with the spirit lover relationship, feeling that I was becoming ungrounded by the contact and perhaps losing my grip on reality. I wanted to experience the embodiment of this work rather than to transcend out of my body into the etheric realms of Spirit. I wanted this process to enable me to come more fully into my body as sacred and holy. I got the idea that if my contact could find a suitable physical host, someone who held a close vibrational frequency with my contact—perhaps as his Divine Self—that my beloved could interact with me through this person. I thought, perhaps, that my contact would move through my husband.

In 2010, I performed a ritual where I asked my contact to reach out to me through a human person. Years later, I would discover that this is a known practice among Ceremonial Magicians. The renowned Southern California occultist and founder of the Jet Propulsion Laboratory (JPL), Jack Parsons, used Ceremonial Magic, specifically the Babylon ritual, to successfully summon a physical embodiment of the Goddess in the person of Marjorie Cameron.[1]

Six months later, my Faery Beloved began to move through the Druid in very profound and demonstrable ways. This man would often become overshadowed by my Faery Beloved, channeling him, so to speak. The intense connection between the two of us was undeniable. I shared with my then-husband what was happening, and, as you know, we decided to open our marriage agreement so that I could be free to cultivate the contact that was developing.

The three of us lived as a triad for several years, but it became increasingly clear that my relationship with the Faery Beloved and the man who aligned with him was excavating deeper levels of my psyche and was requiring more and more of my focus. We had quite a bit of karmic healing work to do together, and the intensity of our relationship didn't seem to fit well into a polyamorous arrangement. As a result, my second husband and I decided to transition our relationship out of legal marriage and into the realm of spiritual cocreators. To this day, he remains one of my dearest friends and staunchest supporters, and I his.

At first, the fact that my Faery Beloved was moving through a human was confusing. I began to think that this man was actually my Faery Beloved or that he was meant to embody him all the time.

However, it quickly became clear that this expectation was not only unreasonable but potentially dangerous to the nervous system of the man. Instead, we began to focus on healing the entanglements and projections that we had brought with us into our relationship. During this time my Faery Beloved receded almost entirely from my awareness. Occasionally, I would have a dream encounter, but for the most part it seemed to me that my Faery Beloved was working with me through the Druid as we worked on our relationship. The relationship with my Faery Beloved became sporadic. Despite all my research and study, I was still uncertain as to his exact name, cosmological location, and identity. I even began to question whether the contact had just been wishful thinking on my part.

Nevertheless, I persisted with my research into spirit marriage. Orion had been counseling me on how to cultivate a relationship with my Faery Beloved, and at this point he encouraged me to develop the practices and rituals that would help me to differentiate and disentangle my experience of my Faery Beloved from that of the Druid. It seems that having my Faery Beloved move through a physical person had been useful to a point, but then became a hindrance to deeper levels of contact. In retrospect, I may have stormed the gates of heaven a bit by requesting my Faery Beloved manifest in human form, as it has been challenging at times both for my Druid partner to host the energy as well as for me not to conflate my Faery Beloved with him. Nevertheless, I learned a tremendous amount from this experience about the nature of spirit contacts and their ability and willingness to meet us where we are.

SEARCHING FOR UNDERSTANDING

I hoped that talking with my different spirit marriage interviewees would help me clarify and hone my understanding of my Faery Beloved and further develop our relationship. The questions I had developed for my interviews were ones that I was unable to answer for myself. I felt sure that hearing my coresearchers' stories would help me to answer them.

Because I had structured the interviews in an open-ended and conversational way, I had the opportunity to share some of my own experiences and musings on the topic of spirit marriage with my coresearchers and get their feedback. In three of my interviews (Orion Foxwood, Bloody Mary, and Frater Lux) a profound self-scrutiny arose wherein important personal information surfaced—not only about my experience of being contacted, but also about the reason and motivation for undertaking this research in the first place. Each interview deepened my personal inquiry and ultimately reframed how I approached the topic, as well as how I interacted with my Faery Beloved. The following are two of the pivotal insights I gained from sharing my personal story and process of inner inquiry with these coresearchers.

Healing My Relationship with the Divine Masculine

I began to realize that part of my hesitancy to accept a proposal of spirit marriage, and one of my unconscious motivations for undertaking this research topic, was that I did not feel safe with the Divine Masculine, or perhaps with the masculine in general. Although I had spent years in therapy working through my history of abusive relationships, at some point it became clear that the wounds I carried around men were coloring my experience of the Divine Masculine as well.

Years of fundamentalist Christian conditioning had left me with a subconscious experience of a Father God who was capricious, authoritarian, and not entirely trustworthy or benevolent. Even his Savior-Son, Jesus, allegedly a champion of love and tolerance, has followers who perform atrocities in his name. Clearly, I had some unresolved issues to work out surrounding entities that present as male. Although, ultimately, noncorporeal entities are perhaps not gendered in the binary way we tend to classify gender, I realized that I had readily embraced a spiritual relationship with the Divine Feminine, even with more nonbinary energies like nature. However, I had avoided developing any kind of relationship with the Divine Masculine. For me to enter into a spirit marriage with my Faery Beloved, that would all need to change.

During my interview with Bloody Mary she asked me what my

deepest fear was about entering into a spirit marriage. I think I surprised both of us by answering that I was afraid of giving up my power. Mary astutely pointed out that perhaps the reason my contact first came to me as a forceful male spirit was to indicate that I needed to do some healing around my relationship with men. Because I had been in abusive relationships with controlling men, I was projecting those qualities onto my spirit contact as well. Her counsel would mark a turning point in my relationship with my Faery Beloved.

It all boils down to you. Why do you attract controlling men? Why do you want that? Why do you need that? Why do you think that you're not worthy to be balanced? Maybe the marriage would balance you. Maybe this is to draw out your fears to find the other side of this person. You're projecting your own image of man onto this spirit or Loa or whoever he is, but you're not giving him a chance because you haven't stopped projecting your incarnational issues with men. . . .

For you to even say "I wouldn't want to give up my power" shows that you look at marriage as giving up your power. And that's not what marriage is. Marriage is not even just about love or sex, marriage is about having somebody in the trenches that's got your back. Marriage is about someone who will record your life, who can validate the things you do, who can say, "I was there, she did this," so it's not just you. Marriage is a union of the spiritual and sacred. It would be far from giving up power, as much as joining forces.

I think the question in the dissertation for you is, What is marriage? Why do I look at this as giving up power? And what is it triggering in me? It's obviously triggering past relationship issues for you to think that. I think that you may have clothed him in a domineering, aggressive, "He's gonna bully me until I marry him" kind of thing.

There are many aspects of this that are you. Part of this might be looking at the outlook of marriage throughout the ages. Sometimes you were placed in a marriage, sometimes you chose and fell in love as in the modern idea of romance. It's a partnership, someone you can depend on and count on. . . . Why are you marrying someone? Is it because you're trying to find yourself in someone else, trying to find a part of you that's deeply buried within? Or are you trying to find something new? But to lose your power, to worry about that, would be the absolute wrong thought pattern and not based on love. . . .

You almost sound like you were coming from the idea of marriage from a [traditionally] male perspective. "What am I giving up?" Maybe you are [your spirit beloved] or were in a past life, and you're trying to get that part of yourself back by marrying it, to balance your male and female sides, to trust in love, in the world again.

Mary's suggestion got me thinking that perhaps something had happened in a past life (or in this one) that tore me apart, and that this research is about reconciling that wound. Given all the physical illness I had experienced since beginning this research—illness that is genetically inherited from my matrilineal line—could my inquiry also be about healing the epigenetic wounds of my mother's line? Might this spirit be somehow attached to my matrilineal inheritance?

During a divination, Orion had once told me that I had already gone through a spirit marriage in a few previous incarnations and that my research would help me reconnect to those past-life memories and vows. I wondered: "Is it possible that this spirit was married to an ancestor, or perhaps even was my ancestor, and has been waiting for me to come along and resurrect our relationship?" Perhaps, as indicated before, this was a *familiar spirit* to my ancestral line, a spirit that had been attached to my bloodline and was passed down through the generations.

Finally, after generations of having been shut out by Christian orthodoxy, was this spirit reaffirming a relationship with me because I am the first in my family to reconnect to our Pagan roots? Perhaps the intensity with which my Faery Beloved showed up in that first contact scared me because of the backlog of family healing work I needed to do for myself and my ancestors.

Mary suggested that sometimes you have to surrender and be torn apart in order to become the true power that you are. Until you finally let go and give up the fight, you can't be rebuilt. It became clear that I would need to redouble the work I had been doing with my ancestors as part of this inquiry. Mary also challenged me by asking, "Why does someone pick a subject for their dissertation? It's something you need to understand within yourself. This is a therapy, this whole dissertation, it's therapy." Truer words were never spoken. I was no longer just collecting other people's stories about spirit marriage and sharing my reactions to their experiences. I was going to have to delve deeper than I had previously anticipated into the uncharted realms of my own ancestral, epigenetic memory to navigate my own story.

Finding the Path to My Ancestors

In 2016 I took a two-week pilgrimage with Orion Foxwood and twenty of my fellow Faery Seers to Albion, the sacred land of my ancestors, more commonly known as Wales, Cornwall, and England. Although I had been to some of these places before (first in 1987 when I was fifteen, then in 2007 on my honeymoon, and again in 2012 with my triad), in 2015 I had started having a series of dreams that were making it abundantly clear that it was time for me to return.

Religious studies scholar Huston Smith states, "The object of pilgrimage is not rest and recreation—to get away from it all. To set out on pilgrimage is to throw down a challenge to everyday life. Nothing matters now but this adventure. . . . There is a stony road to climb on foot—a rough, wild path in a landscape where everything is new. The naked glitter of the sacred mountain stirs the imagination; the adventure of self-conquest has begun. Specifics may differ, but the substance is always the same. . . . Travel brings a special kind of wisdom if one is open to it."[2]

Albion evokes the mystery of megalithic stone structures, subterranean burial chambers, Otherworldly sacred groves, and numinous holy wells. Often referred to as the Pagan holy land, it is the land to which many witches of European descent to remember, reclaim, and reconstitute their memory by accessing the undying records contained within stone, water, and tree.

It's believed that to undertake pilgrimage to a sacred site is to open oneself to the power and potency of that place, wherein one is activated, changed, and expanded by the experience. Like Jerusalem, Mecca, or the Hindu Shakti Pitha, it is in the terra firma of place that we can journey to find ourselves anew. From ancient stone circle to chthonic barrow, the memory of our wild, pre-Christian inheritance is quickened and reshaped by Albion, giving succor once again to the witch's soul. Although most of our grimoires have been destroyed, still the rock, root, and well retain the codex of Pagan knowledge, if we will only quiet down enough to listen.

West Kennet Long Barrow, England
Pilgrimage Account ✳ September 8, 2016

Like almost every other day of the pilgrimage, our last day began much like the others, rising early, piling into two vans, and driving for what seemed like hours to a sacred site. Unlike other days, however, this day we would visit two of the most frequently visited ancient megaliths in Britain—Stonehenge and Avebury.

The sheer number of people crowding into, around, and through Stonehenge is staggering. This wasn't my first visit, but it was the first time I'd been to the recently built visitor's center. Built like a military complex, the entrance area maintains a healthy distance from the sacred site, a good mile away from bathrooms, food, and the rest area—all the things I had been relying on during pilgrimage to keep my nervous system calmed, centered, and balanced. I had to plan carefully what I was going to need with me out at the site, because it was a long walk back for provisions.

The commercial onslaught of tchotchkes and gawkers made this location particularly difficult for me to drop into the desired liminal space that I had been so easily accessing at some of the other less popular sites we'd visited up until then. I resigned myself to "not really feeling it" at Stonehenge, made a perfunctory circumambulation of the stones and waited back at the rest area for the rest of our group, somewhat disappointed by my lack of connection with this ancient site. "Onward to Avebury. Better luck there!" I thought.

The logistics of our excursion and dealing with the ongoing naviga-
tion of a group of twenty travel-weary pilgrims took up a good portion
of the stop. We had grown comfortable enough with each other to feel
like family, both in closeness and in annoyance, and punctuality was just
not one of our strong points. Finally, about an hour after we'd originally
planned to leave, we were on the road to Avebury. After another inter-
minable drive, which was promised to be "only forty-five minutes" and
felt more like two hours, we finally arrived late afternoon to Avebury.
Less populated and restrictive than Stonehenge, we were free to explore
the ancient and massive site of megalithic stones that surround an entire
village. Here, I hoped, I would find that numinous encounter, the spine-
tingling "hallelujah!" moment that would bring all of my other experi-
ences on pilgrimage into sharp relief and open the sky to a flashing bolt
of insight. No small expectations here!

And yet, on this day in the beginning of autumn in Britain, we
experienced unseasonably bright sunshiny weather—even heat!
Wholly unprepared for the warm, bright day, I found myself tired, a
little cranky, and frankly just going through the motions. I wondered at
this point if perhaps my pilgrimage was truly over, the zenith reached
the day before on the side of Glastonbury Tor. Perhaps this day was
just a day of tying up loose ends by doing the due diligence of going to
the "big sites" that are de rigueur for pilgrims. Maybe I had gotten all
the whammy of powerful insights and life-changing revelations that I
would get, and I just needed to sit back and let autopilot navigate me
the rest of the trip?

We ate a leisurely dinner at the only restaurant in Avebury, a medi-
eval pub clearly geared to hungry tourists, and prepared to get on the
road. By my count, we had a two- to three-hour drive back to our hostel,
and many of us just wanted to be back home for a good night's sleep.
However, one of the sites we had meant to visit, one of the oldest intact
burial mounds in Britain—the West Kennet Long Barrow, long con-
nected to the Faery—was less than a mile from Avebury. Well known for
preternatural, some would say alien, sightings, many folks in the group,
including myself, had been waiting to visit this site. And so, although it

was already getting dark, we agreed to at least drive by the barrow and Silbury Hill adjacent to it, to feel into the energy there.

We arrived at West Kennet Long Barrow well after dark. In spite of it being a dark night under a waning moon, the decision was made that we would get out of the vans and climb the hill to see the mound. Most of us had not thought to bring flashlights so camera lights were all we had to navigate by. Shrouded in darkness and in small clusters, we set out on the singular path that led up the hillock. Those who had been there before led the way, and I suddenly realized that this was the first site we'd been to in a while that I had not visited on previous trips. The West Kennet energies were indeed strange, a little foreboding, and pretty unnerving after a day of exerted travel and an intense and physically arduous two-week pilgrimage.

Perhaps due to fatigue, perhaps loosened up by a few too many pints at our pub dinner, perhaps to stave off the eerie feeling of the land, the group reached a kind of pitched jocularity as we ambled up the path. It was at this point that I began to get the uncanny feeling that the night was alive around us and watching our every move. It seemed to be fully aware of our presence and a bit surprised at a somewhat rowdy group of Pagans disturbing hallowed land at such an ungodly hour. But then again, perhaps the night was simply remembering what it was like to be contacted ritually, as I began to increasingly remember what it had once been like to be one with night, human, and other. My senses began to heighten, and I had a premonition that this could become an exceptional experience, an opportunity to slip between the veils with little disturbance, should our group be willing to go there.

The fact that we were walking in the dark toward a reputedly haunted site somehow touched into a deep, slumbering part of my sacred memory, and I broke away from the group and began to walk alone. With each step, I felt myself moving deeper and deeper into trance, as if the closer I got to the barrow the deeper I moved into the Otherworld. At some point it felt as if the air were growing denser, more viscous, even though I was outside. I took my black shawl and wrapped it around my head and shoulders, like a hooded cloak. In my mind's eye, I saw myself the way I had perhaps looked lifetime after lifetime of visiting this place—shrouded, singular, altered.

A chant rose up in my chest, first softly, "Baroom, Baroom," then insistent, "Baroom, Baroom!" Where had I heard this before? "Baroom, Baroom!" Its sound became louder inside of me, until I couldn't help but begin to say it aloud. "Baroom, Baroom!" Again and again it pounded in my head, in my bones, like a drumbeat—ancient, primordial, petitioning. I felt it building, entraining with my every step. Slowly, obliquely, my walk became an open-eyed trance. My feet matched the chant, "Baroom, Baroom!" With each step, each breath, I moved past the membrane of this dimension and into another realm. All the hairs on my body stood at attention. A sense of danger felt imminent. This was no ordinary site, no average encounter. I wrapped this chant around me like a cloak and it kept me focused, attentive, safe.

Nearing the top of the hillock, the sky seemed to open above me, revealing starry velvet, splashes of silver moon, and the incandescence of flora and fauna alive in the night. Then, black as soot against the sky, I saw the barrow. Outcropping of earth, megalithic boulder outlines—the entrance to the barrow loomed large. As I drew closer, it was if something wholly other and yet mine since the beginning of time overtook me. I became entranced, flooded with the bodily memories of the ancient seer, the priestess of the barrow, she who holds open the gates of life and death.

Many in our group had already entered into the barrow, but I knew that I could not go directly in. Instead, the presence I was contacting—a presence that seemed to arise from inside me like a codex illumined in my bones—walked my body clockwise around the mouth of the cave, up the side of the barrow, and onto its top. I have no recollection how I did this with no path and nothing but moonlight, but I found myself standing on top of the barrow, arms raised to the sky—a priestess of infinite mother night. My chant grew louder and louder. My eyes widened, ablaze with moonlight and memory. I felt the palm of each hand open with spirals of energy. It coursed down my arms, into my torso, and down my legs into Earth. With one ceremonious sweep, I dropped my arms downward, connecting sky to Earth in the gesture of invocation known as *Drawing Down the Moon.*

My body felt fully indwelled now with the energy of the ancient priestess, returning and resurrecting inside of me, and I practically floated down the side of the barrow. I sensed a mist growing—was it atmosphere or the silvery mist of Faery now enshrouding me? My face felt lit from within and a small, beatific smile pulled at my mouth, as my eyes remained starry, wide, and staring. Silently, I processed across the giant lintel of the barrow. I could hear chatter inside, mundane conversation that felt out of resonance with the energy I was hosting. So as I reached the entryway to the barrow I resounded loudly, "Baroom, Baroom!"—insistent, commanding, filling up the barrow and all inside with its cadence. As I entered, the group inside began to chant over and over with me, "Baroom, Baroom! Baroom, Baroom!"

Later, I would be reminded that this is the chant that calls the Faery, their ancient sound cue. But in the moment, I simply knew that this was the key, the initiatory sound, that would open the way for us to make contact. We chanted for what felt like an hour, but in truth it was only moments, for after I entered the chamber, our mentor Orion followed. He came into the barrow greeted by our chant, and we all deepened into the inner mystery of this Faery barrow together.

Sometime later we emerged, one by one, some altered, some shaken, some transformed. I hung back and was the last one to depart. I touched the walls of the barrow, the roof, the floor. I thanked and blessed the ancestors for what they had given me this night, for what they had revealed to me. As I emerged from the barrow and crossed the lintel back into the night a fellow pilgrim watched me. Having just witnessed the energy I had embodied and feeling moon and stars and night as our witness, she whispered to me, "You are a High Priestess," a role I had secretly felt attuned to but dared not claim. Later, through a series of synchronicities, I would discover that this high priestess identity was in fact the Divine Self name that I had received in sacred entheogenic ceremony some years earlier. I feel that this energy more fully indwelled inside of me that night on the barrow,

*and because it was witnessed and upheld by my community, I have
felt more permission and alignment to step into my role as Priestess
of Faery.*

One of the first encounters that I had with nonordinary entities
involved a class of Faery beings called the Shining Ones—primordial
beings who show up prominently in Celtic mythology. The Shining
Ones, also called the Sidhe (Ireland) or Sith (Scotland) and pronounced
"Shee," began to appear to me in dreams and visions, and over the years
they revealed to me that they are my primordial ancestors. Apparently,
seeking my ancestral bloodline magic had been, in essence, reaching
back through time to them. Eventually, working with my ancestors
became indistinguishable from working with the Shining Ones.

I shared this insight with Orion during our interview, and his
response was encouraging:

*Look to what our human ancestors look to for guidance. They look to the
plant world. And look to who the plant world looks to for guidance. They
look to the stone world. Look to who the stone world looks to for guidance. They look to the stars. And who is of the stars but living here? The
Sidhe, the Fair Ones, the oldest ancestors of life.*

Orion explained that for me to touch that far back into the current, the living stream of ancestral memory, connected my voltage, my
life-stream, to the vision stream, the soul stream, and the blood stream
simultaneously. By seeking the root of my mother's line, I had connected to all of the streams of consciousness that have pulsed me here
from the unseen to this world. All of it was ancestral.

Orion went on to explain that cultural and folkloric anthropologists
have battled for years over the identity and classification of the Faery.
Are they nature spirits? Are they angels? Are they ancestors of another
race that were smaller in stature and buried in the mounds? Orion's
answer to all of these postulations is "Yes"—all of these categorizations
are Faery. All of that is ancestral.

In Orion's opinion, the anthropologists overlook the fact that Faery work is primarily an under world tradition. The Underworld is the living memory of the world—not the memory of events, but the living memory of the entire unfettered stream of life, the *current*. In folkloric tradition, it is the Underworld, the Faery mounds, that is the abode of the Shining Ones. Orion went on to explain that the under world is about ancestry, whereas the upper world is about divinity.

Remember, the Divine cannot incarnate in terms of becoming a form. For instance, Megan—no matter what divine impulse from the highest strata of the stars, without the genetic memory and the periodic table of elements—is just a hope and a dream, but never a possibility. So the stars need Earth's memory in order to give birth to Megan. . . . It's a deep level of ancestral being and an expanded level of divine being, and those two come together within us. The Divine can't come down until the ancestral rises up. Our job is to be focused on the human-other life to keep humanity tethered to a harmony that these beings never forget. . . .

People think of Faery as simply nature spirits. It's much deeper. It's the entire subtle threshold and invisible dimension of Earth life. All of it. So many of these spirit-beings that humans are in a relationship with— saints, angels, divinities—a great deal of them are part of that same strata that we're calling "Faery." But it's really the rest of the dimensions of Earth life. Earth is much bigger than it appears. It's so much bigger. . . . Your dissertation is a further extension, the next level of what it will take to help make this make sense for people. Because it's going to increase; it's not going to decrease. . . .

Brigh just said something. She said: "You must understand, your species will grow into its glory when it understands you wear the golden lock. The rest of nature has the silver key." She said, "There is but one mind with many brains." There is only one mind, and that mind is this planet. We are little laptops, and that's the mainframe.

I am reminded of a remark made by the ecopsychologist Theodore Roszak in a "Thinking Allowed" interview with Jeffrey Mishlove: "We are living on a planet from which we evolved. We cannot therefore be so alienated from that planet that we can no longer claim some participation in that genetic heritage, that evolutionary heritage, and that ought to become a part of our psychological theory."[3]

Connecting to my Faery Beloved has required a recalibration of my psychological and physical systems to his. This recalibration has been aided by my ancestral work. Orion teaches that there is an attracting force, usually of a divine nature, that underlies this process. This power, which is beyond the human and the Faery, requires that when we reach to each other, we must then calibrate to modulate the energy. For when a human and Faery comingle, it is always done in service to something else—to bring something new to the planet. The human and Faery together must discover the purpose of their cocreation. I would add that this is true of any spirit marriage, Faery or other. Part of the attunement process is the human learning to hear the spirit partner's voice and signature clearly.

Orion also points out that calibrating to a Faery contact and undergoing a marriage are not the same thing—nor does calibrating necessarily lead to marriage. Before marriage, the Faery contact overshadows the human. It may even wrap around or interpenetrate with the human's subtle body, but they don't indwell the human. In the spirit marriage, an indwelling happens, a symbiosis, the grafting of the two into one. The nervous system of the human and the *toradh* of the Fae merge, and the spaces between the human's synapses are filled in with the Fae's honey-like being. From this union a third entity arises: the love child, which is the purpose of that union. This is the mysterious alchemy of the spirit marriage.

A concept begins to take shape, a possible outcome to indicate why spirit marriages are needed now more than ever. This idea constellates around the question, What work do we need to do as a species, as humans, to ready and prepare ourselves for mindfully living on a conscious and evolving planet?

It seems that up to this point most contemporary Westerners have been unconsciously living on a conscious planet. As concepts like the singularity, Gaia theory, and the noosphere have gained popularity, encouraging humanity to seek the oneness in all things, what are the spiritual technologies that we need in order to evolve so that we can actually embody these ideals? I have heard many New Age and spiritual circles talk about nonduality and oneness, about living as part of a holy, intelligent entity called Earth. I can't help but wonder: *Do people really understand the psycho-physiological ramifications of taking an evolutionary leap into immersing oneself in unity consciousness?*

Speaking from the perspective of a highly sensitive person, I believe *what unity consciousness really entails is the ability to stabilize oneself psychologically, physiologically, and psychically while at the same time being acutely attuned to Earth and her morphogenic fields.* This stabilization requires a kind of dialectic between cultivating healthy personal boundaries and simultaneously tracking everyone else around. It seems the work we have to do to truly hold unity consciousness as a species is tremendous. Humans are so physically dense that the work to really embody and fully integrate with the subtle realms is going to require a complete transmutation of our physical bodies and nervous systems. This transmutation is incredibly taxing and time-consuming work. Even though we may understand intellectually—and maybe even emotionally and spiritually—that unity consciousness is where we might be headed as a species, the psycho-spiritual technology that it will take to get us there is significant.

I offer that this is the unique gift of a spirit marriage: *Marriage to a spirit helps us evolve toward greater unity consciousness by teaching us how to refine our subtle senses and attune to realms of nonlocal interdimensionality.* As a result, we embody the full blueprint of what our species is meant to be, moving us from *Homo sapiens sapiens* to the next stage of our evolutionary unfolding, sometimes called *Homo spirictus* or *Homo universalis.*[4]

Just before my second interview with Orion, I had a dream. In the dream, I was visiting my ancestors, and they were talking to my Faery Beloved on the phone. I wanted to speak with Him, but as soon as I got close to the phone there was too much static to hear anything. My ancestors had to relay messages back and forth between us. When I shared this dream with Orion, he felt that it was an important token indicating how my Faery Beloved may be connected to my ancestors. He suggested that this dream might imply that my Faery Beloved has been in my ancestral line and making his way through to me for some time—following the blood thread until he got to me.

Orion elaborates:

I think some of them are grafted to our soul from the very beginning of life. Meaning, we burst from one flame into two different flames. A part of me left the garden; a part of me stayed in the garden. They're the part of us that stayed in the garden; we're the part that went out on a quest, searching. But the calling didn't start just now—it's been going on your whole life.

DEEPENING THE CONTACT

After these revelatory conversations with my interviewees, I began to understand that something had been missing from my inquiry. I had been taking too passive a role in the development of my contact, expecting him to come to me, and as a result not feeling his presence very often. As Kama shared: After she married Kali, she experienced two years of a lost connection to her. She found her way back to Kali through deep, disciplined, ritualized action. Every day she built up her connection through a series of rituals that created a deeper and stronger container for her contact.

Her story reminded me that I had not been doing that for myself. I had left contact with my Faery Beloved up to him. I only interacted with Him when he visited me in dreams. My daily spiritual practice was spotty. I needed to actively engage my Beloved, to solidify my relationship with him through ritualized embodied action.

Slowly I began to build up practices to deepen our relationship. I began a regular movement meditation ritual wherein I connected to and listened for the voice of my Beloved in nature. The following are key deepening encounters that arose as a result of this practice:

Connecting to the Faery Beloved

Ritual ✳ *July 7, 2015*

I went out for a walk along Land's End today with the intention of simply trying to reconnect to Earth, to nature, to green *myself a bit.*

As I walked deeper into the trail, I began to chant a charm that I'd received a few weeks earlier on the summer solstice, a charm that could call my Faery Beloved. "Betwixt and between the sky and the sea / my Faery love, he comes to me / betwixt and between the night and the day / I hold a flame to light his way / Betwixt and between breathe in, breathe out / On the wings of a dove / he arrives with a shout!" The more I chanted this, the stronger the energy became until I began to feel Him arriving as if a flow were streaming forward and connecting us. . . . Nearby was a large cypress tree with branches low enough to the ground that they had been worn smooth from people sitting on them. I climbed onto the tree branch and began to meditate.

I began to sense that this tree is attuned to humans because humans sit on him a lot, but he is not accustomed to humans talking to him. I began to talk to this tree, which had a distinctly male energy. As I talked to the tree and breathed with the tree, I began to feel his bark climb up my arms and spine, as if I was merging with it. This was a little unnerving, because this was the first time a tree had initiated merging with me. Usually I was the one to initiate a merge. It felt like I was being consumed by this tree and although it was a bit scary, I decided to just relax and breathe into it. I let go.

Before me manifested the Peacock God, a beautiful being with curly dark hair, blue skin, and eyes aflame. All I could say was, "Lord, welcome, Lord." And I bowed, not out of subservience, but out of honor and respect. Many different associations began running through my mind as I tried to associate this being, this Faery King, with a deity. At first I thought, "Is this Krishna?" And he responded, "I am like that. Krishna was based on me." And I thought, "Is this Dionysus?" Again, he responded, "I am like that, he is based on me." I then remembered the Peacock God, Dian-y-glas also known as Lucifer, from the Anderson

Feri tradition. Again, he responded, "I am like that. He is based on me."

While I sat with this being, whom I recognized as the Faery Beloved of my dreams, I kept asking "What is your name? What should I call you?" I felt like I had heard his name before in my dreams, that I knew his name, that I'd already learned it but had just forgotten. And so I kept breathing into it, trying to remember his name, but it wasn't coming. At some point he finally said to me, "Just call me HIM, like you call Her [the primordial Goddess], HER." For it was only after years of devotion to Her, to the Divine Feminine within and without, that I finally learned her name, the name of my HGA. My Faery Beloved was requesting similar treatment, get to know him as HIM—His name would be revealed when it was time.

There was something that felt very right about His response. I felt like I finally had an image, an energy, that was definitely different from how He appeared in my dreams. And yet at the same time it was not anything that I had manufactured with a sigil* or a visualization. It was how He was choosing to manifest himself to me. This encounter reminded me of a dream I had had where He and I were sitting together on the cliffs in Ireland. In that dream, I realized I had known Him for many lifetimes.

The Glastonbury Faery Tree

Dream ✳ *November 2, 2015*

I am flying toward a hill where there are two Faery trees, both hawthorns. One is male and one is female. They are covered in silvery lights—will-o'-the-wisps. This hill overlooks a town (Glastonbury), which in my dream is my hometown. I begin to hear/chant, "Betwixt and between the sky and the sea / my Faery love, he comes to me" over and over. I am naked, and I fly toward the male Faery tree and wrap my legs around it. I begin to make love to the tree, and it makes love to

---

*Sigils are sacred symbols charged with mystical properties to summon or transfer spiritual beings and/or energies.

*me. It/he is my Faery Beloved. He penetrates me, and it is both pain
and pleasure. His wood pierces my womb and opens me, and it is exquisite pain. He fills me up like a tree growing inside of me, up my spine,
twining leaves and branches throughout my body. I become hawthorn.
He pierces my heart, and the gaps and pains in my broken heart are
filled in and transformed by his love. My medulla begins to quake with
activation. I am Holy Thorn.*

Learning His Name
Dream ✳ February 22, 2016

*In my dream last night, I encountered Him again. Is He an ancestor? A
Faery? My spirit lover? I knew not, simply that His presence opened to
me, pulled me to him, and he saw me. His appearance was golden, radiant, his eyes full of love. And I felt the quickening of desire, as if I were the
golden lock and He the silver key. And so I opened to Him. I invited Him
inside to fill me. But not from lust or lack, instead from a deep desire
to be filled/wed to his soul; to make the magic that made this world. As
He drew closer and closer coaching me to breathe and subtly move the
energies, I could feel his indwelling begin. Comingling, divine union, He
worshipped me as his Goddess. Later, his mother arrived and blessed us,
and He asked her permission to wed me. I gave him a kiss as my pledge.
And then He filled me, gently, steadily, surely, and he became the seed
inside my womb and whispered his name to me, "Gwyn."*

Gwyn, or Gwyn ap Nudd, is the Welsh Lord of the Dead, the
darkly radiant Faery King of the Underworld, the Lord of the Hunt,
and a Horned One. He is potent, chthonic, fecund, ancient, and a crossroads being. Unfortunately, not much has been written about the specific identity and behavior of this Pagan God. Most of what we know is
from the early Arthurian Welsh tale "Culhwch and Olwen"; the medieval poem "The Dialogue of Gwyn ap Nudd and Gwyddno Garanhir,"
found in the *Black Book of Carmarthen;* and the Middle Welsh prose
stories known as the *Mabinogion,* which were recorded in the twelfth

and thirteenth centuries from the earlier oral tradition. In these various sources Gwyn is said to be Arawn, the ruler of the Welsh Otherworld called "Annwn"[5]; a *psychopomp* and great warrior with a "blackened face"[6]; and the Lord of the Wild Hunt.[7] Although information on Gwyn is limited, there is wider research available on the more generalized figure of the Horned God.

Vivianne Crowley describes the plight of the Horned God:

> The Horned God is an image of great power that has endured in the human psyche through centuries of repression. . . . With the spread of Christianity, the Horned God was suppressed. He was seen as threatening, sexual, and animalistic. His image became associated with that of the Christian devil. The Horned God is not cerebral and celibate, but the phallic hunter god of forest and hill. He is Lord of the Animals. His body is that of a man, but his feet are hooves and his antlers or horns reach up to heaven, capturing within them the power of the Sun. He is strong and powerful; but he is also the shepherd, the caring and protecting father. The God is old, but young; he is strong and steadfast, but he is also light, energy, movement, creativity.[8]

This description seems to suit the dual nature of my contact well. He says he is like Gwyn, but should not be limited to only that cosmology/identity. I had shared the dream about the Glastonbury Faery Tree with Orion, and he shocked me by saying such a tree actually exists and is traditionally connected with Gwyn ap Nudd. The synchronicity of my Faery Beloved revealing his name as Gwyn, after having dreamed of making love to his tree, made my hair stand on end. So in 2016 when the opportunity had arisen to go on pilgrimage with Orion and our Faery Seer community to visit Glastonbury and other sites sacred to our Faery Seership tradition I hadn't hesitated. I had gone with the specific intention of visiting the tree on the side of Glastonbury Tor, the traditional abode of Gwyn ap Nudd, thereby deepening my contact with Gwyn.

Glastonbury Tor

Pilgrimage Account ✳ *September 7, 2016*

On the side of the tor in Glastonbury, England, there is a legendary entry to the Underworld and the residence of Gwyn ap Nudd, Faery King and Lord of the Dead. A large omphalos stone sits at the site of the entry. It is said to be his testicle in the upper world. A twin stone, the other testicle, resides in the Underworld. A hawthorn tree marks the entrance to his Underworld realm, and clooties (sacred prayers and wishes) hang from its branches. Visiting this location, I remembered the dreams I'd had some months before in which my Faery lover told me his name was Gwyn, and of being made love to by a hawthorn in Glastonbury.

I sat down under the tree and asked it if I might have a token from him. His answer was, "Of course, my beloved." I was given a root from the tree, which has become my palm wand. It was like ecstasy sitting under his branches. I sat at his base and wrapped my legs around his trunk. I felt the reveigning again, the green world twining itself up and through my nervous system, as the hawthorn caused my Kundalini energy to rise up my spine and weave itself out into my body. I realize now that all the work I've been doing with the trees has prepared me so that I could go deeper on this pilgrimage and be available for the merging that has happened. I have been made ready to receive the encoded messages from rock, tree, and water.

Another way I have deepened my knowledge and relationship with my Faery Beloved is through formally committing to a relationship with my human partner, the Druid, whose Divine Self aligns closely to Gwyn, the Guardian/Horned One. I believe my Faery Beloved has used this relationship to help calibrate me to his potency, as well as to offer my partner and me the gift of experiencing a divine union.

This calibration was confirmed when, on our pilgrimage to Glastonbury, my partner proposed to me at midnight atop Glastonbury Tor. Although I had not shared with him what was developing between Gwyn and myself at the time, I believe that his intuitive choice of location for the proposal was being guided by Gwyn. It felt as if both of them were asking for my commitment. I replied with a resounding "Yes!" A few days after returning home from pilgrimage, my Faery Beloved reaffirmed his request to marry me. While I meditated atop a giant boulder in San Francisco's Glen Park Canyon, my Faery Beloved spoke to me in the following words.

Proposal at Glen Park Canyon

Poem ✳ *October 10, 2016*

Before the techies showed up in their khaki monochrome
uniforms
Before the church of the arch-demon took up residence on
the corner of anarchy and confusion
Before the flower children camped out on the streets
Before the bongo-clad, finger-snapping beats brought their
word-prose to the coffee halls
Before the painted ladies unfurled their gentle delicacies
Before the pirates brought their stories of gold and fortune
Before the conquistadors, brandishing flags and crosses, laid
their claim
Before the deerskin tribe of Earth wove their baskets and
caught their fish
Before, before, before
I was here
This place. This land.
That you call home.
That has given nurturance and delight to so many who
have come after.
I was here and I remain here, and I will always be here.
Deep within the Earth. Deep within the root, within the
rock.
The very bottom of the well
I lie dreaming

Asleep and awake.
Calling you to rise up. Take my hand.
Calling you to remember, re-member.
Calling you, my love. Hold me.
Let us reweave this fabric together.
Let us re-green and re-convene the fibers of our body, you
 and I,
Into an exquisite tapestry of Leaf and Thorne and Fruit.
Into a place that is haven for all.
Let us go then, you and I,
Let us go there into the shadow,
Into the quiet,
Into the in-between,
And, slipping into that place, find ourselves a bower of
 sanctity and delight.
A space. A womb. An encounter that will leave us both
 alive, anew, refreshed.
Marry me. Mary me. Marry me.
There in that quiet space,
where only the light of our pulse beating in our veins
—yours the blue and mine the silver—
Lights our world.

A few days later, I went on personal retreat to Santa Cruz. I needed some time to integrate the experiences I had had on pilgrimage and the intensity with which the contact was manifesting. I went to the ocean at night with the intention of making contact with my Faery Beloved for guidance.

The following is my account of that experience:

The Waxing Moon

Ritual ✳ *October 13, 2016*

Last night I went to Seacliff Beach in Santa Cruz intending to do some
scrying with my dark mirror. I took an offering of honey and fed it to

the ocean. I washed my dark mirror in the ocean and fed it with moon-light. Almost immediately I began to feel a presence behind me, and as I peered into the mirror I "saw" Him. Tall, dark, and looming behind me. This dark horned figure that seemed to be the Guardian, or like the Guardian. I looked into the mirror again and kept feeling/seeing him there close, so close, as if he were touching me.

After returning to my lodging I sat in the hot tub and took a moon bath. I asked the moon and redwood and night spirits to help me under-stand this contact, to not run away afraid, but to do the work to integrate it—the Dark God—beloved of the Dark Goddess. Gwyn ap Nudd. Black and white. Twins. As if there are two versions of him, upper and lower. Outer and inner. Superficial and deep. And the duality of it all weighs heavy. He has been buried under the projections of two thousand years of prejudice and persecution, and now like the rest of us, he is cleaning that off to resurrect himself. He is known by many names— the Dark Rider, the Guardian, the Horned One, Dalua, Dagan, the Bull God, Gwyn ap Nudd, the Trickster, the Cunning One, Lucifer, the One Who Tests, the Descended Christ, He who is Ensouled in Earth, the Luminous Light of the Underworld, the Goat God, the Man in the Shadows, the Collective Unconscious.

He holds it all. Guardian of our subconscious and our collective shadow, he holds the keys to the mystery of our duality, our "sins," unto death. Daddy Down There knows us and loves us, for he has taken upon himself the burden of humanity, which he has shouldered for us out of love. His power is that he loves us so much he is willing to sit in all our collective darkness until such time that we shall release ourselves, and him, to be transformed, ascended. He is the Christed one who harrows hell, the one who set the captives free, yet remained in the Underworld to embrace the dead and clean them off, guard and guide them, until which point they integrate back into the oneness. His nature is threefold—Star Walker, Surface Walker, Dream Walker—Archangel Michael, Jesus, Lucifer—holding the keys of the ancestors and memory and ancient Earth consciousness.

What about me? Is it the height of arrogance to think I could unite with such a potent force in my body and not be destroyed by it? How do I reconcile who I am, who I understand myself to be, in a relationship with this chthonic force? How do I reconcile my Christian phobias (which I seem to have completely transformed for the Dark Mother) around the Dark Father? I've done so much research on the Dark Goddess, perhaps now it's time to research him, the Dark God.

What was emerging was the revelation of my Faery Beloved as an aspect of the Dark God, what in Faery Seership we call the Guardian, the Father of Earth Life.

Orion describes the Guardian in the Faery Seership tradition:

The traditional image of the Guardian is a great horned male being that stands at the threshold between life and death, coming and going, night and day, humanity and nature. . . . When he is first encountered, he can be terrifying, as he embodies the full force of nature. . . . The Guardian is the high priest of the planet Earth, consort to the high priestess, who is the Weaver of Destiny. He is the Faery King. . . . His presence is most felt in the places of immense natural beauty and solitude. His power marks a place as thinned and the fragrances of musk, pine, amber, cedar, juniper, and other woodland scents often mark his presence. When he enters into this world, most humans feel an initial sense of awe or terror. . . . He can often be encountered where the ocean meets the land, where streams intersect, in graveyards at midnight, and a host of other in-between places.[9]

I find many noteworthy elements in Orion's account, particularly the sense of smell, the place of liminality, and the somatic cues of awe and terror, all of which have also been present with my contact. It is important to note that I had not read the preceding paragraph from Orion until after the above encounters had happened, which I believe adds to the credibility of my contact.

EMBODIMENT:
DEVILS AND MONSTERS

The revelation of my Faery Beloved as an aspect of the God of the Underworld took me to new depths in my self-inquiry. Because my beloved has repeatedly shown himself to encompass both the light and dark, and often shows up as twins or as two beings—one light, one dark—I had to revisit everything I thought I knew about dualism. Although my contact's light identity feels angelic, and his dark identity feels Faery, the somatic response I have to this being—light or dark—is the same. Could He be trying to communicate something through this (non)duality?

My Faery Beloved has also manifested through various forms to reveal different, sometimes contradictory, aspects of his personality. They are the Guardian, Gwyn ap Nudd, the Horned One, Lucifer, the Faery Lover, a black dog, the hawthorn tree, an African man/ancestor/ deity, Jesus, Apollo, Gwythyr ap Greidawl, a Pillar of Flame/Light, a Norse Viking, a Scots-Irish man, and the colors silver and gold. What seems most noteworthy is that his dual nature, the manifestation of him as twins, seems to imply that He is a multifaceted being, while at the same time maintaining wholism.

For many years, I referred to his light face as Hawmosel, which is an acronym for "He Whom My Soul Loves," a *telesmatic* name* I created for him to differentiate his energy from my other contacts. Hawmosel is radiant, like an angelic Apollonian vision. It is worth noting that I created this name about a year before I met my human partner-now-fiancé and imbued the name with the specific qualities that Hawmosel seemed to manifest. Synchronistically, one of the tokens that hastened our relationship was the fact that my human partner closely resembles the qualities I set into the name.

I had more difficulty naming his dark face, which seemed to

---

*A telesmatic name is a name created from a sacred alphabet where the properties of each letter correspond to different attributes of the entity. Similar to a sigil, it is then ritually charged and used for summoning or transference.

encapsulate both the chthonic and Earthy aspects of his presence. A few names emerged over the years but nothing felt right. Finally, once he gave me the name Gwyn, I felt something fall into place with this dark face. Eventually, I began to use the name Gwyn as the overarching name for both his light and dark forms.

Indwelling the Light and Dark Beloveds
Vision ✳ May 18, 2017

I am lying on the massage table. I see my angel (light) contact, Hawmosel, as a being of golden flame with an erect phallus of light. He sits down next to me and then lies back into my body, indwelling inside of me, and we merge. I experience an upswell of indescribable joy, as if my heart will burst, it is so full of love. Then my Faery (dark) contact, Gwyn, appears as dark vines that grow up inside of me. This feels exactly like the haw-thorn dream. I am filled with his loamy presence, and we merge. Again, my heart and now womb are open and full to bursting. I feel whole, com-plete, indwelled by the two-as-one. I realize that when the solar/upper world (light) comes in first, I can relax and allow the lunar/under world (dark) to enter, and I feel safe.

A few days prior to this visitation, I had been meditating on my spirit contact and why I am still in resistance. I realized I am afraid of allowing the contact(s) to indwell. I'm still afraid of being "possessed," of losing my sovereignty and will, and of allowing forces that I'm not one hundred percent sure of to reside in my body. I think this vision came to show me that this can all happen in a way that I will feel safe and supported.

Carl Jung observed: "No tree, it is said, can grow to heaven unless its roots reach down to hell."[10] Instrumental to this inquiry has been my willingness to engage in a lengthy under world descent wherein I have had to acknowledge and address the projected shadow aspects of myself, and perhaps of the human collective. Engaging with my Faery Beloved has meant engaging with the Underworld. This Underworld work has required that I reexamine the assumptions I have held around evil, the devil, demons, and my relationship to the dark, chthonic realms—hearkening back to Caroline's reframe of the Devil card in the tarot. My first Shakta Tantra teacher, Elizabeth Bast, once told me: "Demons are simply angels whose names have been forgotten." To become an eco-sexual priestess, I needed to release old outworn ideas about Deity. At times I have wondered whether this entire journey has been a vehicle for me to transmute and transform shadow pieces for myself, and by so doing, for those who will encounter this book.

Recently I came across preliminary research material I had done on reclaiming and reframing the myths of Lilith and Medusa. In this research I made connections between these mythological figures and potent, fierce Tantric deities like Kali—all of whom are associated with darkness, fangs, and blood. In my research I sought to reframe the label of "monster" placed on these potent chthonic entities. Instead, I desired to show that their role has always been and continues to be fecund, sexual, and wild-force embodiments of the Dark Goddess. I believe it is our fear and rejection of our own potency that causes us to reject and label these energies as "evil." The following poem by the philosopher and theosophist Richard Power eloquently illustrates this principle—specifically, how far the Dark Goddess has fallen from her rightful place in history.[11]

The True Gospel of Lilith

Lilith. Lost Goddess, forsaken Goddess. Goddess of aliases (and stage names). You are the original Other. And in a textbook case of projection, the People of the Lie scapegoated you as the "child killer." Cruelly ironic. You are the Stolen Child, you are Lisbeth Salander, you are the infant sacrifice. Banished from Olympus, banished from the Abrahamic "Heaven," kept at a discrete distance even in Shambhala, you live on in the great rainforests of the South, although known by other names. There, your darkness is cultivated as the very Self of the sacred fire, and all the great rivers empty into that jet black lustre.

Lilith. Goddess of the lost and forsaken. Blinded by your light, the false prophets are terrified and name you "darkness." But they know nothing of either light or darkness. If they did, they would not try to separate the two. Light and darkness are passionate lovers. Separate one from the other, and you extinguish them both.

There is a left-handed path and a right-handed path. Evil is a subterfuge that appears sometimes on the left-hand path and sometimes on the right-hand path. But it belongs to neither. Evil is an abomination born from the sundering of light and darkness. Between before and beginning, you were.

Human history is the long story of a struggle with madness, a madness that issues from within the many divisions imposed on psyche by a mad God masquerading as the progenitor of the right-hand path: spirit divided from matter, light divided from dark, life divided from death, man divided from woman, from nature, from himself.

This madness is not you, Goddess of the daemons, this madness is the absence of you. Lilith. Abused Goddess, runaway Goddess, destitute Goddess, harlot Goddess.

The Gospel of John only got it half-right: "The light was in the darkness, and the darkness comprehendeth it not." I declare the other half of the truth in this Gospel of Lilith: "The darkness was in the light, but the light comprehendeth it not."

Lilith. Goddess of the abused. Goddess of the runaways. Goddess of the destitute. Goddess of the harlots. This true Gospel of Lilith is not written on papyrus, it is inked onto the flesh of her arching back, coiling arms, and undulating belly.

*You catch glimpses of it in the flickering candlelight of her
tent, as the world spins out of control all around you.*

*The true Gospel of Lilith is written in an ancient language
that only the future remembers. Hasten to hear it.*

RICHARD POWER

Certainly there is a long ecclesiastical history of demonizing and
vilifying the Faery people, labeling them as capricious, monstrous,
even demonic. Not surprisingly, this affront coincided with the repression of women and folkloric magic during the Middle Ages and the
Burning Times, and in the oft-cited medieval accusation of witchcraft
as *congressus cum daemones*—"marriage to the devil."[12] However, the
Pagans of that era did not believe in, let alone worship, the Christian
devil. Instead, they revered a vegetative and Earth-based deity, the
Horned One, the Guardian, the Lord of the Hunt and of the Fae.
The church, in fact, fashioned its version of the devil deliberately in
the image of the Horned One to supplant and suppress Pagan spirituality and practice. As Vivianne Crowley asserts: "The attitude [of
monotheism] was uncompromising, and missionaries such as Augustine
preached definite views about the Pagan religions: the worship of Pagan
deities was the worship of devils. . . . The deities of the Old Religion
were made into the devils of the new."[13]

Ultimately, my personal story is about reconciliation with the Dark
Goddess and Dark God. As mentioned earlier, this inquiry has brought
me to a new understanding of evil and seemingly deleterious entities.
Like the belief in unrestful spirits of the dead that cause havoc among
humans by influencing their thoughts and actions,[14] I believe that evil
is not a personified entity (the devil) nor a group of beings (demons). I
offer that evil is the unredeemed, unrepentant actions of individuals,
both incarnate and disincarnate, who seek personal gain and advance-
ment with no regard for the welfare or impact on others or the environment. In this regard, contrary to mainstream monotheistic belief, there
are no evil or malicious angels that fell from a heavenly paradise to be

trapped on Earth as punishment. As Orion/Brigh observed: "Fallen from where to where?" We are all part of the expression of the Creatrix, her children, and her body.

Therefore, the idea of good "versus" evil and light "versus" dark are but a continuum of Her expression, of Her Self. We suffer at the hands of others not because they are inherently evil or bad, but because malicious actions arise from largely unconscious wounds, traumas, in the psyche, resulting chiefly from an unintegrated heart, mind, and vitality; a lack of collective awareness; and fears of lack, loss, and/or separation. This is not to say we should excuse harmful or destructive actions. However, the idea that there are a group of evil entities out to subdue or oppress humanity (a common spiritual belief in the West and especially in New Age circles), I believe, simply adds to the fearmongering and dualism, which ultimately create more separation.[15] Vivianne Crowley would agree:

> Most practitioners of Earth Traditions do not see their deities as good guys opposed by the universe's baddies. The Divine is neither good nor evil, but a force that permeates the universe. It emerges into action out of eternal tranquility and contemplation and returns to stillness once more when each phase of creation is done. There is good and evil, but it is within human beings, not the cosmos. . . . Evil exists not in the form of an external tempter or demon, but in the actions of human beings. The Divine itself is neither good nor evil.[16]

This work, then, seeks to redeem and restore the "fallen" beings labeled as "monsters," "demons," and "devils," who have become encrusted with our human fears and projections of *otherness*. What if, instead of being evil or malicious, they have simply been scapegoated with the psychological refuse of humanity's shadow and are entombed inside the projections of this collective shadow? Perhaps originally these chthonic beings were simply serving a purpose, doing a job, their function to caretake the negative polarity of death, dismemberment, and transformation. Similar to humans dumping toxic waste into pristine waters, with the rise of monotheism we began to dump our collective shadow onto these beings, originally known as "faery," "djinn," "elementals," "daemons," and so on. Human agendas then created stories that cast these beings in the roles of devils or demons, teaching us to fear and revile them.

It seems that one of the underlying motivations for my inquiry, then, has been an attempt to track and transform both personal and societal projections around dark "versus" light, masculine "versus" feminine, upper "versus" lower. One could argue that this entire research endeavor has been an exercise in finding wholeness and integration, a nonbinary cosmology of sorts, uniting a kind of oppositional schism between humans and the realm of chthonic spirits. The more I have ascended to heights of spiritual rapture, the more intense the pull of the Underworld has become, until I could no longer avoid the descent.

This descent first manifested in my life as finding myself face-to-face with the archetypal devil via two abusive relationships. However, through much psycho-emotional support and spiritual practice, this chthonic pull eventually found a more manageable way to express itself through my Shakta Tantric sadhana, my devotion to the Dark Goddess, and my relationship with my Faery Beloved.

Orion Foxwood describes the importance of redeeming our relationship with the Underworld as follows:

> In the philosophy of Faery Seership, there is no other way to the heart of the universal Creator but through hallowing the underworld. By hallowing, I mean you travel into the sacred and primal powers of your underworld through the Ancestor, then bring that stream of living consciousness to the larger ocean of life embodied in the Guardian's natural laws. This process redeems the blood that flows through you and opens your connection to the deep abiding vision and power of the underworld. There is no way into the underworld except by unifying the human natural elements within you in communion with the larger natural world through the Guardian.[17]

A willingness to embrace the dark and sometimes unsettling sexual forces associated with the Dark Goddess has led me to an inevitable relationship with the Dark God. It is here that I find I am being asked to transform the moniker *monster* that is often used to label the dark masculine. If I am, as I suspect, being wooed to marry the Gods of the upper worlds and the under worlds jointly, as a united entity, then perhaps there is a deeper mystery unfolding in the identity and cosmological location of my Faery Beloved. The more I reconcile and heal my assumptions about the Underworld, the more capacity I have to accept his true nature. This spirit marriage, then, is my deepening, my endarkenment, tempering and enhancing my lifelong pursuit of enlightenment.

CONFIRMATION OF THE CONTACT
An Invitation to Be Indwelled
Dream ✳ *October 25, 2016*

Gwyn shows up looking like a Viking/Norse God. He is my other half, my missing piece. Just seeing each other we are magnetically pulled together. He says only now can he fully approach me. He wants to indwell me, to be one, like we've been over and over again, sometimes me inside him, sometimes him inside me, incarnation after incarnation. The ecstasy is palpable, and my heart and soul are wide open to receive him, no hesitation.

CONFIRMATION
An Invitation to be Indwetted
Dream ✳ *October 28, 2016*

On each side of me are male beings. On my right is a light Christ-like being who is full of serenity and compassion. On my left is a dark feisty being—primal and passionate. The Light God wants me to be only his, but the potency and passion of the Dark God is not something I am willing to sacrifice. The Light God asks me who do I think that he is? I look into his eyes and see compassion, Jesus. He tells me God created the world. I correct him. I show him the primal power of nature and say,

"She, the Goddess Mother, created all this! This is Earth manifesting herself!" As much as I love the solar/stellar God of the cosmos, I love Earth Mother and the God of the Underworld, Gwyn. I sit between them mediating the energy, and it is exhausting. I ask them if they can't simply merge into one being, back together, light and dark united. They do, and chaos erupts, a totally unstable being.

They show me this to demonstrate that the two of them simply merging won't work, the system is too unstable. They need a third element— the Divine Feminine—to bring the two into union. And so I merge with their duality and the three of us become one being—light and dark Gods with the transformative, mediating, and stabilizing force of Goddess in between. With me they unite and we become something altogether new and rare. We are three beings and one being, a new Holy Trinity, and we expand to the size of a giant over ten feet tall. We fly up into the sky and out over the world to heal the chaos on the planet. Together we begin to shower down blessings like golden honey onto all we fly over. The last thing I hear before I wake is, "The devil of this time (age) is the epicene Christ."

He Is with Me Always
Dream ✳ June 19, 2017

My Faery Beloved appears. He is only a little taller than I am, and he has shoulder-length golden hair like hay. His skin and clothes look like he is part tree. Perhaps he is related to the Old Faery Grandfather in my Faery family dream who kept regressing back to his tree form. My beloved radiates love for me. He takes me into his arms and speaks to me, to my soul. It is hard to make out exactly what He is saying. I only catch phrases here and there, as if a din is drowning out his words.

He leans in closer and speaks directly into my ear so that I can hear him more clearly. He tells me that his shape is constantly changing, implying that I shouldn't be so fixated on how he appears to me. He tells me I'm needlessly worrying about "how to contact" him. But He is always with me, and in fact, sometimes he is me. (Does this mean He is indwelling inside of me at times?) Now when He appears, instead of feeling an overwhelming erotic energy rise up like a shakti pulse, I feel a deepening thrum, a union, and a completeness inside of me. It's the kind of wholeness that you didn't know was missing until that part is reunited. I have a sense that I have been calibrated to his energy to the point that, when He arrives, it's not such a shock to my system. The fact that I am able to hear his voice more clearly is an indication that all the work I've been doing to attune myself to nature and to Him is working.

Like a multidimensional Christos, my Faery Beloved walks from Cosmos to Earth to Underworld and back, circulating the energy of the three worlds in this movement. This circulation seems to align with Orion Foxwood's British Traditional Witchcraft tradition, which teaches that the Christos is a tripartite constellation of the beings Archangel Michael, Jesus, and Lucifer. Perhaps my Faery Beloved presented himself as the Faery King Gwyn ap Nudd so that I would be free to engage with him without any association to the patriarchal monotheistic dogma that vilifies the Dark God. Perhaps the situation of Gwyn as Lord of the Faery and of the Dead insinuates that he holds a primordial potency devoid of religious labels, giving me a context within which to cultivate the contact outside of Christian cosmology and language. This, in turn, has given me the ability to contact this potent entity in a more unconditioned way—without the personal and collective projection of Christianized fear, worry, and guilt.

Had my Faery Beloved initially shown up stating, "Hi, I'm the Lord of the Underworld. Marry me!" I can only imagine the psycho-spiritual contortions I might have gone through to avoid this contact. Instead, his gradually revealing himself as Gwyn ap Nudd, Lord of the Faery, has enabled me to engage a being of this magnitude, free of the weight of two thousand years of projected "evil." Although this has not absolved me of having to contend with my own assumptions about darkness, it has given me the opportunity to question collectively held beliefs about "the shadow" and "the dark."

It has also allowed this being to show himself to me on his own terms, in his own time, without much overt resistance from me. Because he manifests as "both-and" energy, light and dark, it seems that our work together is meant to transcend and include the totality of the human experience. It is meant to encompass both the darkness and the light, as together we bring all dualities, including masculine and feminine, upper and lower, good and bad, into greater harmony and balance through our relationship. Perhaps, when all is said and done, *the names and exact cosmology of my Faery Beloved are less important than the delicate inner workings of the contact and our numinous capacity for transformation together.*

In January of 2018, six months after I wrote the first draft of my story, a volume entitled *Gwyn ap Nudd: Wild God of Faerie, Guardian of Annwfn* found its way to me. The Celtic Witch and Druid Danu Forest who runs a magical order in Glastonbury, UK, describes Gwyn ap Nudd as a two-faced God, both light and dark.[18] His light counterpart is Gwythyr ap Greidawl, the solar, upper world God to Gwyn's dark, under world God. This was all new information to me. Her research confirmed the encounters and experiences I had been having, and left me awestruck with how accurate my visions, dreams, and encounters had been. They precisely matched her narrative description of this (these) ancient presence(s).

However, what brought me to a heart-pounding, skin-tingling full stop was her description of the Goddess Creiddylad, for whose love Gwyn and Gwythyr compete. Creiddylad is a mysterious Welsh Goddess who represents Earth, the land, and sovereignty. Not much is known about her other than that she is married to, or is a consort of, *both* Light and Dark Gods and that she is considered to be Queen of the Land and of the Faery. It is Creiddylad that the high king would ritually wed to bless the land and restore health and wholeness to his people.[19] Having read this, and then looking back at the way in which my Divine Self and Faery Beloved story has unfolded, I can only wonder if this is, as Craig Chalquist describes in his work on archetypal mythology, the guiding myth of my life finally making itself unequivocally known to me.[20]

MARRYING GWYN

On October 27, 2018, while in the process of finishing my dissertation, I participated in the Spiral Dance, an annual Samhain ritual led by Starhawk and the Reclaiming Pagan community in the San Francisco Bay Area. I have been participating in this ritual annually for over seven years, usually by creating an altar or participating in the ritual invocation. This year, I agreed to cocreate the Necromanteum, an altar-chamber where participants are invited to *scry* (gaze into) mirrors to meet with their beloved dead. Because of my relationship with my Faery Beloved, Gwyn, the Lord of the Dead, and the Fae, I felt led to priestess this altar by acting as an embodiment of Lady Death, anointing participants with a blessing as they entered.

A few weeks before the ritual, I had a dream in which my Faery Beloved took me to his Faery court and introduced me as his betrothed. It was a powerful dream, and I awoke feeling expanded and elated. After having not sensed much contact with him for many months, to have such a dream felt encouraging and affirming.

The Spiral Dance ritual always includes a trance journey during which all three to four hundred participants lie down on the ground and journey together to the Summerlands, also known as the Isle of Apples, the realm of the Faery, and land of the dead. We journey there to meet with our beloved dead and converse with them. I have done this journey many times; typically, my mother or a beloved ancestor has shown up for me. However, this year, something profoundly different happened. When I stepped onto the farther shore I dropped to my knees and sank my hands into the ground. Looking up, I saw the feet of Gwyn, although his feet were part human, part hawthorn tree, as if his feet had roots. Normally, Gwyn assumes a more human form when we interact, but he said to me that this night I would need to come into Fae form to interact with his realm.

Together we became like a stream of liquid light and journeyed through the roots of the tree and into the land of the Fae. There his court was waiting for us, and it was then I realized we were going to be married. I knew this was the perfect time, yet I had not prepared vows or anything special for such a holy event. Yet none of that seemed to matter; the rite was much more energetic than literal. We exchanged vows, which were much more like promises of mutual collaboration and fealty than romantic wedding vows. I promised to take his people as my own and to be a voice and champion for them. He promised to lend me his protection and magic. It was very much like two kingdoms coming together as one. We then exchanged rings and forged a blood bond, his silver blood mixing with my blue blood. Then it was over and complete—just so. Coming back from the trance, Gwyn stayed with me as we danced the spiral. I could feel him basking in the love and beauty of all the amazing human faces that passed before us in the dance, reveling in the joy of our humanity. It was a delight and a celebration.

At the beginning of the ritual, Starhawk had asked us to suspend our disbelief for that night, which is not a request she normally makes. A Druid friend had recently told her: "The Gods are absolutely real, and the Gods are entirely a figment of our imagination." She admitted that she was, herself, something of a skeptic, but that for that evening we needed to suspend our skepticism and let the magic flow. It was almost as if she knew that I would be questioning the validity of my journey and needed that extra nudge to let go and trust.

Still, over the days following the ritual, I pondered this spontaneous union, which had taken so many years to finally manifest. Was it real? Had it truly just happened? How could I have spent all this time researching the protocol for spirit marriages, to have mine happen so spontaneously and without fanfare? I shared my thoughts with a trusted friend who is a psychic medium, and she cast things in a different light. She reminded me that often when people of different countries marry, they have one marriage in their home country and another in the country of their spouse. These marriages may happen months apart, or sometimes years apart.

Marrying Gwyn in the realm of the Fae was the way he acknowledged me and our union among his people. This is what I most needed to happen at this time—to confirm and enjoy a certain recognition in the subtle realms. At some point, a union among my human community may need to be witnessed, depending on whether the human world needs the confirmation of our union. This makes perfect sense to me.

REQUIREMENTS AND PURPOSE
OF THE RELATIONSHIP

As I reflect back upon the requirements and sacrifices my interviewees shared with me about their spirit marriages, I can see how my own story mirrors many of their experiences. Similar to Orion, Kama, and Frater Lux, the biggest requirement of my journey toward a spirit marriage was a total and complete surrender to the process, requiring my undivided time and energy. I was not able to work professionally while I was writing my dissertation; the organic inquiry took over all my waking and sleeping activities.

Surrendering to the chthonic made me practically useless for anything other than doing rituals, being in nature, and spiritual study. It was as if my mind-body-spirit was like a computer, and my inquiry into spirit marriage was a program constantly running in the background—one that required all my resources and left very little space to do anything else. So one of the repeated requests that I made to my Faery Beloved and my helping spirits was for providence, sustenance, and grace. Fortunately, with the support of my community (and a hefty amount of student loans!), I was able to devote myself completely to the research. This allowed me to incubate the dissertation intelligence fully, and as a result, to experience the potent transformation of the organic inquiry process.

One thing that has helped me cultivate my contact has been creating an altar to my Faery Beloved and the Fae. On it I have placed images that remind me of him, as well as items I have collected that hold his vibration. Following Madrone's practice of connecting to Tingan daily, each day when I awake, I try to open the Faery well—a ritual for connecting to the Faery realm—over the altar or in my garden and take a moment to tune into his energy. This ritual helps to anchor the connection between us, so that I can feel his indwelling more clearly.

At this point, I believe the purpose of my relationship with my Faery Beloved is twofold. One, it is preparing and refining me for more of my own *entheosis* (awakening the Divine within) process to take root and unfold. Two, it is rectifying and refining the relationship of humanity to the under world through the transdimensional nature of my Faery Beloved who is the embodiment of integrated duality, dark-light, above-below, good-bad. As in my epicene Christ dream, together we are the Earth Goddess plus upper world God and under world God united. As three in one, we are now integrated to help bring about a wholism that, perhaps, our planet has not experienced since the rise of patriarchy, if ever. *Our job is to transcend and include dualistic thinking, to reclaim and hallow the Underworld beings and God/desses, to wake up the slumbering and disaffected upper world God/desses, and to support humanity in its entheosis.* And this book is the love child of our union.

TRUSTING THE PROCESS

To be honest, I still struggle with wanting to understand and rationalize this phenomenon, instead of letting go, trusting, and surrendering. A huge amount of faith is required when working with the spirit world. Most people, as I have witnessed through my interviews, do not experience flesh and blood manifestations of their spirit-spouses. Instead, they experience them in a much more intuitive way. This is challenging for me. There is still a part of me that wants tangible proof that this is real. I can perceive the subtle realms and their cues, but I also have a keen, logical mind that can undermine my more mystical inclinations if I'm not careful. I believe this makes me a good researcher, because I am open to the paranormal and subtle energies, but rarely get carried away into fantasy. Unfortunately, it can also make me a little thickskulled when Spirit is trying to get my attention. As with Frater Lux, sometimes the spirits have to beat me over the head to drive home a point.

Much of my work with Faery Seership over the past ten-plus years has been trying to relearn and reconnect to the innate mysticism of my childhood, when I trusted myself and my intuition more. Yet I also realize that the human mind has a huge capacity for self-delusion. It seems that a lot of my work has been developing discernment around what is actual contact and what is fancy.

Interestingly, lucid dreams have been an important key to this process. Although one could argue that dreams are the epitome of imagination, lucid dreams for me are numinous encounters in which my thinking mind is shut off. At these times I can allow the visions to arise and guide me without the interruption of logic or analysis— and I can still experience a sense of agency and intentionality in the encounter. Similar to psychedelic research, lucid dreams open the doors of my perception to other realms, worlds, and beings. It is in my dreams that I am most free to explore my Faery Beloved and our relationship.

In undertaking this journey, one of the biggest tasks for me was to keep a meticulous record of all extraordinary dreams wherein I have been contacted or given phenomenological information about the realms of Spirit.

When I began, I jokingly referred to myself as "Pagan-lite," meaning I had some exposure to magical practice and Earth-based teaching but was not on a formal path of any kind, other than my own intuitive explorations. As a result of being contacted, I have formally stepped onto the path of Shakta Tantric self-cultivation, as well as that of a ten-year (and counting) Faery Seership apprenticeship, and have also publicly claimed my identity as an ecospiritual seer, witch, and priestess.

A WORD OF CAUTION

In reading my story, one could question whether the undertaking of a spirit marriage is a way to avoid real intimacy and the trials and tribulations associated with intimate human relationships. This is a fair critique, one that I have wrestled with, asking myself, Am I interested in the subject of spirit marriage because I am wounded from past relationships? Is spirit marriage a way for me to avoid human interaction? Personally, I believe every person who finds themselves wooed by a spirit or who desires to take a spirit lover should ask themselves some form of this question.

For some whose past, like my own, included abuse, marriage to a spirit might offer a way to heal and trust again. In my opinion, this would ideally be a phase or step in the growth process toward greater human connection—not the end point. The temptation to surrender oneself entirely to a spirit marriage as a means of avoiding human relationships can be seductive. For what human could measure up to an all-pervasive and presumably omniscient being? However, it is important to recognize that almost all of my interviewees, including myself, have intimate human partners in addition to spirit partners—and in almost all cases, the spirit marriage enhances and encourages the human relationship.

It is also essential to recognize that neither my interviewees nor I went in search of a spirit marriage or spirit partners; these relationships came to us. This is not to imply that asking for a spirit partner is inappropriate. If that is one's desire, though, one would do well to assess the motivation for seeking an intimate relationship with a spirit-being. Spirit marriage is not a means to avoid intimacy with flesh and blood people, at least not a healthy spirit marriage. Spirit marriage is an adjunct to human relationships, in whatever constellation they may take, giving us an enhanced ability to impact our community and our world.

I believe that much of the spirit world wants to see humanity thrive and evolve as a species. We can do this supported by their wisdom and guidance, but ultimately we must learn how to cocreate and get along with other humans. The cauldron of intimate human relationships is one of the most powerful accelerators of that process. I believe we contribute very little positive social and planetary change by hiding behind our computer screens, social media profiles, or in hermit-like withdrawal. However, *we have the capacity to transform the planet when we as a species—supported by our unseen allies—come together in our vulnerability and imperfections and envision a world that works for everyone.*

And so I end my story with just as much awe and wonder as when I first began it—changed in profound ways, with questions answered, and yet with new questions continually surfacing to take their place. Truly, this is a lifelong inquiry, one that I may never fully comprehend in this lifetime. And I am okay with that.*

---

*Completed on a rainy, windswept evening, during the first quarter moon in the sign of Aquarius, on the eve of St. Valentine's Day, in the Chinese lunar year of the lucky Earth pig.

PART III

The Future

*

**A Druid chant for becoming
a good ancestor**
. . . .
*We are tomorrow's ancestors,
the future of yesterday,
and what we are in the here
and now,
goes rippling out all ways,
goes rippling out always.*

14
Cultivating
a Spirit Marriage

*W*e have parted the velvety curtain, the outer sanctum known as the past. We then stepped into the clarifying light of the inner sanctum, the present. Now let us peer into the radiant splendor, the *sancta sanctorum,* which is the future of spirit marriage.

Finding a path to spirit marriage is perhaps as unique as the individual. There is no one, right, and only way that a spirit marriage may manifest. Some choose to adopt a tradition that practices spirit marriage to help them navigate the relationship. Others choose to go it alone, listening primarily to the voice of the spirits that guide them.

In my case, as I read and reread each of the stories I collected, I began to hear the voices of my coresearchers' spirit-spouses speak to me. To envision the future of spirit marriage, I listened to these voices, meditating on each of their stories until I received a vision that revealed the main themes and important aspects within each of them. I discovered there were five main ideas that each of my coresearchers had shared aspects of in one way or another and which were present in my own journey. I paid attention to each unique expression of those themes and the ways in which the stories informed each other and my inquiry.

However, as you have read their stories, you may have found other themes that called to you, or ideas and inspirations that whisper to you about your own potential for this practice. Fantastic! The idea that this book is a living, breathing entity, or daimon, which will speak to each individual differently is part of the magic of this work. Perhaps the spirit of one of my coresearchers is wooing you. Perhaps your own research muse is inspiring you to pick up a thread of this material and weave it into an inquiry of your own. Wonderful! I encourage further discussion, analysis, and embodied interaction with this material, in hopes that the daimon of this research may speak to and guide you on your quest to deepen with the spirits.

WHY BONDED RELATIONSHIPS WITH SPIRITS ARE NEEDED NOW MORE THAN EVER

I truly believe that the spirits have been wooing us from time immemorial, gently and sometimes more forcefully, so as to reveal to us the mysteries of our Self, our species, and our planet. If we humans are to make our next great evolutionary leap forward, I believe we will do so in consort with our varying spirit lovers/spouses who have been lovingly advancing our consciousness, perhaps since the dawn of our species. Let us now envision where an intimate relationship with Otherworldly beings might take us personally, as a species, and how it might help us better foster a cocreative, regenerative Earth.

THE IMPORTANCE OF COMMUNITY

One of the first themes to reveal itself to me when I began this work was the importance of community involvement in a spirit marriage. Community witnesses uphold and in some instances challenge the practitioner in their commitment to marry. In fact, the Vodou/Voodoo mariage Loa, the Dagara Tingan sob enshrinement, and Orion's Faery marriage all required a community of fellow practitioners for the marriage to take place. For Kama, although her marriage took place spontaneously, her lineage family and community of elders helped her navigate and implement the requirements of her marriage to Kali. In Caroline's case, community provided an important counterpoint to her marriage experience, helping her find her own unique path with Odin (and with the Orisha) beyond and against the prescribed norms of the community. In Frater Lux's story, community fed and protected him while he went on the solitary journey to unite with his HGA. Similarly, a community of people are required to support the Vodouisant during the arduous seven-day met tet ritual. Therefore, it appears that community is also a kind of participant in the spirit marriage.

For most of my coresearchers, the spirit marriage had to become a public relationship, a kind of participatory experience wherein the entire community became involved. Their involvement made the relationship real for both the practitioner and the community. The community helped to hold the practitioner to the vows they publicly took—a commitment that then gave the community a sense of cohesion. Witnessing a spirit marriage can coalesce or deepen a spiritual community, who in turn are fed by the spirit marriage. In Madrone's story, her marriage was actually a requirement for building the West Coast Dagara community, and brought balance, wealth, support, and unity to her community.

By allowing the spirit marriage to be witnessed and upheld by the group, the practitioner becomes a guide and mediator of the spirit-spouse for the community. For Frater Lux, this led to the task of creating "order out of chaos," of figuring out how to bring greater meaning to his community through the guidance of his HGA. For Kama, it led to the cultural "translation project" of Tantra—working out how to translate a historically heteronormative practice for a Western queer audience while still honoring the lineage and tradition of her kula family.

A focus on community can also lead to a tension between community and nonconformity. How is it possible to cultivate a sense of cohesion and agreement within a community when the practice of spirit marriage is, for most, a radical alternative spiritual path? Many practitioners drawn to engage in a spirit marriage are, in the broader context of societal norms, nonconformists, comfortable with going against the grain, and seem to have a high tolerance for transgressing the boundaries of acceptable spiritual practice. For Caroline this has meant working with severe limits on her ability to engage in the Santería community that culturally aligns with some of her spirit-spouses. For Kama, it has meant a deep commitment to self-inquiry wherein she has delved into certain assumptions about her sexuality again and again to uncover deeper truths. Ultimately, a balance (if sometimes tenuous) is struck between finding cohesion within the spiritual community and understanding that not everyone needs to act or look the same. Perhaps this idea is also applicable to the broader conversation on spirit marriage and its variety of manifestations and practices among traditions.

Ultimately, each practitioner must work it out with their copractitioners, determining what levels of cohesion and variance their group can tolerate. As Kama described it: One looks for the auspicious signs, reads the karmic agreements of those involved, and fosters an ongoing dialogue with the various players within the community and the spiritual tradition itself. Ideally, one finds a way to include all the ways a spirit marriage might manifest as a boon to the community. As Henri and Suzette expressed, eventually the marriage contributes to a greater public discourse via creative expression, (re)education about subaltern spirituality, and ideally demystifies and normalizes spirit contact.

To reiterate what was previously touched on in Madrone's story, it seems that the complex and demanding undertaking required to engage and marry an extraordinary being is so potent and destabilizing to the human ego that a community is needed to help ground and uphold that relationship. A spirit marriage may be undertaken by the individual, but everyone else in the community is effectively a part of that relationship as well. Ultimately, this is the case for all forms of relationship, spirit or human—relationships do not function in a vacuum. Healthy relationships flourish with a community around them to help them thrive, flow, and be balanced.

SOVEREIGNTY THROUGH SURRENDER

Another primary theme in most of the stories is the dialectic between surrendering to the guidance of a spirit-spouse and claiming one's personal sovereignty. In almost every interview, reports were made about sacrificing certain aspects of one's life, work, relationship, personality, or possessions—and in some cases, being completely remade via the vehicle of the spirit marriage. In the most extreme example, Orion reports that Brigh "took everything away" until nothing was left but his relationship with her. Kama echoes this sentiment when she reports that her primary relationship with Kali means that everything else in her life comes second.

Frater Lux also experienced a kind of ego dismantling wherein he worked deliberately to release anything that would get in the way of his relationship with his HGA. Careers changed—as in the case of Orion, Suzette, and Kama. Long held ideas about the self shifted, were restructured, and in some cases dissolved, as surrender to the transformation of oneself and one's previous way of life was enacted. Madrone specifically highlighted the importance of surrender as a paramount aspect of the marriage ritual. And yet, once the spirit marriage practitioner was able to fully surrender to the presence and will of the spirit, a sense of newfound personal sovereignty and potency was not long to follow.

In reviewing each story for the themes of sovereignty and surrender, I began to see a common progression through the stages of a spirit marriage, one that many of the coresearchers undertook. To begin with, most of my coresearchers went through an initial phase of *preparedness* wherein the spirit-spouse—often unbeknownst to them—had begun tempering them for the relationship. This preparation was often accomplished through the psychological and physiological readying of the individual for the eventual indwelling of the contact. Sometimes restrictions were placed upon the practitioner, and things like diet, lifestyle, and personal associations changed to better accommodate the newly forming connection with the spirit.

Second, the spirit contacts formally made themselves known and revealed their intention to wed the practitioner. It was during this *contact* phase that several of my coresearchers reported feeling a kind of possessiveness or a "being laid claim to" by the spirit. In many cases this led to the next phase: *resistance* and/or *negotiation*. During the resistance phase, practitioners reported a need to challenge and, in some cases, argue with the spirit to gain further clarity about the spirit's intentions.

As Bloody Mary shared, resistance and/or negotiation are an anticipated developmental stage—in her tradition called the *Voodoo crisis*—which helps to balance and calibrate the two beings to one another. The process of wrestling with the spirit strengthens, shapes, and focuses the connection, whereby the practitioner negotiates the terms of the relationship and develops greater confidence therein. This process of negotiation and boundary setting were also reported as an *ongoing* part of the spirit marriage relationship, taking place not only in some early phase, but over the course of the partnership. For example, recall that Monique shared her need to negotiate around the sleeping arrangement with her husband and spirit-spouses. In fact, many practitioners reported a strong belief that they were not relinquishing power to their spirit-spouse but instead were experiencing greater personal power and agency in the relationship. One does not blindly submit to or engage in worship of a spirit-spouse, but instead collaborates with them via cocreative endeavors.

Eventually the process of negotiation leads to a kind of *sacrifice* or *letting go* phase, in which sufficient trust has been established between the practitioner and the spirit. The practitioner is finally able to surrender into an expanded embodiment with the spirit. In this phase a development of presence or indwelling arises wherein the old habits, thoughts, and life patterns previously clung to by the practitioner are swept away to make room for the consciousness of the spirit-spouse. Through this recalibration, the final phase is reached, one of greater agency and sovereignty, one of productive and enriching interplay, dialogue, and cocreativity. As a result of the marriage, the practitioner is now imbued with the potency and insight of the spirit world and its forces.

The idea of sovereignty gained through spirit marriage hearkens back to the idea of the sacred marriage between the human regent and the land in numerous pre-Christian traditions from ancient Mesopotamia to early Ireland.

Writing on the relationship between sovereignty and the sacred land Druid, Danu Forest writes:

> In Celtic culture, the figure of sovereignty was represented by numerous earth and mother Goddesses who bestowed health and fertility on the land. Evidence suggests that rites of sacred kingship involved ritually or physically mating with her in order to achieve legitimacy. . . . Sovereignty is something that is always fought for; it cannot come easily from birthright or any political system. It is a place of harmony and balance where all is literally "all right with the world," a state of blessedness and heavenly wholeness.
>
> However, this state must be continually in flux. . . . We see how life saps us of sovereignty, drains it away with daily concerns or denies us enough power over our own destinies to encounter such a vivifying presence, and so the quest must begin. If we are not sovereign in our own lives, we can be sure that someone or something else is, and that must be tackled if we are to marry the queen of the land or finally recover our own soul's treasure. . . . Sovereignty is an elusive figure, something that calls to us with an inner yearning, something that will wake us in the night or stir us to tears at a sunset but is easily over looked in the brash light of day.[1]

The stories shared by my coresearchers point to a way in which an individual may achieve personal sovereignty through the rite of the spirit marriage, realizing a more stable state of the harmony, balance, blessedness, and wholeness that Forest suggests we struggle to achieve. Like the struggle to surrender—which most of the coresearchers reported as being present in their betrothal—so the journey toward sovereignty is a quest that typically requires testing, hardship, and duress, all in service to the refinement of the practitioner for the union—and for the greater cocreation that can then be offered to the community and the world.

SEXUALITY AND DIVINE UNION

A third theme to arise was that of erotic engagement with one's spirit-spouse and the potential for divine union. Many of my coresearchers reported the experience of sexual arousal or engagement in some form of sexual contact with their spirit-spouse—to varying degrees and outcomes. Suzette and Nanette both alluded to the idea that a sexual relationship might come as a benefit of being wed to a spirit, inasmuch as the Loa determined that it would be beneficial to the human. In Orion's case, Brigh's presence often elicits a kind of whole-body state of arousal, but he stresses that his experience of union with Brigh is more like "honey flowing through a honeycomb" and less about genital stimulation. On the other hand, Kama's Tantric practice and Caroline's shamanic experience both intentionally cultivate eroticism to generate power and exchange energy. In fact, Caroline explicitly stated that engaging in sexual relationships with her spirit-spouses is a way to comingle and exchange information, empowerments, and healing.

Indeed, as teacher and author Jalaja Bonheim says:

The image of God as lover is ancient, and it permeates all religious traditions. Ecstatics revel in the imagery of sexual love because no other human experience reflects so accurately the nature of what transpires between the soul and God in the secret chambers of the heart. Since the dawn of history, mystics have celebrated this love affair between the transcendent Spirit and the incarnate human soul.[2]

Although an erotic relationship was not the stated end goal of the spirit marriage for any of my interviewees, many did enjoy the deeper unitive experience and activation that a sexual encounter with their spirit-spouse provided. Some even reported that the by-product of an erotic relationship with their spirit-spouse was the cocreation of new ideas, teachings and, in Orion's case, an entire spiritual system of study. In my case, the by-product of my union is this book. It seems that the fecundation provided by a spirit-spouse can birth new creative expression into the world through the human spouse, thereby bringing new ideas and advanced spiritual teachings to humanity.

That said, Frater Lux stressed that his connection to his HGA does not include an erotic component, even though his HGA did give him volumes of material to teach. Although his encounter with his HGA is not overtly erotic, perhaps the indwelled intimacy of his relationship yields similar results to those who do report explicitly erotic encounters. Frater Lux did admit that the idea of sexual contact with entities is not unheard of in his order, but that the Golden Dawn strongly cautioned its magicians against the practice of sex magic with entities because of the unpredictability of astral and noncorporeal beings. As complex as sex with humans can be, he implies that it is doubly so with entities who are not subject to the physical laws of embodiment. If, however, the magician sought such an alliance, it was with the utmost respect, and in most cases was a lifelong commitment.

In my opinion, the pivotal issue seems to be one of how we spatially orient with the entity according to our subtle body senses. The Golden Dawn holds that one can have sex with an entity outside of oneself, whereas one cannot, or perhaps does not, engage in erotic energy with one's Divine Self. I would challenge this idea as particularly Victorian. I would also offer that a postmodern interpretation of knowledge and conversation with one's HGA or Divine Self might, in fact, include the kind of self-love practices that consecrate the body into becoming the ideal host for one's Divine Consciousness to dwell within. In fact, in my experiential study of Shakta Tantra, I have come across certain left-handed Tantric practices that prescribe this very technique. I would also add that binary, three-dimensional spatial orientations like "within/without," "up/down," "near/far," are most assuredly a human construct to which nonphysical forces are not bound.

In her essay "The Sexual Mystic: Embodied Spirituality," former nun Dorothy Donnelly makes the argument that making love with God is a feminist statement. Patriarchal religion has taken God out of the bedroom and pathologized our longing for ecstatic sexual union. "For the feminist mystic . . . whose experiences were so often denigrated or ridiculed by male directors or theologians . . . she discovered in God's lovemaking that the embrace of God's unifying love was not better expressed then in the act of human love. Human love turned out to be the copy! Mystic, unitive love, the original! And that love was eminently cognitive as well as emotional."[3]

I offer that to make love to Spirit is to reconnect to our bodies in a way that vitalizes them, making them temples of divine awakening. Donnelly goes on to claim: "The love we experience for God . . . must happen in a sexual way by dint of the fact that we love embodied. The love of God manifest in our spirituality is influenced and shaped by our sexuality in turn."[4] If a tradition embraces the practice of marriage between humanity and the divine or spirit realms, I offer that then some form of vital exchange between the two realms is an inevitable and necessary part of that tradition—thereby fostering the alchemy of embodied spirituality and erotic mysticism.

As a result, a subtheme arose regarding sexual orientation and gender identity. Three coresearchers shared how their understanding of their sexual orientation was challenged and/or informed by their spirit marriage. Both Orion and Henri, who are gay men, married female spirits. However, neither expressed any misgivings about the heteronormative nature of this practice, which seems to be the traditional approach for both the Faery marriage and the mariage Loa. On the other hand, for Kama as a mostly heterosexual woman, being married to a female deity meant that her entire sexual orientation was brought into question, and she spent quite a bit of time exploring and wrestling with her sexuality. Ultimately, as Orion shared, perhaps the spirits aren't gendered in the way that we humans understand gender. Many of the coresearchers reported the ability of their spirit-spouse to shape-shift into any form they desired. *Gender, then, becomes a (human) language that spirit uses to inform, enhance, or balance needed qualities within the practitioner.*

Finally, I offer a note on polyamory. Caroline was the only coresearcher to touch upon this subject directly in her interview, in which she shared the complexity of negotiating the desires of her various spirit-spouses and their occasional jealousy of each other. Monique also alluded to the idea of polyamory when she discussed the ways in which she and her sister-wives teased each other about their marriage to the same spirit husband. However, I believe that *because most of the coresearchers are in committed human relationships in addition to spirit marriages, in most cases, a kind of polyamory is being practiced whether they name it such or not.* In fact, as previously stated, in the New Orleans Voodoo and Haitian Vodou traditions polyamory is the rule among the Loa—Erzulie Freda is wife to Damballah, Ogou, and the sea king Met Agwe, while the God Ogou wears the rings of both Erzulie Freda and Erzulie Danto. I believe that engaging in a spirit marriage necessarily leads to a reconsideration of the heteronormative assumptions surrounding monogamous (human) relationships.

Furthermore, the projection of Western culture and religious values that devalue or even vilify the practice of polyamory in nonmainstream cultures is a concern that has arisen from this research—a concern that is rooted in feminist, queer, and indigenous scholarship.[5] This is an inquiry worthy of its own research project, but regrettably beyond the scope of this work.

COCREATION AND CONSCIOUS EVOLUTION

As the medieval German mystic Meister Eckhart pointed out, "All who make love with Spirit will conceive and become pregnant with an otherworldly joy. They will nurture a pure, innocent, and unsullied spirit that radiates divine love into the world, and they will give birth to acts of compassion and beauty."[6]

The previous theme of divine union, then, organically unfolds into the theme of cocreative conscious evolution. As the Faery Seer R. J. Stewart once told me: "We need each other. We do what they cannot, and they do what we cannot." The idea that with a spirit-spouse we can achieve so much more than we can as our separate, individual selves is an important outcome reported by most of my coresearchers and certainly tracks with my own experience. Whether in conscious collaboration or conjugal bliss, spirit marriage serves to *allow the human counterpart to reach beyond their finite sense of Self and expand to embrace the realms of consciousness out beyond the reach of ordinary space and time.* There an awakening of mystical forces can happen—forces that are interdependent and interpenetrating. No longer are we limited by our five senses or solely rational ways of knowing. Instead, we become quickened by the presence of the Divine Other, which prompts us to let go of our mundane nature and open to receive the influx of ecstatic anointing— hastening a kind of evolutionary change in our capacities and ourselves.

Orion, Kama, Caroline, and Frater Lux all reported that the process of surrendering their mundane sense of self allowed them to be rebuilt in ways that greatly expanded, enhanced, and facilitated a greater sense of purpose and contribution to the world. Instrumental to this process were the recalibration and attunement of the human to subtler and subtler energies—what some call psychic or extrasensory perception— enabling them to more fully engage and communicate with both human and extraordinary beings. As Caroline and Orion describe it, they believe this sensitization is part of the next evolutionary leap for the human species, one that we must rigorously apply ourselves to or perish. Through the process of conscious evolution informed by union with spirit partners, humanity is given an opportunity to find its way back (or, indeed, forward) into the "Garden of Eden," as Orion puts it, the original blueprint of our garden planet.

A key tool for doing this, one that both Orion and Kama have dedicated much of their teaching to, is devotion to the Divine Feminine— specifically the Dark Goddess who holds the keys to the mysteries of Earth, the womb, and Creation. *Through orienting our relationship to Earth as sacred body and taking on the art of ecospiritual practice, humanity becomes a conscious cocreator in Gaia consciousness, and our own bodies become the interface point for this exchange.*[7]

"Waking up," then, *is not a transcendent state of escape, but a radical indwelling of the Divine within ourselves and our planet.* Worship of the "old Gods and Goddesses," as Caroline described it, supports this

process, as we turn away from forms of religion and spirituality that seek to dominate and exploit the body of Earth and humanity. Instead we turn to forms of Deity that heal and transform us into conscious cocreators in our Gaia-verse. As Frater Lux described it, we expand our consciousness to the point where we touch divinity, thereby awakening one's Self as a vehicle for the Divine. Ultimately, this process led many of my coresearchers to devote their work in the world to the task of awakening all of humanity—a theme that factors strongly into Orion's, Caroline's, Kama's, and Frater Lux's stories, and which Madrone, Henri, and Suzette touched upon as well. This, then, leads us to our final theme—the embodiment of the Divine Self.

ENTHEOSIS:
SPIRITUAL TECHNOLOGIES
FOR EMBODYING THE DIVINE SELF

Psychologist, Pagan scholar, and Wiccan high priestess Vivianne Crowley describes the search for the Divine Self through the lens of transpersonal psychology and individuation:

> Spiritual knowledge is something that unfolds from within us; from accessing that deeper layer of the mind that is the collective unconscious, containing the full repository of all human knowledge—past, present and that which is yet to be revealed. Access to this timeless zone comes from learning the techniques of meditation and finding an interior stillness within ourselves where we commune with the Divine and hear the voice of the spirit penetrating the veil between the conscious and unconscious mind. It is achieving this connection with the deeper levels of the Divine Self within us that is the root of our Earth-centered spirituality. . . . Issues of power, control, and domination of human beings by others are important to Pagans. People no longer want to be told by an elite power group what to think and believe. . . . Instead, we must find new sources of authority by developing links with the

voice of our own inner Divine core and recovering the wisdom deep within us. . . .

Contact with and exploration of the worlds of inward reality have always been one of the goals of mysticism. It is a goal with a clearly-defined end—that of becoming at-one with Goddess or God, of finding the Divine Self which is present within us all, and of uniting our external personality with this Divine center. . . . The Divine is present within us as well as in the world outside and beyond. Jean Hardy in her book *A Psychology with a Soul: Psychosynthesis in Evolutionary Context* explains: "In transpersonal psychotherapy terms, the search for spiritual meaning is also the search for the self, the 'God within,' which is linked to the soul of the world." . . . The discovery, or recovery, of the self, for it is always there, is what Carl Jung described as the process of individuation. This is the process of becoming who and what we really are. . . . Individuation is becoming what we were meant to be from the beginning. . . . In order to find the self, the wiser and deeper part of ourselves, we must make a spiritual journey. This is the process of spiritual initiation.[8]

For me, the most potent theme to arise from this inquiry has been the concept of awakening and/or embodying one's Divine Self as perhaps part of the spirit marriage process—or as I see it, a form of spirit marriage in and of itself. This topic could easily become an entire book on its own, and much has already been written on various understandings of the Divine Self in both spiritual and psychological circles. So here I will focus on the Divine Self technologies that arose organically as part of my coresearchers' stories and my own. Let's look closer, then, at the firsthand accounts of my coresearchers who reported having successfully established a long-term relationship with their Divine Self and who are grounded in a spiritual lineage that supports this endeavor.

Defining Entheosis

As I spoke with my coresearchers, I began to see that many of the traditions that practice spirit marriage also include the concept that one has a personal deity that functions for some like a patron saint and for others like a Higher Self. I considered the possibility that spirit marriage may not be solely limited to the practice of uniting with a foreign or externalized entity but might also include the practice of union with one's Divine Self. As Orion reported in his interview, his elevation to the third degree of British Traditional Witchcraft initiated a descent of the "Godhead," a kind of Divine Self embodiment that hastened the taking of a new name and ultimately led to his marriage with Brigh. Likewise, Kama Devi's search for her ishtadevi, the Vodou/Voodoo concept of the met tet, and Frater Lux's account of meeting his HGA all touch upon this theme. As well, each related to a lineage-specific spiritual technology that they engaged in for cultivation of some kind of personal indwelling of the Divine.

For the purpose of this research, I have termed this type of spiritual technology *entheosis* from the Greek root *entheos* meaning "God within." Therefore, *entheosis is any spiritual process that connects an individual to a divine or rarified aspect of themselves. In so doing, it helps to bring the mundane human consciousness into greater awareness and dialogue with the divine or transpersonal aspect—perhaps even allowing them to embody this consciousness as their way of being in the world.*

To avoid the common pitfalls of ego inflation and false claims to enlightenment, I propose that we first need to redefine the term *divine*. In the context of entheosis, I offer that divinity is not a state of transcendent perfection typified by omnipotence, omniscience, or omnipresence. Instead, the divine human is the fully realized potential of an individual or group that has devoted itself to the greater good in both themselves and their community. In this context, to awaken the Divine within is to be fully human and yet in conscious contact with one's Highest or Divine Self—what has been alternatively called here in the West the *entelechy* by Aristotle, the *Holy Guardian Angel* by MacGregor Mathers, the *True or Individuated Self* by Carl Jung, and in more recent transpersonal psychology terms, the *Unique Self*[9] and the *Universal Self*.[10] Dean Radin in *Real Magic* describes this relationship between the human consciousness and what he calls the Universal Self:

The goal of meditation across many traditions is to achieve a state of awareness where one gains the realization that the personal self and the Universal Self are one (in my shorthand [c] = [C]). . . . Let's assume that the esoteric traditions are correct and that personal consciousness [c] and Universal Consciousness [C] are made out of the same "stuff." Personal consciousness [c] may be thought of not as a tiny piece of [C] that has been broken off and is separate from the rest of the universe, but rather as the tip of an extremely large "iceberg" of consciousness.

Theurgy works because the human physical form is just one of a potentially infinite number of ways that consciousness can be embodied. There is no reason for the "body" that hosts [c] to be necessarily physical, at least not in the way that we currently understand physicality.[11]

Through this research and my personal transformational inquiry into this topic, I contend that *the realization of the Divine Self, the entheotic state, is not an unprecedented experience reserved only for an exceptional few, but the intended birthright of all people on this planet right here, right now.*

Entheosis versus Spirit Marriage

As I reflected upon the relationship one develops with the HGA as shared by Frater Lux, I contemplated whether what Frater Lux described is any different in practice from engaging in a spirit marriage. Certainly, to successfully develop a wedded relationship with an external entity one must also develop the discernment and divinatory skills he outlined. And yet none of my coresearchers shared quite as elaborate or time-consuming a preparatory ritual as Frater Lux described. Both Kama Devi's journey, aided by her sakhi to find her ishtadevi, and Suzette's description of the met tet ritual seem to reflect an ethos similar to that of the HGA operation—all being a *search for the divine identity of the Self.*

That said, many of my coresearchers described their experience of their spirit-spouse in almost the same way as Frater Lux described his experience of his HGA. Question and answer, back and forth, intuitive nudges, signs, and portents were all reported as ways in which both spirit-spouse and Divine Self communicate to human beings. And although the initial goal of the Hermetic practice is to make contact with the HGA, might the outcome of that contact, perhaps over lifetimes, be that the Divine Self becomes increasingly how the practitioner shows up in the world—indwelled and wholly identified with that greater consciousness? The differences between the two technologies start to seem more semantic than anything else. Perhaps spirit-spouses lead their embodied partners into relationship with their Divine Self, and perhaps the Divine Self opens us to potential contact with a spirit-spouse. And in some instances perhaps they are one and the same.

The question then arises: What is the practical difference between uniting in marriage with an entity and uniting with one's Divine Self? Although both can be called divine union technologies, are they in fact different mechanisms for different purposes, or is the difference in name only? Considering my coresearchers' stories from a comparative perspective, I suspect that the biggest differences among them may not be in practice or concept but may, in fact, be cultural. Marriage and marriage-like unions mean different things to different people and have throughout history expressed radically different ideologies. For example, for Vodou/Voodoo practitioners, many have stated that marrying a Loa offers an alliance that brings with it resources and protection. This union makes sense for a population that has been heavily persecuted and oppressed for both their beliefs and their racial identity. For others, a marriage is a way to bring about an alliance or foster a partnership in the Otherworld, as with Caroline's marriage to Odin. Finally, as mentioned previously, marriage can also be about cocreation, balance, and integration, which is also an outcome of uniting with one's Divine Self.

Perhaps the significant difference lies not in the *outcome* of the union but in the *method* by which one achieves the contact, and in the *intention* of the union. This might best be assessed by addressing the various understandings of why one enters into marriage in general, be it marriage to a human or to a spirit. Orion shared the idea that spirit marriage is two beings coming together to form a new, third being. This is the core concept behind spirit marriage practitioners who call themselves "indwelled" by an entity external to their core consciousness. Whereas with regard to the HGA, Frater Lux stressed that a two-way conversation was being cultivated between the magician and the HGA. However, in Kama Devi's story she was both married to and embodying her ishtadevi. Clearly, there is no one, final answer. Perhaps my attempts to tease out the differences between entheosis and spirit marriage are best left to the numinous realm of individual spiritual experience and lineage teachings.

That said, we are still left with three distinct spiritual technologies that my coresearchers shared that help to cultivate one's sense of a Divine Self. As Kama Devi shared in her interview: "Awakened beings still have a personality. Which is why Ammachi operates differently from the Dalai Lama, for example, just to use two well-known examples. The shape of the personality is still there . . . even if the ego clinging has loosened." Following this logic, the technologies used to achieve entheosis can be as unique and varied as the individual undertaking them. Whereas one person might initiate into the path of the Ceremonial Magician and undertake the Abramelin Operation, another might cultivate the ecstasies of the Tantric and woo their ishtadevi. Still another might seek the aid of sacred medicines like psilocybin, 5-MeO-DMT, ayahuasca, or other entheogenic substances—all in service to the awakening of the Divine Self within.

From a cross-cultural perspective, the idea of each of us having a highest, or divinized, expression accessible to our human self seems to be a commonly held belief among many of my coresearchers. However, how one approaches and interacts with that entity varies according to the tradition. Here then are a few of the technologies my coresearchers shared that specifically help to foster and awaken the entheotic state.

The Holy Guardian Angel

Knowledge of and conversation with the HGA, as previously discussed, is primarily an entheotic practice. It is meant to bring the practitioner into dialogue with the Divine Self through tools and techniques that purify the practitioner and helps them distinguish between their mundane consciousness and that of the HGA. Rituals, like the Abramelin Operation, aid the Ceremonial Magician in fostering this relationship, which can take months, sometimes years, to achieve.

When I proposed the idea that perhaps knowledge of and conversation with the HGA is also a form of spirit marriage, Frater Lux admitted that he leans away from the term *marriage* in relation to the HGA not because it's conceptually incorrect but because the term itself is loaded with misconceptions and projections about the purpose of marriage. Perhaps the idea of marrying one's Divine Self, then, is not so dissimilar from marrying an external entity, as I had previously suspected. In both cases the practitioner is contacting something external to the mundane self/ego consciousness, inviting it into deeper intimacy, and in some cases giving it controlling interest in the holistic construction of the Self.

My research suggests that people are embracing these realms, whether they be internal (like a Divine Self) or external (like a spirit-spouse) to the core psyche in order to create something new from that relationship. Spirit marriage and entheosis are spiritual technologies that align the core personality to an expanded and sometimes elevated state of perception, be it on a horizontal or vertical axis. Perhaps the main difference is in the identity and locale of the entity being wed. In the case of the HGA, it is a consciousness that one's mundane self is embedded or nested within, while at the same time sitting above, or transcendent, to egoic consciousness and higher self.

The Met Tet

The concept of the met tet, in both Haitian Vodou and New Orleans Voodoo, seems similar to the concept of the HGA in Ceremonial Magic. During my conversation with New Orleans Voodoo Queen Bloody Mary, we discussed the concept of the met tet as well as some of the finer distinctions between the met tet and the mariage Loa—two complementary yet distinct practices. Mary claimed that marrying a spirit is a much more accessible process than having one's met tet placed. A marriage formally attaches you to a spirit so that you can work more deeply with it, and the marriage can take place in a day with very little expense. To initiate into your met tet on the other hand, requires a six- to seven-night *couché* ritual wherein one is attended to by anywhere from five to twenty different people, all of whom support you through the different stages of the initiation including rituals, baptisms, and divinations. The couché traditionally happens three times over a period of years and can cost thousands of dollars each time. This is the protocol for becoming a mambo or houngan in the Vodou/Voodoo lineage.

A spirit marriage, however, is a onetime event. Vodouisants may choose to undertake a marriage because they want to deepen their practice and their connection to the spirits, or because a spirit has asked them to marry. However, undertaking a mariage Loa does not make one a mambo or a houngan. One might also undergo a dedicatory initiation into a Voodoo house or temple or dedicate oneself to a specific Loa. However, these rituals are initiated by the Vodouisant, whereas the couché and mariage Loa are both instigated by the spirits. Mary admits that she has heard of people undertaking the mariage in lieu of the couché for financial reasons, but marrying a Loa is not recognized as a formal initiation and does not bestow any kind of title or spiritual authority.

Neither is the mariage Loa a requirement for becoming a mambo or houngan. Mary herself is not married to a spirit but has undergone the couché initiation. The mariage Loa is not a requirement of couché, nor is undergoing the couché a requirement of the mariage. They are two separate technologies for different purposes. Unlike some of the ambiguity between Divine Self and spirit marriage that I encountered with some of my other coresearchers, in Vodou/Voodoo the distinction between the two is important and exact. The mariage Loa strengthens your appreciation and understanding of a particular Loa and unites you with that spirit. The couché gives you the indwelling of your guardian spirit(s), uniting you with your met tet—what I understand to be a version of the Divine Self.

The met tet, as previously discussed in Suzette's interview, is a similar concept to the idea of a patron saint or HGA. During the couché ritual this entity is embedded in your head. As in the Abramelin Operation, one goes through an exhaustive process of ritual purification and preparation. During this preliminary process, the identity of the met tet is divined by the mambo or houngan presiding over the ritual. Then, during couché, the head of the initiate is ritually opened, and the Loa is placed inside. This entity becomes the guardian spirit, presumably like an indwelled co-walker.

Interestingly, Mary notes that you can have more than one met tet, and—unlike the HGA relationship—your met tet may change at different times in your life. Although you may have an affinity for a specific Loa and may even have had a met tet divination to determine which Loa are closest to you, that does not guarantee which Loa will initiate into you (be placed as your met tet) during the couché.

Mary elaborates:

They claim you; you don't claim them. Same thing with the mariage: they ask you; you don't ask them. . . . They choose you for whatever reasons that they see in you. Maybe it's what you can do with them. There are a thousand different reasons why the spirit would choose you. Maybe it's also because you're the right one to carry that [deity] in that house, and it's missing in that house. There are a thousand reasons, and different reasons, for why maybe one might want to marry you.

The met tet is more like a relationship that is held inside oneself with the patron saint or Divine Self, whereas the mariage Loa is more externally focused on the spirits that want to marry you so that they can work with you in cocreation. Admittedly, I find the distinction between the two concepts a bit difficult to grasp. On the subject of discarnate entities, the lines between inside, outside, above, and below all seem a little blurred to me. One could argue that union with the met tet is like a marriage par excellence—aspects of you uniting into a greater intelligence, two becoming one, as we previously discussed regarding the HGA.

Mary explains that for the uninitiated the distinction between the met tet and the mariage Loa can indeed be hard to understand. The distinction between the two is not meant to be understood intellectually; understanding comes with experiential knowledge of the practices. *It is in the blurry, in-between spaces that the spirits are waiting to reveal themselves.* What is clear to me is that in Vodou/Voodoo, there is a concrete distinction between the kind of relationship a practitioner holds with a spirit that they marry and the kind of relationship they hold with an initiatory spirit(s) placed inside them during the couché. The Loa themselves might be the same entity from person-to-person, but the nature of an individual's relationship with them determines how they manifest for that individual.

The Ishtadevi

Kama Devi's story stands in stark contrast with both the HGA and the met tet protocols. Unlike the clear delineation made between a spirit marriage and the Divine Self in Voodoo/Vodou, in Tantra it is possible for one's ishtadevi to also be one's spirit-spouse. Indeed, Kali is both Kama's ishtadevi and her wife. Still, there is an underlying commonality between all three divine embodiment technologies—namely, the exhaustive journey one goes on to discover the identity of the divine partner (or the Divine Self). Let's unpack this commonality in light of the Tantric practice a bit further.

As in the search for one's HGA, in the Tantric tradition any one of thousands of deities could potentially be one's ishtadevi. The colloquialism of finding a needle in a haystack feels like an apt metaphor for this process. Therefore, part of the journey to unite with the Divine Self is the exhaustive search for that identity. Similar to the met tet, the Tantric practitioner may also have more than one ishtadevi whom they are involved with and/or married to at different times in their life. As well, the deity who initiates contact with the practitioner may or may not end up being that person's ishtadevi. What appears to be different from both the HGA and the met tet process is that in Tantra once the ishtadevi is found, he or she may also propose marriage to the devotee.

It is clear that in all three traditions a high degree of discernment and responsibility are placed upon the seeker to discover the authentic identity of their Divine Self or spirit mate. This discernment process seems to be de rigueur for anyone embarking on a relationship with spirit forces: caution, patience, and intentionality are paramount.

What seems to be unique about the Tantric concept of the ishtadevi is the fact that the ishtadevi then becomes the center point of spiritual practice. Like the *bindu* point in the middle of a mandala, all other aspects of one's sadhana array themselves around the ishtadevi. It seems that finding one's ishtadevi is essential for development on the Tantric path, whereas on the Hermetic path one can progress quite far without ever undertaking the knowledge of and conversation with the HGA, and one can be a devout practitioner of Vodou/Voodoo without ever going through the couché.

As Kama shared in her story, it is the journey through all the elaborately differentiated versions of Deity that brings one into a sensory engagement with the myriad ways in which Deity manifests. It is from the duality implied in the externalized search for one's ishtadevi that one eventually arrives at an experience of the Deity within.

15
Practices and Precautions

$\mathcal{P}$erhaps you've been drawn to this work because a spirit has been wooing you. Maybe, like myself, you've had problematic romantic relationships with humans and a spirit-spouse sounds like a blessed alternative. Maybe you want to deepen your relationship to an existing spirit contact by making a more formal bond. Whatever your motivation, here are some general practices and a few precautions that can help guide you through navigating and negotiating with your potential spirit-spouse.

CREATE A SOLID CONTAINER

As I mentioned previously, I took an organic inquiry approach to learning about spirit marriage, discovering the identity of my spirit-spouse, and collecting the stories of my coresearchers. Organic inquiry invites you to maintain an open mind about the phenomena you encounter and treats the discovery process itself as having a separate intelligence, one that serves as a cocreator in the inquiry. It's all about personal transformation, and as such requires that you create a strong container, a cauldron, for the work. Paramount to this approach is the excavation of your biography, ancestry, and the meaning-making moments of your life, in addition to your felt-sense and intuition. This process underscores the inquiry itself as a sacred, self-revelatory process.

Organic inquiry was developed by transpersonal psychologists Jennifer Clements, Dorothy Ettling, Dianne Jenett, and Lisa Shields as a feminist methodology designed to bring somatic and intuitive ways of knowing into dialogue with more traditional ways of researching a subject. If we consider "right brain" versus "left brain" ways of thinking, organic inquiry is very right brain. It involves a creative process wherein "the researcher is called to pay attention to the suggestions of the inner voice of the research itself, which speaks by way of dreams, coincidences, or intuitive knowing and to adjust the operation of the method accordingly."[1] The inquiry becomes an intimate and sacred process of chthonic excavation that operates "beyond the confines of ego."[2] Organic inquiry is a whole-person, intuitive way of doing formal research.

For those called to explore a spirit marriage, I encourage using some form of organic inquiry as a container for your exploration. In addition to offering a perfect format for investigating extraordinary reality, it also offers excellent guidelines for developing the critical thinking, self-reflexive critique, and grounded action that are sometimes lacking in many New Age and esoteric circles. Here, then, are a few tips for taking an organic inquiry approach.

Measure Your Success in Personal Growth, Not Data Points

It is tempting to want to hash out all the specifics of your desired spirit paramour before progressing far into a relationship. Unfortunately, finding the name, cosmological orientation, and all the nitty-gritty details of a spirit contact can be one of the hardest things to do, depending on the tradition in which you're working. Spirits are notoriously coy about giving their true names. Folklore is replete with tales of how knowing the true name of something or someone gave the knower control over it. (Remember, it took me over ten years to discover the actual name of my spirit lover!)

So how can you tell if you're having an encounter with a spirit or if you're just hallucinating a good time? Answering this isn't easy and letting your somatic, or felt-sense, intelligence guide you is key.

According to R. J. Stewart, "Who and what they are, and how they seem to appear, are not always the same. When you work with any spiritual contact, it is the sense of what they feel like that is of more significance to us as humans than the visual appearance."[3]

And psychiatrist and transpersonal psychology pioneer Stan Grof has this to say on the subject:

> People report that the experience is unusually vivid and authentic, and there is no confusion about the [spirit] having an identity that is quite independent of the person who envisions it. . . . The person who has a truly transpersonal experience with a [spirit] presence usually resists any efforts to assign symbolic meanings to the experience; it is what it is. . . . They have extraordinary characteristics. . . . They radiate unusual energy . . . and may even manifest by alternating between taking animal and human form.[4]

Generally speaking, and according to Grof, a transpersonal experience with a spirit contact feels unique, extraordinary, and distinct. It often takes place in a dream or a ritual setting like a shamanic journey. Outside that context, at first it might be dismissed as simply a "fantasy." However, in the case of being wooed by a potential spirit-spouse, that same being will show up again and again, eventually causing you to begin to question exactly where these fantasies are coming from and why.

It is in the ongoing cultivation of contact with the spirit lover that a felt-sense knowing of when he, she, or they are making contact is discerned. Also, as R. J. Stewart reports, the costume of the spirit may change, but what they feel like to their partner never alters. This is how contact is recognized.

Best to focus, then, on how you're feeling about the relationship, and the kinds of insights, revelations, and transformations you are experiencing as a result of it. Of primary importance to this process is keeping some kind of record or journal of important contact points and how they affect you. I kept meticulous dream and ritual journals during the development of my contact, both written by hand and on my computer. This allowed me to reflect back and see how the relationship had been developing over the years, as well as how I had been growing as a practitioner. It also helped me to capture some of the more subtle clues my contact had been giving me about his identity, ones I was often missing until I looked back and saw repeated themes and images.

Pay Attention to Your Dreams and Visions

Dream contact seems to be a universal way in which the spirits can reach us, regardless of tradition. These contacts are called visitation dreams. Similar to Grof's felt-sense, it is the knowing or feeling of a visitation dream that marks it as such. For people whose primary means of understanding and working with dreams is through a psychological or archetypal lens, the presence of a spirit contact in a dream can easily be dismissed. Not surprisingly, the cultures and traditions, usually indigenous, who work with dreams as vehicles for contact with the spirit world tend to most often acknowledge and cultivate spirit marriage:

> Dreams have been associated with the spirit world. . . . Visitation dreams seem to represent a transpersonal reality only dimly perceived by humans. . . . In visitation dreams, a deceased person or an entity from a spiritual realm reportedly provides counsel or direction that the dreamer finds of comfort or value . . . [they are] dreams in which the dreamer was greeted by ancestors, spirits, or deities, and given messages or counsel by them. It is through relationships that our spiritual path has its greatest opportunity to express itself. . . . This internal dream journey can actually serve as a sacred venture toward a communion with God.[5]

It is the job of the organic inquirer, then, to listen for the often unfamiliar and sometimes uncomfortable messages of the spirit world that rarely speak above a whisper during waking life but can get through more clearly when we're dreaming or in altered states. Rarely linear or explicit, these messages often arrive in chthonic forms such as dreams, sudden intuitions, even synchronicities, which implies that the inquiry is omnipresent in the life of the seeker. This may require that you devote a good portion of your life to the task at hand. Slowing down, resting your nervous system by unplugging from technology, getting out into nature regularly, and getting ample sleep are all essential activities for cultivating a contact.

Take Your Time

The goal of organic inquiry is for the seed of the inquiry to blossom into a tree of transformation—of perceptions, self-concept, relations with each other and the world. This tree needs time, tending, and resources to grow. According to Craig Chalquist, "[Organic inquiry] focuses on individual and personal transformation that is persistent, pervasive, and profound."[6] Organic inquiry allows us to engage "the spirit of the research topic as a muse or a deity, perhaps a personified image with a twinkle in her eye who knows the truths of the topic under investigation. She holds universal teachings and is ready to share them with the world."[7]

This is a marathon, not a sprint. Just as you would, hopefully, take your time getting to know a human before you decided to marry them, you really need to take the time to learn about your potential spirit-spouse and their impact upon you. Sadly, some spirit-spouse relationships, like that of William Sharp and Fiona Macleod, have had the tendency to burn out the human and shorten their life span considerably. So doing your due diligence about what you're getting yourself into is a must. Remember, you can push back, set limits, and negotiate with the spirits! Also, because this is all done using your subtle senses, developing your intuition, sovereignty, and discernment is key.

One of the most notable side effects of being spirit-touched is the awakening of what is commonly referred to as ESP. A loving relationship with a spirit is often accompanied by extraordinary experiences, from telepathy to precognitive dreams to clairvoyance. Parapsychologists have been examining and validating these phenomena for over a century, but what perhaps remains to be explored is the connection between spirit marriages and parapsychological talent. Orion Foxwood outlines the primary gifts given to humans who walk with a spirit; they include psychic gifts, prophecy, the ability to bless or curse, mediation of healing, shape-shifting, and enchantment.

The development of these gifts and the discernment of the spirits is an art form that many spend lifetimes evolving. Your spirit contact may have a past-life connection to you. They may, as in my case, have been wedded to your ancestral line for generations. Or perhaps you are being asked to wed a specific spirit to bring about a certain kind of healing for your family, community, or the planet. This relationship could have been developing for many, many lifetimes to finally find its culmination in you!

The better you become at using the various divination tools at your disposal (tools like tarot, scrying, automatic writing, astrology, augury, and the like) the clearer you can become about the nature of your spirit contact and whether they are worthy of marriage. Yes, you read that correctly, whether *they* are worthy of *your* hand in marriage. You are a prize, a rare and precious vehicle for Spirit to flow through. Don't give away space in your inner temple to just anyone!

Build Your Magical Body

One of the best ways to create a solid container within and around yourself is to cultivate daily exercises that attune you to greater spirit contact and protect you from unwanted contact. Some call this "grounding and shielding." The point is to establish awareness and control over your inner and outer personal space. It also helps you foster discernment of the spirits you are contacting. I like to think of it as magical bodybuilding. Done on a daily basis, your energy body begins to develop somatic memory that adds strength and vigor to your energetic container.

The techniques for building up the magical body are as varied as the different traditions we've explored in my coresearchers' stories. Ceremonial Magicians use the previously mentioned ritual known as the Lesser Banishing Ritual of the Pentagram, which employs ritualized movements, visualization, and recitation to lay claim to one's energy body and field. (Frater Lux touched on this in his story.) Tantrics use a technique called a *kavacam,* which places protector deities in and around the body. Witches cast a magic circle, sending their grounding cord down to anchor to Earth and then envisioning a protective bubble around themselves.

Whatever technique you use, the result should feel like you are claiming sovereignty over your personal space, so that you may walk through the world with greater discernment of what's in and around you.

✳ Covering

One of my favorite techniques and one that I use on a daily basis is what my mentor Orion Foxwood calls *covering* (which he outlines in detail in his book *The Candle and the Crossroads*). This is a simple, self-anointing ritual that sets your spirit for the day. It helps you to be more aware and in control of what you're thinking, feeling, and doing, rather than being pulled about by the myriad inputs of your mundane self, society, and spirits that are clamoring for your attention. It's simple but potent.

Step 1. Begin by ritually cleansing yourself. This can be done with water, for example just after you've take a cleansing bath or shower; with smoke using incense or herbs;* with fire, by using a flame to sweep light around your body; or any other method of spiritual cleansing, like a sauna or even some form of exercise such as yoga or tai chi. I do this practice every day after I take a shower.

Step 2. Choose an anointing oil of your preference. This doesn't need to be fancy. Some olive oil that you have blessed will do, although traditionally hyssop oil is used.

Step 3. Place the oil on your dominant index finger and touch the back of your head at the base of your skull.

Step 4. Draw a line from the base of your skull across the top of your head, back to front, ending at your third eye.

Step 5. Draw a circle around your head clockwise from your third eye to

---

*I recommend using purifying herbs like mugwort, garden sage, rosemary, or even a high-quality incense like *nag champa* to purify yourself with smoke.

the right temple, from your right temple to the base of your skull, from the base of your skull to your left temple, and from your left temple back to your third eye.

Step 6. Now from your third eye draw a line across your forehead and up to the soft spot on the top of your head. Draw a sacred symbol of your choosing there. This could be a triangle, pentagram, cross, or even a dot, depending on what spiritual system you most resonate with. This is called *crowning* and forms a crown of blessedness over you.

Step 7. Now place a little oil on both index fingers and anoint each elbow. The anointing of your crown and each elbow forms a triangle that is sometimes called the eye of God. Orion explains, "The anointing of each elbow allows you to 'bless what you are reaching for' and 'what reaches for you.' It completes the imprint of the triangle of light (or eye of God) upon your body. This puts you in the watchful eye of the Divine while having the watchful eye guiding you in your works from within [yourself]. This both protects you and brings divine presence to your head—that which you reach for and which reaches to you."[8]

PRACTICE SELF-CARE AS TEMPLE KEEPING

My organic inquiry into spirit marriage required that I calibrate to my own spirit contact and also to those of my coresearchers. The more information I collected and the more beings I was introduced to through my coresearchers, the more downtime and psychic space I needed to create enough room in my nervous system to integrate these energies. Each encounter had evoked a numinous experience wherein I felt profoundly activated and altered. Somatic cues of chills, disorientation, agitation, and expansion were present, as well as emotions like gratitude, ecstasy, uncertainty, and sometimes fear. It was a wholly somatic experience in which I felt I was being enveloped by these vast intelligences. It was overwhelming, and I needed to give myself plenty of time and space to digest it all.

The process of deep self-reflection led to a complete overhaul of my self-care regime. I had to alter the way I ate, slept, and exercised—hastening a total transformation of my relationship to my physical body. I needed to be comprehensively stronger to be the container for this kind of deeply transformative relationship. This seems to be part of the deal we make when we seek to become *supernormal*—to borrow Dr. Dean Radin's term. There are sacrifices that need to be made; disciplines that must be followed. But the discipline typically isn't about suffering or going without. It is often about slowing down, setting boundaries, and taking really good nourishing care of ourselves—becoming the custodian of our inner temple. My first Tantra teacher, Bast, likes to call this *blissipline*—all the nourishing things that support us in having a well-adjusted nervous system and balanced body-mind-spirit.

But self-care isn't about self-indulgence. It's not about fancy manicures, cheat days, or elaborate spa dates. It's about choosing the activities that take you out of a stress response (which, let's face it, is the default for most of us these days) and bringing your parasympathetic nervous system online. Known as the "rest and digest response," this gives your brain chemistry, organs, immune system—pretty much all your vital systems—a chance to recuperate. What elicits this response in you may not do the trick for me. Some folks find meditation apps on their smartphone helpful, but doing anything involving technology stresses me to some degree. So it's up to you to find the things that bring you into the rest and digest zone.

Daily and weekly self-care routines are key. This could be a daily mini ritual like having your morning tea while watching the birds out your window, or a weekly trip to your favorite spot in nature. Routine acupuncture, yoga, and hiking in nature are all part of my personal blissipline regime. Good old-fashioned sweating, whether by exercise or a sauna, seems to also be one of the most effective ways to clear out the old and allow more space in your system for the spirit contact. (Just be mindful that excessive exercise can elicit a stress response, so don't overdo it!) Toxins in your system tend to disrupt spirit communication—as Orion shared in his story when Brigh asked him to stop drinking coffee for a time so she could calibrate to him more easefully.

Am I suggesting you give up coffee? Not necessarily, unless you find that your addiction to caffeine is preventing you from relaxing and dropping into the deeper places we need to reach for spirit contact. Ultimately it's for you (and your spirit contact) to decide what your discipline will be. I have had to stop a lot of things—alcohol, caffeine, gluten, dairy—because as part of my inquiry (which involved getting ancestry and DNA tests) I discovered I have some genetic health issues that make these foods difficult for me to process. However, in exchange for giving them up, I have gained so much more—clarity, potency, vitality, insight, to name just a few gifts—and I *feel* great!

Another aspect of self-care that we don't normally think of as self-care is our psycho-spiritual care, what I like to call *depth care*. Our mental, emotional, and spiritual bodies are all part of the Self. They need tending, sometimes even cleaning, just like our physical bodies do. Once we have attended to our surface self-care, we then gain the ability to slow down and drop in deeper. It is in and through our depths that we gain access to Otherworldly contacts, spiritual insight, and ancestral magic.

When I begin each day with meditation, sacred reading, and simple ritualized actions like lighting a candle and focusing my mind, I enter into an appropriately open and receptive place from which I can drop in deep to hear the voice of my spirit contact better. You will need to find what works for you, but self-care, depth care, and the positive self-regard that is required to claim the time and energy to properly care for yourself are non-negotiables for healthy spirit marriages.

✳ Visioning

One of my favorite ways to care for the temple of my body-mind is to create vision boards for who and what I want to embody. As a former burlesque performer, I learned firsthand the power of the visual and how it can evoke strong emotions. There's magic behind the saying "A picture is worth a thousand words." I choose images that resonate with the felt-sense of who I want to be out in the world and bolster a sense of positive self-regard. When I'm feeling lost or doubting myself, I turn back to my boards for inspiration. They serve as a reminder of who I'm choosing to become. Fortunately, nowadays you don't need to cut up a bunch of magazines to create a vision board. Apps like Pinterest, Canva, PicCollage, and Wishboard all offer easy ways to create one. In fact, the late self-help guru Louise L. Hay at Hay House even created a free downloadable vision board app. The only limitation is your ability to dream up different search terms that describe your vision!

DEEPEN THROUGH RITUALIZED MOVEMENT MEDITATIONS

Sacred movement like ecstatic dance, yoga, tai chi, chi kung—any kind of mindful movement practice—is instrumental in not only preparing your physical body for spirit contact but also in deepening an experience of your Self as Divine. And the more we experience our Divine Self, the more we become an attractive potential partner to the spirit world. Ritualized movement creates a dialogue between your body, Earth, and the spirits—thus cultivating an embodied awareness of your spirit contact. A daily movement practice creates more space in your body for the intelligence of the spirit contact to settle in, as well as helping to shift some of the personal and ancestral trauma that usually manifests at some point during this kind of work. Sacred movement also helps to incubate and digest the information you're receiving, and connects you to greater numinous intelligences. The best way I can illustrate the importance and efficacy of sacred movement is to tell you a story.

Through the years, it became clear that one of the most important ways I could interact with my spirit contact(s) was through movement. Daily yoga practice and dance became a natural way to create more space in my body for the intelligence of the work to settle in. After a few years of daily movement practice, I found that my movement meditations in nature were becoming deeper and more intense. A simple walk in nature to commune with my spirit contact was no longer sufficient.

Through a series of synchronicities and dreams, it became clear that I needed to begin making regular offerings to the spirits of this book.

Although I had been alternating among a few natural places in the San Francisco Bay Area to do these movement meditations, I was now being guided to deepen my terrapsychological approach by focusing on one location specifically. This was a natural canyon area in San Francisco called Glen Park Canyon, not far from my home. It is one of the oldest, underdeveloped wild places in San Francisco. It also has a natural creek, Islais Creek, that runs through it—one of only two creeks left in the city. Islais Creek was, at one point, a major river that provided food and shelter for the indigenous people who lived in Yerba Buena prior to Spanish settlement.

Early on in my Faery Seership apprenticeship, I'd had a dream about this location as a place of contact for the Faery energies and for my Faery contact in particular. Not long after I had this dream, while hiking the canyon, I found an altar that someone had created to the Faeries. It was an old oak stump with many hollows and roots where offerings were often left. This oak became a focal point for my rituals in the canyon. During the drought of 2014–2016, I went to the canyon and made water offerings to the oak, the ancestors of place, and to the dry creek bed, praying for rain. Eventually—because of my regular terrapsychological contact with the canyon—the spirits of the land began to open to me.

I deepened my relationship with this canyon, increasingly visiting her. It has a very feminine, yonic energy for me, being a deep crevasse in the land through which water flows. Here I would make offerings and prayers and, when I did so, she responded to me.

It was during this time that I'd gone on pilgrimage to Wales, Cornwall, and Glastonbury, which, as I shared in my story, had a profound effect upon my ecospiritual practice. When I returned home, I brought back with me many of the sacred insights from my pilgrimage and began to apply them to my relationship with the land in San Francisco. Through song, movement, and ritual offerings I connected to the land and to its ancestors—both human and Fae. I sought to integrate the experiential knowledge I had gained into an embodied nature practice through regular, intentional contact with the canyon and its oaks, boulders, and creek. Five places of power revealed themselves to me in the canyon, and it became my routine to circumambulate it, performing specific rituals at each of these sites.

Much of the ritualized movement that I performed was informed by my study of Shakta Tantra, which teaches about the shakti pitha, the sacred Goddess sites of India, and how we can interact with Earth as the body of the Goddess. Yet, almost equally, my work with the canyon was intuitive and instinctual. Working in this way deepened my ability to quiet my thinking mind and pierce the veil of forgetfulness so that an almost wild, primordial sense of my Self began emerging—an aspect of me that seemed to sense energy patterns in nature, people, and the cosmos, and decode the messages therein.

This led to an ah-ha moment. Up to that point I had been laboring under the assumption that connecting with nature meant that I had to go somewhere other than my home (which is situated in the middle of the City) to find a wild patch of land upon which to do ritual. Driving somewhere out in nature on a daily basis was not always realistic. Therefore, when our downstairs neighbors moved out, leaving our backyard a barren dirt patch, I began to cultivate my own backyard as a space for ritual contact.

I took it upon myself to revitalize the backyard by planting flowers and herbs that are sacred to the Faery. Also, inspired by Orion's teaching, I built a small Faery cairn out of rocks in the corner of the garden and activated it for work with the Fae. Over the next six months, the garden flourished, filling with the scents of rose, lavender, rosemary, and sage. From previously exhausted soil, the garden now produced lush foliage in a riot of color, erupting as dahlias, roses, marigolds, foxglove, and a variety of herbs. Daily I gardened and performed Faery Seership rituals to encourage the growth of the plants and to contact the wild-force energy, the *genus loci* of the land—an entity that was also revealing itself to be closely linked with my Faery Beloved.

This development was a revelation. It felt like a confirmation of my seasoning as a seer and witch, for I discovered that the plants and land told me exactly what they wanted planted, when, and where. The more I turned inward and relied upon my innate resourcing and sacred connection to the land, the stronger my intuition grew, and the more clearly my spirit contact spoke to me. I was reaching maturation as a Faery Seer. I no longer needed to go on pilgrimage, escape the city, or even search out wild places. I could now raise the wild-force energy anywhere, even in my own previously barren backyard.

I hope that these pages give you a few ideas about how you might engage your own form of ritualized movement meditations. They can be shared by a group or tradition, like yoga or tai chi, or performed alone. They could be your own unique actions made sacred by your solitary intention, like gardening, hiking, or creating art. The only limit is your imagination and the key ingredient is your intention.

✳ Offerings

Leaving offerings for the spirits, particularly ones you want to develop an ongoing relationship with, is a good way to get their attention. Regular offerings left in the same place and in the same manner demonstrate to the spirit realm that you are serious about making contact. It also shows them that you're interested in a reciprocal relationship: you're willing to give something, not just show up and make demands, as Suzette shared in her story. However, not all spirits like the same offerings and some kinds of offerings are just a bad idea. Here then, are some tips for proper offerings, particularly when making them in public or wild places.

- ◆ Try not to leave anything that isn't perishable. Suitable offerings are usually milk, honey, alcohol, dried herbs, corn meal, ash, and home-baked goods. Avoid processed and high sugar foods, which are horrible for the wildlife. When in doubt, water is a great offering to leave; it's known as "pouring a libation." In the absence of anything else, your saliva is a perfectly acceptable offering! It holds your DNA and is part of the nourishing waters of your body.
- ◆ Always ask the genus loci, the guardian spirit of the place, for permission to leave anything. It's also a good idea to know the name of the indigenous people who lived on the land before you were

there, and acknowledge their ancestral presence, leaving them an offering as well. In fact, there's an app called Native Land that will tell you which tribe was indigenous to the land you're currently on. However, if you are on land that is sacred to the indigenous people of that place, like Panther Meadow at Mount Shasta, it's best not to leave offerings unless you are with or have been guided by the indigenous caretakers of that land on how to properly do so. When in doubt, say a prayer of thanks, sing a song, breathe with the Earth, or do something else that leaves no trace.

♦ Never leave chocolate! Chocolate is toxic to most wildlife, dogs, and other critters that might come in contact with it.

♦ Experiment with creating designs with your offerings. Some people like to make elaborate mandalas using found objects like leaves, sticks, and petals. I like to keep it simple. I typically draw a Faery cairn out of cornmeal and leave my offerings in its center ring. I also have crystals and rocks that I place around and inside its four points. I use the same ones in the same places each time I create a cairn. They come home with me after each offering is made and therefore hold a charge from all the cairns I've ever made.

EXPLORE YOUR SACRED STORY

One of the most rewarding parts of exploring a potential spirit marriage is the sleuthing work you do to trace how your contact may have been reaching out to you your entire life, perhaps lifetimes. While not everyone may discover that this is, in fact, the case, it is well worth considering how your life may have been leading you up to this moment of divine union. Narrative approaches to research underscore the importance of not only how we see the world, but how we see ourselves.

Our personal story is one of our most powerful modes of communication. We can learn much about ourselves by searching our life's narrative to uncover the guiding influences that may have had a hand in our growth and evolution from before our birth. We may even uncover ways in which we are embedded in larger mythological narratives wherein our life may mirror key elements of the story of a deity, archetype, or esoteric framework, what Craig Chalquist calls the "personal myth." I strongly encourage the undertaking of writing out your sacred story, the moments in your life when something numinous touched you and caused you to rethink or perhaps transform your view of Self, community, and/or planet. That said, not everyone enjoys writing, and almost no one finds the act of writing easy. So if you haven't been religious about keeping a journal or book of shadows, taking meticulous notes about your esoteric interactions, don't fret! Here are some tips for creating your sacred story.

Talk It Out

One of the most rewarding methods I discovered in the process of creating my story was to take long walks in nature with a tape recorder, and to tell my story through talking. I would then use voice-to-text translation software to put the recording into written form (Otter is a great app for this). This could also be done with a trusted friend, coach, or therapist, by devoting a period of sessions to unpacking the parts of your story that hold the scent of a spirit contact, and recording them. These story fragments may not be overtly obvious—your spirit companion appeared in a cloud of luminescence and begged to marry you—but you may have an intuition or felt-sense that something extraordinary was afoot. Great! Explore that more deeply. Feel into it. Dream into it. This leads us to our next technique.

Practice Dream Tending

Try using the techniques of depth psychologist Stephen Aizenstat's process called Dream Tending, in which you sit with a dream—or in this case some juicy part of your story—and meditate on it, asking it to speak to you from deeper and deeper levels to reveal its truth. In my case, I went back to dream journals I had been keeping since the onset of the spirit proposal and highlighted the important entries and most salient revelations that related to my spirit contact.

You can also practice dream incubation, in which you focus on a specific idea or question as you fall asleep and ask a dream to come to you that reveals something about the subject matter. Just make sure to keep a notebook next to your bed in case you wake up in the middle of the night and need to record something!

Ritualize It

I ritualized my story collection process—which took me about a month—by beginning and ending it on new moons. I participated in powerful community rituals during that time, one wherein I *aspected,* or channeled, Mary Magdalene, and another called a Serpent Ceremony wherein I danced with snakes. I touched into the snake's transformative power to amplify an intention—mine being to uncover my sacred story. These rituals helped to soften my conscious mind and move me into a trance-like state for most of the story collection period. It was also instrumental at this time to take a social media fast and to greatly limit time spent on technology in general.

I share these techniques not as a prescription for how to collect your story, but as an example of how creative and versatile the process can be. I had thought I'd relate my own story by sitting down each day and putting words onto the page. Instead, the process required me to surrender to the chthonic intelligence of my experience as it arose out of my unconscious in nonlinear and highly unstructured ways. Most of the actual writing happened in the middle of the night, around three in the morning. I would wake with the beginning of a story taking shape in my mind. So I would go into the living room, lie on the couch, and dictate into a recorder. It was as if I were being fed each sentence by an Otherworldly contact. In this way each section of the narrative arose, spontaneously and organically, from a kind of supraconscious intelligence that dictated to me which portions to share.

This process of self-knowledge, and particularly the discovery of the identity of the Divine Self and spirit-spouse, is a journey, lasting maybe a lifetime. The more we can do to support our bodies, minds, and spirits to be receptive to the voices of extraordinary reality, the greater clarity we tend to get. This often means slowing down and perhaps taking a period of withdrawal or retreat so as to go deep to hear the subtle inner and outer realms more clearly. In this we discover a greater sensitization of the Self. Most importantly, we undertake every step with a dedication to this Great Work.

✳ Time Line

One tool that I found very useful in helping me conceive of and structure my story was to create a time line of my life. This is a great way to get a bird's-eye view of your sacred story and create a record of your transformational journey. It can be added to as you remember things, and becomes an ongoing document of your spiritual experience.

Step 1. Create a time line. No doubt there are apps that will help you do this, but I just taped together about five sheets of printer paper end to end and drew a horizontal line across them.

Step 2. Divine the time line up in five- to ten-year increments. The key memories and experiences you have had then become little hash marks along the time line.

Step 3. On the time line add any major life events: marriages, births, deaths, divorces, significant jobs, for example. Also add any life-altering or significant spiritual events—both the highs and the lows. I added things like when my parents went bankrupt when I was 10; when I had my kundalini awakening at 30; when I initiated into Ceremonial Magic; when I went back to school to obtain a Ph.D.; when my mom died; when I went to Burning Man for the first time; when I did my first medicine journey, met my spiritual mentor, met my Faery Beloved, and so forth— basically any life event that had an important psycho-spiritual impact.

Step 4. Color-code each life event according to the psycho-emotional quality of that event. Was it transformational? Devastating? Paradigm-shifting? Life-altering? Shameful? Liberating? The categories you choose are up to you but try to keep it to five categories or less, as this keeps the stories manageable.

Step 5. Now look at each category and the events contained therein. This should give you a clear road map for the sacred stories you want to develop, as well as a general sense of the feeling tone of your life to date. You may begin to get a sense of an overarching metaphor for your life. You can even use these story elements to excavate your own personal myth, perhaps revealing the personal deity or mythological character with whom you are presently aligned.

AVOID THE POTENTIAL SHADOWS OF SPIRIT MARRIAGE AND ENTHEOSIS

Seeking to enhance or replace one's mundane consciousness with an extraordinary or divine consciousness is an admirable pursuit, perhaps one of the greatest spiritual quests one can undertake. Apotheosis, or the God/dess-making endeavor, has been a part of our collective awareness since the birth of recorded civilization, most commonly seen in the imperial cults of kings and queens as divine beings, also known as *euhemerism*.[9] And yet, for the Western audience, we face some distinct challenges in pursuit of the embodiment of divine consciousness. To this end, I offer a few areas of caution around potential pitfalls for students of indwelling and divine embodiment practices and those who might seek to embark on this journey.

Self-Aggrandizement

Your spiritual achievements are nobody else's business. Reflecting upon the words of caution I received when looking to interview someone who had achieved knowledge and conversation with their HGA: the fact that someone achieves union with their Divine Self and then publicly announces it could potentially be a red flag.* It calls to mind transpersonal psychologist Mariana Kaplan's work on premature claims to enlightenment.[10] The claim of knowing the way to achieve

---

*I wrestled quite a bit with how much to share of my own HGA journey. It was only after receiving feedback from my early readers, as to its importance and utility to the narrative, that I decided to include it in this book.

embodiment of one's divinity, or of having successfully done so, can lead the practitioner down a slippery slope of entitlement and an exaggerated sense of self-importance.

I have personally witnessed women who, upon going through a spiritual awakening to their inner Goddess, find it confusing when they discover they are still being treated like a mortal by the rest of the world. I have watched women and men demand that partners treat them like a God/dess, while treating others as subjects, pawns, or acolytes in their service. Surely this is not what the embodiment of divinity should look like. Respect and recognition are essential qualities in any healthy relationship, but these qualities are typically earned by our behavior, our treatment of ourselves and others. Surely being revered is something one inspires in others through how we display a compassionate and wise nature in day-to-day life.

The New Age movement has popularized the concept that we are both human and divine. Coupled with that, there is a trend here in the West to move away from transcendence and toward immanence—which I wholeheartedly celebrate. However, if we're not careful, deity embodiment practices may become a seductive outlet to make us feel special, important, worthy, and often a tad self-righteous. Because we are divine, we feel entitled. I wonder, is this truly what it means to be human and divine? Perhaps, if we want to be treated as the Divine, we must first adopt the behaviors that inspire others to respect and observe the divinity within us.

The myths of the Gods and Goddesses may be partly to blame. Many of our examples of Deity, at least in the West, have portrayed vindictive, tyrannical beings who, aside from having supernatural powers, seem quite human. Female deities in particular have undergone a kind of patriarchal revisionism wherein an ancient primordial life-giving Goddess like Aphrodite was turned into a petty, vain diva.[11]

Nevertheless, I believe we can learn a lesson from both the Hermeticists and the Tantrics in this regard. Both lineages require a vow of silence or a *samaya* promising that the details and accomplishments of one's spiritual practice will not be publicly broadcast or discussed, sometimes for the duration of a working, sometimes never. Should we undertake the process of embodying our Divine Self, or be graced with an ongoing indwelled relationship with a divine consciousness, it would be best to let that relationship manifest in the way we live our lives and interact with others. We shouldn't automatically assume that it qualifies us to special treatment—or even to teach this process to others. This brings us to the second pitfall of divine embodiment claims: the cult of personality.

Competition

We either all get there together, or not at all. Who we think we are and what we think we know have become a kind of currency here in the West, and nowhere is this more apparent than in the self-help and spirituality movements. Many cultivate spiritual accomplishments to bolster a brand identity. Claims of studying with such and such a teacher, and/or receiving initiations, empowerments, or secret teachings from a certain guru, are then used to sell products, services, and experiences. The commodification of spirituality is not a new thing. What is germane to this critique is the idea that claiming embodiment of one's Divine Self might tempt a practitioner to use this as a way to gain a competitive edge.

Free market capitalism has co-opted spirituality. Seekers, aspirants, and supplicants become market consumers—"potential customers" shopping around for a spiritual practice like we shop for a new pair of shoes. We compare prices, claims, durability, even styles, all hoping to finally find the perfect fit. This is in stark contrast to Kama's story wherein she reported that she is actually prohibited from promoting herself as a spiritual teacher by her lineage family in India. She is only allowed to teach if someone asks her for a teaching. What might our Western spiritual landscape look like if teachers only taught because others observed the fruits of their practice in their lives and then begged them to share their secrets?

In an overly saturated market, with almost every spiritual teaching and practice imaginable now available at the click of a button, special attention should be paid to the lineage and authenticity of anyone claiming to embody or teach embodiment of the Divine. *Perhaps a radically new way of assessing the validity and authenticity of a spiritual teacher or system is not what they themselves claim to be able to offer or teach, but what their community, their relationships, and their lived experience reveal about them.*

We should consider looking first to the lifestyle habits of a potential teacher or spiritual system and assessing how successfully they embody the fruits of their claims. I suggest we need to demand a new kind of vulnerability and transparency from anyone offering spiritual teachings and trainings. What is needed is nothing less than the kind of candid openness that requires the teacher to name and own their shadow and unresolved issues as well as, perhaps, fully disclosing their financial and criminal records to their potential students! I also suggest that this is doubly important for teachers who offer divine embodiment technologies, as the nature of that practice is potentially charged with problems of abusing power as well as *spiritual bypassing.*

This kind of shadow exposure would, admittedly, require a level of disclosure and transparency that some might find uncomfortable. But I would offer that if a teacher is not comfortable with letting potential students see the inner workings of their personal practice, then perhaps they are not truly qualified to be a teacher of divine embodiment. In my opinion, teachers of spiritual development, and especially of entheosis practices, ought to be held to a higher standard of conduct.

We need to stop turning a blind eye to the bad behavior of spiritual teachers because we like what they teach but not how they live. Yes, even entheosis teachers are human, and though striving to be their divine selves, they are still working out their issues. Knowing what those issues are up front—because the teacher has taken an account and assumed total personal responsibility for naming and addressing their shadow—is deeply empowering to the student, who then goes into the relationship with eyes wide-open.

Paramount to this discussion is the Tantric worldview (at least in Kama's lineage practice) that no one gets left behind. Entheosis is not a competition to see who can embody their God/dess self the best or the fastest. As a planet, we are faced with collective extinction. Threats like global warming, famine, and pollution impact us all equally, and a small group of individuals can affect the entire planet for good or ill. We will either survive as a species because we all pull together and make a collective change, or we will equally all become extinct. Survival of the human race is at stake, and embodying our Divine Self in such a way that we transform our lives and our world for the better is a key technology for the survival of life on Earth.

Pagan scholar Vivianne Crowley echoes this sentiment, stating: "In the religions of the Piscean Age, the focus was on the salvation of the individual. In the 21st century, the lives of the whole human species and of the planet on which we live are threatened by environmental catastrophe. The issue is not our individual needs, but the needs of the world as a whole. We seek the Grail in order to become it—that we may become vessels so that others too may drink from that source."[12]

Superiority

Everyone has a Divine Self that is trying to get their attention. As we strive to become more aligned and attuned to the divine impulse that courses through our consciousness, let us not forget that this same pulse is beating in the heart of every being on this planet—yes, even the non-human ones to varying degrees. We can no longer afford the kind of dualism that creates "insider/outsider" thinking, wherein one group is considered "awake," "enlightened," or "saved" and others are not. Every group believes that its agenda is righteous and noble. Everyone has a rationale for their beliefs. Those who practice Divine Self technologies are no exception. The fact that some are attempting to embody the highest or wisest consciousness they can access does not mean that they are inherently better than someone who is not. The Divine Self reaches out to touch us whether or not we are aware of it and reach back.

To assume that someone else is devoid of divinity or disconnected from their Divine Self is to make a grave and dangerous assumption—perhaps just as dangerous as publicly claiming oneself to be divine. Just because we do not approve of the actions another person takes or what they stand for, they are not necessarily bad or wrong. Perhaps they are embodying exactly the energy that they came into this life to express, be it authoritarian, repressive, saturnine, or militaristic. Perhaps they are expressing the epigenetic trauma of their upbringing or ancestry. We may not like it, we may even need to actively work to prevent them from doing harm, but we need to be extremely careful in dismissing the individual as devoid of their divine spark. As Frater Lux, Suzette, and Kama all reported, Deity can express itself in many ways. Some manifestations we may like, and some we may not. However, our not liking someone does not mean they are evil, even if their actions are hurting others and need to be curtailed. One could go so far as to suggest that even so-called demons have a job they are performing in service to the divine whole.

It seems that many people flock from teacher to teacher thinking that the next guru/coach/shaman will somehow unlock the very mystery of their being, never stopping to question whether perhaps that job should rest solely upon their own shoulders. As with the search for the HGA and the ishtadevi, no one can tell us who we are here to embody. It is our sacred work to discover that for ourselves.

✳ Self-Excavation

I often use the concept of the archeological dig as a metaphor for working within the various layers of the psyche. One goes slowly and is conscientious and methodical about how one approaches the territory. Nothing is discarded outright, and pieces that fit together to form a cohesive whole are often spread across the terrain, buried in various places and at differing levels.

One of the best ways I've found to keep my ego in check and avoid the pitfalls of self-aggrandizement, competition, and superiority is a process I call *self-excavation*. This is a deepening process that helps to neutralize habituated thinking patterns and get to the heart of the Self. Although it can be used to set aside difficult thoughts and emotions *for the moment,* it is *not* meant to spiritually bypass important aspects of our psycho-emotional well-being. Instead, it gives us some breathing room from habituated thoughts and feelings and invites us to look closely at our assumptions by tapping into something deeper. We can then see from the perspective of the Higher Self, and perhaps even connect into our Divine Self. There are many tools and techniques for getting into your essence. The self-excavation process arises out of my work as a hypnotherapist, and I personally use it on a regular basis.

Here's how to begin:

Step 1. Sit or lie down in a relaxed position.

Step 2. Begin by taking deep, prolonged inhalations and exhalations. Try to make the inhale and exhale equal in length, pausing briefly in between. Do this for a few breath cycles, until you feel you are relaxed but still alert.

Step 3. Now scan your body for any areas that feel tight, stuck, numb, closed, turbulent, clogged, or perhaps simply in need of attention. Often when we touch into these areas, we discover thoughts or emotions that linger in these spaces. Sometimes they arise spontaneously. If not, we can simply ask ourselves, "What's hanging out in here?" Keep breathing deeply and stay open to whatever arises.

Step 4. When a thought or emotion arises—whatever the quality, difficult or beneficial—breathe into it and invite it to soften. Don't analyze it, just breathe into and around it. Invite it to relax. This isn't about assessing the truth or origin of the thought. This is about giving yourself and your thought processes some breathing room.

Step 5. Continue scanning and breathing into the body until all the challenging areas feel open and relaxed. At some point you may begin to get a sense of the Self beneath the self, what some call the witness consciousness. Great! Breathe into that and see if there is anything beneath it. Conversely, you may find it difficult to relax your thoughts, discovering that the mind comes up with endless scenarios or ideas to distract you. Fine. Keep breathing into them and inviting them to relax until you feel complete.

When you're first starting out you may want to set a timer for, say, fifteen to thirty minutes, as the relaxation part of this process can sometimes cause you to fall asleep. If you do, no worries! When you wake up, just pick up where you left off until the timer goes off or you feel complete. There is no right or wrong way to do this process. It's simply about softening your awareness and letting go of any rigidity in your thinking so that you can drop into deeper and deeper layers of discovery.

This kind of deep mental relaxation helps us get out of dualistic thinking and decouple our thoughts from our sense of Self. Remember, this is a process of self-discovery, one that you will get more out of the more you practice it. With time you may find that you can drop into this expanded space at will, accessing it whenever you're having a strong reaction to something, thereby giving yourself a wider perspective.

CULTIVATE DEVOTION, DISCERNMENT, AND DISCIPLINE

Finally, I leave you with three overarching keys to cultivating extraordinary spiritual contact—whether it be to a spirit or your Divine Self. First, one must have an unwavering *devotion* to the Great Work of embodying the Divine Self and entering into intimate union with a spirit. Devotion to aligning with the Divine Self—and as Frater Lux noted, to the idea that one actually has a divine identity that is actionable—is first and foremost. It follows that uniting with one's Divine Self may then open one to a suitable spirit marriage partner.

Key questions to contemplate in the further study of devotion as it is related to spirit marriage might be: What aids us in the cultivation and enactment of devotion? What inspires us to seek a devotional relationship with the Divine Self or an extraordinary being? What examples do we have to show that an intimate relationship with one's Divine Self is possible?

Second, one must cultivate *discernment* of both external and internal influences, or "inputs." One must learn how to discern one's unique thoughts among the myriad inputs from society and family; one's own inner aspects, ancestral patterns, and various levels of personality; and the voices of subtle forces and entities that increased sensitization to extraordinary realms may induce.

Key questions to contemplate in the further study of discernment as it is related to spirit marriage might be: What systems and worldviews teach us to perceive and control both external and internal inputs? What technologies are useful in assessing the quality and force of the subtler realms and our relationship to them? What systems of divination help the discernment process, and what systems might make this more challenging?

Finally, one must cultivate *discipline* upon the path. Having experienced the desire to pursue divine embodiment or a spirit marriage, devoted oneself to the work, and adopted practices and methods for discerning the identity and influence of the Divine Self/spirits against many other voices, one must then discipline oneself to the journey unwaveringly. This is most often achieved through reorganizing one's life to fuel the pursuit. Discipline can require a broad range of actions. For Kama it was taking vows, her *samaya,* regarding daily spiritual practice. For Orion it was observing a geas, abstaining from caffeine. And for Frater Lux it was taking vows of silence and anonymity. To quote Orion and his witchcraft lineage: "For the Tree of Silence bears the fruit of wisdom. He/She who speaks, knows not. He/She who knows, speaks not. Ever be ye mindful: though sound is the beginning of Creation, silence is the beginning of power."

Key questions to contemplate in the further study of discipline as it is related to spirit marriage might be: What forms of discipline are generative to the process of divine embodiment/spirit marriage, and what forms might be contraindicated? Is there a one-size-fits-all disciplinary approach that might work for everyone? Or might the tools and methods used for cultivation differ according to a person's age, personality, gender, culture, ancestry, and so on? What might discipline look like for a practitioner who is navigating this technology within a tradition that does not formally teach this practice, or for a practitioner who is outside of a tradition altogether?

✳ Automatic Writing

Another activity that I found instrumental in cultivating devotion, discernment, and discipline was the practice of daily automatic writing, sometimes called stream of consciousness writing. This is slightly different from keeping a journal, given that you aren't chronicling what is going on in your life, like diary keeping, and you aren't necessarily writing about what *you* are thinking. Instead, it is a concentrated conversation with your Divine Self, primary deity, or spirit contact. Some people approach automatic writing with a question in mind, like, What do you want me to know right now about my life? Others simply sit down, tap into their contact, and let the words flow. Here's how I like to practice automatic writing (an exercise that greatly influenced the writing of this book):

Step 1. Begin by grounding and centering yourself. Perform any clearing and covering exercises you use to set aside your own mundane thoughts or those of the collective so that you can tune into Spirit. This is the *discernment* aspect of the practice.

Step 2. Close your eyes and feel into the energy of your contact. Visualize them before you or, in the case of your Divine Self, sense their presence around and within you. Personally, I like to light a candle, make offerings, and have an altar or an image nearby dedicated to the being I'm contacting. This is the *devotional* aspect of the practice.

Step 3. Begin to write from the perspective of this being. Their voice is generally loving and wise. They often share insights and encouragement about you, your life, and the path you are on. If you begin to write words that berate or criticize you, it's probably not your Divine Self or a benevolent spirit who's talking—you may be tapping into a part of yourself that is hurt or an aspect of the collective consciousness that needs healing. If this happens, invite that voice to step outside into a "waiting room" and invoke your chosen spirit again by going back to step 1. (Talking to hurt aspects of yourself or the collective isn't wrong, it's just a different exercise called Parts Dialogue.) When establishing a relationship with your spirit contact, this exercise should be done daily. This is the *discipline* aspect of the practice.

This is by no means a comprehensive list of all the practices one could use to cultivate a relationship with their Divine Self and/or spirit beloved. Some of these practices were taught to me, and others I intuitively explored as a way to make contact. Unlike many initiatory traditions, none of these practices are prescribed or set in stone (except, perhaps, the Covering Practice, which requires specific movements). I encourage you to experiment, adapt, and expand upon them as you see fit—or create your own rituals and practices. This work should not feel like drudgery. Remember, this is about falling in love with your Divine Self or your spirit beloved! Most of all, become curious, cultivate wonder, and have fun.

CONCLUSION

Normalizing
the Paranormal

*I*t was in the final few months of writing this book that some of the most profound questions regarding spirit marriage arose. These are questions that can only be answered with the passage of time—the time that this material will take to mature out in the world and gain its own footing. In the West, so much of the world of holistic healing and spiritual growth seems to be cordoned off behind a velvet rope of economic and social privilege. So how shall we take the transpersonal and somewhat esoteric material outlined in this work and make it approachable and accessible to everyone who needs it?

I believe it begins with what I call *normalizing the paranormal*—helping our communities understand that perception and interaction with Otherworldly forms and forces is part of our normal, albeit expanded, human capabilities. In this book I have given you many examples of spirit marriage throughout history and shared contemporary stories of, in some cases, highly educated individuals who hold spirit marriages. I've also given you a solid foundation for how to develop your own contacts. All of this is in hope that you will begin to see this practice as a healthy and normal part of our psycho-spiritual evolution as a species.

As Dr. Martin Luther King Jr. extolled, "Our goal is to create a beloved community, and this will require a qualitative change in our souls as well as a quantitative change in our compassionate action."[1] I often ask myself, How can this work support the creation of Dr. King's vision of the beloved community? I believe this material demonstrates the many ways one may transform the quality of one's soul in cocreation with Spirit. From that union, greater compassion for Self and others seems to naturally follow as we realize that we are each a fractal contributing to the greater intelligence of the cosmos. Ultimately, it is my fervent hope that our definition of "cocreative" and "beloved community" will expand to include all the many beings we share our beautiful planet with—physical and Otherworldly.

I am reminded that this ending of the book is, in fact, just a beginning. The activations that have been transmitted, the tests and trials that my fellow spirit marriage practitioners and I have shared, and the tools and techniques we have explored have all been in service to the laboratory of experiential learning known as *embodied spirituality,* so that we may contribute something of value to our planet. This type of inquiry is both involution and expansion, like a mandala. The mandala that has formed began with the love relationship between myself and my Faery Beloved. It then expanded out to my fellow practitioners and their spirit-spouses, and it now includes you and your inquiry.

We sit in the *bindu* point at the center of the mandala with our personal stories, and bit by bit, they expand outward into varying configurations of collective stories and cross-cultural conversations. Our job becomes learning how to relax and breathe through the sometimes uncomfortable process of expansion. This sacred configuration will hopefully continue to expand its energy outward to encompass our beautiful, blue-green Earth and foster the awakening and transformation of our planet into a world that works for everyone—all beings, all species, all time lines, the All in THE ALL.

If I have done my job correctly, you will have discovered that spirit marriage practices are a widespread part of Earth-based spirituality, albeit often circumspect, as well as present in many traditional religions. You will understand that to this day spirits still beckon and guide humans toward what indigenous researcher Polly Walker describes as a greater balance and harmony amid the web of relationships among humans and the natural and spirit worlds that sustains us all.[2] You will now have a cosmology and worldview that both honors and respects spirit marriage as a powerful transpersonal agent for change. And perhaps you will have been inspired to pursue your own inquiry or deepening practice to explore your own Divine Self/Divine Other relationship.

OUR SHARED STORIES

This book was informed, in large part, by the contribution of other people's stories. So I asked my fellow spirit marriage practitioners, and a few people close to the material, to read each of the stories and share how it impacted them. I wanted to get a sense of the transformative potential for this work.

Most of my fellow spirit marriage practitioners reported feeling surprised to learn that they were part of a larger phenomenon and a broader community of practitioners that reached far beyond their own traditions. They reported feeling a greater sense of being seen, and that seeing the commonalities and differences between the different practitioners had a clarifying effect on their own story. One coresearcher noted: "A soothing salve to my soul was to see the unknown fellowship between us as we faced challenges and rose to meet them."

A few people shared how the material profoundly activated them, citing somatic experiences like "falling into rapture," being opened, heightened, and brightened, and of having a sense of the Self expanded and validated. This clued me into the magical nature of this text, and the fact that the voices of these spirits are alive and transmitting their power through these stories. This material has the potential to be liberating, activating, and galvanizing—if we are willing to open to the possibility of being loved by the spirits. In fact, one early reader claimed that decades-long cycles of suffering, disappointment, worry, and other energy leakages had been healed as a result of encountering this research.

At the very least, I believe that hearing others' stories can help us step into greater personal sovereignty and to acknowledge the importance of telling our own stories. Ultimately, through encountering the many beings in this material, we can find deep companionship on the journey, a sense of being accompanied—not only by the spirits—but as one reader put it "by an ever-widening swath of humanity willing and ready to talk frankly about embodied spirituality." A new kind of fellowship is forming, one in which we traverse these ancient and yet unfamiliar waters together, holding each other up along the way through the power of our shared experience.

Personally, I discovered that as a highly sensitive person, I am not alone in having these extraordinary experiences. Many of the qualities associated with being an HSP are foundational to having extraordinary spiritual experience, and specifically to the practice of spirit marriage. Increasingly, research into highly sensitive people is showing that almost a quarter of the population share qualities of expanded perception, heightened sensation, and awareness of subtle cues and changes in one's environment.[3] Twenty-plus percent is hardly a marginalized or isolating number. I offer that these HSP qualities are all foundational to extraordinary spiritual experiences and specifically the practice of spirit contact.

The current cultural paradigm, specifically here in the West, devalues and ridicules the qualities and habits of sensitive people, who are sometimes ridiculed as "snowflakes," thereby making them feel unwelcome and alienated. This alienation then leads to the polarizing dynamic of either feeling "outcast and weird" or "special and more evolved"—two extremes of an outsider complex. It is my hope that now that you have heard stories that, perhaps, mirror your own, you will be less likely to label your extraordinary experiences as either "weird" or "exceptional." Hopefully you will simply understand that they go with the territory of your being, in all probability, an HSP.

All in all, I hope this material affirms the range of extraordinary experience that involve intimate contact and communication with extraordinary beings and intelligences. Ultimately, although mainstream psychology and the hard sciences tend to disregard extraordinary encounters as make-believe or pathological, this research has confirmed for myself, my early readers, and my coresearchers that one is not alone in the perception of and belief in spirit contacts. And, as we have seen, many of these spirits are eager to betroth themselves to humans in order to foster cocreative alliances and planetary well-being. Panpsychism—"the idea that matter at all levels, including fundamental particles, has an inherent property of sentience, or mind"[4] is currently receiving, like its cousin animism, increased serious attention in both science and the humanities. As ecopsychologist Theodore Roszak claims: "Animism is irrepressible because it is a valid perception of the natural world as having dignity, vitality, and mentality."[5] Spirit contact and intimate union with extraordinary beings is but a facet of animism, which understands Earth to be a living, breathing intelligence full of animate life of all strata of consciousness.

KEY TAKEAWAYS

The material contained in this book, I know, has been a tremendous amount of information to digest. Some parts may have resonated deeply with you, and others may have slipped by unnoticed. Here, then, is a quick summary of what I believe the key learnings of this book demonstrate—insights that are perhaps unique to this material or bear highlighting in summary.

- ◆ Spirit marriage allows the human counterpart to reach beyond their finite sense of self and expand to embrace the realms of consciousness that are beyond the reach of ordinary space and time.
- ◆ To make love to a spirit is to reconnect to our bodies in a way that vitalizes them, making them temples of divine awakening and thereby fostering the alchemy of embodied spirituality.
- ◆ Spirits use gender as a kind of language to inform, enhance, or balance needed qualities within the practitioner.
- ◆ Because most of the coresearchers are in committed human rela-

tionships in addition to spirit marriages, in most cases a kind of polyamory is being practiced, whether they name it as such or not.

◆ Through honoring our relationship to Earth as a sacred body and engaging in the art of ecospiritual practice, humanity becomes a conscious cocreator in Gaia consciousness, and our own bodies become the interface point for this exchange. "Waking up," then, is not a transcendent state of escape, but a radical indwelling of the Divine within ourselves and our planet.

◆ Entheosis is any spiritual process that connects an individual to a divine or rarified aspect of themselves and helps to bring the mundane human consciousness into greater awareness and dialogue with the divine or transpersonal aspect—perhaps even allowing them to embody this consciousness as their way of being in the world.

◆ The realization of the Divine Self, the entheotic state, is not an unprecedented experience reserved only for an exceptional few, but the intended birthright of all people on this planet, at this time.

◆ The spirit-spouse relationship might naturally enhance and even require cultivating and claiming one's own spiritual sovereignty. And mirroring this, stepping into one's spiritual sovereignty perhaps activates and awakens the practitioner to the point of attracting a spirit-spouse.

◆ Marriage to a spirit helps us evolve toward greater unity consciousness by teaching us how to refine our subtle senses and attune to realms of nonlocal interdimensionality.

◆ What unity consciousness really entails is the ability to stabilize oneself psychologically, physiologically, and psychically while at the same time being acutely attuned to Earth and her morphogenic fields.

◆ We have the capacity to transform the planet when we as a species—supported by our unseen allies—come together in our vulnerability and imperfections and envision a world that works for everyone!

CONTRIBUTIONS

Each individual who reads this book will derive their own meaning and conclusions from the material. This is by design. The magical nature of any transformative text is that it takes on a life of its own and lives out beyond the author. That said, here are some overarching assertions that are important to me as the cocreator of this work and to which I'd like to draw your attention.

First, although the practice of spirit marriage has been upheld predominantly through oral tradition or in the *twilight* or coded language of metaphor, it's important to understand that it has persisted as a transformational spiritual practice since the dawn of recorded history (probably earlier); it's practiced on almost every continent; and is still relevant today—particularly to contemporary practitioners of Earth-based traditions.

Second, spirit marriage practices have led, and continue to lead, to the development of a cocreative consciousness between humanity and suprahuman intelligences—a dynamic that has helped evolve the human species toward cultivation of extraordinary powers, acceleration of evolutionary development, and progression of people. As a result, spirit marriage practitioners often report a sense of personal awakening and self-sovereignty as the by-product of their union.

Third, undertaking a spirit marriage leads to greater autonomy and power, and to becoming one's own spiritual authority. Spirit marriage results in a kind of self-governance. This allows the practitioner to claim their personal power and act in full agency for themselves and their community. These actions stand over and against whatever dominating, "culturally normative" forces may have been telling them. Spirit marriage leads to audacity of spirit, spiritual transformation, and even social change. I contend, then, that the primary goal of spirit marriage is not only liberation and transformation of the individual but ultimately the transformation of society and evolution of the planet toward what futurist Barbara

Marx Hubbard refers to as the *Homo spiritus* or *Homo universalis.*

Fourth, the door is now open for a transcultural conversation among various spirit marriage traditions, one wherein practitioners of spirit marriage who previously have felt more guarded or protective of this subaltern practice now may feel a greater sense of being seen and validated. As well, they may be feeling a sense of being in community with practitioners of other traditions. Along these lines, it seems that various deities from vastly different pantheons are now urging us toward greater transcultural understanding, advocacy, and tolerance among their practitioners. Some spirit marriage practitioners are engaging with multiple traditions and deities in cross-pantheon practices. Therefore, it is my hope that spirit marriage practitioners will cultivate a broader dialogue among their various spirit marriage traditions so that we can better hear the voices of these marginalized religions and groups.

Fifth, it would behoove those of us who are prone to needing validation or proof of the reality of spirit-beings to grow quiet and listen as each practitioner speaks from inside their own tradition and experience. We need to hear these voices. We need to learn from their years of experience working in the shadow of hegemonic religions. We need to allow them to tell us how best to undertake a conversation of inclusivity and cocreation without a need to validate things scientifically.

Finally, we each have a Divine Self that we can awaken and/or embody, and this is a legitimate expression of spirit marriage. However, I am *redefining divinity as the fully realized potential of an individual or group that has devoted itself to the greater good of both themselves and their community.* In this context, to awaken the Divine within is to be fully human and yet in conscious contact with one's highest or Divine Self. I contend that the realization of the Divine Self, or entheosis, is not an unprecedented experience reserved only for an exceptional few, but the intended birthright of all people on this planet, at this time.

RECOMMENDATIONS

For those of you who are ready to embark on a spirit-spouse adventure, I'll leave you with a few recommendations that helped me tremendously on my own voyage.

+ Find a mentor who has been through this process and/or a community to support you in stepping into a relationship with an extraordinary being. This is paramount to grounding and validating the relationship, as well as helping you steer clear of some of the shadowy areas of spirit contact.
+ Likewise, particularly for a Westerner, it can be beneficial to have the support of a psychologist or other counselor well versed in the paranormal and/or indigenous or Earth-based spirituality—someone who can help tease out the finer points of interaction with the subtle realms without pathologizing the more extraordinary aspects of spirit communication.
+ Although not every seeker may be wooed into a spirit marriage per se, the search for and establishment of a relationship with one's Divine Self is an endeavor that every person may undertake. You have a Divine Self that is at this very moment reaching through to you. Now go out and find Her/Him/Them!

FINAL THOUGHTS

It is my hope that this book has served to guide like-minded seekers in the cultivation of a spirit marriage, particularly those who do not have access to one of the aforementioned traditions. Now is the time for toppling paradigms that are old, outdated, and useless. Too much of our attention and consciousness has been co-opted by dualistic thinking and a scarcity mentality. Many extraordinary beings want us to know we have all the tools we need to build sustainable, enlivening, and just societies, based on the values of sharing, cocreation, and love. To do this, we must plumb the depths of our assumptions about "us versus them," "in versus out," "upper versus lower," "good versus bad," and "light versus dark." The only way to restore our Earth and save our species is through unity, and the primary power that will get us there is love. We can restore Earth and save our species through intimate relationships with each other, the seen, and the unseen.

Reaching out—or perhaps reaching in—to the indwelling of a spirit empowers us to move beyond our previously held beliefs about reality and encourages us to look with new eyes at the horizon of possibility. The world around us becomes animated with many varied mysteries just waiting to be explored. By taking a literal approach to the existence of spirit-beings and the possibility of spirit marriage, we empower the world around us to embody its own mystery—to live beyond us—out beyond the field of our bounded knowing. We make sacred all existence, from the tiniest atom to the largest tree. We are no longer the center, or master, of Creation; instead we are its beloved, waiting to be wooed by its ardent desire for our embrace.

Glossary

Abramelin Operation: The Abramelin Operation is a ritual ordeal designed to bring the magician into knowledge of and conversation with the Holy Guardian Angel. Occult practitioners also may use the "Bornless Ritual" and/or the "Liber Samekh" rituals to achieve similar results.

animism: The belief that Earth, specifically, and the cosmos, in general, are living, breathing intelligences full of animate intelligent life at all strata of being. As such, humanity is but one species in relationship with both the seen and unseen aliveness of the world around us.

archetype: Psychological concept introduced by the Swiss psychiatrist Carl Jung (1875–1961), who believed that archetypes were models of people, behaviors, or personalities. Archetypes, he suggested, are inborn tendencies that play a role in influencing human behavior.

asana: A Sanskrit word meaning "postural practice," "posture," or "seat."

autoethnography: A research method that uses personal experience to describe and interpret cultural texts, experiences, beliefs, and practices.

crossroads: The liminal space between this world and the "other world." The place where two or more roads meet and create an intersecting point is considered by practitioners of Voodoo/Vodou, Witchcraft, and other folk magic traditions to be a powerful place for magic to occur.

daimon: Also *daemon.* According to Plato's *Symposium,* the daimon is a benevolent, guiding spirit or benign nature spirit similar to a ghost, chthonic hero, spirit guide, force of nature, or deity.

darshan: A Sanskrit word that means "the opportunity or occasion of seeing a holy person or an image of a deity."

Dasa-Mahavidya: A group of ten wisdom Goddesses in the Tantric tradition.

ecofeminism: A branch of feminism that examines the connections between women and nature.

egregore: An occult concept representing a thought-form or collective group mind, an autonomous psychic entity made up of, and influencing, the thoughts of a group of people.

enchantivism: As defined by terrapsychologist Craig Chalquist, enchantivism is an activist approach that seeks to inspire deep societal change, whether locally or more widely, by working with story, myth, dream, and the presence of place to inspire and envision alternative possibilities for our future as a species and a planet.

entheogen: From the Greek root *entheos* meaning "God within." An entheogen, also called a *psychedelic,* is a chemical substance, typically of plant origin, that is ingested to produce a nonordinary state of consciousness for religious or spiritual purposes.

entheosis: From the Greek root *entheos* meaning "God within." The *entheotic process* is any spiritual process that connects an individual to a divine or rarified aspect of themselves. In so doing, it helps to bring the mundane human consciousness into greater awareness and dialogue with the divine or transpersonal aspect.

Faery: Also spelled *Feri, Faerie,* and/or *Fae*—terms used to specifically denote a class of Otherworldly entities, of which terms like *fairy,* more properly known as *sylphs,* are a subcategory of elemental beings. The spelling of *Faery* and its variations have been adopted by practitioners of magick to distinguish magical practice and teachings from the diminutive folktale entities commonly found in fairy tales.

folk magic: A form of folk religion or vernacular religion that comprises various forms and expressions of religion that are distinct from the official doctrines and practices of organized religion. Generally of a practical nature, folk magic is meant to address the common ills of the community: healing the sick, bringing love or luck, driving away evil forces, finding lost items, bringing good harvests, granting fertility, reading omens, and so on.

Gaia theory: Also referred to as the *Gaia hypothesis* or the *Gaia principle,* it proposes that living organisms interact with their inorganic surroundings on Earth to form a synergistic and self-regulating, complex system that helps to maintain and perpetuate the conditions for life on the planet.

geas: Also *geis, géis, deas;* plural *geasa.* An idiosyncratic taboo, whether of obligation or prohibition, akin to being bound to a vow. The plural is also used to specifically mean a spell prohibiting some action, which is common in Irish folklore and mythology.

gris-gris: In Voodoo/Vodou both the act and the object of magical supernatural power.

Heathenry: Also termed *Heathenism, Contemporary Germanic Paganism,* or *Germanic Neopaganism,* Heathenry is a modern Pagan religion modeled on the pre-Christian belief systems adhered to by the Germanic peoples of the Iron Age and early medieval Europe.

Hieros Gamos: A form of sacred marriage, often involving the sexual union between a Priest/Priestess/Ruler and a God/Goddess, that may or may not incorporate a spirit marriage.

Holy Guardian Angel (HGA): The part of one's Self that is akin to a God Self. The identity of the HGA is distinct from the mundane consciousness as well as the Higher Self. According to British occultist MacGregor Mathers, the highest part of the Higher Self overlaps with the lowest part of the HGA.

houngan: A male priest in the Vodou/Voodoo tradition.

indigenous feminism: An intersectional theory and practice of feminism that focuses on decolonization and indigenous sovereignty in the context of indigenous cultural values and priorities rather than white, mainstream, patriarchal ones.

ishtadevi/a: Also *istadevata*. A Sanskrit word that means "one's chosen or primary deity."

Kabbalah: An esoteric method, discipline, and school of thought that originated with Judaism and that has been adopted, some might argue appropriated, by the practitioners of Ceremonial Magic. In Kabbalah, *Kether* is the formless divine, or unmanifest realm, and *Malkuth* is the manifest or incarnated realm.

karma: A Sanskrit word meaning "action," "work," or "deed," it also refers to the spiritual principle of cause and effect in which the intent and actions of an individual influence the future of that individual.

kula: A Sanskrit word that means "community," "lineage," or "family."

Kundalini Shakti: In yogic philosophy this refers to the Divine Feminine shakti or the life-energy made corporeal. Kundalini is described in Eastern religious or spiritual traditions as an indwelling spiritual energy that resides coiled like a snake in the sacrum of the spinal column. This energy can be awakened in order to purify the subtle system and ultimately to bestow a state of divine union or awakening upon the seeker. In some Tantric traditions Kundalini Shakti is also believed to be an indwelling Goddess who lives within the life-force of the practitioner.

left-handed Tantra: Practices that are considered taboo or unclean by mainstream or *right-handed* Tantrics. These taboo practices may include the eating of meat, intoxication, cultivating sexual arousal, and engaging with practitioners of a different caste.

Loa: Alternatively spelled *Lwa,* Loa are the spirits and/or deities of Haitian Vodou and Louisiana Voodoo.

magick: Magick with a *k* was first used by the Ceremonial Magician Aleister Crowley to differentiate occult magick from stage magic and is defined as "the science and art of causing change to occur in conformity with will."

mahasiddha: A Sanskrit term for a Tantric practitioner who has gained sufficient empowerments and teachings to act as a guru or Tantric master.

mambo: A female priestess of Vodou/Voodoo.

mantra: A Sanskrit word or sound repeated to aid in meditation or concentration.

mariage Loa: The Vodou/Voodoo term for the ritual marriage to a Loa.

masculinism: The adherence to or promotion of attributes (opinions, values, attitudes, habits) regarded as typical of men and boys.

matrka: Also *Matrika*. A Sanskrit word that means "mothers," it commonly refers to a group of eight primordial Hindu Goddesses who are always depicted together, and known as the "little mothers" of creation.

mendhi: A traditional Indian art form that uses pigment to dye the skin with elaborate designs.

morphogenic or morphogenetic: The collective, or group mind. Morphogenic fields are fields of thought created by everything in existence; such a field is the input and output of Creation and it also holds within itself the full potential of that creation.

met tet: In Vodou/Voodoo the patron deity received by a Vodouisant during initiation. Similar to the ishtadevi or a patron saint, this deity is closely aligned with one's personality and path in life and becomes a guide and mentor in the spirit realms.

murti: A Sanskrit word that means "sacred statue" or "icon."

nefer: An Egyptian hieroglyph used to convey the concepts of Perfection, Completion, Goodness, and Beauty.

noosphere: The sphere of human consciousness and mental activity, especially regarding its influence on the biosphere and in relation to evolution.

paranthropology: The social-scientific approach to the study of paranormal experiences, beliefs, and phenomena as coined by anthropologist Jack Hunter. The paranthropological approach is devoted to an open-minded and exploratory perspective on a wide range of experiences, beliefs, and phenomena often called paranormal, supernatural, or anomalous.

polyamory: Typically defined as the practice of, or desire for, intimate relationships with more than one partner at a time, with the knowledge and consent of all partners involved.

prana: Breath, life-force, and/or universal energy that circulates in currents in and around the body.

psychopomps: Creatures, spirits, angels, deities, or people who escort newly deceased souls from Earth to the afterlife.

puja: A Sanskrit word that means "reverence," "honor," "homage," "adoration," and "worship." It is commonly used to refer to a ritual or ceremony.

pujarini: A female priestess or one who offers puja.

reenchantment: Reenchantment is a response to the increasing *disenchantment,* or devaluation of religion and spirituality, that has arisen as a result of modernized, bureaucratic, secularized Western society where scientific understanding is more highly valued than belief, and processes are oriented toward rational goals. Reenchantment calls for a *resacralization,* or making sacred again, the stories, myths, meaning, and mysteries of life, as a necessary tonic for a sick and dying world. In the reenchanted worldview, humanity becomes a participant in the cosmos—grounded in a real and intimate connection between humans and nature, not an isolated observer.

sadhana: A Sanskrit word that can be translated as a means of accomplishing something. It is commonly used to refer to a daily spiritual practice.

sakhi: A Sanskrit word that means "true or bosom friend," "companion," or "life partner."

Samhain: Pronounced "saw-wen," Samhain is the Pagan celebration for the ancestors and beloved dead, the root of the holiday we now celebrate as Halloween.

Santería: Also known as Regla de Ocha, Santería is an Afro-American religion of Caribbean origin that developed in the Spanish colonies among West African descendants.

santero: A Cuban priest of Santería.

scientism: The dogmatic belief that a narrow interpretation of today's scientific worldview is infallibly correct.

Seidr: Also *seidhr, seidh, seithr, seith,* or *seid.* A form of Norse magic concerned with divination, prophecy, and magic-working.

Shakta Tantra: A sect of Tantra that emphasizes the relationality of the human to transpersonal or divine forces through the worship of the female principle (shakti)—embodied both as the human yoni (vulva/womb) and Earth—as the prime mover at the foundation of all Creation.

shakti: The primordial cosmic energy representing the dynamic forces that are thought to move through the entire universe as the Divine Feminine or the life-energy. (See Kundalini Shakti.)

shaktipat: The transmission (or conferring) of spiritual energy upon one person by another.

shakti pitha: A Sanskrit term that refers to the veneration of specific sacred sites in India as the physical body of the Goddess.

siddhi: A person who attains the realization of siddhis—psychic and spiritual abilities and powers.

Sidhe: Also *Sith.* Primordial Faery beings also known as the Shining Ones.

sindur: Also called *kumkum,* sindur is a red powder applied to the center hair part or as a dot in the center of the forehead; it can be used as a devotional offering. Marking the center hair part with sindur is a gesture commonly performed in a traditional Hindu marriage ceremony.

singularity or technological singularity: The idea that technology will eventually eclipse human evolution, specifically when artificial intelligence surpasses human intelligence.

spiritual bypass: An avoidance technique in which one focuses solely on the highly attractive exterior images of spirituality in an effort to avoid the darker, painful, and more exhausting aspects of the spiritual path.

telesmatic: A name that is created to develop images for visualization of a nonphysical entity for Ceremonial Magical purposes. It is based on the letters of the name of the entity to be given an image.

terrapsychology: A growing field of imaginative studies, ideas, and practices for reenchanting our relations with the natural world and therefore with each other and ourselves, originally developed by depth psychologist Craig Chalquist.

theurgy: From the Greek meaning "God-work," it involves methods for evoking and communicating with the spirits.

toradh: A Gaelic term for life-force, similar to chi, prana, or orgone energy.

transpersonal: A term used by different schools of philosophy and psychology to describe experiences and worldviews that extend beyond the personal level of the psyche and beyond mundane worldly events.

transpersonal psychology: A subfield or "school" of psychology that integrates the spiritual and transcendent aspects of the human experience with the framework of modern psychology. It is also possible to define it as "spiritual psychology."

yogini: A Sanskrit word that refers both to a female practitioner of yoga as well as a group of female Tantric wisdom beings or Goddesses.

Notes

FOREWORD

1. Macleod, *The Mystic's Prayer.*
2. Quoted in Clark, *Einstein,* 422.

PREFACE

1. Hallowell, quoted in Hunter, *Engaging the Anomalous,* 73.

INTRODUCTION. FEMINIZING AND DECOLONIZING OUR PERCEPTIONS OF REALITY

1. Nissinen and Uro, *Sacred Marriages,* 1–6.
2. For further reading on this, please see Mathers, *The Book of the Sacred Magic;* Crowley, Aleister, *Magick Without Tears.*
3. For further reading on this, please see Chilisa, *Indigenous Research Methodologies,* 3–6.
4. For more background on the concept of the *Enchanted Universe,* see Caroline Merchant's *The Death of Nature;* Landy and Saler's *The Reenchantment of the World;* Sharon Blackie's *The Enchanted Life;* and Craig Chalquist's "Declaration of Enchantment." Also relevant to this approach is Lisa Christie's 2012 dissertation "Re-membering the Cosmological Self: Toward an Ecological-Postmodern Feminist Process Philosophy and Goddess Thealogy," in which she provides a spiritual ecofeminist philosophical framework in which these experiences might be understood as valid and natural.
5. Hunter, *Engaging the Anomalous,* 17.
6. Merchant, *The Death of Nature.*
7. Chalquist, "Enchantivism," par. 9.

CHAPTER 1. HIDDEN IN PLAIN SIGHT

1. Eliade, *Shamanism,* 72–73.
2. Sarbacker, "Indo-Tibetan Tantrism," 33.
3. Eliade, *Shamanism,* 67.
4. Sarbacker, "Indo-Tibetan Tantrism," 33–34.
5. For a discussion of the influence of the witch trials on Celtic folk magic, see Randolph Conner's 2007 dissertation entitled "The Pagan Muse: Its Influence in Western Culture—Embodying and Transmitting Ancient Wisdom from the Middle Ages Through the Early Twentieth Century," 14–15; and Lizanne Henderson's chapter "Witch-Hunting and Witch Belief in the Gàidhealtachd" in *Witchcraft and Belief in Early Modern Scotland,* 95–118.
6. For a further discussion of contemporary Faery belief and theory see Neil Rushton's 2020 online article "The Faerie Phenomenon in Folklore and Modern Experience."
7. Sherma, "Sacred Immanence," 89–90, 95, 107.
8. For a discussion of these entities and others, see, for example, Fortune, *Psychic Self-Defense;* Eliade, *Shamanism;* McCarthy Brown, *Mama Lola: A Vodou Priestess in Brooklyn;* Foxwood, *The Faery Teachings;* Dominquez Jr., *Spirit Speak: Knowing and Understanding Spirit Guides, Ancestors, Ghosts, Angels, and the Divine;* and Rachel, "Ecologies of the Soul."

CHAPTER 2. HISTORY, FOLKLORE, AND RELIGION

1. Teppo, "Sacred Marriage," 75.
2. Herodotus, *Histories,* 181.
3. Herodotus, *Histories,* 182.
4. Green, *Elf Queens and Holy Friars,* 15.
5. Green, *Elf Queens and Holy Friars,* 2.
6. Cited in Green, *Elf Queens and Holy Friars,* 85.
7. Cited in Green, *Elf Queens and Holy Friars,* 99–100.
8. Wilby, *Cunning Folk,* 105.
9. Wilby, *Cunning Folk,* 105.
10. For further reading, please see Crowley, Vivianne, *A Woman's Guide to Earth Traditions;* Green, *Elf Queens and Holy Friars.*
11. Wilby, *Cunning Folk,* 106.
12. Eliade, *Shamanism,* 71.
13. Herbert, "Goddess and King," 264.
14. Dehijia, *Yogini Cult and Temples,* 85.
15. Topley, "Ghost Marriages," 92.

16. Eliade, "Mystical Marriage," 437–38.

17. Eliade, *Shamanism,* 125n, 168, 257, 329, 351–52, 395, 461.

18. Eliade, *Shamanism,* 351.

19. Conner, Sparks, and Sparks, *Encyclopedia of Queer Myth,* 27.

20. Conner, Sparks, and Sparks, *Encyclopedia of Queer Myth,* 28–29.

21. Marglin, *Wives of the God-King,* 7.

22. Marglin, *Wives of the God-King,* 1–21.

23. von Rospatt, "Remarks on the Consecration Ceremony," 237–43; Allen, "Girls' Pre-Puberty Rites," 221–28.

24. Rigoglioso, *The Cult of the Divine Birth,* 21–27.

25. Rigoglioso, *The Cult of the Divine Birth,* 31; *Virgin Mother Goddesses,* 25, 141.

26. Bolle, "Hieros Gamos," 319.

27. Plutarch, "Parallel Lives," 4.2.

28. Apuleis, *Metamorphoses,* 4.28–31.

29. Gibson, "The Offspring," 282.

30. Gibson, "The Offspring," 285.

31. Heaney, *Over Nine Waves.*

32. Stewart, *EarthLight.*

33. Davies, Phillipa, "The Physicians of Myddfai."

34. Harman, *The Sacred Marriage,* 116–17.

35. Harman, *The Sacred Marriage,* 117.

36. Clapp, *Sheba*; Heschel, "Lilith," 17–20; Scholem, "Demons, Demonology," 572–78.

37. Collins, Andrew, *From the Ashes of Angels;* Radin, *Real Magic.*

38. Wise, Abegg, and Cook, *The Dead Sea Scrolls.*

39. Sullivan, *Wrestling with Angels,* 216–17.

40. Sullivan, *Wrestling with Angels,* 225.

41. Sullivan, *Wrestling with Angels,* 66n.

42. Collins, John, "The Sons of God," 263, 273.

43. Collins, Andrew, *From the Ashes of Angels,* 1996.

44. St. Teresa, *Collected Works,* Volume 3, Chapter 29, Part 17.

45. Case, "Tracking the Vampire," 5.

46. Quoted in Bowie, *Beguine Spirituality,* 1:23, 57.

47. Bowie, *Beguine Spirituality,* 5:30, 76.

48. Bowie, *Beguine Spirituality,* 96.

49. Hadewijch, "Visions," 195.

50. Hadewijch, "Visions," 195–96.

51. Hadewijch, "Visions," 196.

52. Hadewijch, "Letters," 1986a, 189–90.

53. Brown, *Immodest Acts,* 66–74.

54. Brown, *Immodest Acts,* 112–13.

55. Brown, *Immodest Acts,* 118–23.

56. Brown, *Immodest Acts,* 126–28.

57. Dalai Lama, "Tantra," 200–207; Lama Yeshe, *Introduction to Tantra,* 94–95, 183; Frawley, *Inner Tantric Yoga,* 9–16, 28, 110.

58. Frawley, *Inner Tantric Yoga,* 13–16, 110.

59. Sarbacker, "Indo-Tibetan Tantrism," 33, 38.

60. Lewis, *Arguments with Ethnography,* 109–11.

61. Sarbacker, "Indo-Tibetan Tantrism," 35.

62. Conner, Sparks, and Sparks, *Encyclopedia of Queer Myth*; Crowley, Vivianne, *Woman's Guide to Earth Traditions.*

63. Koleva, "A Marriage," par. 11.

64. Filan, "I married a Lwa."

65. René and Houlberg, "My Double Mystical Marriages," 299.

66. Conner, Sparks, and Sparks, *Encyclopedia of Queer Myth,* 5.

CHAPTER 3. THE OCCULT
AND PSYCHO-SPIRITUAL PRACTICE

1. Moreman, *The Spiritualist Movement,* 102–3.

2. Craddock, "Heavenly Bridegrooms," 62–63.

3. Blamires, *Chronicles of the Sidhe,* 11–14.

4. Macleod, *Iona,* 155.

5. Macleod, *The Winged Destiny,* 367–90.

6. Blamires, *Chronicles of the Sidhe,* 107–8.

7. Blamires, *Chronicles of the Sidhe,* 108.

8. Fortune, *Psychic Self-Defense,* 69–70, 150.

9. Fortune, *Psychic Self-Defense,* 150–51.

10. Fortune, *Psychic Self-Defense,* 69–70.

11. Fortune, *Psychic Self-Defense,* 71; Rigoglioso, *The Cult of Divine Birth,* 91.

12. Fortune, *The Esoteric Philosophy,* 74.

13. Tyson, *Sexual Alchemy,* 25.

14. Foxwood, personal communication with the author, November 20, 2010.

15. Foxwood, *Faery Teachings,* 236–37.

16. Foxwood, *Faery Teachings,* 238–43.

17. Foxwood, *Faery Teachings,* 243.

18. Espinoza, "Erotic Intelligence of Plants," 116.

19. Quoted in Gabriel, "Did Rudolf Steiner Channel," par. 34.

20. Quoted in Gabriel, "Did Rudolf Steiner Channel," par. 13.

21. Quoted in Corbett, "The Holy Grail of the Unconscious," par. 13.
22. Cited in Corbett, "The Holy Grail," par. 39
23. Jung, *Memories, Dreams and Reflections,* 191.

CHAPTER 5. THE FAERY SEER

1. Macleod, *The Immortal Hour,* Act 1, scene 111.
2. Wilson, "Trembling in the Dark," 201.
3. René and Houlberg, "My Double Mystical Marriages"; Although outside the scope of this book, I am keen to see an exploration of the topic of spirit marriage and polyamory undertaken. Because polyamory can be a triggering and often misunderstood topic, I suggest using a postfeminist/queer lens to question the practice of traditional marriage, as well as a decolonizing lens to critique the projection of Western culture and religious values onto the practice of polyamorous cultures and spirit marriage.

CHAPTER 6. THE SHAKTA TANTRIC

1. There has been some ambiguity about the difference between Kali and Kamakhya in my conversations with Kama. Are they distinct entities or aspects of each other? And if Kama is married to Kali, how is it that the real sadhana began when she met her lineage family at Kamakhya's temple? Kama seems intentionally ambiguous about these distinctions, as well as the various lineages she holds, and the identity of her sadhana family. She says it is to protect the lineage.

CHAPTER 7. THE WEST AFRICAN
SHRINE KEEPER

1. Chalquist, "Declaration of Enchantment."

CHAPTER 8. THE WASHINGTON, DC,
WITCHDOCTOR

1. According to the Anti-Defamation League's hate symbols database, white supremacists have appropriated the runic alphabet, in large part, because Nazi Germany sometimes used runes in its symbology.

CHAPTER 9. THE NEW ORLEANS
VOODOO MAMBO

1. Panepinto, "Cultural Appropriation vs. Cultural Appreciation."

CHAPTER 11. THE CEREMONIAL MAGICIAN

1. Ceremonial Magicians traditionally refer to each other as Frater (Brother) so-and-so or Soror (Sister) so-and-so. I have chosen to use the name Frater Lux, which is akin to calling him Brother Light, in keeping with the convention of how Ceremonial Magicians refer to each other.

2. This concept is similar to *Patanjali's Yoga Sutra* 1.3 *tadā draṣṭuḥ svarūpe avasthānam.* B. K. S Iyengar translates this sutra as: "The seer, or the *ātman,* dwells in his home. When the coverings of the *ātman*—namely, the five elements and their counterparts (the body, organs of action, senses of perception, mind, intelligence and consciousness)—are quietened, the core *puruṣa* (*bindu*) reveals himself. Then he moves to surrender himself to God (*Īśvara pranidhāna*)."

3. Mathers used the least-reliable manuscript copy of *The Book of Abramelin* as the basis for his translation, and so it contains many errors and omissions. The later English translation by Steven Guth and Georg Dehn (von Worms), based on the earliest and most complete sources, is more scholarly and comprehensive. Although Abraham von Worms is traditionally attributed as the author of this work, in their translation Dehn and Guth postulate that the actual authorship of *The Book of Abramelin* was by Rabbi Yaakov Moelin (ca. 1365–1427), a German Jewish Talmudist.

CHAPTER 12. THE EROTIC MYSTIC: JOURNEY TO MY DIVINE SELF

1. Foxwood, *Tree of Enchantment,* 29, 84.
2. Radin, *Real Magic,* 4, 216.
3. Wohlleben, *Hidden Life of Trees;* Gagliano, *Thus Spoke the Plant.*
4. Chitgopekar, "The Unfettered Yoginis," 88–89.

CHAPTER 13. THE EROTIC MYSTIC: ENCOUNTERS WITH MY FAERY BELOVED

1. Lipschutz, *Cameron,* 9–17.
2. Cousineau and Smith, *The Art of Pilgrimage,* ix.
3. Roszak, "Towards an Eco-Psychology," 26:16.
4. Hubbard, "Homo Universalis."
5. Davies, *Mabinogion,* 189–99.
6. Forest, *Gwyn ap Nudd,* 72–79.
7. Forest, *Gwyn ap Nudd,* 67–69.
8. Crowley, Vivianne, *Woman's Guide to Earth Traditions,* 119–20.

9. Foxwood, *Tree of Enchantment,* 104–5.

10. Jung, *Aion,* 43.

11. Power, *Wyrds of Power,* 180–81.

12. For further reading on this, please see Hoak, "Great European Witch-Hunts"; Conner, "The Pagan Muse"; Henderson, "Witch-Hunting and Witch Belief."

13. Crowley, Vivianne, *Woman's Guide to Earth Traditions,* 21.

14. See, for example, the Indian *chudail,* the Japanese *yūrei,* the Chinese *yuan gui,* and the Celtic *green lady.*

15. For further reading on this, please see Levy, Paul, *Dispelling Wetiko.*

16. Crowley, Vivianne, *Woman's Guide to Earth Traditions,* 182, 184.

17. Foxwood, *Tree of Enchantment,* 123.

18. Forest, *Gwyn ap Nudd,* 48–49.

19. Forest, *Gwyn ap Nudd,* 52–55.

20. For further reading on this, please see Chalquist, *Storied Lives.*

CHAPTER 14. CULTIVATING A SPIRIT MARRIAGE

1. Forest, *Gwyn ap Nudd,* 54–55.

2. Bonheim, *Aphrodite's Daughters,* 16.

3. Donnelly, "The Sexual Mystic," 134–35.

4. Donnelly, "The Sexual Mystic," 135–36.

5. Ferrer, "Mononormativity, Polypride."

6. Bonheim, *Aphrodite's Daughters,* 23.

7. Lovelock, "The Quest for Gaia," 304–9; Roszak, "Towards an Eco-Psychology," 26:16.

8. Crowley, Vivianne, *Woman's Guide to Earth Traditions,* 9, 192, 197–98.

9. Gafni, *Your Unique Self,* 4.

10. Hubbard, "Homo Universalis"; Radin, *Real Magic,* 76.

11. Radin, *Real Magic,* 76, 192–94.

CHAPTER 15. PRACTICES AND PRECAUTIONS

1. Clements et al., *Organic Inquiry,* 2–3.

2. Clements et al., *Organic Inquiry,* 2–3.

3. Stewart, *EarthLight,* 32.

4. Grof, *Holotropic Mind,* 146.

5. Krippner, Bogzaran, and Percia de Carvalho, *Extraordinary Dreams,* 147–55.

6. Chalquist, personal communication with the author, November 12, 2012.

7. Clements et al., *Organic Inquiry,* 3.

8. Foxwood, personal communication with the author, May 28, 2021; *Candle and the Crossroads,* 141.

9. For further reading, see Marglin, *Wives of the God-King;* Effland and Lerner, "The World of God Kings"; Rigoglioso, *The Cult of Divine Birth.*

10. Kaplan, *Halfway Up the Mountain.*

11. Cashford and Baring, "Goddesses of Greece," 349–59.

12. Crowley, Vivianne, *Woman's Guide to Earth Traditions,* 199.

CONCLUSION.
NORMALIZING THE PARANORMAL

1. King, "Nonviolence," para. 5.

2. Walker, "Research in Relationship" 299–316.

3. Stony Brook University, "Sensitive? Emotional? Empathetic?" paragraph 1; Aron, *Highly Sensitive Person.*

4. Radin, *Real Magic,* 189.

5. Roszak, "Towards an Eco-Psychology," 7:09.

Bibliography

Allen, Michael. 2000. "Girls' Pre-Puberty Rites among the Newars of Kathmandu Valley." In *Ritual, Power, and Gender: Explorations in the Ethnography of Vanuatu, Nepal, and Ireland*, 211–51. Sydney Studies in Society and Culture 19. Sydney: Sydney Association for Studies in Society and Culture. Available at Sydney Studies in Society and Culture online.

Anti-Defamation League (ADL). 2019. "Runic Writing (racist)." In *Hate on Display™ Hate Symbols Database*. Available at Anti-Defamation League online.

Apuleis, Lucius. 2013. *Metamorphoses: The Golden Ass*. Translation by A. S. Kline. Available at Poetry in Translation online.

Aron, Elaine. 1996. *The Highly Sensitive Person: How to Thrive When the World Overwhelms You*. New York: Broadway Books.

Beckwith, Michael B (lecturer). 2008. *The Moses Code*. Interview with James Twyman, director. DVD. Carlsbad, CA: Hay House.

Blackie, Sharon. 2018. *The Enchanted Life*. Toronto: House on Anansi Press.

Blamires, Steven. 2008. *The Little Book of Great Enchantment*. Arcata, CA: R. J. Stewart Books.

———. 2012. *The Chronicles of the Sidhe*. Cheltenham, UK: Skylight Press.

Bolle, Kees. 1987. "Hieros Gamos." In *The Encyclopedia of Religion, Vol. 6*, edited by Mircea Eliade et al., 317–21. New York: Macmillan.

Bonheim, Jalaja. 1997. *Aphrodite's Daughters: Women's Sexual Stories and the Journey of the Soul*. New York, NY: Simon and Schuster.

———. 2001. *The Hunger for Ecstasy: Fulfilling the Soul's Need for Passion and Intimacy*. London: St. Martin's Press.

Bowie, Fiona. 1990. *Beguine Spirituality: Mystical Writings of Mechthild of Magdeburg, Beatrice of Nazareth, and Hadewijch of Brabant*. New York: The Crossroad Publishing Company.

———. 2010. "Methods for Studying the Paranormal (and Who Says What Is

Normal Anyway?).” *Paranthropology: Journal of Anthropological Approaches to the Paranormal* 1 (1): 4–6.

Bramly, Serge. 1975. *Macumba: The Teachings of Maria-José, Mother of the Gods.* San Francisco: City Lights Books.

Braud, William, and Rosemarie Anderson, eds. 1998. *Transpersonal Research Methods for the Social Sciences: Honoring Human Experience.* Thousand Oaks, CA: Sage.

———. 2011. *Transforming Self and Others through Research: Transpersonal Research Methods and Skills for the Human Sciences and Humanities.* SUNY series in Transpersonal and Humanistic Psychology. Albany: State University of New York Press.

Brown, Judith. 1986. *Immodest Acts: The Life of a Lesbian Nun in Renaissance Italy.* New York: Oxford University Press.

Bubant, N. 2009. “Interview with an Ancestor: Spirits as Informants and the Politics of Possession in North Maluku.” *Ethnography* 10 (3): 291–316.

Case, Sue-Ellen. 1991. “Tracking the Vampire.” *Differences: A Journal of Feminist Cultural Studies* 3, no. 2 (Summer): 1–20.

Cashford, Jules, and Anne Baring. 1993. “The Goddesses of Greece: Aphrodite, Demeter and Persephone.” In *The Myth of the Goddess: Evolution of an Image,* 349–90. London: Arkana.

Chalquist, Craig. 2009. *Storied Lives: Discovering and Deepening Your Personal Myth.* Walnut Creek, CA: World Soul Books.

———. n.d.-a. “Declaration of Enchantment.” Accessed August 30, 2019. Available online at Chalquist’s personal website.

———. n.d.-b. “Enchantivism: Transmutation through Inspiration.” Accessed August 30, 2018. Available online at Chalquist’s personal website.

———. n.d.-c. “What is Terrapsychology?” Accessed October 22, 2019. Available online at the Terrapsychology website.

Chappell, Vere. 2010. *Sexual Outlaw, Erotic Mystic: The Essential Ida Craddock.* San Francisco: Red Wheel/Weiser.

Chilisa, Bagele. 2012. *Indigenous Research Methodologies.* Los Angeles: SAGE Publications.

Chitgopekar, Nilima. 2002. “The Unfettered Yoginis.” In *Invoking Goddesses: Gender Politics in Indian Religion,* edited by Nilima Chitgopekar, 82–111. Delhi: Shakti Books.

Christie, Lisa. 2012. “Re-membering the Cosmological Self: Toward an Ecological-Postmodern Feminist Process Philosophy and Goddess Thealogy.” Ph.D. diss., California Institute of Integral Studies.

Clapp, Nicholas. 2002. *Sheba: Through the Desert in Search of the Legendary Queen.* New York: Mariner Books.

Clark, Ronald W. 2007. *Einstein: The Life and Times.* New York: William Morrow.

Clements, Jennifer, Dorothy Ettling, Dianne Jenett, and Lisa Shields. 1999. *Organic Inquiry: If Research Were Sacred.* Palo Alto, CA: Serpentina.

Collins, Andrew. 1996. *From the Ashes of Angels: The Forbidden Legacy of a Fallen Race.* Rochester, VT: Bear & Company.

Collins, John. 2008. "The Sons of God and the Daughters of Men." In *Sacred Marriages: The Divine-Human Sexual Metaphor from Sumer to Early Christianity,* edited by Marti Nissinen and Risto Uro, 259–74. Winona Lake, IN: Eisenbrauns.

Conner, Randolph. 2007. "The Pagan Muse: Its Influence in Western Culture— Embodying and Transmitting Ancient Wisdom from the Middle Ages Through the Early Twentieth Century." Ph.D. diss., California Institute of Integral Studies.

Conner, Randolph P., David Hatfield Sparks, and Mariya Sparks. 1997. *Cassell's Encyclopedia of Queer Myth, Symbol, and Spirit.* New York: Cassell.

Corbett, Sara. 2009. "The Holy Grail of the Unconscious." *New York Times,* September 16, 2009. Available at New York Times online.

Cousineau, Phil, and Huston Smith. 1998. *The Art of Pilgrimage: The Seeker's Guide to Making Travel Sacred.* San Francisco, CA: Red Wheel/Weiser.

Craddock, Ida. 1894. "Heavenly Bridegrooms." Unpublished manuscript. Available online at the Ida Craddock website.

Crowley, Aleister. 1973. *Magick Without Tears.* Reprint, Woodbury, MN: Llewellyn. First published 1954.

Crowley, Vivianne. 2001. *A Woman's Guide to Earth Traditions: Exploring Wicca, Shamanism, Paganism, Native American and Celtic Spirituality.* London: HarperCollins.

Curry, Deah, and Steven J. Wells. 2013. *An Organic Inquiry Primer for the Novice Researcher: The Who, What, When, Why, and How of a Sacred Approach to Disciplined Knowing.* West Conshohocken, PA: Infinity Publishing.

Dalai Lama XIV. 2005. "Tantra: Deity Yoga." In *The Essential Dalai Lama: His Important Teachings,* edited by Rajiv Mehrotra, 200–207. New York: Penguin Books.

Davies, Phillipa. 2016. "The Physicians of Myddfai revisited." *National Botanic Garden of Wales,* July 11, 2016. Available at National Botanic Garden of Wales online.

Davies, Sioned, trans. 2007. *Mabinogion.* Oxford: Oxford University Press.

Dehejia, Vidya. 1986. *Yogini Cult and Temples: A Tantric Tradition.* New Delhi: National Museum New Delhi.

Dominguez, Jr., Ivo. 2008. *Spirit Speak: Knowing and Understanding Spirit Guides, Ancestors, Ghosts, Angels, and the Divine.* Franklin Lakes, NJ: New Page Books.

Donnelly, Dorothy. 1982. "The Sexual Mystic: Embodied Spirituality." In *The Feminist Mystic, And Other Essays on Women and Spirituality,* edited by Mary E. Giles, 120–42. New York: Crossroad.

Eden, Amnon H., and James H. Moor. 2012. *Singularity Hypotheses: A Scientific and Philosophical Assessment.* Dordrecht, Netherlands: Springer.

Effland, Richard, and Shereen Lerner. 1997. "The World of God Kings: Buried Cities and Lost Tribes." Mesa Community College. Available at Internet Archive Wayback Machine online.

Eliade, Mircea. 1994. *Rites and Symbols of Initiation: The Mysteries of Birth and Rebirth.* Translated by Willard R. Trask. Putnam, CT: Spring Publications. First published 1958.

———. 1964. *Shamanism: Archaic Techniques of Ecstasy.* Translated by Willard R. Trask. Princeton: Princeton University Press.

———. 1977. "Mystical Marriage of a Siberian (Goldi) Shaman." In *From Primitives to Zen: A Thematic Sourcebook of the History of Religion,* 437–38. New York, NY: Harper & Row.

Espinoza, Yalila. 2013. "The Erotic Intelligence of Plants: A Heuristic Inquiry of Women's Sexual/Spiritual Experiences with Sacred Amazonian Plant Teachers." Ph.D. diss., California Institute of Integral Studies.

Ettling, Dorothy. 1998. "Levels of Listening." In *Transpersonal Research Methods for the Social Sciences: Honoring Human Experience,* edited by William Braud and Rosemarie Anderson, 1–32. Thousand Oaks, CA: Sage.

Evans, John Gwenogvryn. 2013. *The Black Book of Carmarthen.* Reprint, Toronto: University of Toronto Libraries. First published 1906.

Extraordinary. 2019. In *Merriam-Webster Online Dictionary.* 11th ed. https://www .merriam-webster.com/dictionary/extraordinary.

Fearnow, Benjamin. 2018. "Number of Witches Rises Dramatically Across US as Millennials Reject Christianity." *Newsweek,* November 18, 2018. Available at Newsweek online.

Ferrer, Jorge. 2017. *Participation and the Mystery: Transpersonal Essays in Psychology, Education, and Religion.* Albany: State University of New York Press.

———. 2018. "Mononormativity, Polypride, and the 'Mono–Poly Wars.'" *Sexuality and Culture* 22, no. 3 (September): 817–36. Available at Springer Link online.

Filan, Kenaz. (2004) 2013. "I married a Lwa: The sacred nuptials of Haitian Vodou." *Witches of the Craft,* January 12, 2013. Available online at the Witches of the Craft website.

Foor, Daniel. 2002. *Animist Psychology: Healing Self and Culture Through the Path of Relationship*. Self-published ebook.

Forest, Danu. 2017. *Gwyn ap Nudd: Wild God of Faerie, Guardian of Annwfn*. Pagan Portals series. Winchester, UK: Moon Books.

Fortune, Dion. 2000. *The Esoteric Philosophy of Love and Marriage*. Reprint ed. York Beach, ME: Weiser Books. First published 1930.

———. 2001. *Psychic Self-Defense: The Classic Instruction Manual for Protecting Yourself Against Paranormal Attack*. Reprint ed. York Beach, ME: Weiser Books. First published 1930.

Foxwood, Orion. 2007. *The Faery Teachings*. Arcata, CA: R. J. Stewart Books.

———. 2008. *The Tree of Enchantment: Ancient Wisdom and Magic Practices of the Faery Tradition*. San Francisco, CA: Red Wheel/Weiser.

———. 2012. *The Candle and the Crossroads: A Book of Appalachian Conjure and Southern Root Work*. San Francisco, CA: Red Wheel/Weiser.

Frawley, David. 2008. *Inner Tantric Yoga: Working with the Universal Shakti: Secrets of Mantras, Deities, and Meditation*. Twin Lakes, WI: Lotus Press.

Gabriel, Douglas. 2017. "Did Rudolph Steiner Channel The Masters?" *Our Spirit*, February 24, 2017. Available online at the Neoanthroposophy blog.

Gafni, Marc. 2012. *Your Unique Self: The Radical Path to Personal Enlightenment*. Tucson: Integral Publishers.

Gagliano, Monica. 2018. *Thus Spoke the Plant: A Remarkable Journey of Groundbreaking Scientific Discoveries and Personal Encounters with Plants*. Berkeley: North Atlantic Books.

Gibson, H. N. 1953. "The Offspring of the Human-Faery Marriage." *Folklore* 64, no. 1 (March): 282–85.

Goff, Philip. 2017. "Panpsychism Is Crazy, but It's Also Most Probably True." Edited by Nigel Warburton. *Aeon*, March 1, 2017. Available at Aeon online.

Goslinga, Gillian. 2006. "The Ethnography of a South Indian God: Virgin Birth, Spirit Possession and the Prose of the Modern World." Ph.D. diss., University of California Santa Cruz.

Green, Richard F. 2016. *Elf Queens and Holy Friars: Fairy Beliefs and the Medieval Church*. Philadelphia: University of Pennsylvania Press.

Grof, Stanislav, and Hal Zina Bennett. 1993. *The Holotropic Mind: The Three Levels of Human Consciousness and How They Shape Our Lives*. San Francisco: Harper San Francisco.

Guilford, Gwynn. 2018. "Germany Was Once the Witch-Burning Capital of the World. Here's Why." *Quartz*, January 24, 2018. Available at Quartz online.

Hadewijch of Brabant. 1986a. "Letters to a Young Beguine." Translated by Eric

Colledge. In *Medieval Women's Visionary Literature,* edited by Elizabeth Petroff, 189–94. New York: Oxford University Press.

———. 1986b. "Visions: Vision 7. Oneness in the Eucharist." Translated by Mother Columba Hart. In *Medieval Women's Visionary Literature,* edited by Elizabeth Petroff, 195–99. New York: Oxford University Press.

Harman, William. 1992. *The Sacred Marriage of the Hindu Goddess.* New Delhi: Motilal Banarsidass.

Heaney, Marie. 1994. *Over Nine Waves: A Book of Irish Legends.* London: Faber and Faber.

Henderson, Lizanne. 2008. "Witch-Hunting and Witch Belief in the Gàidhealtachd." In *Witchcraft and Belief in Early Modern Scotland,* edited by Julian Goodare, Lauren Martin, and Joyce Miller, 98–118. New York: Palgrave Macmillan.

Herbert, Máire. 1992. "Goddess and King: The Sacred Marriage in Early Ireland." In *Women and Sovereignty,* edited by Louise Olga Fradenburg, 265–75. Edinburgh: Edinburgh University Press.

Herodotus. 1920. *Histories.* Book 1. Translated by A. D. Godley. Cambridge: Harvard University Press.

Heschel, Susannah. 2007. "Lilith." In Vol. 13 of the Encyclopaedia Judaica, edited by Fred Skolnik and Michael Berenbaum, 17–20. 2nd edition. Farmington Hills, MI: Thomson Gale.

Hoak, Dale. 1983. "The Great European Witch-Hunts: A Historical Perspective." *American Journal of Sociology* 88, no. 6 (May): 1270–74.

Holy Bible. 1962. Revised Standard Version. Cleveland, OH: The World Publishing Company.

Hubbard, Barbara Marx. 2018. "Homo Universalis: Awakening the New Species in Us." Interview by Raymond Moody. *Legacy,* November 28, 2018. Video, 32 min. Available at Gaia online.

Hunter, Jack. 2010. *Paranthropology: Journal of Anthropological Approaches to the Paranormal* 1 (1): 2–3.

———. 2018. *Engaging the Anomalous: Collected Essays on Anthropology, the Paranormal, Mediumship and Extraordinary Experience.* Hove, UK: August Night Books.

Iyengar, B. K. S. 2012. *Core of the Yoga Sutras: The Definitive Guide to the Philosophy of Yoga.* London: HarperCollins.

Jung, Carl. 1959. *Aion: Researches into the Phenomenology of the Self.* Volume 9, Part 2 of *The Collected Works of C. G. Jung.* Edited and translated by Gerhard Adler and R. F. C. Hull. Princeton: Princeton University Press.

———. 1969. *The Archetypes and the Collective Unconscious.* Volume 9 Part 1 of

The Collected Works of C. G. Jung. Edited and translated by Gerhard Adler and R. F. C. Hull. Princeton, NJ: Princeton University Press. First published 1934–1954.

———. 1971. *Psychological Types.* Volume 6 of *The Collected Works of C. G. Jung.* Edited and translated by Gerhard Adler and R. F. C. Hull. Princeton, NJ: Princeton University Press. First published 1921.

———. 1989. *Memories, Dreams and Reflections.* Edited by Aniela Jaffe. Translated by Richard and Clara Winston. New York: Vintage Books.

———. 2009. *The Red Book: Liber Novus.* Edited by Sonu Shamsadani. Translated by Mark Kyburz and John Peck. New York: W. W. Norton.

Kaplan, Marianna. 1999. *Halfway Up the Mountain: The Error of Premature Claims to Enlightenment.* Prescott, AZ: Hohm Press.

Kaufman, Stuart A. 2016. *Humanity in a Creative Universe.* New York: Oxford University Press.

King, Martin Luther Jr. 1966. "Nonviolence: The Only Road to Freedom, May 4, 1966." *Ebony,* October 1966, 27–34.

Koleva, Gergana. 2006. "A Marriage, When the Spirit Moves Them." *New York Times,* February 19, 2006. Available at New York Times online.

Krippner, Stanley, Fariba Bogzaran, and Andre Percia de Carvalho. 2002. *Extraordinary Dreams and How to Work with Them.* Albany, NY: SUNYPRESS.

Kyle, Richard. 1995. The New Age Movement in American Culture. Lanham, MD: University Press of America.

Lama Yeshe. 1987. *Introduction to Tantra: The Transformation of Desire.* Edited by Jonathan Landaw. Somerville: Wisdom Publications.

Landy, Joshua, and Michael Saler, eds. 2009. *The Reenchantment of the World: Secular Magic in a Rational Age.* Stanford: Stanford University Press.

Lapinkivi, Pirjo. 2008. "The Sumerian Sacred Marriage and Its Aftermath in Later Sources." In *Sacred Marriages: The Divine-Human Sexual Metaphor from Sumer to Early Christianity,* edited by Marti Nissinen and Risto Uro, 7–42. Winona Lake, IN: Eisenbrauns.

Levy, Paul. 2013. *Dispelling Wetiko: Breaking the Curse of Evil.* Berkeley, CA: North Atlantic Books.

Levy, Robert. 1990. *Mesocosm: Hinduism and the Organization of a Traditional Newar City in Nepal.* Berkeley: University of California Press.

Lewis, I. M. 1999. *Arguments with Ethnography: Comparative Approaches to History, Politics & Religion.* London: The Athlone Press.

Lipschutz, Yael. 2014. *Cameron: Songs for the Witch Woman.* Santa Monica, CA: Cameron Parsons Foundation.

Loprieno, Antonio. 1995. *Ancient Egyptian: A Linguistic Introduction.* Cambridge, UK: Cambridge University Press.

Lovelock, James. 1975. "The Quest for Gaia." *New Scientist* 65 (938): 304–9.

Macleod, Fiona [William Sharp]. 1904. *The Winged Destiny: Studies in the Spiritual History of the Gael*. London: Chapman and Hall. Available at Internet Archive online.

———. 1900. "Iona" in *The Divine Adventure: Iona, By Sundown Shores, Studies in Spiritual History*. London: Chapman and Hall. Available at Internet Archive online.

———. 1907. "The Mystic's Prayer" in *The Hour of Beauty*. Portland, ME: Thomas B. Moser.

———. 2017. *The Immortal Hour, A Drama*. Miami, FL: HardPress. First published 1908.

Marglin, Frédérique Apffel. 1985. *Wives of the God-King: The Rituals of the Devadasi of Puri*. Oxford: Oxford University Press.

Masters, Robert Augustus. 2010. *Spiritual Bypassing: When Spirituality Disconnects Us from What Really Matters*. Berkeley, CA: North Atlantic Books.

Maté, Gabor. 2008. *In the Realm of Hungry Ghosts: Close Encounters with Addiction*. Vancouver: Knopf Canada.

Mathers, Samuel L. MacGregor. 2010. *The Book of the Sacred Magic of Abramelin the Mage*. Reprint, New York: Cosimo Classics. First published 1900.

McCarthy Brown, Karen. 1991. *Mama Lola: A Vodou Priestess in Brooklyn*. Berkeley: University of California Press.

Mennesson-Rigaud, Odette. 1953. "Notes on Two Marriages with Voudoun Loa." In *Divine Horsemen: The Living Gods of Haiti*, by Maya Deren, 263–79. New York: Thames and Hudson.

Merchant, Carolyn. 1980. *The Death of Nature: Women, Ecology, and the Scientific Revolution*. San Francisco: HarperSanFrancisco.

Moreman, Christopher. 2013. *The Spiritualist Movement: Speaking with the Dead in America and Around the World*. Santa Barbara: ABC CLIO.

Morgan, Adam. 1999. "Sahaja Yoga: An Ancient Path to Modern Mental Health." Ph.D. thesis, University of Plymouth. Available at University of Plymouth PEARL database online.

Moustakas, Clark. 1990. *Heuristic Research: Design, Methodology and Applications*. Newbury Park, CA: Sage.

Nissinen, Marti, and Risto Uro. 2008. *Sacred Marriages: The Divine-Human Sexual Metaphor from Sumer to Early Christianity*. Winona Lake, IN: Eisenbrauns.

Panepinto, Lauren. 2019. "Cultural Appropriation vs. Cultural Appreciation." *Muddy Colors: Art, Education, Community*. Accessed October 3, 2020. Available at Muddy Colors online.

Plato. n.d. "On the Daimon, between God and Man." *Symposium,* 202b–203a. Accessed October 22, 2019. Available at Mesa Community College online.

Plutarch. 2014. *The Complete Collection of Plutarch's Parallel Lives.* Translated by John Dryden. CreateSpace.

Pope Francis. (2018, July 4). "Ecclesiae Sponsae Imago" on the "Ordo Virginum" (Papal instruction). Vatican City: Holy See Press Office.

Power, Richard. 2017. *Wyrds of Power: New Language for A New Reality.* CreateSpace.

Rachel, Alex. 2012. "Ecologies of the Soul: A Study of the Relationships Between the Human Psyche and Nonphysical Entities." Ph.D. diss., California Institute of Integral Studies.

Radin, Dean. 2018. *Real Magic: Ancient Wisdom, Modern Science, and a Guide to the Secret Power of the Universe.* New York: Harmony Books.

Reese, Thomas. 2017. "Beyond Halloween: Witches, Devils, Trials and Executions." *National Catholic Reporter,* October 25, 2017. Available at National Catholic Reporter online.

René, George, and Marilyn Houlberg. 1995. "My Double Mystical Marriages to Two Goddesses of Love." In *Sacred Arts of Haitian Vodou,* edited by Donald J. Cosentino, 287–99. Los Angeles: UCLA Fowler Museum of Cultural History.

Rhys, John. 2012. *Celtic Folklore: Welsh and Manx.* Vol. 1. London: Forgotten Books.

Rigoglioso, Marguerite. 2009. *The Cult of Divine Birth in Ancient Greece.* New York: Palgrave Macmillan.

———. 2010. *Virgin Mother Goddesses of Antiquity.* New York: Palgrave Macmillan.

Roszak, Theodore (lecturer). 1992. "Towards an Eco-Psychology, Part 3." Interview by Jeffrey Mishlove, August 10, 1992. *Thinking Allowed* (TV series), directed by Arthur Bloch. DVD. Part 3. 7:09, 26:16.

Rushton, Neil. 2020. "The Faerie Phenomenon in Folklore and Modern Experience." *Graham Hancock.* Accessed October 3, 2020. Available at Graham Hancock online.

Sarbacker, Stuart Ray. 2011. "Indo-Tibetan Tantrism as Spirit Marriage." In *Perceiving the Divine through the Human Body: Mystical Sensuality,* edited by Thomas Cattoi and June McDaniel, 29–44. New York: Palgrave Macmillan.

Scholem, Gershom. 2007. "Demons, Demonology." Vol. 5 of *Encyclopaedia Judaica,* 2nd ed., 572–78. Farmington Hills, MI: Gale.

Schwartze, Lucas J. 2010. "Grave Vows: A Cross-Cultural Examination of the Varying Forms of Ghost Marriage among Five Societies." *Nebraska Anthropologist* 60. Available at University of Nebraska Lincoln Digital Commons online.

Scott, (Sir) Walter. 1900. *The Complete Poetical Works of Sir Walter Scott.* Boston: Houghton Mifflin Company.

Sheldrake, Rupert. 2003. *The Sense of Being Stared At: And Other Aspects of the Extended Mind.* New York: Harmony Books.

Sherma, Rita Dasgupta. 1998. "Sacred Immanence: Reflections of Ecofeminism in Hindu Tantra." In *Purifying the Earthly Body of God: Religion and Ecology in Hindu India,* edited by Lance E. Nelson, 39–132. Albany: State University of New York Press.

Sprinkle, Annie, and Beth Stephens. 2021. *Assuming the Ecosexual Position: The Earth as Lover.* Minneapolis: University of Minnesota Press.

St. John of the Cross. 1959. *The Poems of St. John of the Cross.* Translated by John Frederick Nims. New York: Grove.

St. Teresa of Avila. 1985. *The Collected Works of St. Teresa of Avila.* Vol. 3. Translated by Kieran Kavanaugh and Otilio Rodriguez. Washington, DC: ICS Publications.

Stegman, Judith. 2014. "Virginial Chastity in the Consecrated Virgin." Master's thesis, Catholic Distance University.

Stewart, R. J. 1998. *EarthLight: The Ancient Path to Transformation, Rediscovering the Wisdom of Celtic and Faery Lore.* Lake Toxaway, NC: Mercury Publishing.

———. 2006. *The Well of Light.* Arcata, CA: R. J. Stewart Books.

Stony Brook University. "Sensitive? Emotional? Empathetic? It could be in your genes." ScienceDaily. Accessed August 16, 2021. Available at ScienceDaily online.

Sullivan, Kevin. 2004. *Wrestling with Angels: A Study of the Relationship between Angels and Humans in Ancient Jewish Literature and the New Testament.* Boston, MA: Brill.

Teppo, Saana. 2008. "Sacred Marriage and the Devotees of Ištar." In *Sacred Marriages: The Divine-Human Sexual Metaphor from Sumer to Early Christianity,* edited by Marti Nissinen and Risto Uro, 75–92. Winona Lake, IN: Eisenbrauns.

Topley, Marjorie. 1956. "Ghost Marriages among the Singapore Chinese: A Further Note." *Man* 56 (May): 71–72.

Turner, Edith. 1993. "The Reality of Spirits: A Tabooed or Permitted Field of Study?" *Anthropology of Consciousness* 4, no. 1 (March): 9–12.

———. 2010. "Discussion: Ethnography as a Transformative Experience." *Anthropology and Humanism* 35, no. 2 (December): 218–26.

Turner, Judy Ann. 1983. "Hiereiai: Acquisition of Feminine Priesthoods in Ancient Greece." Ph.D. diss., University of California, Santa Barbara.

Tyson, Donald. 2000. *Sexual Alchemy: Magical Intercourse with Spirits.* St. Paul, MN: Llewellyn.

Vernadsky, Vladimir Ivanovich. 1997. *Scientific Thought as a Planetary Phenomenon.* Moscow: Nongovernmental Ecological V. I. Vernadsky Foundation.

von Rospatt, Alexander. 2010. "Remarks on the Consecration Ceremony in Kuladatta's Kriyāsa grahapañjikā and Its Development in Newar Buddhism." In *Hindu and Buddhist Initiations in India and Nepal,* edited by Astrid Zotter and Christof Zotter, 197–260. Wiesbaden: Harrassowitz Verlag.

von Worms, Abraham. 2015. *Book of Abramelin: A New Translation.* Translated by Steven Guth and edited by Georg Dehn. Lake Worth, FL: Ibis Press.

Walker, Polly. 2013. "Research in Relationship with Humans, the Spirit World, and the Natural World." In *Indigenous Pathways into Social Research: Voices of a New Generation,* edited by Donna M. Mertens, Fiona Cram, and Bagele Chilisa, 299–316. Walnut Creek, CA: Left Coast Press.

Washburn, Michael. 2003. *Embodied Spirituality in a Sacred World.* Albany: SUNY Press.

White, David Gordon. 2003. *Kiss of the Yogini: Tantric Sex in its South Asian Contexts.* Chicago, IL: University of Chicago Press.

Wilby, Emma. 2005. *Cunning Folk and Familiar Spirits: Shamanistic Visionary Traditions in Early Modern British Witchcraft and Magic.* Brighton, UK: Sussex Academic Press.

Williamson, Marianne. 1992. *Return to Love: Reflections on the Principles of a Course in Miracles.* London: HarperCollins.

Wilson, A. P. 2004. "Trembling in the Dark: Derrida's Mysterium Tremendum and the Gospel of Mark." In *Derrida's Bible: Religion/Culture/Critique,* edited by Yvonne Sherwood, 199–214. New York: Palgrave Macmillan.

Wise, Michael, Martin Abegg, and Edward Cook, trans. 1996. *The Dead Sea Scrolls: A New Translation.* San Francisco: Harper San Francisco.

Wohlleben, Peter. 2015. *The Hidden Life of Trees: What They Feel, How They Communicate, Discoveries from a Secret World.* Vancouver: Greystone Books.

Wolynn, Mark. 2016. *It Didn't Start with You: How Inherited Family Trauma Shapes Who We Are and How to End the Cycle.* New York: Penguin Books.

Woolever, Megan. 1995. "The Beguine Movement: Lovers of God or God's Lovers?" Unpublished manuscript. Berkeley, CA: Graduate Theological Union.

Index

About the Author

*I*n addition to her academic credentials (Ph.D. in Psychology, M.A. in Religion), Megan Rose is a full-tilt Highly Sensitive Person (HSP) and erotic mystic. Her spirituality has always been intertwined with her sexuality. She is also a Visionary Heretic, which means she's conscious about how what we choose to believe in shapes who we are and the world we create. And, finally, she's a Badass Nerd. You don't grow up in the SF Bay Area without developing some hardcore nerd skills! Hers manifest as a deep understanding of psycho-spiritual systems, academic prowess, and a penchant for supernatural sci-fi, flamboyant costuming, and outrageous theater.

She has dedicated more than twenty years of her life to researching and practicing erotic mysticism and spirit communication. She now helps other Erotic Mystics, Visionary Heretics, and Badass Nerds cultivate safe, sane, and secure relationships with the spirits (okay, and sometimes with humans, too) so they can more fully express their own sexy, weird Self! Learn more at www.drmeganrose.com.